T0072345

PENGUIN CLASSICS

QUAKER WRITINGS

THOMAS D. HAMM is professor of history and archivist/curator of the Friends Collection at Earlham College. A native of New Castle, Indiana, he received his Ph.D. in history from Indiana University in 1985. After teaching two years at Indiana University-Purdue University-Indianapolis, he joined the Earlham faculty. He is the author of numerous works on Quaker history, and his most recent book, *The Quakers in America*, was published by Columbia University Press in 2003.

Quaker Writings

AN ANTHOLOGY
1650–1920

Edited with an Introduction by
THOMAS D. HAMM

PENGUIN BOOKS

PENGUIN BOOKS
Published by the Penguin Group
Penguin Group (USA) Inc., 375 Hudson Street, New York, New York 10014, U.S.A.
Penguin Group (Canada), 90 Eglinton Avenue East, Suite 700, Toronto, Ontario, Canada M4P 2Y3
(a division of Pearson Penguin Canada Inc.)
Penguin Books Ltd, 80 Strand, London WC2R 0RL, England
Penguin Ireland, 25 St Stephen's Green, Dublin 2, Ireland (a division of Penguin Books Ltd)
Penguin Group (Australia), 250 Camberwell Road, Camberwell, Victoria 3124, Australia
(a division of Pearson Australia Group Pty Ltd)
Penguin Books India Pvt Ltd, 11 Community Centre, Panchsheel Park, New Delhi - 110 017, India
Penguin Group (NZ), 67 Apollo Drive, Rosedale, North Shore 0632, New Zealand
(a division of Pearson New Zealand Ltd)
Penguin Books (South Africa) (Pty) Ltd, 24 Sturdee Avenue, Rosebank, Johannesburg 2196,
South Africa

Penguin Books Ltd, Registered Offices:
80 Strand, London WC2R 0RL, England

First published in Penguin Books 2010

Selections from records of West Branch Monthly Meeting of Friends. Used by permission.

"The Vision of John Beals" (ca. 1796). Courtesy of Friends Historical Collection, Guilford College,
Greensboro, North Carolina.

LIBRARY OF CONGRESS CATALOGING IN PUBLICATION DATA
Quaker writings : an anthology, 1650–1920 / edited with an introduction by Thomas D. Hamm.
p. cm.—(Penguin classics)
ISBN 978-0-14-310631-9
1. Society of Friends—History—Sources.   I. Hamm, Thomas D.
BX7631.3.Q35 2010
289.609—dc22   2010044561

Set in Sabon

146122990

Contents

PART II: MATURING, 1661–1690

PART III: QUIETISM, 1690–1820

PART IV: CREATIVITY AND CONTROVERSY, 1820–1870

PART V: SEPARATE WAYS, 1870–1920

PART VI: PEACE

Introduction

The People Called Quakers

They began amidst uncertainty, conflict, upheaval, and even personal torment. They were one of dozens of strange, sometimes bizarre sects that sprang up in England in the 1640s and 1650s, as common folk—farmers, smiths, cobblers, shopkeepers, wives, and mothers—took advantage of civil war and the breakdown of government control to assert the right to seek God, read the Bible, and find truth in their own ways. In what hostile observers called "a world turned upside down," both the learned and the illiterate challenged accepted orthodoxies: political, social, and religious. Yet of all the sects that flourished in this generation—Diggers and Levelers, Ranters and Muggletonians, Brownists, Familists, and Fifth Monarchists, to name just a few—only one has survived to the present day. At first it had no name, then came to refer to itself as Children of the Light, then Friends of the Light, and finally the Religious Society of Friends. Detractors labeled them "Quakers," an insulting nickname that the Friends would, for the most part, eventually embrace.

The early Quaker world was one of conflict. In 1642, Great Britain was plunged into a civil war that pitted King Charles I against Parliament. Although the power of king versus Lords and Commons was central, so was religion. Charles was a staunch supporter of a state-supported, ritualistic Protestant church ruled by bishops with him at their head. Parliament was dominated by Puritans, champions of a purer, Reformed church in which bishops would be abolished and ritual would be minimal. By 1650, the king was dead and the old Church of England no longer existed. Now the terms of the religious debate shifted. Would there be a new state church along Puritan lines, or would some form of religious toleration and liberty become the rule?

Coming of age amidst this uncertainty was a young man from

a Puritan family in Leicestershire, George Fox. Born in 1624, Fox was by his own account an unusually solemn, pious youth. He was tormented by the claims of the competing groups around him, convinced that if he made the wrong choice in faith, a just and jealous God would damn him. So he embarked on a kind of spiritual pilgrimage, seeking out both clergy and laypeople with reputations for piety, yet, as he put it, "none spoke to my condition." By 1646, his journey took him onto the moors of Yorkshire and Lancashire. There he had a series of experiences that we today would call revelations—he called them "openings"—in which Fox was certain that God spoke directly to him. As he described it later: "when all my hopes . . . were gone, so that I had nothing outwardly to help me, nor could tell what to do, then, Oh then, I heard a voice which said, 'There is one, even Christ Jesus, that can speak to thy condition.'"

Over the next few years, Fox's "openings" continued, laying the foundations for the Quaker movement. Key was the idea of direct revelation, that God spoke directly to human beings through the Holy Spirit, just as he had in the days of the Hebrew prophets and the apostles. While Fox was a devout student of the Bible—a Friend later said that if all the Bibles in the world were somehow lost, it could be reconstructed from George Fox's memory—he insisted that the same spirit that inspired the scriptures still inspired believers. Fox gave equal weight to the centrality of the experience of the light of Christ. This light, he argued, was inward. He wrote, "every man was enlightened by the divine light of Christ, and I saw it shine through all, and they that believed in it came out of condemnation and came to the light of life, and became the children of it, but they that hated it, and did not believe in it, were condemned by it, though they made a profession of Christ." If Friends were obedient to this light within them, then they would know salvation; but if they disobeyed it, they would be damned. Radically, Fox and other early Friends argued that this light was in all, even those who had never heard of Jesus, and that obedience to it would bring anyone salvation, even without any knowledge of Christianity.

Such beliefs led Friends in other directions. While they valued preaching, and gave deep respect to their own ministers, they repudiated any conception of an ordained clergy. All that was necessary was a call from God, and no human action could confer more legitimacy. Particularly radical was the Quaker conviction that women as well as men could be called to preach and minister. Few features of early Quakerism were as controversial as the place of women within it. Fox's first convert was a woman, Elizabeth Hooton, who herself became a well-known Quaker preacher.

Commitments to direct revelation and the ministry of all believers also shaped Quaker worship. It had no predetermined form; ritual was entirely absent. Quaker worship included no preset prayers or recitations of formulas or creeds, no singing of hymns or psalms. Friends gathered in utterly plain, unornamented buildings, waiting in silence, confident that if God had something to be shared with the gathered meeting, then he would inspire someone present to speak. Theoretically, that might be any member of the congregation. In practice, however, most of the speaking or preaching was done by "Public Friends," Friends who had "a gift in the ministry." Such Friends' status, however, came entirely from their gifts as preachers and their reputations for piety and spiritual wisdom, what Friends came to refer to as "weight." While Public Friends exercised considerable authority and constituted the movement's leadership, they did not assume pastoral offices.

Early Friends did not lack confidence in their inspiration. Many, particularly Fox, argued that it was possible for humans, through obedience to the light and the leadings of the Holy Spirit, to achieve perfection, the sinless state of Adam and Eve in the Garden of Eden before the Fall. They took other radical positions, most notably on the nature of the sacraments. Friends argued that baptism and communion should be understood as purely spiritual, that "outward" observances such as water baptism and "the supper" with bread and wine were unnecessary and could even detract from real spirituality and Christian experience.

This determination to achieve perfect obedience and avoid anything that might detract from the guidance of the inward light and the Holy Spirit manifested itself in other ways. Friends became known for their commitments to distinctive practices that set them apart from many of their neighbors. They shunned outward decoration and display. Even relatively well-to-do Friends were expected to live simply, not using dress or ostentation to cast themselves as socially superior. One manifestation was the Quaker refusal to use courtesy titles such as "Mister" or "Your Honor" or "My Lady" or "Your Excellency" that were considered both good manners and appropriate social deference in seventeenth-century England. While not committed to a leveling of all social ranks, Friends believed that the use of such "compliments" encouraged sinful pride and vanity. Similarly, Quaker men refused to doff their hats to their "betters." Perhaps best known was the Quaker insistence on addressing others as "thee" and "thou." Grammatically, this was the singular of "you," but it had become customary to use "you" to show respect to parents and social superiors. Friends, however, refused to follow such practices. Another Quaker peculiarity was refusal to swear legal oaths, which Friends believed implied that one could be trusted to speak truthfully only in certain situations.

Friends saw all of their activities as embraced in what they labeled "the lamb's war," the lamb being Jesus Christ. They were convinced that they were called to play a central role in advancing the kingdom of God on earth. Many shared an apocalyptic expectancy that it would happen in their lifetimes.

Friends also proved aggressive in advocating and seeking converts to their beliefs. Between 1647 and 1652, Fox appealed to small groups of religious radicals in the north of England, many of whom described themselves as "seekers." By 1652, however, the foundations for a movement were laid. He felt inspired by a vision that he had on Pendle Hill in Lancashire, where he saw "a great people to be gathered." Fox attracted a capable group of supporters, of whom the most important were James Nayler, a farmer from Yorkshire, and Margaret Fell, a Lancashire gentlewoman whose home, Swarthmore Hall, became the effective headquarters of the movement, and who in 1669 married Fox. Cadres of Public Friends, who later became collectively known as the "Valiant Sixty," took the Quaker message south, making thousands of converts. By 1660, London and Bristol had come to rival Yorkshire and Lancashire as Quaker centers.

The rapid growth of such a radical movement was not unopposed. The very name "Quaker" was first used as an insult for Friends in 1650, from a widespread conviction that Friends would shake and quake under the influence of the Holy Spirit. By 1653, Puritan ministers were issuing pamphlet attacks on the movement with titles such as *The Irreligion of the Northern Quakers*. Dozens of such works appeared before 1660. The sources of opposition were varied. Some critics saw Quakers as blasphemers who made themselves equal to Christ. Friends often invited such attacks with their self-assertion and combativeness. An example is Mary Fell, the daughter of Quaker leader Margaret Fell, writing to a local minister: "Lampitt, the plagues of God shall fall upon thee and the seven vials shall be poured out upon thee and the millstone shall fall upon thee and crush thee as dust beneath the Lord's feet. How can thou escape the damnation of hell?" Mary Fell was eight years old. Some Friends interrupted services of other groups to point out their shortcomings. A few Friends were led to "go naked as a sign," either for self-abasement or to demonstrate their own spiritual innocence. Most controversial was James Nayler, who before 1656 rivaled Fox as a Quaker leader. That year, however, Nayler and a group of followers made a bizarre entry into Bristol that appeared calculated to reenact Christ's entry into Jerusalem, leading many observers to accuse Nayler of blasphemy. Nayler was jailed, tried by Parliament, and severely punished. Hundreds of other Friends found themselves imprisoned before 1660.

The restoration of the monarchy in 1660 worsened the situation of Friends. The new king, Charles II, without firm religious views himself, sometimes found Quaker effrontery amusing, but the gentry-dominated Parliament equated religious dissent with sedition. As Friends struggled to find their place in the new order, one response was to solidify a repudiation of violence that had appeared in the thought of many Friends in the 1650s, what would become known as the "Peace Testimony." Some historians see this as a calculated response to political change, others as simply a strengthening of a basic Quaker belief. Early in 1661, after a failed radical uprising in London, Fox and other leading Friends issued a statement: "All bloody principles and practices, we . . . do utterly deny, with all outward wars and strife and fightings with outward weapons, for any end or under any pretense whatsoever." Pacifists were unlikely supporters of armed rebellion. Nevertheless, Parliament between 1661 and 1664 passed a series of laws that effectively outlawed Quaker worship. As a result, thousands of Friends were fined and imprisoned over the next three decades, and many died in prison.

The Quaker response was complex. To aid the suffering, and to promote group solidarity, Friends became more organized, creating a series of monthly, quarterly, and yearly business meetings, with the yearly meeting as the highest authority. The monthly and quarterly meetings were remarkable for including women Friends, albeit in separate groups. Friends also became adept in using the English legal system, showing themselves quite willing to take advantage of technicalities to escape punishment. Friends with gentry connections, such as Margaret Fell, employed them to Quaker advantage.

After 1660, Quakerism changed in other ways. By 1664, several important early leaders, such as James Nayler, were dead. The survivors, led by Fox, lost some of their earlier sense of apocalyptic urgency. Friends no longer expected to convert the entire world, or initiate the kingdom of God. Friends continued to attract converts but not at the same rate as in the 1650s. Two Friends "convinced" (the Quaker term for converted) in the 1660s would be especially important. One was William Penn (1644–1718), an Oxford-educated son of an admiral who would become a leading minister, a prolific writer, and a visible Quaker politician. The other was Robert Barclay (1648–1690), a Scot trained by Jesuits who would become the new movement's most important systematic theologian. His 1676 treatise, *An Apology for the True Christian Divinity,* would increasingly define the boundaries of Quaker faith.

Between 1660 and 1690, the geographic boundaries of Quakerism expanded. Public Friends had traveled widely in the 1650s—two even made it to Constantinople with the goal of converting the Ottoman emperor. More attention, however, went to British colonies in North America. Friends faced bitter persecution in Massachusetts and Connecticut—four, including one woman, Mary Dyer, were hanged in Boston between 1659 and 1661. In other places, Friends were banished, fined, and imprisoned. But by the 1670s, meetings had been established in the British West Indies, the Chesapeake, Rhode Island, Long Island, and Albemarle Sound. George Fox himself traveled widely in the Caribbean and from New England to the Carolinas in 1672 and 1673.

Most important for Quaker development would be the Delaware Valley. In 1675, a group of British Quakers had purchased about half of the future state of New Jersey—what was then called West Jersey—from an English nobleman. Quaker migration to the east side of the Delaware River began soon afterward, and Burlington and Salem became important Quaker settlements. In 1681, William Penn received a large grant of land that would become Pennsylvania. Penn's framework for government was a mix of Quaker idealism and feudal autocracy. He saw himself in many ways as a benevolent dictator. But he guaranteed religious liberty, opened office-holding to all Protestants, tolerated Roman Catholics and Jews, instituted an enlightened criminal code, and made liberal provisions for landownership. Power quickly passed into the hands of a Quaker-dominated assembly. Penn took pains to negotiate with the Native American inhabitants, and for the next seventy-five years relations between Europeans and American Indians would be better than in any other British colony.

By the time of George Fox's death in 1691, Quakerism's survival was no longer in question. In 1689, Parliament instituted religious freedom. While Quaker scruples against bearing arms, swearing oaths, and paying tithes to the established church still caused problems, Quaker worship was now legal. Second- and third-generation Friends, generally more prosperous than most of their neighbors, found themselves respectable. On both sides of the Atlantic, Friends responded by turning inward.

Historians usually refer to the period from roughly 1690 to 1820 as the era of "quietism." "Quietist" has become a convenient term for a Quaker outlook that focused on the preservation of group discipline and fear of what Friends referred to as "creaturely activity." Friends saw obedience to God and attention to the inward light as virtually depriving them of any right to heed human inclination, will, or intellect. They strove to become empty vessels, devoid of any desire to think, say, or do anything that was not clearly revealed as the divine will. Increasingly, Friends saw salvation as something to be achieved gradually, through a lifelong process of growth into holiness, sanctification, or perfection, which fitted believers for heaven. Friends advanced their growth through introspection, avoiding "diversions" and "outward activity," and experiencing periods of mental suffering and depression that they referred to as "baptisms." Silence became more common in meetings for worship, as even Friends who felt called to preach were terrified that they might speak without a clear leading. The creation of the office of elder, charged with overseeing the ministry—encouraging fledgling ministers but also discouraging those who apparently had mistaken their gifts—strengthened such tendencies. While new members continued to join, they were relatively few compared with the early period.

What historians refer to as a "reformation" between 1750 and 1780 reinforced this direction. In both Great Britain and America, Friends gave increasing attention to the enforcement of the rules and regulations that were embodied in the "discipline." Friends had always condemned moral lapses such as drunkenness or fornication, but they now became less tolerant of deviations from Quaker peculiarities, particularly marrying nonmembers. Friends were disowned even for erecting tombstones for spouses. Statistical analysis suggests the loss of thousands of members, although high birth rates meant that the number of Friends continued to grow.

Paradoxically, the era of quietism was also one of innovation in Quaker attempts to influence the larger world. Although war in Pennsylvania ended peace with Native Americans, Friends shifted their attention to attempting to defend Indian rights. English Friends became pioneers in humane treatment of the mentally ill. English and American Friends were at the forefront of prison reform movements. And Quakers were at the heart of the eighteenth-century antislavery movement. By 1784, Friends had ruled that no member could own a slave and that Friends who did own slaves must free them unconditionally. American Friends John Woolman and Anthony Benezet are recognized as central to eighteenth-century antislavery, while British Friends were at the heart of the movements to abolish first the slave trade in 1807 and then slavery in the British Empire in 1833.

By the early nineteenth century, however, signs of strain were becoming apparent on both sides of the Atlantic, especially in the United States. Its sources have been debated by Friends then, and historians now, but by 1828 Quakerism would fracture in a division that has endured to the present.

By the 1820s, Elias Hicks, a Quaker minister from Long Island, had become the most controversial figure in the Quaker world. An old man, born in 1748, Hicks was in most respects a staunch quietist whose writings show an intense desire to subordinate any hint of his own will to the leadings of the inward light. Hicks often felt led to travel and before his death in 1830 had visited most of the Quaker communities in North America.

By the 1820s, Hicks had become convinced that Quakerism was under siege, threatened by forces in the larger world. These ranged from commercialism (Hicks opposed construction of the Erie Canal as unnatural) to slavery to general "worldliness." Hicks's particular concern, however, was what he saw as the growing influence of non-Quaker evangelicalism on Friends. He argued that Friends who had formed ties with Episcopalians, Presbyterians, Methodists, and others through business or reform work had imbibed many of their ideas and were endangering true Quakerism. Hicks pointed to the increasing emphasis that some Friends were placing on the authority of the Bible, which he saw as diminishing the centrality of direct revelation and the inward light. From time to time, Hicks also advanced ideas about the nature of the divinity of Christ that some Friends saw as dangerous and at odds with historic Quakerism. Some Friends accused him of denying the Virgin Birth, a charge that Hicks denied. But Hicks was clear that he viewed Jesus Christ as unique because he was the only human who had ever been perfectly obedient to the inward light. This obedience made him the Christ; he was not born as Christ. To counter the inroads of "the world," Hicks argued, Friends needed to undergo a reformation to restore the Society of Friends to its original basis.

Many Friends perceived this as simply historic Quaker doctrine, but others, both in North America and in the British Isles, denounced Hicks's views as un-Quakerly, unchristian, and even atheistic. While maintaining their commitment to distinctive Quaker doctrines such as the inward light, they argued that Friends had always understood Jesus to have been born as the Christ. Moreover, salvation was achieved through faith in the efficacy of his blood shed on the cross, an understanding that Hicks denounced. Such Friends became known as Orthodox. By the early 1820s, leading Friends in Philadelphia were denouncing Hicks and urging New York Friends to silence him. Traveling Friends from Great Britain, where Hicks's ideas found little support, strengthened the Orthodox. Social divisions may also have played a role. Studies have found that in the Philadelphia area, Orthodox Friends tended to be more prosperous and more likely to live in the city, while rural communities were Hicksite strongholds. This pattern is not clear in other yearly meetings.

In spring 1827, the Philadelphia yearly meeting split, with

Hicksites withdrawing to "reorganize" what they claimed was the true historic meeting. The division obliged other yearly meetings to decide which one they would recognize and thus take sides. This produced splits in New York, Baltimore, Ohio, and Indiana yearly meetings. New England, Virginia, and North Carolina sided with the Orthodox, as did Friends in the British Isles. Estimates are that Hicksites were about 40 percent of all American Friends.

The separations of 1827–28 set a pattern for the rest of the century. In the 1830s and 1840s, both Hicksite and Orthodox Friends in America faced bitter controversies, as did, to a lesser extent, Friends in the British Isles. While Orthodox Friends agreed in viewing Elias Hicks as dangerous, they soon found themselves divided over what their relationship with the larger Protestant world should be. Some, especially in England, came to question the doctrine of the inward light; the most extreme, who became known as Beaconites, were disowned by the larger body of British Friends. But other Friends began to articulate a vision of Quakerism that found common ground with evangelical Protestantism, subordinating the inward light to the guidance they found in the Bible, and urging Friends to be open to ties with other evangelicals. The most articulate advocate of such views was a wealthy English minister and banker, Joseph John Gurney (1788–1847), whose sister, Elizabeth Fry (1780–1845), won international fame as a prison reformer. Like-minded Orthodox Friends became known as Gurneyites. A minority of deeply conservative Orthodox Friends, in England and North America, saw such views as dangerous innovation, condemning Gurney. In North America, the most articulate critic was a New England minister, John Wilbur (1774–1856), who lent his name to the opponents of Gurney. When other New England Friends disowned him for what they saw as his unfair attacks, Wilbur and his supporters separated, producing another series of splits among Orthodox Friends. In turn, these critics of innovation often argued among themselves over points of theology or their relationships with other yearly meetings. This produced a bewildering series of splits among Wilburites, Middleites, Maulites, Kollites, Otisites, and Primitive Friends.

Hicksites were not immune to these tendencies. In the aftermath of the separation, they were a heterogeneous group of conservatives opposed to what they saw as Orthodox innovation, incipient liberals who questioned the inspiration of some parts of the Bible, and ambivalent members who had simply followed the majority in their meetings without any deep sense of commitment. In the 1830s and 1840s, some Hicksites, most notably the Philadelphia minister Lucretia Mott (1793–1880), became active in reform movements such as temperance, nonresistance, and, most of all, the radical antislavery movement. All agreed that slavery was an evil, but conservatives argued that to join non-Quakers in reform causes endangered Quaker distinctiveness and would introduce influences similar to those that Orthodox Friends had embraced. The conservatives were a majority, and some radicals separated in the 1840s and 1850s to form groups that they called Congregational or Progressive Friends. Others, like Mott, remained within the larger Hicksite bodies. Hicksite women would be in the forefront of the women's rights movement for the rest of the century. Four of the five women who organized the first women's rights convention in American history—at Seneca Falls, New York, in 1848—were Hicksite Friends or had Hicksite ties. Of the three most influential women's rights activists of the nineteenth century—Elizabeth Cady Stanton, Lucretia Mott, and Susan B. Anthony—the last two were Hicksite Friends. By 1860, however, the Progressive groups of Friends had dwindled, with most either returning to the larger Hicksite bodies or joining other denominations. Many became Spiritualists.

The American Civil War saw almost all Friends firmly supportive of the Union. English Friend John Bright, a Member of Parliament, was unrelenting in his opposition to Confederate attempts to gain British support. The relatively small number of Friends in the Confederacy, all in Virginia, North Carolina, and Tennessee, opposed secession, and many young Quaker men fled north rather than be conscripted into the Confederate army. In the North, hundreds of Friends disregarded the strictures of their meetings and joined the Union army. Many other Friends, both men and women, went south during and after the war to work with the freed people as teachers or nurses.

The late nineteenth century was a period of change for most Friends. Most visible were those among American Gurneyites. Beginning in the late 1860s, most Gurneyite Friends in the United States were swept up in a wave of revivalism that transformed their lives and worship. The roots of this movement lay in an openness to influences from the larger religious world that Gurneyites had embraced since the 1830s. In the 1860s, many were urging a relaxation of some traditional rules, especially those against marrying a non-Quaker. But the driving force of the revival would be the interdenominational Holiness movement that had a profound impact on American Protestantism between 1850 and 1900. Its advocates argued that all Christians should have two separate, instantaneous experiences, both made possible by faith in the efficacy in the atoning blood of Christ. First they would be converted, born again, or "justified." Then would come the experience of sanctification, or holiness, in which any propensity to sin would be eradicated. In the 1860s and 1870s, this movement drew many Gurneyite Friends. The best known, Hannah Whitall Smith of Philadelphia, had an uneven relationship with Friends. Others, such as David B. Updegraff, Luke Woodard, John Henry Douglas, and Esther Frame, used the message and revivalist techniques of the Holiness movement to revolutionize Quakerism. By 1890, most Gurneyites, an overwhelming majority of American Friends, had changed dramatically. The plain life was restricted mainly to the elderly. Pastors had taken charge of worship, and music had become central to it. Gurneyites followed the lead of other evangelicals in becoming aggressive proponents of missionary work. By 1920, they had established missionary outposts in Mexico, the Caribbean, China, Japan, and East Africa.

Such changes did not come without controversy. The revivals produced a new round of separations between 1877 and 1904, as traditionalist Friends left revived bodies to preserve the old ways. Gradually, they formed common cause with the older Wilburite bodies and became known as Conservative Friends.

Change also came to British Quakerism, although not as dramatically. Although by midcentury, the prevailing ministry and theology was strongly evangelical, most British Friends perceived Quakerism as declining. Unlike their American counterparts, a revival movement did not develop among them, but British Friends did establish evening schools and mission meetings with paid staffs that not only brought in some new members but also gave many younger Friends a sense of purpose. Similarly, English Friends began missionary work in Palestine, Madagascar, and India.

As evangelical Friends innovated and transformed themselves, a liberal Quaker renaissance was emerging in the late nineteenth century. It had two sources. One was the Hicksite wing of American Quakerism. While rejecting revivalism and pastors, American Hicksites were receptive to other changes, significantly relaxing the rules on dress, amusements, and marriage to non-Quakers. By the 1880s, most identified themselves as liberal Protestants and reached out to Unitarians and other religious liberals. A parallel movement began in the London yearly meeting in the 1880s. A turning point came at a conference in Manchester in 1895, after which it was clear that liberal Friends would have the upper hand. In turn, by the early twentieth century, a small but influential group of liberal American Gurneyite Friends, led by Haverford College professor Rufus Jones, had emerged.

While differing on some issues, these liberals shared certain fundamental views about Christianity and Quakerism. They embraced modernist, critical study of the Bible. They emphasized the love and mercy of God, envisioning the death of Christ not as an atoning sacrifice but as an ultimate act of love. They became adherents of the Social Gospel, arguing that Quakerism required social activism on behalf of the poor and disadvantaged. While embracing modern life, however, they also embraced the Quaker past. Liberal Friends produced major works of Quaker history and gave new emphasis to traditional Quaker doctrines, particularly that of the inward light, which they used to argue for the essential goodness of humanity.

By the early twentieth century, Quakerism was becoming increasingly diverse. For the first time in its history, it included significant numbers of Africans, Asians, and Latin Americans. Theologically, it ranged from pastoral Friends who saw themselves as part of the emerging fundamentalist Protestant movement to liberal Friends who embraced Darwinian evolution and critical study of the Bible, with other Friends at almost every point on the doctrinal spectrum between these two extremes. Today, this diversity remains true of Quakerism worldwide, even as all claim spiritual descent from Fox and the "First Publishers of Truth."

THOMAS D. HAMM

Suggestions for Further Reading

PRIMARY SOURCES

Barbour, Hugh, and Arthur O. Roberts, eds. *Early Quaker Writings, 1650–1700*. Wallingford, Pa.: Pendle Hill, 2004.

Barclay, Robert. *An Apology for the True Christian Divinity*. Glenside, Pa.: Quaker Heritage Press, 2002.

Garman, Mary, et al., eds. *Hidden in Plain Sight: Quaker Women's Writings, 1650–1700*. Wallingford, Pa.: Pendle Hill, 1996.

Moulton, Phillips P. *The Journal and Major Essays of John Woolman*. New York: Oxford University Press, 1971.

Nickalls, John L., ed. *The Journal of George Fox*. Philadelphia: Religious Society of Friends, 1995.

SECONDARY SOURCES

Bacon, Margaret Hope. *Mothers of Feminism: The Story of Quaker Women in America*. San Francisco: Harper and Row, 1986.

Barbour, Hugh. *The Quakers in Puritan England*. New Haven: Yale University Press, 1964.

Barbour, Hugh, and J. William Frost. *The Quakers*. Rev. ed. Richmond, Ind.: Friends United Press, 1995.

Birkel, Michael. *Silence and Witness: The Quaker Tradition*. Maryknoll, N.Y.: Orbis, 2004.

Brinton, Howard. *Friends for 350 Years: The History and Beliefs of the Society of Friends Since George Fox Started the Quaker Movement*. Rev. ed. Wallingford, Pa.: Pendle Hill, 2002.

Dandelion, Pink. *An Introduction to Quakerism*. Cambridge: Cambridge University Press, 2007.

Hamm, Thomas D. *The Transformation of American Quakerism: Orthodox Friends, 1800–1907*. Bloomington: Indiana University Press, 1988.

Ingle, H. Larry. *Quakers in Conflict: The Hicksite Reformation*. Knoxville: University of Tennessee Press, 1986.

Kennedy, Thomas C. *British Quakerism, 1860–1920: The Transformation of a Religious Community*. Oxford: Oxford University Press, 2002.

Larson, Rebecca. *Daughters of Light: Quaker Women Preaching and Prophesying in the Colonies and Abroad, 1700–1775*. New York: Knopf, 1999.

McDaniel, Donna, and Vanessa Julye. *Fit for Freedom, Not for Friendship: Quakers, African Americans, and the Myth of Racial Justice*. Philadelphia: Quaker Press, 2009.

Marietta, Jack D. *The Reformation of American Quakerism, 1748–1783*. Philadelphia: University of Pennsylvania Press, 1984.

Moore, Rosemary. *The Light in Their Consciences: Early Quakers in Britain, 1646–1666*. University Park: Penn State University Press, 2000.

Punshon, John. *Portrait in Grey: A Short History of the Quakers*. London: Quaker Books, 2006.

Weddle, Meredith Baldwin. *Walking in the Way of Peace: Quaker Pacifism in the Seventeenth Century*. New York: Oxford University Press, 2001.

A Note on the Texts

The texts used in this collection are, with one exception, taken from published works no longer under copyright. While modern editors have, in many cases, produced editions that are more literally correct or consistent with original manuscripts, in no case have I reproduced texts that are not true to the original meaning or intent of the authors. In some cases, I have modernized spelling and inserted punctuation to enhance readability. "The Vision of John Beals" is reproduced with permission of the Friends Historical Collection, Guilford College, Greensboro, North Carolina.

Quaker Writings

PART I

BEGINNINGS

1645–1660

FOUNDERS

GEORGE FOX

While historians debate whether George Fox was the founder of Quakerism, no one disputes that he was at the center of the movement from the 1640s until his death in 1691. In the 1670s, Fox recorded his memories of his early life and of the beginnings of the Quaker movement.

The Journal of George Fox; Being an Historical Account of His Life, Travels, Sufferings, and Christian Experiences (London, 1902).

I was born in the month called July, 1624, at Drayton-in-the-Clay, in Leicestershire. My father's name was Christopher Fox: he was by profession a weaver, an honest man; and there was a seed of God in him. The neighbours called him Righteous Christer. My mother was an upright woman; her maiden name was Mary Lago, of the family of the Lagos, and of the stock of the martyrs.

In my very young years I had a gravity and staidness of mind and spirit, not usual in children; insomuch, that when I saw old men behave lightly and wantonly towards each other, I had a dislike thereof raised in my heart, and said within myself, "If ever I come to be a man, surely I shall not do so, nor be so wanton."

When I came to eleven years of age, I knew pureness and righteousness; for while a child I was taught how to walk to be kept pure. The Lord taught me to be faithful in all things, and to act faithfully two ways, viz., inwardly to God, and outwardly to man; and to keep to Yea and Nay in all things. For the Lord showed me, that though the people of the world have mouths full of deceit, and changeable words, yet I was to keep to Yea and Nay in all things; and that my words should be few and savoury, seasoned with grace; and that I might not eat and drink to make myself wanton, but for health, using the creatures in their service, as servants in their places, to the glory of Him that created them; they being in their covenant, and I being brought up into the covenant, as sanctified by the Word which was in the beginning, by which all things are upheld; wherein is unity with the creation. . . .

Afterwards, as I grew up, my relations thought to make me a priest; but others persuaded to the contrary: whereupon I was put to a man, a shoemaker by trade, but who dealt in wool, and was a grazier, and sold cattle; and a great deal went through my hands. While I was with him, he was blessed; but after I left him he broke, and came to nothing. I never wronged man or woman in all that time; for the Lord's power was with me, and over me to preserve me. While I was in that service, I used in my dealings the word Verily, and it was a common saying among people that knew me, "If George says Verily, there is no altering him." When boys and rude people would laugh at me, I let them alone, and went my way; but people had generally a love to me for my innocency and honesty.

When I came towards nineteen years of age, being upon business at a fair, one of my cousins, whose name was Bradford, a professor, and having another professor with him, came to me and asked me to drink part of a jug of beer with them, and I, being thirsty, went in with them; for I loved any that had a sense of good, or that sought after the Lord.* When we had drunk each a glass, they began to drink healths, calling for more, and agreeing together, that he that would not drink should pay all. I was grieved that any who made profession of religion, should do so. They grieved me very much, having never had such a thing put to me before, by any sort of people; wherefore I rose up to go, and putting my hand into my pocket, laid a groat on the table before them, and said, "If it be so, I will leave you." So I went away; and when I had done what business I had to do, I returned home, but did not go to bed that night, nor could I sleep, but sometimes walked up and down, and sometimes prayed and cried to the Lord, who said unto me, "Thou seest how young people go together into vanity, and old people into the earth; thou must for-

---

*[Fox means one who professes religion. —ed.]

sake all, both young and old, and keep out of all, and be as a stranger unto all."

Then at the command of God, on the ninth day of the seventh month, 1643, I left my relations, and broke off all familiarity or fellowship with old or young. I passed to Lutterworth, where I stayed some time; and thence to Northampton, where also I made some stay: then to Newport-Pagnell, whence, after I had stayed a while, I went to Barnet, in . . . June 1644. As I thus traveled through the country, professors took notice and sought to be acquainted with me; but I was afraid of them, for I was sensible they did not possess what they professed.

Now during the time that I was at Barnet, a strong temptation to despair came upon me. Then I saw how Christ was tempted, and mighty troubles I was in; sometimes I kept myself retired in my chamber, and often walked solitary in the chace, to wait upon the Lord. I wondered why these things should come to me; and I looked upon myself and said, "Was I ever so before?". . . Temptations grew more and more, and I was tempted almost to despair; and when Satan could not effect his design upon me that way, he laid snares for me, and baits to draw me to commit some sin, whereby he might take advantage to bring me to despair. I was about twenty years of age when these exercises came upon me; and I continued in that condition some years, in great trouble, and fain would have put it from me. I went to many a priest to look for comfort, but found no comfort from them. . . .

When I was come down into Leicestershire, my relations would have had me marry, but I told them I was but a lad, and I must get wisdom. Others would have had me into the auxiliary band among the soldiery, but I refused; and I was grieved that they proffered such things to me, being a tender youth. Then I went to Coventry, where I took a chamber for a while at a professor's house, till people began to be acquainted with me; for there were many tender people in that town. After some time I went into my own country again, and was there about a year, in great sorrows and troubles, and walked many nights by myself.

Then the priest of Drayton, the town of my birth, whose name was Nathaniel Stevens, came often to me, and I went often to him; and another priest sometimes came with him; and they would give place to me to hear me, and I would ask them questions, and reason with them. And this priest Stevens asked me a question, viz., Why Christ cried out upon the cross, "My God, my God, why hast thou forsaken me?" and why he said, "If it be possible, let this cup pass from me; yet not my will, but thine be done"? I told him that at that time the sins of all mankind were upon Him, and their iniquities and transgressions with which He was wounded, which He was to bear, and to be an offering for, as He was man, but He died not as He was God; and so, in that He died for all men, and tasted death for every man, He was an offering for the sins of the whole world. This I spoke, being at that time in a measure sensible of Christ's sufferings, and what He went through. And the priest said, "It was a very good, full answer, and such a one as he had not heard." At that time he would applaud and speak highly of me to others; and what I said in discourse to him on the weekdays, he would preach on the first-days; for which I did not like him. This priest afterwards became my great persecutor.

After this I went to another ancient priest at Mancetter, in Warwickshire, and reasoned with him about the ground of despair and temptations; but he was ignorant of my condition; he bade me take tobacco and sing psalms. Tobacco was a thing I did not love, and psalms I was not in a state to sing; I could not sing. Then he bid me come again, and he would tell me many things; but when I came he was angry and pettish, for my former words had displeased him. He told my troubles, sorrows, and griefs to his servants; which grieved me that I had opened my mind to such a one. I saw they were all miserable comforters; and this brought my troubles more upon me. Then I heard of a priest living about Tamworth, who was accounted an experienced man, and I went seven miles to him; but I found him only like an empty hollow cask. I heard also of one called Dr. Cradock, of Coventry, and went to him. I asked him the ground of temptations and despair, and how troubles came to be wrought in man? He asked me, Who was Christ's father and mother? I told him, Mary was his mother, and that he was supposed to be the son of Joseph, but he was the Son of God. Now, as we were walking together in his garden, the alley being narrow, I chanced, in turning, to set my foot on the side of a bed, at which the man was in a rage, as if his house had been on fire. Thus all our discourse was lost, and I went away in sorrow, worse than I was when I came. I thought them miserable comforters, and saw they were all as nothing to me; for they could not reach my condition.

After this I went to another, one Macham, a priest in high account. He would needs give me some physic, and I was to have been let blood; but they could not get one drop of blood from me, either in arms or head (though they endeavoured to do so), my body being as it were, dried up with sorrows, grief and troubles, which were so great upon me that I could have wished I had never been born, or that I had been born blind, that I might never have seen wickedness or vanity; and deaf, that I might never have heard vain and wicked words, or the Lord's name blasphemed. When the time called Christmas came, while others were feasting and sporting themselves, I looked out poor widows from house to house, and gave them some money. When I was invited to marriages (as I sometimes was), I went to none at all, but the next day, or soon after, I would go and visit them; and if they were poor, I gave them some money; for I had wherewith both to keep myself from being chargeable to others, and to administer something to the necessities of those who were in need.

About the beginning of the year 1646, as I was going to Coventry, and approaching towards the gate, a consideration arose in me, how it was said that, "all Christians are believers, both Protestants and Papists"; and the Lord opened to me that, if all were believers, then they were all born of God, and passed from death to life, and that none were true believers but such; and though others said they were believers, yet they were not. At another time, as I was walking in a field on a first-day morning, the Lord opened to me, "that being bred at Oxford or Cambridge was not enough to fit and qualify men to be ministers of Christ"; and I wondered at it, because it was the common belief of people. But I saw it clearly as the Lord opened it to me, and was satisfied, and admired the goodness of the Lord who had opened this thing unto me that morning. This struck at priest Stevens' ministry, namely, "that to be bred at Oxford or Cambridge was not enough to make a man fit to be a minister of Christ." . . . But my relations were much troubled that I would not go with them to hear the priest; for I would get into the orchards, or the fields, with my Bible by myself. I asked them, Did not the apostle say to believers, that "they needed no man to teach them, but as the anointing teacheth them?" And though they knew this was Scripture, and that it was true, yet they were grieved because I could not be subject in this matter, to go to hear the priest with them. I saw that to be a true believer was another thing than they looked upon it to be; and I saw that being bred at Oxford or Cambridge did not qualify or fit a man to be a minister of Christ: what then should I follow such for? So neither these, nor any of the Dissenting people, could I join with, but was as a stranger to all, relying wholly upon the Lord Jesus Christ.

At another time it was opened in me, "That God, who made the world, did not dwell in temples made with hands." This at first seemed a strange word, because both priests and people used to call their temples or churches, dreadful places, holy ground, and the temples of God. But the Lord showed me clearly, that he did not dwell in these temples which men had commanded and set up, but in people's hearts: for both Stephen and the apostle Paul bore testimony, that he did not dwell in temples made with hands, not even in that which he had once commanded to be built, since he put an end to it; but that his people were his temple, and he dwelt in them. This opened in me as I walked in the fields to my relations' house. When I came there, they told me that Nathaniel Stevens, the priest, had been there, and told them "he was afraid of me, for going after new lights." I smiled in myself, knowing what the Lord had opened in me concerning him and his brethren; but I told not my relations, who though they saw beyond the priests, yet they went to hear them, and were grieved because I would not go also. But I brought them Scriptures, and told them, there was an anointing within man to teach him, and that the Lord would teach his people himself. I had also great openings concerning the things written in the Revelations; and when I spoke of them, the priests and professors would say that was a sealed book, and would have kept me out of it: but I told them, Christ could open the seals, and that they were the nearest things to us; for the Epistles were written to the saints that lived in former ages, but the Revelations were written of things to come.

After this, I met with a sort of people that held women have no souls, (adding in a light manner), no more than a goose. But I reproved them, and told them that was not right; for Mary said, "My soul doth magnify the Lord, and my spirit hath rejoiced in God my Saviour."

Removing to another place, I came among a people that relied much on dreams. I told them, except they could distinguish between dream and dream, they would confound all together; for there were three sorts of dreams; multitude of business sometimes caused dreams; and there were whisperings of Satan in man in the night-season; and there were speakings of God to man in dreams. But these people came out of these things, and at last became Friends.

Now though I had great openings, yet great trouble and temptation came many times upon me; so that when it was day, I wished for night, and when it was night, I wished for day: and by reason of the openings I had in my troubles, I could say as David said, "Day unto day uttereth speech, and night unto night showeth knowledge." When I had openings, they answered one another, and answered the Scriptures; for I had great openings of the Scriptures: and when I was in troubles, one trouble also answered to another.

About the beginning of the year 1647, I was moved of the Lord to go into Derbyshire, where I met with some friendly people, and had many discourses with them. Then passing further into the Peak-country, I met with more friendly people, and with some in empty, high notions. Travelling on through some parts of Leicestershire and into Nottinghamshire, I met with a tender people, and a very tender woman, whose name was Elizabeth Hooton; and with these I had some meetings and discourses. But my troubles continued, and I was often under great temptations; I fasted much, and walked abroad in solitary places many days, and often took my Bible, and went and sat in hollow trees and lonesome places till night came on; and frequently, in the night, walked mournfully about by myself: for I was a man of sorrows in the times of the first workings of the Lord in me.

During all this time I was never joined in profession of religion with any, but gave myself up to the Lord, having forsaken all evil company, and taken leave of father and mother, and all other relations, and traveled up and down as a stranger in the earth, which way the Lord inclined my heart; taking a chamber to myself in the town where I came, and tarrying sometimes a month, more or less, in a place; for I durst not stay long in any place, being afraid both of professor and profane, lest, being a tender young man, I should be hurt by conversing much with either. For which reason I kept myself much as a stranger, seeking heavenly wisdom and getting knowledge from the Lord; and was brought off from outward things, to rely wholly on the Lord alone. Though my exer-

cises and troubles were very great, yet were they not so continual
but that I had some intermissions, and was sometimes brought
into such a heavenly joy, that I thought I had been in Abraham's
bosom. As I cannot declare the misery I was in, it was so great
and heavy upon me; so neither can I set forth the mercies of God
unto me in all my misery. O, the everlasting love of God to my
soul, when I was in great distress! when my troubles and torments
were great, then was his love exceedingly great. "Thou, Lord, makest a fruitful field a barren wilderness, and a barren wilderness a
fruitful field; thou bringest down and settest up; thou killest and
makest alive; all honour and glory be to thee, O Lord of glory; the
knowledge of thee in the Spirit, is life; but that knowledge which
is fleshly, works death." While there is this knowledge in the flesh,
deceit and self-will conform to anything, and will say yes, yes, to
that it doth not know. The knowledge which the world hath of
what the prophets and apostles spoke, is a fleshly knowledge; and
the apostates from the life, in which the prophets and apostles
were, have gotten their words, the Holy Scriptures, in a form, but
not in their life nor Spirit that gave them forth. So they all lie in
confusion, and are making provision for the flesh, to fulfill the
lusts thereof; but not to fulfill the law and command of Christ in
his power and Spirit; this, they say, they cannot do; but to fulfill
the lusts of the flesh, that they can do with delight.

Now after I had received that opening from the Lord, that "to
be bred at Oxford or Cambridge was not sufficient to fit a man to
be a minister of Christ," I regarded the priests less, and looked
more after the Dissenting people. Among them I saw there was
some tenderness; and many of them came afterwards to be convinced, for they had some openings. But as I had forsaken the
priests, so I left the separate preachers also, and those esteemed the
most experienced people; for I saw there was none among them all
that could speak to my condition. When all my hopes in them and
in all men were gone, so that I had nothing outwardly to help me,
nor could I tell what to do; then, O! then I heard a voice which
said, "There is one, even Christ Jesus, that can speak to thy condition"; and when I heard it, my heart did leap for joy. Then the
Lord let me see why there was none upon the earth that could
speak to my condition, namely, that I might give him all the glory;
for all are concluded under sin, and shut up in unbelief, as I had
been, that Jesus Christ might have the pre-eminence, who enlight-

ens, and gives grace, and faith, and power. Thus when God doth work, who shall hinder it? and this I knew experimentally. My desires after the Lord grew stronger, and zeal in the pure knowledge of God, and of Christ alone, without the help of any man, book, or writing. For though I read the Scriptures that spoke of Christ and of God, yet I knew him not, but by revelation, as he who hath the key did open, and as the Father of Life drew me to his Son by his Spirit. Then the Lord gently led me along, and let me see his love, which was endless and eternal, surpassing all the knowledge that men have in the natural state, or can obtain from history or books and that love let me see myself, as I was without him. I was afraid of all company, for I saw them perfectly where they were, through the love of God, which let me see myself. I had not fellowship with any people, priests, or professors, or any sort of separated people, but with Christ, who hath the key, and opened the door of Light and Life unto me. I was afraid of all carnal talk and talkers, for I could see nothing but corruptions, and the life lay under the burthen of corruptions. When I myself was in the deep, shut up under all, I could not believe that I should ever overcome; my troubles, my sorrows, and my temptations were so great, that I thought many times I should have despaired, I was so tempted. But when Christ opened to me, . . . that through his power, light, grace, and Spirit, I should overcome also, I had confidence in him; so he it was that opened to me, when I was shut up, and had no hope nor faith. Christ, who had enlightened me, gave me his light to believe in; he gave me hope, which he himself revealed in me, and he gave me his Spirit and grace, which I found sufficient in the deeps and in weakness. Thus, in the deepest miseries, and in the greatest sorrows and temptations, that many times beset me, the Lord in his mercy did keep me. I found that there were two thirsts in me; the one after the creatures, to get help and strength there; and the other after the Lord, the Creator, and his Son Jesus Christ. I saw all the world could do me no good; if I had had a king's diet, palace, and attendance, all would have been as nothing; for nothing gave me comfort, but the Lord by his power. I saw professors, priests, and people, were whole and at ease in that condition which was my misery; and they loved that which I would have been rid of. But the Lord stayed my desires upon himself, from whom came my help, and my care was cast upon him alone. Therefore, all wait patiently upon the Lord, what-

soever condition you be in; wait in the grace and truth that comes
by Jesus: for if ye so do, there is a promise to you, and the Lord
God will fulfill it in you. Blessed are all they that do indeed hunger
and thirst after righteousness, they shall be satisfied with it. I have
found it so, praised be the Lord who filleth with it, and satisfieth
the desires of the hungry soul. O let the house of the spiritual Israel say, "His mercy endureth forever!" It is the great love of God
to make a wilderness of that which is pleasant to the outward eye
and fleshly mind; and to make a fruitful field of a barren wilderness. This is the great work of God. But while people's minds run
in the earthly, after the creatures and changeable things, changeable ways and religions, and changeable, uncertain teachers, their
minds are in bondage, they are brittle and changeable, tossed up
and down with windy doctrines and thoughts, and notions and
things; their minds being out of the unchangeable truth in the
inward parts, the Light of Jesus Christ, which would keep them
to the unchangeable. He is the way to the Father; and in all my
troubles he preserved me by his Spirit and power; praised be his
holy name forever! . . .

One day when I had been walking solitarily abroad, and was
come home, I was wrapped up in the love of God, so that I could
not but admire the greatness of his love. While I was in that condition it was opened unto me by the eternal Light and Power, and I
saw clearly therein, "that all was done, and to be done, in and by
Christ; and how he conquers and destroys this tempter, the Devil,
and all his works, and is above him; and that all these troubles
were good for me, and temptations for the trial of my faith, which
Christ had given me." The Lord opened me, that I saw through all
these troubles and temptations; my living faith was raised, that I
saw all was done by Christ, the Life, and my belief was in Him.
When at any time my condition was veiled, my secret belief was
stayed firm, and hope underneath held me, as an anchor in the
bottom of the sea, and anchored my immortal soul to its Bishop,
causing it to swim above the sea, the world, where all the raging
waves, foul weather, tempests, and temptations are. But, O! then
did I see my troubles, trials, and temptations more clearly than
ever I had done. As the light appeared, all appeared that is out
of the light; darkness, death, temptations, the unrighteous, the
ungodly; all was manifest and seen in the light. After this, a pure
fire appeared in me: then I saw how he sat as a refiner's fire and as

fullers' soap;—then the spiritual discerning came into me, by which I did discern my own thoughts, groans, and sighs; and what it was that veiled me, and what it was that opened me. That which could not abide in the patience, nor endure the fire, in the light I found it to be the groans of the flesh, that could not give up to the will of God, which had veiled me; and that could not be patient in all trials, troubles, and perplexities;—could not give up self to die by the cross, the power of God, that the living and quickened might follow him; and that that which would cloud and veil from the presence of Christ—that which the sword of the Spirit cuts down, and which must die, might not be kept alive. I discerned also the groans of the Spirit, which opened me, and made intercession to God; in which Spirit is the true waiting upon God, for the redemption of the body and of the whole creation. By this Spirit, in which the true sighing is, I saw over the false sighings and groanings. By this invisible Spirit I discerned all the false hearing, the false seeing, and the false smelling which was above the Spirit, quenching and grieving it; and that all they that were there, were in confusion and deceit, where the false asking and praying is, in deceit, in that nature and tongue that takes God's holy name in vain, wallows in the Egyptian sea, and asketh, but hath not; for they hate his light and resist the Holy Ghost; turn grace into wantonness, and rebel against the Spirit; and are erred from the faith they should ask in, and from the Spirit they should pray by. He that knoweth these things in the true Spirit, can witness them. The divine light of Christ manifesteth all things; the spiritual fire trieth all things, and severeth all things. Several things did I then see as the Lord opened them to me; for he showed me that which can live in his holy refining fire, and that can live to God under his law. He made me sensible how the law and the prophets were until John; and how the least in the everlasting kingdom of God is greater than John.

The pure and perfect law of God is over the flesh, to keep it and its works, which are not perfect, under, by the perfect law; and the law of God that is perfect, answers the perfect principle of God in every one. This law the Jews, and the prophets, and John were to perform and do. None know the giver of this law but by the Spirit of God; neither can any truly read it, or hear its voice, but by the Spirit of God; he that can receive it, let him. John, who was the greatest prophet that was born of a woman, did bear witness to the light, which Christ, the great heavenly prophet, hath enlightened every man that cometh into the world withal; that they might believe in it, and become the children of light, and so have the light of life, and not come into condemnation. For the true belief stands in the light that condemns all evil, and the Devil, who is the prince of darkness, and would draw out of the light into condemnation. They that walk in this light, come to the mountain of the house of God, established above all mountains, and to God's teaching, who will teach them his ways. These things were opened to me in the light. . . .

About this time there was a great meeting of the Baptists, at Broughton, in Leicestershire, with some that had separated from them; and people of other notions went thither, and I went also. Not many of the Baptists came, but many others were there. The Lord opened my mouth, and the everlasting truth was declared amongst them, and the power of the Lord was over them all. For in that day the Lord's power began to spring, and I had great openings in the Scriptures. Several were convinced in those parts, and were turned from darkness to light, from the power of Satan unto God; and many were raised up to praise God. When I reasoned with professors and other people, some became convinced.

I was still under great temptations sometimes, and my inward sufferings were heavy; but I could find none to open my condition to but the Lord alone, unto whom I cried night and day. I went back into Nottinghamshire, and there the Lord showed me that the natures of those things, which were hurtful without, were within, in the hearts and minds of wicked men. The natures of dogs, swine, vipers, of Sodom and Egypt, Pharaoh, Cain, Ishmael, Esau, &c.; the natures of these I saw within, though people had been looking without. I cried to the Lord, saying, "Why should I be thus, seeing I was never addicted to commit those evils?" and the Lord answered, "That it was needful I should have a sense of all conditions, how else should I speak to all conditions?" and in this I saw the infinite love of God. I saw also, that there was an ocean of darkness and death; but an infinite ocean of light and love, which flowed over the ocean of darkness. In that also I saw the infinite love of God, and I had great openings. . . .

Then came people from far and near to see me; but I was fearful of being drawn out by them; yet I was made to speak, and open things to them. There was one Brown, who had great prophecies and sights of me upon his deathbed. He spoke openly of what I should be made instrumental by the Lord to bring forth. And of others he spoke, that they should come to nothing, which was fulfilled on some, who then were something in show. When this man was buried, a great work of the Lord fell upon me, to the admiration of many, who thought I had been dead; and many came to see me for about fourteen days. I was very much altered in countenance and person, as if my body had been new moulded or changed. . . .

From 1648 to 1652, Fox traveled through the north of England, sharing his vision of faith. He preached wherever he found listeners, and continued to have revelations and ecstatic experiences. Although facing fierce opposition, and thrown into jail in Derby in 1650 as a blasphemer, he found followers. From his experience of the light to his convictions about English grammar, these would become foundations of Quakerism.

After this I went again to Mansfield, where was a great meeting of professors and people; here I was moved to pray; and the Lord's power was so great, that the house seemed to be shaken. When I had done, some of the professors said it was now as in the days of the apostles, when the house was shaken where they were. After I had prayed, one of the professors would pray, which brought deadness and a veil over them: and others of the professors were grieved at him and told him, it was a temptation upon him. Then he came to me, and desired that I would pray again; but I could not pray in man's will.

Soon after there was another great meeting of professors, and a captain, whose name was Amor Stoddard, came in. They were discoursing of the blood of Christ; and as they were discoursing of it, I saw, through the immediate opening of the Invisible Spirit, the blood of Christ. And I cried out among them, and said, "Do ye not see the blood of Christ? See it in your hearts, to sprinkle your hearts and consciences from dead works, to serve the living God"; for I saw it, the blood of the New Covenant, how it came into the heart. This startled the professors, who would have the blood only without them, and not in them. But Captain Stoddard was reached, and said, "Let the youth speak; hear the youth speak"; when he saw they endeavoured to bear me down with many words. . . .

Then I heard of a great meeting to be at Leicester, for a dispute, wherein Presbyterians, Independents, Baptists, and Common-prayer-men were said to be all concerned.* The meeting was in a steeple-house; and thither I was moved by the Lord God to go, and be amongst them. I heard their discourse and reasonings, some being in pews, and the priest in the pulpit; abundance of people being gathered together. At last one woman asked a question out of Peter, What that birth was, viz., a being born again of incorruptible seed, by the Word of God, that liveth and abideth for ever? And the priest said to her, "I permit not a woman to speak in the church"; though he had before given liberty for any to speak. Whereupon I was wrapped up, as in a rapture, in the Lord's power; and I stepped up and asked the priest, "Dost thou call this (the steeple-house) a church? Or dost thou call this mixed multitude a church?" For the woman asking a question, he ought to have answered it, having given liberty for any to speak. But, instead of answering me, he asked me what a church was? I told him, "The church was the pillar and ground of truth, made up of living stones, living members, a spiritual household, which Christ was the head of: but he was not the head of a mixed multitude, or of an old house made up of lime, stones, and wood." This set them all on fire: the priest came down out of his pulpit, and others out of their pews, and the dispute there was marred. But I went to a great inn, and there disputed the thing with the priests and professors of all sorts; and they were all on a fire. But I maintained the true church, and the true head thereof, over the heads of them all, till they all gave out and fled away. One man seemed loving, and appeared for a while to join with me; but he soon turned against me, and joined with a priest, in pleading for infants' baptism, though he himself had been a Baptist before; and so left me alone. Howbeit, there were several convinced that day; and the woman that asked the question was convinced, and her family; and the Lord's power and glory shone over all. . . .

* [Fox means those who followed the Church of England's *Book of Common Prayer.* —ed.]

Moreover, I was moved to go to several courts and steeple-houses at Mansfield, and other places, to warn them to leave off oppression and oaths, and to turn from deceit to the Lord, and do justly. Particularly at Mansfield, after I had been at a court there, I was moved to go and speak to one of the most wicked men in the country, one who was a common drunkard, a noted whore-master, and a rhyme-maker; and I reproved him in the dread of the mighty God, for his evil courses. When I had done speaking, and left him, he came after me, and told me, that he was so smitten when I spoke to him, that he had scarcely any strength left in him. So this man was convinced, and turned from his wickedness, and remained an honest, sober man, to the astonishment of the people who had known him before. Thus the work of the Lord went forward, and many were turned from the darkness to the light, within the compass of these three years, 1646, 1647, and 1648. Divers meetings of Friends, in several places, were then gathered to God's teaching, by his light, Spirit, and power; for the Lord's power broke forth more and more, wonderfully.

Now was I come up in Spirit through the flaming sword, into the paradise of God. All things were new; and all the creation gave another smell unto me than before, beyond what words can utter. I knew nothing but pureness, and innocency, and righteousness, being renewed into the image of God by Christ Jesus, to the state of Adam, which he was in before he fell. The creation was opened to me; and it was showed me how all things had their names given them, according to their nature and virtue. I was at a stand in my mind, whether I should practice physic for the good of mankind, seeing the nature and virtues of things were so opened to me by the Lord. But I was immediately taken up in Spirit, to see into another or more steadfast state than Adam's innocency, even into a state in Christ Jesus, that should never fall. And the Lord showed me that such as were faithful to him, in the power and light of Christ, should come up into that state in which Adam was before he fell; in which the admirable works of creation, and the virtues thereof, may be known, through the openings of that divine Word of wisdom and power, by which they were made.

Great things did the Lord lead me into, and wonderful depths were opened unto me, beyond what can by words be declared; but as people come into subjection to the Spirit of God, and grow up in the image and power of the Almighty, they may receive the Word of Wisdom, that opens all things, and come to know the hidden unity in the Eternal Being. . . .

Now the Lord God opened to me by his invisible power, "that every man was enlightened by the divine light of Christ"; and I saw it shine through all; and that they that believed in it came out of condemnation to the light of life, and became the children of it; but they that hated it, and did not believe in it, were condemned by it, though they made a profession of Christ. This I saw in the pure openings of the light, without the help of any man; neither did I then know where to find it in the Scriptures, though afterwards, searching the Scriptures, I found it. For I saw in that Light and Spirit which was before the Scriptures were given forth, and which led the holy men of God to give them forth, that all must come to that Spirit, if they would know God, or Christ, or the Scriptures aright, which they that gave them forth were led and taught by. . . .

I was sent to turn people from darkness to the light, that they might receive Christ Jesus: for, to as many as should receive him in his light, I saw that he would give power to become the sons of God; which I had obtained by receiving Christ. I was to direct people to the Spirit, that gave forth the Scriptures, by which they might be led into all truth, and so up to Christ and God, as they had been who gave them forth. I was to turn them to the grace of God, and to the truth in the heart, which came by Jesus; that by this grace they might be taught, which would bring them salvation, that their hearts might be established by it, and their words might be seasoned, and all might come to know their salvation nigh. I saw that Christ died for all men, and was a propitiation for all; and enlightened all men and women with his divine and saving light; and that none could be a true believer, but who believed in it. I saw that the grace of God, which bringeth salvation, had appeared to all men, and that the manifestation of the Spirit of God was given to every man, to profit withal. These things I did not see by the help of man, nor by the letter, though they are written in the letter, but I saw them in the light of the Lord Jesus Christ, and by his immediate Spirit and power, as did the holy men of God, by whom the Holy Scriptures were written. Yet I had no slight esteem of the Holy Scriptures, but they were very precious to me, for I was in that Spirit by which they were given forth: and what the Lord opened in me, I afterwards found was agreeable to them. I could speak much of these things, and many volumes might be written, but all would prove too short to set forth the infinite love, wisdom, and power of God, in preparing, fitting, and furnishing me for the service he had appointed me to; letting me see the depths of Satan on the one hand, and opening to me, on the other hand, the divine mysteries of His own everlasting kingdom.

Now, when the Lord God and his son Jesus Christ sent me forth into the world, to preach his everlasting gospel and kingdom, I was glad that I was commanded to turn people to that inward light, Spirit, and grace, by which all might know their salvation, and their way to God; even that Divine Spirit which would lead them into all truth, and which I infallibly knew would never deceive any.

But with and by this divine power and Spirit of God, and the light of Jesus, I was to bring people off from all their own ways, to Christ, the new and living way; and from their churches, which men had made and gathered, to the church in God, the general assembly written in heaven which Christ is the head of; and off from the world's teachers, made by men, to learn of Christ, who is the way, the truth, and the life, of whom the Father said, "This is my beloved Son, hear ye him"; and off from all the world's worships, to know the Spirit of Truth in the inward parts, and to be led thereby; that in it they might worship the Father of spirits, who seeks such to worship him; which Spirit they that worshipped not in, knew not what they worshipped. And I was to bring people off from all the world's religions, which are vain; that they might know the pure religion, might visit the fatherless, the widows, and the strangers, and keep themselves from the spots of the world; then there would not be so many beggars, the sight of whom often grieved my heart, as it denoted so much hard-heartedness amongst them that professed the name of Christ. I was to bring them off from all the world's fellowships, and prayings, and singings, which stood in forms without power; that their fellowship might be in the Holy Ghost, and in the Eternal Spirit of God; that they might pray in the Holy Ghost, and sing in the Spirit, and with the grace that comes by Jesus; making melody in their hearts to the Lord, who hath sent his beloved Son to be their Saviour, and caused his heavenly sun to shine upon all the world, and through them all, and his heavenly rain to fall upon the just and the unjust (as his outward rain doth fall, and his outward sun doth shine on all), which is God's unspeakable love to the world. I was to bring people off from Jewish ceremonies, and from heathenish fables, and from men's inventions and windy doctrines, by which they blew the people about this way and the other way, from sect to sect; and from all their beggarly rudiments, with their schools and colleges for making ministers of Christ, who are indeed ministers of their own making, but not of Christ's; and from all their images and crosses, and sprinkling of infants, with all their holy days (so called) and all their vain traditions, which they had instituted since the apostles' days, which the Lord's power was against: in the dread and authority of which, I was moved to declare against them all, and against all that preached and not freely, as being such as had not received freely from Christ.

Moreover, when the Lord sent me forth into the world, he forbade me to put off my hat to any, high or low; and I was required to Thee and Thou all men and women, without any respect to rich or poor, great or small. And as I traveled up and down, I was not to bid people good morrow or good evening; neither might I bow or scrape with my leg to any one; and this made the sects and professions to rage. But the Lord's power carried me over all to his glory, and many came to be turned to God in a little time; for the heavenly day of the Lord sprung from on high, and broke forth apace, by the light of which many came to see where they were.

But O! the rage that then was in the priests, magistrates, professors, and people of all sorts; but especially in priests and professors! for, though Thou, to a single person, was according to their own learning, their accidence, and grammar rules, and according to the Bible, yet they could not bear to hear it: and as to the hat-honour, because I could not put off my hat to them, it set them all into a rage. But the Lord showed me that it was an honour below, which he would lay in the dust, and stain;—an honour which proud flesh looked for, but sought not the honour which came from God only;—an honour invented by men in the fall, and in the alienation from God, who were offended if it were not given them; and yet they would be looked upon as saints, church-members and great Christians: but Christ saith, "How can ye believe, who receive honour one of another, and seek not the honour that cometh from God only?" "And I (saith Christ) receive not honour of men": showing that men have an honour, which men will receive and give; but Christ will have none of it. This is the honour which Christ will not receive, and which must be laid in the dust. . . .

About this time I was sorely exercised in going to their courts to cry for justice, and in speaking and writing to judges and justices to do justly; in warning such as kept public-houses for entertainment, that they should not let people have more drink than would do them good; and in testifying against their wakes or feasts, May-games, sports, plays, and shows, which trained up people to vanity and looseness, and led them from the fear of God; and the days they had set forth for holy-days were usually the times wherein they most dishonoured God by these things. In fairs, also, and in markets, I was made to declare against their deceitful merchandise, cheating, and cozening; warning all to deal justly, to speak the truth, to let their yea be yea, and their nay be nay; and to do unto others as they would have others do unto them; forewarning them of the great and terrible day of the Lord, which would come upon them all. I was moved also to cry against all sorts of music, and against the mountebanks playing tricks on their stages, for they burdened the pure life, and stirred up people's minds to vanity. I was much exercised, too, with schoolmasters and schoolmistresses, warning them to teach their children sobriety in the fear of the Lord, that they might not be nursed and trained up in lightness, vanity, and wantonness. Likewise I was made to warn masters and mistresses, fathers and mothers in private families, to take care that their children and servants might be trained up in the fear of the Lord; and that they themselves should be therein examples and patterns of sobriety and virtue to them. For I saw that as the Jews were to teach their children the law of God and the old covenant, and to train them up in it, and their servants, yea, the very strangers were to keep the Sabbath amongst them, and be circumcised, before they might eat of their sacrifices; so all Christians, and all that made a profession of Christianity, ought to train up their children and servants in the new covenant of light, Christ Jesus, who is God's salvation to the ends of the earth, that all may know their salvation: and they ought to train them up in the law of life, the law of the Spirit, the law of love and of faith; that they might be made free from the law of sin and death. And all Christians ought to be circumcised by the Spirit, which puts off the body of the sins of the flesh, that they may come to eat of the heavenly sacrifice, Christ Jesus, that true spiritual food, which none can rightly feed upon but they that are circumcised by the Spirit. Likewise, I was exercised about the star-gazers,* who drew people's minds from Christ, the bright and the morning star; and from the Sun of righteousness, by whom the sun, and moon, and stars, and all things else were made, who is the wisdom of God, and from whom the right knowledge of all things is received. . . .

> *By 1652, Fox had gained a core of followers, many of whom would be leaders of the Quaker movement for the next decade. Traveling from Yorkshire into Lancashire in spring 1652, Fox had one of his most critical visions, of "a great people to be gathered," which many regard as the beginning of Quakerism as a movement.*

As we traveled through the country, preaching repentance to the people, we came into a town on the market-day. There was a lecture there that day; and I went into the steeple-house, where were many priests, professors, and people. The priest that preached, took for his text those words of Jeremiah, chap. v., ver. 31: "My people love to have it so," leaving out the foregoing words, viz., "The prophets prophesy falsely, and the priests bear rule by their means." So I showed the people his deceit, and directed them to Christ, the true Teacher within; declaring, "that God was come to teach his people himself, and to bring them off from all the world's teachers and hirelings, that they might come to receive freely from him." Then warning them of the day of the Lord, that was coming upon all flesh, I passed from thence without much opposition.

The next day we passed on; for the Lord had said unto me, "If but one man or woman were raised up by His power, to stand and live in the same Spirit that the prophets and apostles were in, who gave forth the Scriptures, that man or woman should shake all the country in their profession for ten miles round." For people had the Scriptures, but not in that same light, and power, and Spirit, which they were in that gave forth the Scriptures; and so they neither knew God, nor Christ, nor the Scriptures aright; nor had

---

* [Astrologers. —ed.]

they unity one with another, being out of the power and Spirit of God. Therefore as we passed along we warned all people, wherever we met them, of the day of the Lord that was coming upon them.

As we traveled we came near a very great hill, called Pendle Hill, and I was moved of the Lord to go up to the top of it; which I did with difficulty, it was so very steep and high. When I was come to the top, I saw the sea bordering upon Lancashire. From the top of this hill the Lord let me see in what places he had a great people to be gathered. . . .

At night we came to an inn, and declared truth to the man of the house, and wrote a paper to the priests and professors, declaring "the day of the Lord, and that Christ was come to teach people himself, by his power and Spirit in their hearts, and to bring people off from all the world's ways and teachers, to his own free teaching, who had bought them, and was the Saviour of all them that believed in Him." The man of the house spread the paper abroad, and was mightily affected with the truth. Here the Lord opened unto me, and let me see a great people in white raiment by a riverside, coming to the Lord; and the place that I saw them in was about Wensleydale and Sedbergh.

The next day we traveled on, and at night got a little fern or brackens to put under us, and lay upon a common. Next morning we reached a town, where Richard Farnsworth parted from me; and then I traveled alone again. I came up Wensleydale, and at the market town in that Dale, there was a lecture on the market-day. I went into the steeple-house; and after the priest had done, I proclaimed the day of the Lord to the priest and people, warning them to turn from darkness to the light, and from the power of Satan unto God, that they might come to know God and Christ aright, and to receive his teaching, who teacheth freely. Largely and freely did I declare the word of life unto them, and had not much persecution there. Afterwards I passed up the Dales, warning people to fear God, and preaching the everlasting gospel to them.

In my way I came to a great house, where was a schoolmaster; and they got me into the house. I asked them questions about their religion and worship; and afterwards I declared the truth to them.

They had me into a parlour, and locked me in, pretending that I was a young man that was mad, and had run away from my relations; and that they would keep me till they could send to them. But I soon convinced them of their mistake, and they let me forth, and would have had me to stay; but I was not to stay there. Then having exhorted them to repentance, and directed them to the light of Christ Jesus, that through it they might come unto him and be saved, I passed from them, and came in the night to a little ale-house on a common, where there was a company of rude fellows drinking. Because I would not drink with them, they struck me with their club; but I reproved them, and brought them to be somewhat cooler; and then I walked out of the house upon the common in the night. After some time one of these drunken fellows came out, and would have come close up to me, pretending to whisper to me; but I perceived he had a knife; and therefore I kept off him, and bid him repent, and fear God. So the Lord by His power preserved me from this wicked man; and he went into the house again. The next morning I went on through other Dales, warning and exhorting people everywhere as I passed, to repent and turn to the Lord: and several were convinced. . . .

As I traveled through the Dales, I came to a man's house, whose name was Tennant. I was moved to speak to the family, and declare God's everlasting truth to them; and as I was turning away from them, I was moved to turn again, and speak to the man himself; and he was convinced, and his family, and lived and died in the truth. Thence I came to Major Bousfield's, who received me, as did also several others; and some that were then convinced have stood faithful ever since. I went also through Grisdale, and several others of those Dales, in which some were convinced. And I went into Dent, where many were convinced also. From Major Bousfield's I came to Richard Robinson's, and declared the everlasting truth to him.

The next day I went to a meeting at Justice Benson's, where I met a people that were separated from the public worship. This was the place I had seen, where a people came forth in white raiment. A large meeting it was, and the people were generally convinced, and continue a large meeting still of Friends near Sedbergh; which was then first gathered through my ministry in the name of Jesus.

In the same week there was a great fair, at which servants used to be hired; and I declared the day of the Lord through the fair. After I had done so, I went into the steeple-house yard, and many of the people of the fair came thither to me, an abundance of priests and professors. There I declared the everlasting truth of the Lord, and the word of life for several hours, showing that the Lord was come to teach his people himself, and to bring them off from all the world's ways and teachers, to Christ the true teacher, and the true way to God. I laid open their teachers, showing that they were like them that were of old condemned by the prophets, and by Christ, and by the apostles. I exhorted the people to come off from the temples made with hands; and wait to receive the Spirit of the Lord, that they might know themselves to be the temples of God. Not one of the priests had power to open his mouth against what I declared: but at last a captain said, "Why will you not go into the church? This is not a fit place to preach in." I told him, I denied their church. Then stood up one Francis Howgill, who was a preacher to a congregation: he had not seen me before, yet he undertook to answer that captain, and soon put him to silence. Then said Francis Howgill of me, "This man speaks with authority, and not as the scribes." After this I opened to the people, that that ground and house was no holier than another place; and that that house was not the church, but the people, whom Christ is the head of. After a while the priests came up to me, and I warned them to repent. One of them said I was mad, and so they turned away. But many people were convinced there that day, and were glad to hear the truth declared, and received it with joy. Amongst these was one Captain Ward, who received the truth in the love of it, and lived and died in it.

The next First-day I came to Firbank Chapel, in Westmoreland, where Francis Howgill, before named, and John Audland, had been preaching in the morning. The chapel was full of people, so that many could not get in. Francis Howgill said, he thought I looked into the chapel, and his spirit was ready to fail, the Lord's power did so surprise him; but I did not look in. They made haste, and had quickly done, and they and some of the people went to dinner, but abundance stayed till they came again. Now John Blakelin and others came to me, and desired me not to reprove them publicly; for they were not parish teachers, but pretty tender men. I could not tell them whether I should or not (though I had not at that time any drawings to declare publicly against them), but I said they must leave me to the Lord's movings. While the others were gone to dinner, I went to a brook and got a little water; and then came and sat down on the top of a rock hard by the chapel. In the afternoon the people gathered about me, with several of their preachers. It was judged there were above a thousand people amongst whom I declared God's everlasting truth and word of life freely and largely, for about the space of three hours, directing all to the Spirit of God in themselves, that they might be turned from darkness to the light, and believe in it, that they might become the children of it; and might be turned from the power of Satan, which they had been under, unto God; and by the Spirit of truth might be led into all truth, and sensibly understand the words of the prophets, and of Christ, and of the apostles; and might all come to know Christ to be their teacher, to instruct them, their counselor to direct them, their shepherd to feed them, their bishop to oversee them, and their prophet to open divine mysteries to them; and might know their bodies to be prepared, sanctified, and made fit temples for God and Christ to dwell in. In the openings of heavenly life, I explained unto them the prophets, and the figures, and shadows, and directed them to Christ, the substance. Then I opened the parables and sayings of Christ, and things that had been long hid, showing the intent and scope of the apostles' writings, and that their epistles were written to the elect. When I had opened that state, I showed also the state of the apostasy since the apostles' days; that the priests have got the Scriptures, but are not in that Spirit which gave them forth, and have put them into chapter and verse, to make a trade of holy men's words; and that the teachers and priests now are found in the steps of the false prophets, chief priests, scribes, and Pharisees of old, and are such, us the true prophets, Christ, and his apostles cried out against, and so are judged and condemned by the Spirit of the true prophets, and of Christ, and of his apostles; and that none, who are in that Spirit, and guided by it now, can own them. Now there were many old people, who went into the chapel and looked out at the windows, thinking it a strange thing to see a man preach on a hill, and not in their church, as they called it; whereupon I was moved to open to the people, that the steeple-house, and the ground whereon it stood, were no more holy than that mountain; and that those temples, which they called the dreadful houses of God, were not set up by the command of God and of Christ; nor their priests called, as Aaron's priesthood was; nor their tithes appointed by God, as those amongst the Jews were; but that Christ was come, who ended both the temple and its worship, and the priests and their tithes; and that all should now hearken unto him; for he said, "Learn of me"; and God said of him, "This is my beloved Son, in whom I am well pleased, hear ye him." I declared unto them that the Lord God had sent me to preach the everlasting gospel and word of life amongst them, and to bring them off from all these temples, tithes, priests, and rudiments of the world, which had been instituted since the apostles' days, and had been set up by such as had erred from the Spirit and power the apostles were in. Very largely was I opened at this meeting, and the Lord's convincing power accompanied my ministry, and reached the hearts of the people, whereby many were convinced; and all the teachers of that congregation (who were many), were convinced of God's everlasting truth.

JAMES NAYLER

In the 1650s, James Nayler (1616–1660), Yorkshire farmer and former Parliamentarian soldier, ranked second only to Fox among "Public Friends"; some historians have argued that in the first half of the decade, his influence may have been as great. Nayler became a center of public debate in 1656, when he and a small group of Friends felt led to reenact Jesus' triumphal entry into Jerusalem, suggesting that Nayler was Christ returned to earth. Nayler was tried and imprisoned by Parliament and rebuked by Fox, and his stock fell accordingly among Friends. Yet he continued to write, as these two works show.

A Collection of Sundry Books, Epistles and Papers, Written by James Nayler; with an Impartial Relation of the Most Remarkable Transactions Relating to His Life (Cincinnati, 1829).

The Lamb's War against the Man of Sin.

The end of it, the manner of it, and what he wars against.
His weapons, his colours, and his kingdom.
And how all may know whether they be in it, or no: and whether
the same Christ be in them, that is, was, and is to come, and
their faithfulness or unfaithfulness to him.

The Lord God Almighty, to whom belongs all the kingdoms in
Heaven and earth, doth nothing therein but by his son, the lamb,
by him he creates and governs; by him he saves and condemns,
judges and justifies; makes peace, and makes war, and whatsoever
he doth, he is at his right hand in all places, who in him hath long
suffered the burthen of iniquity, and oppression of wickedness that
hath abounded for many generations, till it be come to the full
measure, as in the days of old: and now his appearance in the lamb
(as ever it was when iniquity was full) is to make war with the God
of this world, and to plead with his subjects concerning their revolt
from him their creator, who ordered their beginning, and gave
them a being, and their breaking the order that was in the beginning, and giving up their obedience to the worldly spirit, and the
inventions thereof, till they become so far one with it, as that it
hath not only defiled their souls and bodies, blinded their eyes,
stopt their ears, and so made the creature utterly unprofitable to
God, and unfit for a temple for him to be worshipped in, or to hear
the voice, or understand the mind of the eternal spirit, by which
they were created, but that they are also become open enemies to
every check and reproof of that spirit which should lead them to
God, and doth testify against their evil deeds, and are not afraid
to speak against it as a thing not worth the minding, nor able to
lead them in the way of truth. Thus hath God lost the creature out
of his call and service, and he is become one with the God of this
world, to serve and obey him in ways that do despite to the spirit
of grace; and now use the creation against the creator. Now against
this evil seed, and its whole work brought forth in that nature,
doth the lamb make war, to take vengeance of his enemies.

The End of His War Is,

To judge this deceiver openly before all the creation, shewing that his ways, fashions, and customs, are not what God ordered for man to live in, in the beginning, to bind him, and to redeem him out of his captivity, all who will but believe in the lamb, and are weary of this service and bondage to his enemy, and who will but come forth and give their names and hearts to join with him, and bear his image and testimony openly before all men, and willingly follow him in such ways wherein the father hath given him victory over this power, for himself, and all that follow him, to redeem them to God; and the rest who will not believe and follow him, and bear his image, them to condemn with the destroyer into everlasting destruction, and to restore all things, and make all things new, as they were in the beginning, that God alone may rule in his own work.

The Manner of His War Is,

First, that he may be just who is to judge all men and spirits, he gives his light unto their hearts, even of man and woman, whereby he lets all see (who will mind it) what he is displeased with, what is with him; and what is against him; what he owns, and what he disowns, that so all may know what is for destruction, to come out of it, lest they be destroyed with it, that so he may save and receive all that are not wilfully disobedient, and hardened in the pleasures of this world, against him; all who are deceived, who are willing to be undeceived; all who are captivated, who are willing to be set free; all that are in darkness, and are willing to come to light. In a word all that love righteousness more than the pleasures of sin, that he may not destroy them, nor they fight against him, and know it not, but that he may receive them, to be one with him against that which hath misled and deceived them; and as many as turn at his reproof, he doth receive, and give them power in spirit and life to be as he is, in their measure, but all in watching, and wars against that which hath had them, and now has the rest of the creation in bondage, that he may restore all things to their former liberty.

What They Are to War Against.

And that is, whatever is not of God, whatever the eye (which loves the world) lusts after; whatever the flesh takes delight in, and whatever stands in respect of persons (as saith the Scripture) the lust of the eye, the lust of the flesh and the pride of life, these are not of God; and whatever the God of the world hath begotten in men's hearts to practise or to plead for, which God did not place there, all this the lamb and his followers war against, which is at enmity with it, both in themselves, and wherever they see it; for in the work of God alone is his kingdom, and all other works will he destroy. So their wars are not against creatures, they wrestle not with flesh and blood which God hath made, but with spiritual wickedness, exalted in the hearts of men and women, where God alone should be, and pleaded for, by which they become enemies to God, and their souls are destroyed. Indeed their war is against the whole work and device of the God of this world, his laws, his customs, his fashions, his inventions, and all which are to add to, or take from the work of God, which was in the beginning; this is all enmity against the lamb and his followers, who are entered into the covenant which was in the beginning; and therefore no wonder why they are hated by the God of this world, and his subjects, who come to spoil him of all at once, and to destroy the whole body of sin, the foundation and strength of his kingdom, and to take the government to himself, that God may wholly rule in the heart of man, and man wholly live in the work of God.

What Their Weapons Are.

And as they war not against men's persons, so their weapons are not carnal, nor hurtful to any of the creation; for the lamb comes not to destroy men's lives, nor the work of God, and therefore at his appearance in his subjects, he puts spiritual weapons into their hearts and hands; their armour is the light, their sword the spirit of the father and the son, their shield is faith and patience, their paths are prepared with the gospel of peace, and good-will to-wards all the creation of God; their breastplate is righteousness and holiness to God, their minds are girt with godliness, and they are covered with salvation, and they are taught with truth. And thus the lamb in them, and they in him, go out in judgment and righteousness, to make war with his enemies, conquering and to conquer, not as the prince of this world in his subjects, with whips and prisons, tortures and torments on the bodies of creatures, to kill and destroy men's lives, who are deceived, and so become his enemies; but he goes forth in the power of the spirit with the word of truth, to pass judgment, upon the head of the serpent, which doth deceive and bewitch the world, and covers his own with his love, whilst he kindles coals of fire on the head of his enemies; for with the spirit of judgment and with the spirit of burning will he plead with his enemies; and having kindled the fire, and awakened the creature, and broken their peace and rest in sin, he waits in patience to prevail to recover the creature and stay the enmity, by suffering all the rage, and envy, and evil entreatings, that the evil spirit that rules in the creature can cast upon him, and he receives it all with meekness, and pity to the creature, returning love for hatred, wrestling with God against the enmity, with prayers and tears night and day, with fasting, mourning and lamentation, in patience, in faithfulness, in truth, in love unfeigned, in long suffering, and in all the fruits of the spirit, that if by any means he may overcome evil with good, and by this his light in the sight of the creature, that the eye may come to be opened, which the god of this world hath blinded, that so the creature might see what it is he thus hates, and what fruits he himself brings forth, that the creature may be convinced he is no deceiver, but hath with him the life and power of innocency and holiness, in whom he rules. And this preaching hath a power in it, to open the eye of all that are not wilfully blind, because they love the deed of darkness, and such are left without excuse forever. And thus he in his members many times wrestles, and preaches to the spirits in prison, with much long suffering towards the world, a nation, or a particular person, before he gives them up, and numbers them for destruction; yea, sometimes, till their rage against him, and cruelty exercised upon his members be so great, that there be no remedy, as in the days of old, 2 Chron. 36.15, 16.

And These Fruits Are His Colours He Holds Forth to All the World, in Such as He Reigns In.

As they come to obey him, he covers them with love, gentleness, faith, patience and purity, grace and virtue, temperance and self-

denial, meekness and innocency all in white, that follow him, in
whom he is, who walk themselves as he walked, in all things con-
forming to God, with boldness and zeal, owning the lamb to
be their leader, with him testifying against the world, that the
deeds thereof are evil, themselves the mean while covered with his
righteousness, against all the storms and tempests that they must
be sure to meet withal, who bear that testimony which the lamb
hath ever borne, in whom he appeared to the convincing of the
world; that he is the same that ever he was from the beginning,
that all that will believe and love holiness, may see where it is to
be found, and come forth to him, and be saved, that the whole
world become not as Sodom in the day of wrath, which ever
comes upon a people, or a nation, after Christ hath thus appeared,
and been rejected thereof.

What His Kingdom Is.

The power, the glory and compass of it is not comprehended with
mortal understanding, which was before all beginnings, and en-
dures forever, who orders and limits all spirits in Heaven and
earth, who rules in the rulers of the earth, and in all heavenly
places, though many spirits know him not, till they have felt his
reproof for their rebellion against him; his sufferings are free for
loves sake, which is naturally in him to the creation, being his
offspring, for which cause he becomes meek and lowly, that he
may bear the infirmities of the creation, which doth no way take
from his power, who is equal with the father, but doth manifest
his power to be unlimited, in that he beareth all things, his dominion he hath amongst the heathen, and his hands are in the
counsels of the kings of the earth, and there is no place where he
is not, who descends below all depths, and ascends far above all
Heavens, that he may fill all things.

But his kingdom in this world, in which he chiefly delights to
walk, and make himself known, is in the hearts of such as have
believed in him, and owned his call out of the world, whose hearts
he hath purified, and whose bodies he hath washed in obedience,
and made them fit for the father to be worshipped in. And in such
he rejoices and takes delight, and his kingdom in such is righteousness and peace, in love, in power and purity, he leads them
by the gentle movings of his spirit, out of all their own ways and

wills, in which they would defile themselves, and guides them into the will of the father, by which they become more clean and holy; deeply he lets them know his covenant, and how far they may go and be false, he gives them his laws and his statutes, contrary in all things to the god of this world, that they may be known to be his before all his enemies; if they keep his counsel they are false, but if they refuse, he lets them know the correction of the father, his presence is great joy to them of a willing mind, but with the froward he appears in frowardness; the kisses of his lips are life eternal, but who may abide his wrath? The secrets of the father are with him, and he maketh all his subjects wise; he makes them all of one heart, and with himself of the same mind; his government is wholly pure, and no unclean thing can abide his judgments. As any come into his kingdom they are known, and their change is to be seen of all men; he keeps them low in mind, and a meek spirit doth he beget in them; and with his power he leads them forth against all the enmity of the evil one, and makes all conditions comfortable to them who abide in his kingdom.

Now these are the last times, and many false Christs there must appear, and be made manifest by the true Christ, with their false prophets, false ways and false worships, and false worshippers, which though they be at wars one with another, yet not the lamb's war. Now seeing he hath appeared, who is from everlasting and changeth not, here is an everlasting trial for you all, all sorts of professors, whether you profess him from the letter or the light; come try whether Christ is in you, measure your life, and weigh your profession with that which cannot deceive you, which hath stood, and will stand forever, for he is sealed of the father.

Now, in truth to God and your own souls, prove your work in time, lest you and it perish together. First, see if your Christ be the same that was from everlasting to everlasting, or is he changed according to the times, in life, in death, in peace and wars, in reigning, in suffering, in casting out and receiving in; and if you find the true Christ, then prove your faithfulness to him in all things; doth he whom you obey as your leader, lead you out to war against this world, and all the pride and glory, fashions and customs, love and pleasures, and whatever else is not of God therein? And to give up your lives unto death, rather than knowingly to yield your obedience thereto? Doth he justify any life now, but what he justified in the prophets and apostles, and saints

of old?—Doth he give his subjects liberty now to bow to the god
of this world, and his ways, in things that he hath denied in the
saints of old, and for denying whereof many, both then and now,
have suffered? Is he at peace in you whilst you are in the fleshly
pleasures, or whilst you have fellowship with the unclean spirits
that are in the world? Doth he not lead out of the world, and to
strive against it in watchings, fastings, prayers, and strong cries to
the father, that you may be kept, and others delivered from the
bondage and pollutions of it? Is his kingdom the same in you?
And doth he give out the same spiritual laws against all the laws
and customs of the man of sin in you, as he hath done in his subjects in all ages? Doth he beget in your hearts a new nature, contrary to the world's nature in all things, motions and delights like
himself, whereby he works out the old nature that inclines to the
world, and can beat peace therein? And now your peace is wholly
in him, and that which crucifies the world to you, and you to it,
is your joy and delight? Hath he called you out of this world, to
bear his name before the powers thereof, and put his testimony
into your hearts, and the same weapons into your hands as were
used by the saints of old against the powers of darkness, whereby
you have power given to overcome evil with good? And many
other fruits you may find, which he ever brought forth in his chosen, whereby they were known to be in him, and he in them; for
which the world hates them. By all which you may clearly know,
if he be the same in you to day, as he was yesterday in his people,
and forever; for he changeth not, nor conforms to the world, nor
the will of any creature, but changes all his followers, till they
become in all things like himself; for they must bear his name and
image before all men and spirits.

Now if you profess the same as was, and is, and is to come, the
same for evermore, the same Christ, the same calling in you that
was in all the people of God, then prove your faithfulness in answering and obeying: who is it that sees not that wars are begun?
And to whom hath not the sound gone forth? The children of light
have published the gospel of light throughout the world, and the
prince of darkness hath shown his enmity against it; the lamb hath
appeared with his weapons as before mentioned, in much long suffering, and the God of this world hath appeared to withstand him
with his weapons, and hath prevailed unto blood with much ea-
gerness, and the lamb hath prevailed unto suffering with much

meekness and patience, each of them in their subjects, in whom these contrary spirits act one against another; and now see what part you take, who hath hired you, and whose work are you in, or are you idle, looking on? Or are you gone out with the beast of the field, and regard nothing but your bellies and pleasures? Doth it not greatly concern you to try your states, seeing all must come speedily to an account for their lives and service? Are you such as spend your time and strength in watching and praying to the father of spirits for yourselves and the people of God, that they may be kept in the time of temptation, and assaults of the evil one, who seeks his advantage on the weak brethren; and for your enemies, that they may be delivered from under his power, who are captivated by him at his will, to fulfil his lusts and envy, and satisfy his wrath upon the innocent.

And do you deny yourselves of your pleasures, profits, ease and liberty, that you may hold forth a chaste conversation in the power and life of gentleness, meekness, faithfulness and truth, exercising a conscience void of offence towards God, and all men, that thereby you may shine forth in righteousness, so as to convince your enemies whom you pray for; thus following him who laid down his life for his enemies. Is this your war, and these your weapons? Is this your calling, and are you faithful to him that hath called you hereto, so as you can by no means bow to the God of this world, nor his ways, though it were to save your lives or credit in the world, or estates, and yet can serve the meanest creature in God's way, though to the loss of all? I beseech you be faithful to your own souls herein: do you find nothing in you that calls or moves this way, or reproves the contrary? If there be, are you not such as quench the spirit, and put out your own eye, and deny the lamb's call against your own lives? And if there be not, then are you not dead members, cut off from Christ, and all your profession is but a lie, and without Christ you are in the world? O that you would prove your own selves; for there be many deceitful workers at this day of his appearance, who do the work of the Lord negligently and deceitfully, and many do their own work instead of his; and many are called, and for a while abide, but in the time of hardship prove deceitful, and return to serve in the world again, and take pleasure therein; others are called and convinced, but come half out of the world, even as far as they can do it without loss or shame, but keep their covenant therewith still, in what makes most for their gain, or earthly advantage or credit: others have answered their call, and been faithful in the covenant of the lamb against the prince of this world, so far as they have seen; but not minding the watch against the enemy, and not keeping low in the fear, and zealous in the light, have suffered the simplicity to be deceived, and are led back to the old beggarly rudiments of the world again, and take that for their perfection and growth, which once they had vomited up; and these expect great things in their work; but they are blinder than the rest, and more to be pitied, because of the simplicity that is deceived.

Many other grounds there be that bring not fruit to perfection, who are not found faithful to him that hath called them therein; so that now the truth is, that many are called, but few chosen and faithful; many are ashamed at the lamb's appearance, it is so low, and weak, and poor, and contemptible, and many are afraid, seeing so great a power against him; many be at work in their imaginations, to compass a kingdom, to get power over sin, and peace of conscience, but few will deny all to be led by the lamb in a way they know not, to bear his testimony and mark against the world, and suffer for it with him. Now deceit hath taught you to say, and may be you think it also, God forbid but you should suffer with Christ till death; but come to the trial in deed and truth; doth not he suffer under all the pride and pleasures of the flesh, by all manner of excess, by all manner of customs and fashions, not of God, but of the world? Is not all against him that is not of him and the father? Is not the lust of the eye, and of the flesh, and pride of life, his oppressors? And do you that live in these things, and fashions, and plead for them, suffer with him by them, or war with him against them? Then would you be weary of them, and not practice nor plead for them against him: this you will find true in the end, you cannot suffer with him, and serve his enemies.

Can you live at ease, and in your pleasures and profits, and cover yourselves with worldly glory, whilst Christ Jesus is glorified in his temples with mockings, stockings, stonings, whipping, and all manner of evil intreatings; cast into holes, pits and dungeons, having none on earth to take his part, nor plead his righteous cause, nor once to take notice of his innocent sufferings; but who as will, may tread down his precious life in the open streets, without resisting; and this for no other thing, but for testifying against the deeds of the world, that they are evil: the pride and oppression, false ways and false worships, never set up by him but in the will of man, and so maintained against him, which he must judge with a contrary appearance, e'er he come to his kingdom; and do you suffer with him herein, who have a heart consenting to these things, if not a hand deeply in them; secret or open, either in this cruelty acting or contriving, or in cursed and scornful speeches condemning them that bear witness, as a foolish ignorant people, and that they bring their sufferings upon themselves, by their own wills, and so shoot your poisoned arrows one way or other against that spirit which leads, and hath ever led such as do not resist and disobey him, into the same testimony, and so in secret you become worse than open persecutors.

Or it may be some few become as far as Pilate, who washed his own hands, whilst others shed the innocent blood; and these are few indeed, who thus far will openly confess the just and innocent Lord before his accusers, in what vessel he is thus honoured.

But will the best of these stand in judgment as sufferers with him? Or will he know you at his appearance, by this mark? Are these his steps you follow? Or is this his image, or power, war or weapons? Will this suffering bring you to reign with him, or he in you to your peace? Or will this cross crucify you to the world, and the world to you? Do you walk as he walked, or hath he left you such example to follow? Search the scriptures, and read the life of them, and your own lives, with the light of Christ Jesus, and cease to blaspheme any longer, in saying you are christians, while in Christ you are not, but in a contrary spirit, and contrary life. And your fellowship is not with him in suffering, but with them by whom he suffers.

Were ever christians at their ease and worldly delights, whilst Christ hath not where to rest his head; thrust out of your meeting places, towns, and markets, and every assembly, if he do but testify against the evil thereof? Are you asleep in the world, and doth it not awaken you, to see or hear how sudden a return that bloody spirit hath made, lately in part cast out? And with what power he is now entering, like to exceed seven-fold what he hath this many generations, making daily havoc of the lambs? Is it a time for you to riot in, to satisfy your lusts, to eat and drink, and rise up to play, and spend your time and strength (many of you) so as modest heathens would blush at, and then say you are christians, and suffer with Christ. Surely were you members of that body, or sensible of his sufferings herein, you would not add thereto a greater weight, nor join to his adversary the devil, whose works these are, but on the Lord's part every one up and be armed in the light, with the armour of the lamb, as before mentioned, to withstand these and other the temptations of his enemy, and in sufferings witness against them. Do you not daily read of such a testimony in the scriptures, born against the murderer by the lamb?

How long shall it be e'er the life of what you profess, be seen in the face of your conversation, teachers, and people? When will you teachers approve yourselves as the ministers of God, and sufferers with Christ, (as saith the scripture which you profess) in much patience, in afflictions, in necessities, in distresses, in stripes above measure, in prisons frequently, in deaths often, in tumults, in labours, in watchings, in hunger, in fastings oft, in cold and nakedness, in poverty, in long suffering, and love unfeigned, in honour and dishonour, in evil reports and good reports, as deceivers (yet true) as unknown, sorrowing, chastened, poor, having nothing, yet coveting no man's money, making it your reward to keep the gospel without charge, and much more of this self-denying nature, which is the armour of righteousness the ministers of Christ put on, and with such weapons they went out to fight with beasts, and belly gods, false prophets, greedy dogs, hirelings, and all sorts that went after the error of Balaam for wages, gifts or rewards. And by these marks of Christ they were ever to be known from Baal's priests, and such as the world called and set up in the will of man, and in the spirit of Christ did openly war against them with the sword of his mouth, and do to this day, even to the day of judgment. In whom the scriptures are fulfilled, which cannot be broken.

Now why will you not measure yourselves with this measure, seeing this only is sealed to all generations of God's ministers, (witness the scriptures). Nay, why are you so exceedingly blind, and wicked above measure, that if you be found in the contrary nature, life and practice, and God send some to warn you thereof, and hold forth the lamb's testimony against you, you presently suffer the evil one to get up in you, and in rage and madness, not minding this to be obedience to God in them, and his love and faithfulness to your souls, seek to cast some of these things before mentioned upon them; and so your revenge turns to their double honour, and doubles a witness against yourselves, to your own condemnation, and that you have not the spirit of Christ in you. And some of you exceed in this, above your forefathers; for whom the lambs of God have a lamentation; yet must God be justified when he comes to judgment, for you will be found far off the suffering with Christ, though with your lips you honor him.

Surely he that hath a living conscience, may much admire how you get over these scriptures in your teaching of others, and not to wound yourselves, or pierce your hearts with fear, and your faces with blushing, who are found so absolute in contradiction thereto, in conversation, and unlike in your lives, in the sight of every open eye. Or how you can muzzle your consciences while you pass your prayers, that your own mouth do not condemn you? It's no wonder why you are such enemies to the light within, every one that doth evil hateth the light.

And you hearers of all sorts, how long will it be e'er you hearken to what the Lord saith to your soul? Who is no respecter of persons, but every one that bears not the image of his son in well-doing, he hates, though with Cain you sacrifice, or with Esau you pray with tears.—That with the light of Christ in your own hearts you may see how the world's lusts have spoiled your souls of that heavenly image, and hath captivated your minds into itself, and likeness, and how you lie dead in sin, covered with earth, and daubed over with the words of men. Oh! that you would awake, before wrath awaken you, and put on the armour of God, not relying any longer on men that beat the air, to fight your battles, against him who is got into your hearts; but that yourselves, as soldiers of Christ, may all come to use the spiritual weapons against the spiritual wickedness exalted in the temple of God, so that you can neither see nor serve God therein, being filled with wicked and worldly cumbrances.

That's the spiritual weapon which captivates every thought to the obedience of Christ, and this is the true warfare, and is mighty through God, to cast down the strong holds of the man of sin in you; and having in a readiness to revenge all disobedience; knowing that he that will not be led by the spirit of God is for condemnation. And only these weapons are effectual to cleanse the heart of all that exalts itself against the life and knowledge of God, and to make way for his appearance; which no man's words who is in the same evils hath power to do; for this power is only in Christ his light and life. And only blessed are they who feel and find this treasure working in the earthen vessel, such shall approve their own work to God, and have praise thereof, not of man. So should you come to see what others have said in scripture, concerning the lamb of God, who takes away the sins of the world, and savingly feel the power of his cross, of his death and resurrection, and the everlasting purity of his life, and that eternal love the father bears thereto, an everlasting inheritance to all who learn him, and attain his appearance, whose beauty is blessed forever.

Called, chosen and faithful are the servants and subjects of Christ's kingdom, in whom at this day, he maintains war against the prince of this world, the beast and his seat, with the false prophet, and all that serve under his dominion, and obey his laws which he hath set up.

Now you that cry, the kingdoms of this world are become the kingdoms of the Lord and of his Christ; see that it be truth in you, and that you lie not within yourselves. The lamb's war you must know, before you can witness his kingdom, and how you have been called into his war, and whether you have been faithful and chosen there or no. He that preaches the kingdom of Christ in words, without victory, is the thief that goes before Christ. So take heed that your own words condemn you not, but mind your calling, and how you have answered, and whether you have been faithful in that whereunto you have been called, THE WAR; Christ hath a war with his enemies, to which he calls his subjects to serve him therein, against all the powers of darkness of this world, and all things of this old world, the ways and fashions of it will he overturn, and all things will he make new, which the god of this world hath polluted, and wherewith his children hath corrupted themselves, and do service to the lust, and devourer; this the lamb wars against, in whomsoever he appears, and calls them to join with him herein in heart and mind, and with all their whole might. And for that end he lights his candle in their hearts, that they may find out every secret evil that the man of sin hath there treasured up, even to every thought and intent of the heart, to cast out the enemy with all his stuff, and to subject the creature wholly to himself, that he may form a new man, a new heart, new thoughts, and a new obedience, in a new way, in all things therein to reign, and there is his kingdom.

Now many are called to this war, but few are chosen and faithful. They that are faithful in their calling, them he chooses, and in them he reigns, and with them he makes war against his enemies on every side, under what colour soever they appear, if they be not subjects to him, all in whom he reigns are at war with them in Christ, and the sword of his spirit he hath put into their hands, his word into their mouths, whereby they are at wars with all the world, and the world with them, and he that's faithful will make no peace nor agreement, neither will he bow nor yield agreement, till there be a subjection to Christ. These are faithful to him that hath called them.

So you that are much in words, prove your own selves; if you be in his kingdom, or of his subjects, then are you at work with him in this his day, wherein he is coming in thousands of his saints to take vengeance into his hands, and inflict it upon his enemies.

Now you who are asleep, and at ease in the flesh, are not of his kingdom; for by suffering in the flesh doth he make war, and slays the man of sin.

You that are at peace in the world's ways and fashions, invented and maintained by the man of sin, you are not in his kingdom, for he hath given an alarm against all those things, which hath caused the dragon to whet his teeth, and all the devouring spirits are stirred up, their Lord's kingdom to defend, every one with such weapons as they have, against the lamb in his kingdom, in what vessel soever he reigns; and he is but one in all his, against all these.

Now you that are making peace where these things are upholden, you are false-hearted, and betray the lamb, as that of God in you shall witness, you are at peace-making with his enemies.

But say you, God is love, and we are commanded to love all, and seek peace with all, &c.

I say, is God's love in you otherwise than it hath ever been in Christ, and all his saints, whom the world ever hated, whom God loved, and in whom he testified against the world unto death, and unto bonds, and persecution, were not they in God's love? Did not they keep his commandments? Will you take their words in your mouths, and condemn their lives by your practices?

The lamb's war is not against the creation, for then should his weapons be carnal, as the weapons of the worldly spirits are, for we war not with flesh and blood, nor against the creation of God, that we love, but we fight against the spiritual powers of wickedness, which wars against God in the creation, and captivates the creation into the lust which wars against the soul, and that the creature may be delivered into its liberty, prepared for the sons of God. And this is not against love, nor everlasting peace, but that without which there can be no true love, nor lasting peace.

Love to God and man constrains us to be faithful in this war. Nor is God's love to that seed of bondage, nor did he ever command you to seek the peace of it. For the love of the world is enmity with God, as saith the scripture.

And were you not fallen into self-love which is utterly blind (as to the love of God) you would see a great difference between the creature, and that which keeps the creature in bondage, and out of the love of God; can you love that, and not hate the creature, and God also? This all who fight in the lamb's battles know, who are in the true love. Doth not the spirit of pride, gluttony, drunkenness, pleasures, envy and strife, keep that in bondage which thou shouldst love by the command of God? Doth not the creature groan to be delivered from the vanity, customs and fashions of this generation? Is not the whole time of man taken up in service of the lusts and inventions which the man of sin hath found out; inventions in meats and drinks, inventions in apparel, inventions in worships, in sports and pleasures, &c. Is not the whole creation captivated under this spirit of whoredom, and so man's whole life spent in vain? So that men and women come into the world, and depart out of it again, as though they were made for no other end but for vanity and selfishness. Scarce one of ten thousand knows any call from God to any service for him, or hath an ear to hear his voice; but if any do hear, and obey, they all conclude him deceived, and are ready to devour him, because he testifies against the evils which destroy men's souls, and make void man's service to his creator, and devours the creation.

And can you love this spirit, bow and conform to it, or suffer it to reign in yourselves, or your brethren, and you be silent, under a pretence of seeking love and peace, and obeying God's command; and boast in high words about Christ's kingdom, counting it a low and foolish thing in such as faithfully and zealously bear testimony for God, and against these evils? And will not God find you out, and your deceit and unfaithfulness in your generation; shall not God break your peace, and disannul your covenant, which you are making with the world, to settle yourselves in ease and pleasure, and bring you out with true judgment, where it shall be seen what nature your love is of, whose kingdom you are in, and whom you love and serve.

The day is dawned, and the sun is risen to many that shall not set, nor shall he cease his course, until he have rightly divided between the precious seed, and the children of whoredoms and deceit. And now the holy seed is called forth, to appear in its colours against the man of sin; and with the sword of his mouth doth he make war, and with the spirit of judgment and the spirit of burning, doth he consume the filthy and unclean spirits. And all that are faithful have their armour on ready, day and night to follow the lamb, as he moves, counting nothing hard to undergo, so as they may but have hopes of reconciliation betwixt God, and the creature that is fallen to the prince of the world, and led captive at his will. And this is love indeed, to lay down all for such as are yet enemies.

Go on and prosper in the name of the Lord, and in righteousness make war; and all that are zealous for truth and purity shall say amen: but the slothful, the lukewarm, and all unclean persons, shut themselves out, as not for this work, nor worthy to be counted faithful nor chosen.

His Last Testimony, Said to Be Delivered by Him about Two Hours before His Departure out of This Life; Several Friends Being Present.

There is a spirit which I feel, that delights to do no evil, nor to revenge any wrong, but delights to endure all things, in hope to enjoy its own in the end: Its hope is to outlive all wrath and contention, and to weary out all exaltation and cruelty, or whatever is of a nature contrary to itself. It sees to the end of all temptations: as it bears no evil in itself, so it conceives none in thoughts to any other: If it be betrayed it bears it; for its ground and spring is the mercies and forgiveness of God. Its crown is meekness, its life is everlasting love unfeigned, and takes its kingdom with intreaty, and not with contention, and keeps it by lowliness of mind. In God alone it can rejoice, though none else regard it, or can own its life. It's conceived in sorrow, and brought forth without any to pity it; nor doth it murmur at grief and oppression. It never rejoiceth, but through sufferings; for with the world's joy it is murdered. I found it alone, being forsaken; I have fellowship therein, with them who lived in dens, and desolate places in the earth, who through death obtained this resurrection and eternal holy life.

J. N.

MARGARET FELL

If George Fox and James Nayler were the foremost male Friends of the first generation, few would question that Margaret (Askew) Fell (1614–1702) was the foremost of early Quaker women. Her home, Swarthmore Hall in Lancashire, became the closest thing the early Quaker movement had to a headquarters. In 1669, by then a widow for more than a decade, she and Fox were married. Late in her life she described how she first encountered Fox and became a Friend.

Margaret Fell Fox, "The Testimony of Margaret Fox Concerning Her Late Husband George Fox," in *A Journal or Historical Account of the Life, Travels, Sufferings, Christian Experiences & Labour of Love in the Work of the Ministry of That Ancient, Eminent and Faithful Servant of Jesus Christ, George Fox* (London, 1694).

And in the year 1652, it pleased the Lord to draw [George Fox] towards us; so he came on from Sedbergh, and so to Westmorland, as Firbank Chapel, where John Blaykling came with him: and so on to Preston, and to Grayrig, and Kendal, and Underbarrow, and Poobank, and Cartmel, and Staveley; and so on to Swarthmore, my Dwelling-House, whither he brought the blessed tidings of the everlasting Gospel, which I, and many hundreds in these parts, have cause to praise the Lord for. My then husband, Thomas Fell, was not at home, but gone [on] the Welsh Circuit, being one of the judges of assize. And our house being a place open to entertain ministers and religious people at, one of George Fox's friends brought him hither, where he stayed all night. And the next day, being a lecture or fast day, he went to Ulverston steeple house, but came not in, till people were gathered; I and my children had been a long time there before. And when they were singing before the sermon, he came in; and when they had done singing, he stood upon a seat or form, and desired, that he might have the liberty to speak. And he that was in the pulpit, said he might. And the first words that he spoke were as followeth: He is not a Jew that is one outward, neither is that circumcision which is outward. But he is a Jew that is one inward, and that is circumcision which is of the heart. And so he went on and said how Christ was the Light of the World, and lighteth every man that cometh into the world; and that by this Light they might be gathered to God, etc. And I stood up in my pew, and wondered at his doctrine; for I had never heard such before. And then he went on, and opened the Scriptures and said, the Scriptures were the prophets' words, and Christ's and the Apostles' words, and what, as they spoke, they enjoyed and possessed, and had it from the Lord. And said, "Then what had any to do with the Scriptures, but as they came to the Spirit that gave them forth. You will say, Christ saith this, and the Apostles say this; but what canst thou say? Art thou a Child of Light, and has walked in the Light, and what thou speakest, is it inwardly from God?" . . . This opened me so, that it cut me to the heart; and then I saw clearly, we were all wrong. So I sat down in my pew again, and cried bitterly. And I cried in my spirit to the Lord, "We are all thieves, we are all thieves; we have taken the Scriptures in words, and know nothing of them in ourselves." So that served me, that I cannot well tell what he spoke afterwards; but he went on in declaring against the false prophets, and priests, and deceivers of the people. And there was one John Sawrey, a justice of the peace, and a professor, that bid the churchwarden, "take him away." And he laid his hands on him several times, and took them off again, and let him alone; and then after a while gave over, and came to our house again that night. And he spoke in the family amongst the servants, and they were all generally convinced. . . . And I was stricken into such a sadness, I knew not what to do; my husband being from home. I saw it was the truth, and I could not deny it; and I did, as the Apostle saith, I received the truth in the love of it; and it was opened to me so clear, that I had never a tittle in my heart against it; but I desired the Lord, that I might be kept in it, and then I desired no greater portion. . . .

But the priests were all in a rage. And about two weeks after James Nayler and Richard Farnsworth followed him, and enquired

him out, till they came to Swarthmore, and there stayed a while
with me at our house, and did me much good; for I was under
great heaviness and judgment. But the power of the Lord entered
upon me, within about two weeks, that he came; and about three
weeks-end my husband came home. And many were in a mighty
rage. And a deal of the captains and great ones of the country went
to meet my then husband, as he was coming home, and informed
him, that a great disaster was befallen among his family, and that
they were witches; and that they had taken us out of our religion;
and that he might either set them away, or all the country would
be undone. . . .

So my husband came home greatly offended. And any may think
what a condition I was like to be in, that either I might displease
my husband, or offend God; for he was very much troubled with
us all in the house and family, they had so prepossessed him against
us. But James Nayler and Richard Farnsworth were both then at
our house, and I desired them to come and speak to him; and so
they did very moderately and wisely. But he was at first displeased
with them, till they told him, they came in love and good will to
his house. And after he had heard them speak he was better satisfied, and they offered as if they would go away; but I desired them
to stay, . . . for George Fox will come this evening. . . .

And then at night George Fox came, and after supper my husband was sitting in the parlour, and I asked him, if George Fox
might come in? And he said, yes. So George came in without any
compliment, and walked into the room, and began to speak presently; and the family, and James Nayler, and Richard Farnsworth
came all in; and he spoke very excellently, as ever I heard him;
and opened Christ and the Apostles' practices, which they were
in, in their day. And he opened the Night of Apostacy since the
Apostles' days, and laid open the priests and their practices in
the Apostacy; that if all in England had been there, I thought,
they could not have denied the truth of those things. And so my
husband began to see more clearly the truth of what he spoke, and
was very quiet that night, and said no more, and went to bed. And
next morning came Lampitt, priest of Ulverston, and got my husband into the garden, and spake much to him there. But my husband had seen so much the night before, that the priest got little
entrance upon him. And when the priest, Lampitt, was come into
the house, George spoke sharply to him, and I asked him, when

God spoke to him, and called him to go and preach to the people? But after a while the priest went away. This was on a Sixth-day of the week about the Fifth Month 1652. And at our house divers Friends were speaking one to another, how there were several convinced hereaways, and we could not tell, where to get a meeting. My husband being also present, he overheard, and said of his own accord; you may meet here if you will. And that was the first meeting we had, that he offered of his own accord. And then notice was given that day and the next to Friends, and there was a good large meeting the First-day, which was the first meeting, that was at Swarthmore: and so continued there a meeting, from 1652, till 1690.

> *Much of Margaret Fell's Quaker ministry came through letters. Modeled on the New Testament Epistles of Paul and other early Christians, they combined advice, exhortation, and theology.*

A Brief Collection of Remarkable Passages and Occurrences Relating to the Birth, Education, Life, Conversion, Travels, Services, and Deep Sufferings of That Ancient, Eminent, and Faithful Servant of the Lord, Margaret Fell
(London, 1710).

An Epistle to Friends, 1654

To all my dear brethren and sisters, who are in the Light, Children of the Light, who are obedient to the Light, which is the head of the whole body; in which Light, every particular, dwell and stand single, and you shall see the whole body full of Light. For this leads into the unity and oneness, which is in the body, though many members. So my dear hearts, in that which is the Light of the whole body, which leads into the unity, to that be subject and obedient, that you may be serviceable to the whole body, and give up freely to the service of he head, which is one, and but one in all; and who are faithful, the one Spirit makes subject. Even so are ye called in one hope of your calling, where there is one Lord, one Faith, one Baptism, one God and Father of all, who is above all, and through all, and in you all.

So all my dear brethren and sisters, in this which is eternal, and leads into the unity and oneness, be faithful and obedient; be of one mind, and live in peace. For the promise is but to one Seed; and you are all one in Christ Jesus, who have faith in him, to whom all the promises are yea and amen. And now is the Lord's Day made manifest, wherein he requires of you, in your particular measures, to be serviceable to the body, in your respective places. For there are many members, and but one body; and the head cannot say to the feet, "I have no need of you"; for every one, in their measures, may be serviceable to the whole body, in what is called for, and required; and who dwells in the Light, it makes subject, to be serviceable to the body. And now, that nothing may be kept back, but as you have received freely, so freely you may administer, in obedience to the one Eternal Light; you may be serviceable to the whole body. And as the Lord hath loved you with his everlasting love, and visited you, and hath made manifest his Eternal Light in you, which is the Way that leads to the Father, and hath raised up the Eternal Witness in you, of his everlasting love. So let that love constrain you to love one another, and be serviceable to one another; and that everyone may be made willing to suffer for the body's sake, and that there may be no rent in the body, but that the members have the same care one over another; and where one member suffers, all the members may suffer with it. And here is the unity of the Spirit, and the bond of peace. And that you cannot be unmindful, nor are you ignorant of the present suffering and service of many members of the body in this our day, who are in bonds and imprisonment, and hard persecution and cruelty, which is acted in the will of man, upon the righteous Seed, which is of the body. And others there are, that are sent forth into the service of the most high God, as lambs among wolves, who are made willing and subject to give their backs to the smiter; yea, to lay down their lives for the body's sake. And great and hard persecutions have been suffered for the testimony of the Lord Jesus.

Now, that every particular member of the Body may be sensible of the hardship and sufferings of others, and be willing and serviceable in their places, in what the Lord requires; and to remember those that are in bonds, as bound with them; and them that suffer adversity, as you being yourselves also in the body; and that you may bear one another's burdens, and be equally yoked in the suffering. Our Friends in Westmorland have borne the heat of the day, and many have been sent forth into the Lord's service from thence, and that hath caused the burden to lie heavy upon the rest of the Friends thereabouts; and most of all on our Friends at Kendal, who have been very serviceable in their places to the Truth, to the whole body, to those who have been sent forth in to the ministry, and to them that have suffered imprisonment, and for dispersing books, and several other things that have been needful, wherein they have been serviceable to the Truth, I bear them record.

I see in the Eternal Unchangeable Light of God, that all and every members, who are of the body, ought to be serviceable in their places, and to administer freely, according to their ability, as they have received of the Lord freely. For Jerusalem, which is from above, is free, which is the Mother of us all; and who are here, are one. So, my dear brethren and sisters, let Brotherly Love continue; that every one, as the Lord moves you, and opens your hearts, you may administer; that you may come into the oneness in all things, and in that abide, which dwells in love and unity, which is one for evermore. And so you come to the fulfilling of the Scriptures, in your measures, and the practice of all the saints in the Light, that ever went before.

So God Almighty of Life and Power, preserve and keep you in his everlasting Love and Unity.

YOUR DEAR SISTER IN THE EVERLASTING TRUTH.

M. F.

DECLARING THE WORD
OF THE LORD

FIRST PUBLISHERS OF TRUTH

In the 1650s, Public Friends took the Quaker message to all parts of England, yet the north of England remained the Quaker heartland. Early in the eighteenth century, Friends recorded how Quakerism came to the Richmondshire region of Yorkshire.

Norman Penney, ed., *First Publishers of Truth* (1907).

About ye latter part of ye year 1652, did Richard Hubberthorn, from Yealand in Lancashire, in ye drawing of ye Love of God, come to Countersett, in Wensladale, to ye house of Richard Robinson, who gladly received him, being already convinced of ye blessed Truth, for he had been under deep travail of Spirit after ye substance of religion some years before, & hearing (at a distance) what G. Fox preached for doctrine, he joined with it in his mind, & went abroad to some meetings, where he heard the truth declared, & was fully satisfied, though, that we know of, there was none else so convinced of ye Truth thereabouts, till ye coming of ye aforesaid Richard Hubberthorne, who stayed some weeks & had several meetings thereabouts, as at Bainbridge, & at a market town called Askrigg, where many of ye people were exceeding rude, yet ye Lord's Power Prevailed and several people was convinced of ye Truth, and a meeting was settled about this time here, which has continued ever since & considerably increased & is called Wensladale Meeting.

And after this time, ye aforesaid Richard Robinson (who had now given up his house freely to receive ye messengers & servants of ye Lord, both for entertainment & to keep meetings in), travelling in spirit deeply and secretly before ye Lord, who was fitting him for his service, came under a concern (in ye requirings of ye Lord) to go to many steeple houses & market places, unto which exercise he gave up & went (as ye Lord drew him) into many parts of ye North Country especially, & some in ye South, preaching repentance, & calling to priests & people to forsake their evil doing, & turn to ye Lord, & sometimes almost naked as a sign to ye people. And great was his sufferings & hardships in that day, being often cruelly beaten & sorely bruised at several places, yet ye Lord was his helper, & supported him through all, and made him a very serviceable instrument in ye meeting whereunto he belonged, & to many more where he was concerned to travail both in verbal testimony bearing (which was living & comfortable), and in labouring for ye establishing of men & women's meetings, and was a good example in a sober conversation, & also was truly valiant in bearing his testimony for ye Truth, both under ye Conventicle Act* & against tithes & steeplehouse assessments, &c, and also for not paying as sending to ye militia, for which faithfulness upon these accounts he suffered deeply & cheerfully both by imprisonment & spoiling of goods for ye Lord's sake, who was his rich rewarder. And growing infirm of body by reason of age & his many sore travails and sufferings, he one time signified to a Friend that he thought his time here was much over; and after some time, at a meeting at his own house, he was zealously concerned to exhort friends to faithfulness & diligence in preparing to meet the Lord, & when that his service was over, he desired to lay down upon a bed (which he did), & in a little time he quietly departed this life, steadfast in ye faith for which he had earnestly contended, ye 31st Day of ye 10th mo, 1693, aged about Sixty-five Years.

There was also a woman, named Elizabeth Routh, lived at Bainbridge aforesaid, who did early receive the truth in ye Love of it, whom ye Lord did concern to go to several steeplehouses in several places to testify against ye evil practices & dark ways of ye priests & people, for which testimony she sometimes suffered great hard-

* [The Conventicle Act of 1664 banned dissenting worship in groups of more than five and imposed harsh penalties for anyone refusing to swear a loyalty oath. —ed.]

ships & abuse, and she was made very serviceable in ye women's meetings & in several other respects, being a zealous woman (according to her measure) for ye propagating of truth & righteousness for many years together, even till (by death) she was Removed from us, which was on ye 8th day of ye 1st mo, 1699, about ye 70th year of her age.

In or about ye year 1653, did ye Lord move upon ye hearts of James Nayler & Robert Withers to come into Swaledale to preach ye everlasting truth, being ye first that we know of that came there with that testimony in this latter age, & several were convinced thereabouts, & Nicholas Row received them. And soon after, did ye same James Nayler, & Robert Withers, & Thomas Taylor, pretty near one another, come to Healay in Swaledale aforesaid, & preached ye Truth, & James Alderson received them; and we believe soon after there was a meeting settled thereabouts which has continued ever since & is called Swaledale Meeting. We think fit also to signify that ye aforesaid Nicholas Raw stood a faithful man to ye Truth till his death, which was in prison at York, for his testimony against that antichristian yoke of tithes.

And about ye above said year, 1653 (as far as can be remembered), did one Richard Lancaster, from about Countersett in Wensladale, (occasionally) come to Carleton in Coverdale, being the first (called a Quaker) that came there, to ye house of Richard Geldart, who, through some discourse or agreement about the principles of Truth, both he and his wife was convinced of it. And then abouts did Gervise Benson and John Blaykling, both from about Sedbergh, in the drawings of Truth come (though not just together, or at one time) to the aforesaid Richard Geldart's House, who gladly received them. And they had some meetings thereabouts, & preached ye everlasting Gospel, & several were convinced; & in some short time after, there was a meeting settled thereabouts, which has continued ever since, & is called Coverdale Meeting.

And about five or six years after, was Richard Robinson, from Countersett above mentioned, concerned to preach the Truth in the street of a neighbouring town (called) Carperby, & suffered great abuse by ye people, yet some years after, he had a meeting or meetings here again, & about that time or near then abouts, there was several families convinced of ye truth, & joined themselves to ye above said Coverdale Meeting.

The aforementioned Richard Geldart (in ye strength & virtue of ye Truth) did grow up a zealous, serviceable man, & bore a faithful testimony for ye Truth in its several branches, which he fully demonstrated by suffering, for he died a prisoner in York Castle, because for conscience sake he could not pay tithes.

CALLS TO WITNESS

KATHARINE EVANS AND
SARAH CHEVERS

Two of the most adventurous early Friends were Katharine Evans and Sarah Chevers. Evans was from Somerset, Chevers from Wiltshire. In 1659, they took a ship for Egypt, feeling called to preach in Alexandria and Jerusalem. When their ship touched at the Mediterranean island of Malta, however, they felt led to disembark and preach. A suspicious Inquisition soon seized them and held them for three years.

Katharine Evans, *This is a Short Relation of Some of the Cruel Sufferings (for the Truth's Sake) of Katharine Evans & Sarah Chevers, in the Inquisition in the Isle of Malta* (London, 1662).

We were at sea, between London and Plymouth, many weeks, and one day we had some trials, and between Plymouth and Leghorn [Italy] we were 31 days, and we had many trials and storms within and without; but the Lord did deliver us out of all. And when we came to Leghorn, with the rest of our friends, we went into the town after we had product, and stayed there many days, here we did service every day; for all sorts of people came into, but no man did offer to hurt us, yet we gave them some books and having got passage in a Dutch ship we sailed toward Cyprus, intending to go to Alexandria, but the Lord had appointed something for us to do by the way, as he did make it manifest to us, as I did speak, for the master of the ship had no business in the place; but being in company with another ship which had some business at the city of Malta (in the island of Malta where Paul suffered shipwreck), and being in the harbour, on the first day of the week, we being moved of the Lord, went into the town, and the English consul met us on the shore, and asked us concerning our coming, and we told him truth, and gave him some books, and a paper, and he told us there was an Inquisition, and he kindly entreated us to go to his house, and said all that he had was at our service while we were there. And in the fear and dread of the Lord we went, and there came many to see us, and we called them to repentance, and many of them were tender; but the whole city is given to idolatry. And we went a shipboard that night, and the next day we being moved to go into the city again, dared not to flee the cross, but in obedience went, desiring the will of God to be done. And when we came to the governor, he told us that he had a sister in the nunnery did desire to see us if we were free; and in the fear of God we went, and talked with them, and gave them a book, and one of their priests was with us (at the nunnery) and had us into their place of worship, and some would have us bow to the high altar, which we did deny; having a great burden, we went to the consul again, and were waiting on the Lord what to do, that we might know.

And the Inquisitors sent for us, and when we came before them, they asked our names, and the names of our husbands, and the names of our fathers and mothers, and how many children we had; and they asked us, Wherefore we came into that country? And we told them, we were servants of the living God, and were moved to come and call them to repentance; and many other questions, and they went away, but commanded that we should be stayed there. And the next day they came again, and called for us, and we came, but they would examine us apart, and called Sarah, and they asked, whether she was a true Catholic? She said, she was a true Christian that worshippeth God in spirit and in truth; and they proffered her the crucifix, and would have had her swear that she would speak the truth; and she said, she should speak the truth, but she would not swear, saying, "Swear not at all." And the English consul persuaded her with much entreating to swear, saying, none should do her any harm. But she denied; and they took some books from her, and would have had her swear by them, but she would not. And they asked, where from she brought the books? And she said, because we could not speak their language, and they might know wherefrom we came; and

they asked of her, what George Fox was; and she said, he was a
minister. And they asked, wherefore she came thither? She said,
to do the will of God, as she was moved of the Lord. And they
asked, how the Lord did appear unto her? And she said, by his
Spirit. And they asked, where she was when the Lord appeared
unto her? And she said, upon the way. And they asked, whether
she did see his presence, and hear his voice? And she said, she did
hear his voice, and saw his presence, and they asked, what he said
to her? and she said, the Lord told her, she must go over the seas
to do his will; and then they asked, how she knew it was the Lord?
and she said, he bid her go, and living presence should go with her,
and he was faithful that had promised, for she did feel his living
presence; and so they went away.

Two days after they came again, and called for me, and offered
me the crucifix, and told me that magistrate commanded me to
swear that I would speak the truth. And I told them I should speak
the truth, for I was a witness for God; but I should not swear; for
a greater than the magistrate saith, "Swear not at all, but let your
yea be yea, and your nay be nay, for whatsoever is more, cometh
of evil." But said they, "You must obey the justice, and he commands you to swear. I said, "I should obey Justice, but if I should
swear, I should an unjust thing; for (the just) Christ said, "'Swear
not at all.'" And they asked me, whether I did own that Christ
which died at Jerusalem. I answered, We owned the same Christ,
and no other, he is the same yesterday, today and forever.

And they asked me, what would I do at Jerusalem? I said I did
know that I should go there, but I should go to Alexandria; and
they said, what to do? And I said, to do the will of God; and if the
Lord did open my mouth, I should call them to repentance, and
declare to them the day of the Lord, and direct their minds from
darkness to Light. Then they asked me, whether I did tremble
when I did preach? And I told them, I did tremble when the power
of the Lord was upon me. And they asked, whether I did see the
Lord with my eyes? I said, God was a Spirit, and he was spiritually discerned. . . .

The next second day came a magistrate, two friars, and the man
with the black rod, and a scribe, and the keeper, to the Inquisition, to sit upon judgment, and examined us apart concerning
our faith in Christ. The magistrate would have had us to swear,
and we answered, no; Christ said, "Swear not at all"; and so said

James the Apostle. He asked if we would speak truth. We said, yea. He asked, whether we did believe the Creed? We said, we did believe in God, and in Jesus Christ, which was born of the Virgin Mary, and suffered at Jerusalem under Pilate, and arose again from the dead the third day, and ascended to his Father, and shall come to judge the quick and the dead. He asked, how we did believe the Resurrection? We answered, we did believe that the just and the unjust should arise, according to the Scriptures. He said, do you believe in the saints, and pray to them? We said, we did believe the Communion of Saints; but we did not pray to them, but to God only; in the name of Jesus Christ. He asked, whether we did believe in the Catholic Church? We said, we did believe the true Church of Christ; but the word *catholic* we had not read in Scripture. He asked, if we believed a purgatory? We said, no; but a heaven and a hell. The friar said, we were commanded to pray for the dead; for those that were in heaven had no need; and they that were in hell there is no redemption; therefore there must be a purgatory. He asked, if we believed their holy sacrament? We said, we never read (the word) *sacrament* in Scripture. The friar replied, where we did read in our Bibles sanctification, it was sacrament in theirs. He said, their holy sacrament was blood and wine, which they converted into the flesh and blood of Christ by the virtue of Christ. We said, they did work miracles then, for Christ's virtue is the same as it was when he turned water into wine at the marriage in Cana. He said, if we did not eat the flesh, and drink the blood of the Son of God, we had no life in us. We said, the flesh and blood of Christ is spiritual, and we do feed upon it daily; for that which is begotten of God in us, can no more live without spiritual food, than our temporal bodies can without temporal food. He said, that we did never hear mass. We said, we did hear the voice of Christ, he only had the words of eternal life, and that was sufficient for us. He said, we were heretics and heathens. We said, they were heretics that lived in sin and wickedness, and such were heathens that knew not God. He asked about our meetings in England. And we told them the truth to their amazement. And they asked, who was the head of our church? We said, Christ. And they asked, what George Fox is? And we said, he is a minister of Christ. They asked, whether he sent us? We said, no, the Lord did move us to come. The friar said we were deceived, and had not the faith; but we had all virtues. We said, that faith was the ground from whence virtues do proceed. They said, if we would take their holy sacrament, we might have our liberty, or else the people would not leave us for millions of gold, but we should lose our souls and our bodies too. We said, the Lord had provided for our souls, and our bodies were freely given up to serve the Lord. They asked us, if we did not believe marriage was a sacrament? We said, it was an ordinance of God. They asked us, if we did believe men could forgive sins? We said none could forgive sins but God only. They brought us that Scripture, "Whose sins ye remit in earth, shall be remitted in heaven." We said, all power was God's, and he could give it to whom he would (that were born of the Eternal Spirit, and guided by the same; such have power to do the Father's will, as I answered a friar also in the city of Naples), and they were silent, the power greatly working. We asked them wherein we had wronged them, that we should be kept prisoners all days of our lives, and said, our innocent blood would be required at their hands.

The friar said, he would take our blood upon him, and our journey into Turkey too. We told him, the time would come he would find he had enough upon him without it. They said, the Pope was Christ's vicar, and we were of his church, and what he did, was for the good of our souls. We answered, the Lord had not committed the charge of our souls to the Pope, nor to them; for he had taken them into his own possession, glory was to his name forever. They said, we must be obedient. We said, we were obedient to the government of Christ's Spirit. The friar said, none had the true Light but the Catholics; the Light that we had, was the spirit of the Devil. We said, woe to him that calleth Jesus accursed. Can the Devil give power over sin and iniquity? Then he would destroy his own kingdom. He said, we were laughed at, and mocked at of everyone. We said, what did become of the mockers? It was no matter. He said, we did run about to preach, and had not the true faith. We said, the true faith is held in a pure conscience void of offence towards God and man, and we had the true faith. And he said, there was but one faith, either theirs or ours; and asked us which it was? We said, everyone had the true faith, that did believe in God, and in Jesus whom he had sent but they that say they do believe, and do not keep his commandments, are liars, and the truth is not in them. He said it was true; but he did thirst daily for our blood, because he would not turn, and urged us much about

faith and sacrament, to bring us under their law; but the Lord preserved us.

They said, it was impossible we could live long in that hot room.
So the next week they sat in council; but oh how the swelling sea
did rage, and the proud waves did foam even unto the clouds of
heaven, and proclamation was made at the prison gate, we did not
know the words, but the fire of the Lord flamed against it, my life
was smitten, and I was in a very great agony, so that sweat was
as drops of blood, and the righteous one was laid into a sepulcher, and a great stone was rolled to the door; but the prophesy
was, that he should arise again the third day, which was fulfilled.
But the next day they came to sit upon judgment again, [but I say
in the true judgment they sat not, but upon it they got up un-
justly above the righteous, and upon the same they sat; a child of
Wisdom may understand] and they brought many propositions
written in a paper, but the friar would suffer the magistrate to
propound but a few to us, for fear the Light would break forth;
but they asked how many friends of ours were gone forth in the
ministry, and into what parts. We told them we did not know. They
said, all that came where the Pope had anything to do, should
never go back again. We said, the Lord was as sufficient for us, as
he was for the children in the fiery furnace, and our trust was in
God. They said, we were but few, and had been but a little while,
and they were many countries, and had stood many hundred
years, and wrought many miracles, and we had none. We said,
we had thousands at our meetings, but none (of us) dare speak a
word, but as they are eternally moved of the Lord; and we had
miracles, the blind receive their sight, the deaf do hear, and the
dumb do speak, the poor do receive the Gospel, the lame do walk,
and the dead are raised. He asked, why I looked so, whether my
spirit was weak? I said, nay, my body was weak, because I eat no
meat [I was in their Lent]. He offered me a license to eat flesh. I
said I could not eat anything at all. The terrors of death were
strongly upon me; but three nights after, the Lord said unto me,
about the 11th hour, arise, and put on your clothes. I said, "When
wilt thou come Lord?" He said, "Whether at midnight, or at cock
crow, do thou watch." My friend and I arose, and the Lord said,
"Go stand at the door. And we stood at the door in the power of
the Lord. I did scarce know whether I was in the body, or out
of the body; and about the 12th hour there came many to the

prison gate. We heard the keys, and looked when they could come in. They ran to and fro till the 4th hour; the Lord said, he had smote them with blindness, they could not find the way. And we went to bed, there I lay night and day for 12 days together, fasting and sweating, that my bed was wet, and great was our affliction.

The tenth day of my fast there came two friars, the chancellor, the man with the black rod, and a physician, and the keepers; and the friar commanded my dear friend to go out of the room, and he came and pulled my hand out of the bed, and said, "Is the devil so great in you, that you cannot speak?" I said, "Depart from me thou worker of iniquity, I know thee not; the power of the Lord is upon me, and thou callest him Devil." He took his crucifix to strike me in the mouth; and I said, "Look here!" and I asked him, whether it were that Cross which crucified Paul unto the World, and the World unto him? And he said, it was. I denied him, and I said, the Lord had made me a witness for himself against all workers of iniquity. He bid me be obedient, and went to strike me. I said, "Wilt thou strike me?" He said, he would. I said, "Thou art out of the Apostles' doctrine, they were no strikers; I deny thee to be any of them who went in the name of the Lord." He said, he had brought me a physician in charity. I said, the Lord was my physician, and my saving health. He said I should be whipped and quartered, and burnt that night in Malta, and my mate too; wherefore did we come to teach them? I told him I did not fear, the Lord was on our side, and he had no power but what he had received; and if he did not use it to the same end the Lord gave it to him, the Lord would judge him. And they were all smitten as dead men, and went away.

And as soon as they were gone, the Lord said unto me, "The last enemy that shall be destroyed is Death"; and the Life arose over Death, and I glorified God. The friar went to my friend, and told her, I called him worker of iniquity. "Did she?" said Sarah. "Art thou without sin?" He said he was. "Then she hath wronged thee." (But I say, the wise reader may judge.) For between the eighth and ninth hour in the evening, he sent a drum to proclaim at the prison gate; we know not what it was, but the fire of the Lord consumed it. And about the fourth hour in the morning they were coming with a drum and guns; and the Lord said unto me, "Arise out of thy grave-clothes." And we arose, and they came up to the gate to devour us in a moment. But the Lord lifted up his own Spirit (of Might) and made them to retreat, and they fled as dust before the wind, praises and honour be given to our God forever. I went to bed again, and the Lord said unto me, "Herod will seek the young child's life to destroy it yet again"; and great was my affliction; so that my dear fellow and laborer in the Work of God, did look every hour when I should depart of body for many days together, and we did look every hour when she should be brought to the stake day and night, for several weeks, and Isaac was freely offered up. But the Lord said, he had provided a ram in the bush. Afterwards the friar came again with his physician; I told him, that I could not take anything, unless I was moved of the Lord. He said, we must never come forth of that room while we lived, and we might thank God and him it was no worse, for it was like to be worse. We said, if we had died, we had died as innocent as ever did servants of the Lord. He said, it was well we were innocent. They did (also) look still when I would die.

The friar bid my friend take notice what torment I would be in at the hour of death, thousands of devils (he said) would fetch my soul to hell. She said, she did not fear any such thing.

And he asked if I did not think it expedient for the elders of the church to pray over the sick? I said, yea, such as were eternally moved of the Spirit of the Lord. He fell down on his knees and did howl, and with bitter wishes upon himself if he had not the true faith; but we denied him. The physician was in a great rage at Sarah, because she could not bow to him, but to God only.

The last day of my fast I began to be a hungry, but was afraid to eat, the enemy was so strong; but the Lord said unto me, "If thine enemy hunger, feed him; if he thirst, give him drink, in so doing thou shalt heap coals of fire upon his head; be not overcome of evil, but overcome evil with good." I did eat, and was refreshed, and glorified God; and in the midst of our extremity the Lord sent his holy angels to comfort us, so that we rejoiced and magnified God; and in the time of our great trial, the sun and earth did mourn visibly three days, and the horror of death and the pains of hell was upon me: the sun was darkened, the moon was turned into blood, and the stars did fall from heaven and there was great tribulation ten days, such as never was from the beginning of the world; and then did I see the Son of Man coming in the clouds, with power and great glory, triumphing over his enemies; the heavens were on fire, and the elements did melt with fervent heat, and the trumpet sounded out of Zion, and an alarm was struck up in Jerusalem, and all the enemies of God were called to the great day of battle of the Lord. And I saw a great wonder in heaven, the woman clothed with the sun, and had the moon under her feet, and a crown of 12 stars upon her head, and she travailed in pain ready to be delivered of a man-child; and there was a great Dragon stood ready to devour the man-child as soon as it was born; and there was given to the woman two wings of a great eagle to carry her into the desert, where she should be nourished for a time, times, and half a time; and the Dragon cast a flood out of his mouth, etc. And I saw war in heaven, Michael and his angels against the Dragon and his angels, and the Lamb and his army did overcome them; and there was a trumpet sounded in heaven, and I heard a voice saying to me, "The city is divided into three parts," and I heard another trumpet sounding, and I looked and saw an angel go down into a great pool of water, and I heard a voice saying unto me, "Whosoever goeth down next after the troubling of the waters, shall be healed of whatsoever disease he hath." And I heard another trumpet sounding, and I heard a voice saying, "Babylon is fallen, is fallen, Babylon the great is fallen." And I looked, and saw the smoke of her torment, how it did ascend; and I heard another trumpet sounding, and I heard a voice saying unto me, "Behold!" and I looked, and I saw Pharaoh and his host pursuing the Children of Israel, and he and his host were drowned in the sea.

Dear Friends and people, whatsoever I have written, it's not because it is recorded in the Scripture, or that I have heard of such things; but in obedience to the Lord I have written the things which I did hear, see, tasted and handled of the good Word of God, to the praise of his name forever.

The Quaker historian William C. Braithwaite provides the happy ending to the story of these two determined women:

After the Restoration the Queen-Mother, Henrietta Maria, who was a Roman Catholic, lived for some years in London, and had as Lord Almoner Lord d'Aubigny, a priest in orders, who had much influence in Malta. Gilbert Latey and Fox saw him, and at his instance the two Friends were at length liberated, and after a wait of eleven weeks in the English consul's house were carried home in an English frigate by way of Leghorn and Tangier, reaching England about the end of 1662, after three and a half year's confinement. On their release they knelt down and prayed God not to lay to the charge of the officers of the Inquisition the evil they had done to them, and on arriving in London they went with Latey to thank Lord d'Aubigny for his intercession. He replied with the courtesy of a high-bred and spiritually-minded Catholic: "Good women, for what service or kindness I have done you, all that I shall desire of you is that when you pray to God you will remember me in your prayers."

ADVICES

ADVICES OF THE ELDERS OF BALBY

As the Quaker movement grew, Friends began to think in terms of organization. Although the system of monthly, quarterly, and yearly meetings did not emerge for another decade, by 1656 many, although not all, Friends already perceived themselves as a spiritual community defined by certain common practices. One of the earliest articulations came from a meeting of Friends at Balby, Yorkshire, in 1656. The closing words are often quoted by Friends today.

Abram R. Barclay, ed., *Letters, Etc., of Early Friends, Illustrative of the History of the Society* (London, 1841).

The Elders and Brethren Send Unto the Brethren in the North These Necessary Things Following; to Which, If You, in the Light Wait, to Be Kept in Obedience, You Will Do Well.

1. That the particular meetings, by all the children of the light, be duly kept and observed, where they be already settled, every First-day of the week; except they be moved to other places. And that general meetings be kept in order and sweet in the life of God, on some other day of the week than on the First-day, unless there be a moving to the contrary: that so in the light and life, the meetings be kept, to the praise of God.

2. That care be taken, that as any are brought into the Truth, meetings be in such places amongst them, as may be for the most

convenience of all, without respect of persons: and that hands be laid on none suddenly, lest the Truth suffer.

3. That if any person draw back from meetings, and walk disorderly, some go to speak to such as draw back; to exhort and admonish such with a tender, meek spirit, whom they find negligent or disorderly. And if any, after admonition, do persist in the thing not good, let them again be admonished and reproved before two or three witnesses; that by the mouth of two or three witnesses, everything may be established. And if still they persevere in them, then let the thing be declared to the church: and when the church hath reproved them for their disorderly walking, and admonished them in the tender and meek spirit, and they do not reform, then let their names and the causes, and such as can justly testify the truth therein, and their answers, be sent in writing to some whom the Lord hath raised up in the power of his Spirit to be fathers, His children to gather in the light,—that the thing may be known to the body; and with the consent of the whole body, the thing may be determined in the light.

4. That as any are moved of the Lord to speak the word of the Lord at such meetings, that it be done in faithfulness, without adding or diminishing. And if at such meetings, anything at any time be otherwise spoken by any out of the light, whereby the seed of God cometh to be burdened; let the person or persons in whom the seed of God is burdened, speak in the light (as of the Lord they are moved), in meekness and godly fear, to him; but let it be done in private, betwixt them two, or before two or three witnesses, and not in the public meetings, except there be a special moving so to do.

5. That collections be timely made for the poor, (that are so indeed,) as they are moved, according to order,—for relief of prisoners, and other necessary uses, as need shall require: and all moneys so collected, an account thereof to be taken; from which every need may be supplied, as made known by the overseers in every meeting: that no private ends may be answered, but all brought to the light, that the gospel be not slandered.

6. That care be taken for the families and goods of such as are called forth into the ministry, or [who] are imprisoned for the Truth's sake; that no creatures be lost for want of the creatures.

7. That as any are moved to take a brother or a sister in marriage,— (marriage being honourable in all, and the bed undefiled), let it be made known to the children of the light, especially to those of the meeting of which the parties are members; that all in the light may witness it to be of God. And let them be joined together in the Lord and in His fear, in the presence of many witnesses; according to the example of the holy men of God in the Scriptures of Truth recorded, (which were written for our example and learning); that no scandal may rest upon the Truth, nor anything be done in secret; but all things brought to the light, that Truth may triumph over all deceit; and that they who are joined together in the Lord, may not by man be put asunder, whom God hath joined together. That there may be a record in writing, witnessing of the day, place, and year, of such things, kept within that meeting, of which the one or both of them are members; under which writing the witnesses present may subscribe their names, or so many of them as be convenient; for the stopping of the mouths of gainsayers, and for the manifesting the truth to all who are without.

8. That a record be kept in every meeting of the births of the children of such who are members of that meeting, and of the burials of the dead (who die in the Lord), as they depart out of the body; which be done after the manner of the holy men of God, recorded in the Scriptures of Truth; and not after the customs of the heathen, who know not God.

9. That husbands and wives dwell together according to knowledge, as being heirs together of the grace of life. That children obey their parents in the Lord; and that parents provoke not their children to wrath, but bring them up in the nurture and fear of the Lord, walking before them as good examples, in gravity and godliness; providing things honest in the sight of God and man.

10. That servants be obedient to them that are their masters in the flesh, in things that are good, in singleness of heart as unto Christ; not with eye-service, as men-pleasers, but as the servants of Christ;

doing the will of God from the heart: with good-will doing service, as to the Lord, and not to men; knowing whatsoever good thing any man doth, the same shall he receive of the Lord, whether he be bond or free. And that masters give to their servants that which is just and equal; forbearing threatening, knowing that their Master is also in heaven; neither is there respect of persons with Him.

11. That care be taken that none who are servants depart from their masters, but as they both do see in the light: nor any master to put away his servant, but by the consent of the servant: and if any master or servant in their wills do otherwise, it is to be judged with Friends in the light.

12. That the necessities of the poor, widows and fatherless, may be truly supplied, and that such as are able to work, and do not, may be admonished: and if, after admonition, they refuse to work, then let them not eat. And that the children of such as are in necessity, be put to honest employment; that none be idle in the Lord's vineyard.

13. That care be taken, that as any are called before the outward powers of the nation, that in the light, obedience to the Lord be given.

14. That if any be called to serve the commonwealth in any public service, which is for the public wealth and good, that with cheerfulness it be undertaken, and in faithfulness discharged unto God: that therein patterns and examples in the thing that is righteous, they may be, to those that be without.

15. That all Friends that have callings and trades, do labour in the thing that is good, in faithfulness and uprightness; and keep to their yea and nay in all their communications: and that all who are indebted to the world, endeavour to discharge the same, that nothing they may owe to any man but love one another.

16. That no one speak evil of another, neither judge one against another; but rather judge this, that none put a stumbling-block or occasion to fall in his brother's way.

17. That none be busybodies in other's matters, but each one to bear another's burdens, and so fulfill the law of Christ; that they be sincere and without offence, and that all things which are honest, be done without murmurings and disputings: that they may be blameless and harmless, the sons of God without rebuke, in the midst of a crooked and perverse nation, amongst whom they may shine as lights in the world.

18. That Christian moderation be used towards all men; that they who obey not the word, may be won [by] those that in the word dwell, to guide in an holy life and godly conversation.

19. That the Elders made by the Holy Ghost, feed the flock of God, taking the oversight thereof willingly, not by constraint, but of a willing mind; neither as lords over God's heritage, but as examples to the flock of Christ.

20. That the younger submit themselves to the elder,—yea all be subject one to another, and be clothed with humility; for God resisteth the proud but giveth grace to the humble.

From the Spirit of Truth to the children of light, to walk in the light; that all in the order be kept in obedience to God; that He may be glorified, who is worthy over all, blessed for ever—Amen!

Dearly beloved Friends, these things we do not lay upon you as a rule or form to walk by; but that all, with a measure of the light, which is pure and holy, may be guided: and so in the light walking and abiding, these things may he fulfilled in the Spirit, not in the letter; for the letter killeth, but the Spirit giveth life.

OPPOSITION

FRANCIS HIGGINSON

Almost from the moment that George Fox and other "First Publishers" began to preach, they faced opposition. Critics attacked them as blasphemers, social revolutionaries, witches, and madmen and -women. One of the earliest such attacks was the work of Francis Higginson (1617–1670), the Puritan pastor at Kirkby Stephen at Kendal in Westmorland, a region where Friends made many converts. While the piece is clearly hostile, Quaker historians Hugh Barbour and Arthur Roberts describe it as among the best early descriptions we have of Quaker preaching and writing.

Francis Higginson, *A Brief Relation of the Irreligion of the Northern Quakers, Wherein Their Horrid Principles and Practices, Doctrines and Manners, as Far as Their Mystery of Iniquity Hath Yet Discovered Itself, Are Plainly Exposed to the View of Every Intelligent Reader* (London, 1653).

The last summer there came, or rather crept unawares, into the county of Westmorland, and some parts of Yorkshire and Lancashire adjacent to it, George Fox, James Nayler, one Spoden, and one Thornton, all of them Satan's seeds-men, and such as have prosperously sowed the tares of that enemy in the forementioned fields, as shall be, with God's assistance, in this ensuing relation manifestly declared.

These men, together with some others (who, being affectors of novelty in religion more than verity, were quickly made their proselytes) have powerfully seduced multitudes of people in these parts from the truth, and true worship of God, to embrace their doctrines of devils, and follow their pernicious ways.

This sort of people are vulgarly, and not unaptly, distinguished from others by the name of Quakers, the reason of which appellation I shall show you hereafter.

Now to the end it may be as apparent as the day, that the guides of this sect, notwithstanding their fair pretensions of an immediate, and extraordinary mission, and the great opinion their deluded followers have conceived of them, are not the servants of the Lord Jesus, but in very deed the emissaries and ministers of Satan, and that their way is not the good old way, the way of God, but as contrary to it as the darkness to the light, I shall take some pains to acquaint my reader. . . .

Of the Horrid Blasphemies of the Quakers against God and His Christ

George Fox, the father of the Quakers of these parts, hath avowed himself over and over, to be equal with God; being asked by Doctor Marshall, in the presence of Master Sawre, Colonel Tell, and Colonel West, Justices of the Peace in the County of Lancashire, at a private sessions in the town of Lancaster, whether or no he was equal with God, as he had before that time been heard to affirm: his answer was this, *I am equal with God.* . . .

And well may he affirm himself to be equal with God, when he . . . lays down this blasphemous proposition definitely: He that hath the same Spirit that raised up Jesus Christ from the dead, is equal with God. . . . This Fox hath also professed himself to be the judge of the world.

James Nayler, another of Satan's Nuncios, and principal spokesman in these parts, affirmeth that he was as holy, just, and good, as God himself. This was, I hear, attested at Kendal by two witnesses. . . .

It seems if a man be of their way, although a blasphemer and false prophet, by their own confession, yet with them he is excusable.

One Williamson's wife, a disciple of Milner's, when she came to see him at Appleby, said in the hearing of divers there . . . that she was the eternal Son of God. And when the men that heard her, told her that she was a woman, and therefore could not be the Son of God, she said, no, you are women, but I am a man. These last words I insert, that the Reader may see how strongly the spirits of some of these people are transported, and how ready they are to affirm any thing how ever impious, or absurd.

Of the Erroneous Opinions of the Quakers . . .

1. They hold that the holy scripture, the writings of the prophets, evangelists, and apostles, are not the word of God, and that there is no written word of God; but they say, using a foolish distinction of their own coining, that they are a declaration of the word only in those that have the faith.

2. They hold their own speakings are a declaration of the word (Christ) in them, thereby making them, though they be for the most part full of impiety and nonsense, to be of equal authority with the holy scriptures.

3. They hold that no exposition ought to be given of the holy scripture, and that all expounding of scripture is an adding to it, and that God will add to such a one all the plagues written in that book. Opening, and applying the scripture, is one thing they mainly declaim against, wherever they come.

4. They teach poor people that whosoever takes a text of scripture and makes a sermon of or from it is a conjurer, and that his preaching is conjuration. Fox, in his printed answer to this *(Saul's Errand)* . . . says thus:

> *All that study to raise a living thing out of a dead, to raise the spirit out of the letter are conjurers, and draw points and reasons, and so speak a divination of their own brain. . . . For their doctrine doth not profit the people at all, for it stands not in the counsel of God, but it is a doctrine of the devil, and draws people from God.*

5. They affirm that the letter of the scripture is carnal.

6. That he that puts the letter for light is blind.

7. That the word is not the rule, whereby to try their spirits; they will not allow of comparing of that watcher (they say) they have within, with the written word in Scripture.

8. They call the written word of God, the World's word, the World's light, touchstone, rule, and say, outward Scriptures and glorious gospel is dull. Some of them have affirmed, it was not great matter if all the Bibles in England were burnt.

9. It is a doctrine general with them, that the soul is part of God, or of the divine essence; and was actually existent long before it was conveyed into the body. . . .

10. The denial of any distinction of persons in the ——head is common with them. Fox, . . . affirms that it is best a busy mind to enquire whether there be one individual God, distinguished into Father, Son, and Holy Ghost.

11. They hold that Christ hath no body but his church.

12. They hold that Jesus Christ is come into their flesh, that he is in them as man, that the man Christ dwells in them. . . .

14. They hold that Christ is a light within every man, and that every man must mind that light and teacher within, and follow no teacher without. . . .

15. They hold that all men in the world, have in them a light sufficient to salvation, Turks, Indians, yea, such as never had, or ever shall have any outward means to reveal Christ to them. . . .

16. Some of them have argued that the man Christ is not ascended into heaven. . . .

21. They hold that in conversion there is no new nature, no habit of grace, or seed of God involved, but that Christ that was in man before, is then raised up in them out of prison.

22. They hold that there is a fullness of glory in this life, that they enjoy God here, and Christ here, the Resurrection, Judgment, an-

gels, glory, and all they look for they enjoy in this life, and mock at those that speak of another world, or life to come, or a better kingdom.

23. They deny many of them the resurrection of the body.

24. They hold that there is no local heaven, or hell.

25. They hold many of them, that they have attained to a state of perfection, and that they neither do, nor can sin. . . .

28. They hold the office of teaching to be utterly useless in the Church of God, and tell the most ignorant people where they come, that they have no need that any man should teach them, and therefore dissuade them from hearing any of our ministers whatever, telling them they shall be damned if they do so; and that all that go the bell houses to hear them, shall be turned like chaff and stubble, and charge people not to believe a word that any of them speak. And for themselves when they speak, they say, they do not teach or preach, but only declare the revelations of God within them.

29. They hold that Fox and all the rest of their speakers are immediately called. . . . Fox says they were moved to come into these parts by the Lord, and the Lord let them see he had a people here before they came. Nayler also at the last sessions at Appleby, January 1652, affirmed in the face of the court, that when he was at plow in barley seed time, meditating on the things of God, he suddenly heard a voice commanding him to go out from his country, and from his father's house, and had a promise given with it. And being demanded whether he heard the voice, he said he heard it himself, but those who were with him heard it not. Being asked again whether it was an audible voice, he answered, "No, friend, it was not a carnal voice, audible to the outward ear." . . .

30. They deny all ordinances, and their practice is suitable to this their wicked tenet. An honest minister in Westmorland, discoursing with Fox, asked him whether he did believe prayer, preaching, the sacraments, meditation, holy conference to be ordinances of God. No, says he, away with them, I deny them all.

31. They call the worship of God used in our public assemblies a beastly worm-eaten form, a heathenish way; and worship fleshly, carnal, etc.

32. They hold that the sprinkling of infants is Antichristian, and their baptism the mark of the beast, spoken of in the Revelation, which those that worship the beast receive in their foreheads.

33. They affirm that there is not one word in scripture that speaks of a sacrament, and that they are unlawful; that a little bread and a little wine in a sacrament is the world's communion, and that in the true church of God there is no talk of such carnal things.

34. They hold it unlawful to sing the Psalms of David, and call them the World's Psalms, carnal Psalms, and say we sing David's quakings, and tremblings, and that we put David's conditions into rhyme, and meter, and sing them to the dishonor of God.

35. They deny the Lord's Day to be the Christian Sabbath, and say, the Sabbath is a mystery which we understand not.

36. They hold it unlawful to worship God in our churches (commonly and metonymically so-called) and term them idols' temples, beasts' houses, where God is not worshiped, but the worship of the Beast is upheld, and that the Beasts of the field meet there, night-birds, screech owls.

37. For the office of the magistracy, though they do not yet openly declaim against it, fearing they should be quickly called to account for such an attempt, yet their opinions which some of their lavish tongues have manifested touching it, as also this rude irreverence, saucy deportment towards magistrates, wherein they show not so much as any common respect to them; their bold & impious predictions of the ruin of all in authority whatsoever, and raising predictions against them, do easily evidence them to be none of the best friends to it. . . . One Leonard Till, of their way in Lancashire, affirmed, that one man ought not to have power over another. Another principal man of the sect in our county, affirmed to a justice of the peace, there would be Quakers in Westmorland, when there should never be a justice of the peace in it. . . . Those

of the sect at York, now prisoners, railed against them the judges, calling them scarlet colored beasts, etc., while sitting on the bench. . . .

38. They hold that all things ought to be common, and teach the doctrine of leveling privately to their disciples. . . . Several of them have affirmed there ought to be no distinction of estates, & one above the rest denied the property of estates; a third affirmed that wheresoever Christ came, he came to destroy all property.

39. They hold to quote [early church] Fathers and authors in preaching is antichristian.

40. They are of the opinion that it is unlawful to call any man Master or Sir.

41. They hold it unwarrantable to salute any man by the way.

42. They account it unlawful to use the civility of our language, in speaking to a single person in the plural number.

Of the Wicked Practices of the Quakers, and First of Their Meetings, and Speakings

I shall now go on to present my reader with a brief view of their black wicked practices, the natural fruits of such corrupt principles as are above mentioned. In doing of which I shall principally take notice of their meetings, speakings, quakings, fastings, revelings, censoriousness, lyings, inconstancy in their own opinions, enmity to learning, idleness, incivilities, bloody, barbarous, and turbulent practices, for their ways have not been altogether in the clouds, nor their deeds of darkness always done in corners. . . .

And first for their meetings, and the manner of them. They come together on the Lord's Days, or on other days of the week indifferently, at such times and places as their speakers or some other of them think fit. Their number is sometimes thirty, sometimes forty, or sixty, sometimes a hundred or two hundred in a swarm. The places of their meetings are, for the most part, such private houses as are most solitary and remote from neighbors, situated in dales and by-places. Sometimes the open fields, sometimes the top of a hill, or rocky hollow places, on the sides of mountains are the places of their rendezvous. In these their assemblies, for the most part they use no prayer, not in one meeting of ten. When they do, their praying devotion is so quickly cooled that when they have begun, a man can scarce [count] to twenty before they have done. They have no singing of psalms, hymns, or spiritual songs—that is an abomination. No reading or exposition of holy scripture, that is also an abhorrency. No teaching or preaching—that is in their opinion the only thing that is needless. No administration of sacraments—with them there is no talk, they say, of such carnal things; not so much as any conference by way of question is allowed of; that which asks, they say, doth not know, and they call propounding of any question to them a tempting of others. They have only their own mode of speaking (that is all the worship I can hear of) which they do not call, but deny to be, preaching, nor indeed doth it deserve that more honourable name. If any of their chief speakers be among them, the rest give place to them; if absent, any of them speak that will pretend a revelation. Sometimes girls are vocal, . . . while leading men are silent. Sometimes they are segregated, there is . . . not a whisper among them for an hour or two or three together. This time they are waiting which of them the Spirit shall come down upon in inspirations and give utterance to. Sometimes they only read the epistles of Fox and Nayler, which according to their principles are to them of as great authority as the epistles of Peter and Paul.

They exceedingly affect night meetings, which are usually of both sexes very lately, and not infrequently continued all night long. Their holies, they think, are best dispersed while others are asleep. These unreasonable dark assemblies of theirs . . . have been in some places a just cause of afrightment to the neighboring inhabitants that are not of their way, who have professed they could scarcely sleep in their beds without fear. . . .

For the manner of their speakings, their speaker for the most part uses the posture of standing, or sitting with his hat on, his countenance severe, his face downward, his eyes fixed mostly towards the earth, his hands and fingers expanded, continually striking gently on his breast. His beginning is without a text, abrupt and sudden to his hearers, his voice for the most part low, his sentences incoherent, hanging together like ropes of sand, very frequently full of impiety and horrid errors, and sometimes full of sudden pauses, his whole speech a mixed bundle of words and heap of nonsense. His continuance in speaking is sometimes short, sometimes very tedious, according to the paucity or plenty of his revelations. His admiring auditors who are of his way stand the while like men astonished, listening to every word, as though every word was oraculous, and so they believe them to be the very words and dictates of Christ speaking in him.

Sometimes some of them, men or women, will more like frantic people than modest speakers of the Gospel, . . . run through or stand in the streets or market place, or get upon a stone and cry, "Repent, repent, woe, woe, the judge of the world has come, Christ is in you all, believe not your priests of Baal, they are liars, they delude you. Kendal, and many other towns in these northern parts, are witnesses of these mad speakings and practices. . . .

Of Their Quaking Fits, and the Manner of Them

Now for their quakings, one of the most immediate notable fruits . . . of their speakings. Though their speakings be a very chaos of words and errors, yet very often while they are speaking, so strange is the effect of them, in their unblest followers, that many of them, sometimes men, but more frequently women and children, fall into quaking fits. The manner of which is this: those in their assemblies who are taken with these fits fall suddenly down, as it were in a swoon, as though they were surprised with an epilepsy or apoplexy, and lie groveling on the earth, and struggling as it were for life, and sometimes more quietly as though they were departing. While the agony of the fit is upon them their lips quiver, their flesh and joints tremble, their bellies swell as though blown up with wind, they foam at the mouth, and sometimes purge as if they had taken physic. In this fit they continue sometimes an hour or two, sometimes longer, before they come to themselves again, and when it leaves them they roar out horribly with a voice greater than the voice of a man—the noise, those say that have heard it, is a very horrid fearful noise, and greater sometimes than any bull can make. . . .

George Fox, the ringleader of this sect, hath been and is vehemently suspected to be a sorcerer.

Of Their Railings

They are also as horrible railers as ever any age brought forth, a generation whose mouths are full of bitterness, whose throats are open sepulchers, etc. The Billingsgate oyster-women are not comparable to them. It is ordinary with them in the letters they write to other men to call them fools, sots, hypocrites, vain men, beasts, blasphemers, murderers of the just. It is a customary thing with this gang of people in their discourse with others to tell them they are dogs, heathen, etc. . . .

They affirm that all the ministers in England who preach in steeple-houses are liars of Jesus Christ; they uphold the kingdom of Antichrist, that they do all for filthy lucre. . . .

They accuse them of being brought up at Oxford and Cambridge; they say, they know nothing but natural books and natural things, the scripture letter, Hebrew and Greek, which is all natural; that the ungodly, unholy, proud priests and professors must be scorned who know not the power of the word. . . .

They say the Lord is coming to beat up their quarters, the son of thunder is coming abroad to sound trumpets, to call to battle against the great day of the Lord, and their kingdom must be taken from them, and that their downfall is near at hand. Some of them have said they hope within a year's time to see never a minister left in England. . . .

Of Their Idleness, Savage Incivilities, and Their Irreligious, Bloody, Barbarous, and Turbulent Practices

To what has been hitherto related of their impieties and disorderly walkings, it may be added that they are many of them notorious for idleness in their callings, working not at all sometimes for whole weeks and months together. . . .

A son, if turned a Quaker, will not use the usual civility of the world that is Christian in putting off his hat to his father or mother, will give them no civil salutations. To bid him a good morrow that begat him, or farewell, that brought him forth, is with them accounted a wickedness. . . .

They do not give any title or colour of respect to those who are their superiors in office, honour, estate—such as Master or Sir, etc., but call them by their naked name—Thomas, or William, or Gervase, or Dorothy, and ignorantly mistake it to be disagreeable to the word of truth.

They go to their meals for the most part like heathen, without any prayer or thanksgiving. . . .

To go naked is with some of them accounted a decency becoming their imagined state of innocency better than apparel; the ablest of them plead for this obscenity.

One of this sort in Kirkbymoorside, a market town in Yorkshire, ran stark naked to the [market] cross in the view of many, and stood in that posture . . . speaking to the people.

Two others of their society, a man and a woman, that called themselves Adam and Eve, went for some while as some uncivilized heathen do, discovering their nakedness to the very eye of every beholder, and when they were publicly examined at the assizes for their brutish practice, the man wickedly affirmed that the power of God was upon him, he was commanded to do it. . . .

One of their gang in Westmorland, on Friday the eighth of April last, ran like a mad man naked, all but his shirt, through Kendal, crying, "Repent, repent, woe, woe, come out of Sodom, remember Lot's wife," with other such stuff. . . .

But to linger nowhere in particulars. This one thing to me doth plainly evidence the way of these apostalates to be of the Devil. No sooner is any one became a proselyte to their sect but he is possessed with a spirit of malice, and wrath, and turns enemy to all men that are not of their way. Especially those that appear against it. To such they use menacing speeches as of a day that is coming wherein they shall be avenged, and talk frothily sometimes of levying forces, choosing colonels and captains, etc.

SUFFERINGS

GEORGE BISHOP

*While Friends faced death from assault and miserable condi-
tions in jails, the worst persecution was in Massachusetts. Puritan authorities there regarded Quakers as the most pestilential
plague Satan had unleashed on earth and responded with fero-
cious laws. Their barbarity only drew Friends determined to
testify against such persecution. In 1659, two Friends were
hanged in Boston. Two others would follow in 1660 and 1661.
English Friend George Bishop excoriated Massachusetts authorities in a long account published in 1661, which Friends
subsequently revised and republished.*

George Bishop, *New England Judged by the Spirit of the Lord* (London, 1703).

Now, I am come to the bottom of your work and the height of this
your gradual proceeding, from banishment unto death; and in the
instance of those three servants of the Lord, viz., William Robinson, Marmaduke Stevenson, and Mary Dyer, two of whom, viz.,
William Robinson and Marmaduke Stevenson, ye confess to have
executed; and the third, viz., Mary Dyer, to have sentenced to
death, but reprieved, whom ye have since put to death. I shall now
proceed to the relation of their sufferings and the merits of their
deaths. . . .

William Robinson, a merchant of London, and Marmaduke
Stevenson, a countryman of . . . Yorkshire, being moved of
the Lord, in the Fourth month, 1659, to go from Rhode Island
into your jurisdiction, came thither accordingly; whom ye soon
apprehended, and with them one Nicholas Davis, who came from

Plymouth Patent, of which he was, to reckon with those with whom he traded in Boston, and to pay some debts, and Patience Scott, daughter to Catharine Scott, a girl of about eleven years of age, whose business to you, from her father's house in Providence, was, "To bear witness against your persecuting spirit." And ye sent them to prison, there to remain until the sitting of the Court of Assistants; during which time Mary Dyer, aforesaid, was moved of the Lord to come from Rhode Island to visit the prisoners, whom ye also imprisoned, and at the sitting of the said Court of Assistants, banished, together with William Robinson, Marmaduke Stevenson, and Nicholas Davis, upon pain of death, if after the 14th of the Seventh month following they should be found in your jurisdiction. The child, it seems, was not of years as to law, to deal with her by banishment, but otherwise in understanding, for she confounded you; and some of you consent that ye had many children, and they had been well educated, and that it were well if they could say half so much for God as she could for the devil. So ye blasphemed the Holy Ghost, the Spirit of Truth that spake in her, saying, "It was an unclean spirit." For, saith the Son of God, "All sins shall be forgiven unto the sons of men, and blasphemies wherewith soever they shall blaspheme: but he that shall blaspheme against the Holy Ghost hath never forgiveness, but is in danger of eternal damnation: because they said, He hath an unclean spirit."—See Mark iii. 22–30. For they said, he cast out devils by Beelzebub, the prince of devils; and that he had a devil. . . .

As for the four before mentioned, on the 12th of the Seventh month, two days before the expiration of the time limited by you, after which, if found in your jurisdiction, they should suffer death,—what a hard measure is here, to allow a man but two days to remove for his life, and upon so slight an account, or, rather, none at all,—ye caused to be turned out of prison, to try your law upon them; two of whom, viz., Nicholas Davis and Mary Dyer, found freedom to depart your jurisdiction, the one to Plymouth Patent, and the other to Rhode Island; but the other two, viz., W. Robinson and M. Stevenson, were constrained, in the love and power of the Lord, not to depart, but to stay in your jurisdiction, and to try your bloody law unto death. So, on the 13th, they passed out of prison to Salem, and remained there and at Piscataway, and the parts thereabout, in the service of the Lord, till you took them

up, your cruelty and monstrous inhumanity toward them being
such, when ye sentenced them to banishment, that a handkerchief
was put into the mouth of William Robinson to keep him from
speaking for himself, contrary to all law; and when he yet attempted to speak, ye caused him to be had down, in a great rage,
and twenty cruel stripes to be given him, on his naked back, with
a three-fold corded whip with knots, and then sent him to prison
with his fellow-sufferer, M. Stevenson, in order to death, if they
were found again in your jurisdiction, after the limitation of the
days set by you. Such inhumanities as these have hardly been
heard of in any generation, where men have pretended to law or
truth; but are found upon thee, O New England! and the head of
thy colonies, the Bay of Massachusetts! . . .

Not long after, viz., the 8th of the Eighth month following, Mary
Dyer, whom you had banished upon pain of death, and Hope Clifton, both of Rhode Island, came to Boston, on the First day of the
week, to visit Christopher Holder, who was then in prison. On the
next morning after they came in, they were espied, and carried by
the constable to the House of Correction; who, after your worship
was ended, came again, and charged the keeper, "body for body,
life for life," with Mary Dyer, till further order. So Mary was continued without being sent for, but Hope Clifton was had before
your deputy-governor the next morning, who recommitted her, and
one Mary Scott, a daughter of R. and C. Scott, of Providence aforesaid, who came also to visit the said imprisoned Christopher
Holder, whom the same constable apprehended while she was in
the prison to visit her friend; and your governor also committed
Robert Harper, of Sandwich, though he came about his outward occasions, the one to the prison, and the other to the House
of Correction.

And now the time of the sitting of your Court drawing near,
wherein you acted this bloody tragedy, W. Robinson and M. Stevenson came to Boston, viz., on the 13th day of the Eighth month, and
with them Alice Cowland, who came to bring linen wherein to
wrap the dead bodies of those who were to suffer, and Daniel
Gould, from Salem, William King, Hannah Phelps, the wife of
Nicholas Phelps aforesaid, and Mary Trask and Margaret Smith, of
the same town,—all these, as one, came together, in the moving and
power of the Lord, to look your bloody laws in the face, and to accompany those who should suffer by them; whom ye apprehended

and sent to prison, as aforesaid, and Provided Southwick, daughter of Lawrence and Cassandra Southwick, coming to see her sister, then in prison, and being met in the street and known to your deputy-governor, was asked by him "Whether she was a Quaker?" and she replying, "That she was one that was so called," he committed her also.

So your prisons began to fill, as aforesaid, and on the 19th of the same month, W. Robinson, M. Stevenson, and Mary Dyer were had before your Court, and demanded of by you, "Why they came again into your jurisdiction, being banished upon pain of death?" To which having severally answered, and declared that the ground or cause of their coming was of the Lord, and in obedience to Him, your governor said, "That he desired not their death," and "that they had liberty to speak for themselves, why they should not be proceeded with, as to the giving of sentence against them"; yet he bid the jailer take them away.

The next day—after your worship was ended, being heated by your priest and prepared to shed the blood of the innocent—you sent for them again, and your governor, speaking faintly, as a man whose life was departing from him, for the hand of the Lord was upon him, said to this effect, "We have made many laws, and endeavoured by several ways to keep you from us; and neither whipping, nor imprisonment, nor cutting off ears, nor banishment upon pain of death, will keep you from among us." And he said, "I desire not your death"; yet presently he said, "Give ear, and hearken to your sentence of death," and then made a stop. Whereupon W. Robinson desired that he might be suffered to read a paper amongst them, which was a declaration of his call to Boston, and the reason why they stayed within that jurisdiction after your sentence of banishment; which your governor denied, and said in a great rage, "You shall not read it, nor will the Court hear it read." Then William laid it on the table among them, and it was handed to your governor, who read it to himself and, after he had done, said, "W. Robinson, you need not keep such an ado to have it read, for you spoke yesterday more than is here written"; which was not so, and, if it had been, yet a man may be permitted to speak the same words over again; and the law allows it, viz., for a man to speak for himself ere sentence is given, and the clerks of the court usually proclaim that liberty, but you would not grant it. W. Robinson said, "Nay," and desired again it might be read, that all the people might hear the cause of their coming and of their stay there, and wherefore they were put to death, which was but what the law allowed. But you would not suffer it,—a very hard case; you would not be so dealt with, yet so ye have dealt with the innocent,—and your governor said to him, "Hearken to your sentence of death. You shall be had back to the place from whence you came, and from thence to the place of execution, to be hanged on the gallows till you are dead."

Then M. Stevenson was called, and your governor said to him, "If you have anything to say, you may speak"; and he standing still and giving no answer, for the Lord had shut him up, your governor pronounced the sentence of death against him, saying, "You shall be had to the place from whence you came, and from thence to the gallows, and then be hanged till you are dead." Which being pronounced, M. Stevenson's mouth was opened by the Lord, and he said, "Give ear, ye magistrates, and all who are guilty; for this the Lord hath said concerning you, who will perform His word upon you, that the same day ye put His servants to death, shall the day of your visitation pass over your heads, and you shall be accursed for evermore,—the mouth of the Lord of hosts hath spoken it. Therefore, in love to you all, I exhort you to take warning before it be too late, that so the curse may be removed; for, assuredly, if you put us to death, you will bring innocent blood upon your own heads, and swift destruction upon you." After he had spoken which, he was had to prison.

Then Mary Dyer was called, and your governor said to her to this effect:—"Mary Dyer, you shall go to the place whence you came, and from thence to the place of execution, and be hanged there until you are dead." To which she replied, "The will of the Lord be done." Then your governor said, "Take her away, Marshal." She answered, "Yea, joyfully shall I go." So she was brought to the House of Correction again, and there continued, with her other two friends, in prison, till the 27th of the same month; during which time many people resorted to the prison-windows, these things affecting them,—which struck such a fear in you, that ye set a guard about the prison by night, lest they should be taken away, and on W. Robinson and M. Stevenson you put chains of iron. And, on the 27th of the Eighth month aforesaid, ye caused the drums to beat, to gather your soldiers together for the execution; and after your worship was ended, your drums beat again,

and your captain, James Oliver, came with his band of men, and
the Marshal and some others, to the prison, and the doors were
opened. And your Marshal and jailer called for W. Robinson and
M. Stevenson, and had them out of the prison, and Mary Dyer
out of the House of Correction; who parted from their friends in
prison full of the joy of the Lord, who had counted them worthy
to suffer for His name, and had kept them faithful unto death.
And having embraced each other, with fervency of love and gladness of heart, and peace with God and praises to the Lord, they
went out of your prisons, like innocent lambs out of the butcher's
cart, to the slaughter; and your captain, with his band of men, led
them out by the back way,—it seems that you were afraid of the
front way, lest it should affect the people too much,—to the place
of execution, and caused the drums to beat when they attempted
to speak, (hard work!) and placed them near the drums, that the
people, who flocked about them in great multitudes, might not
hear them when they spoke,—as you used to imprison any that
you found looking in at the prison-windows, when they came there
to visit them, thinking thereby to keep the Seed of God under, and
their testimony from having a place in the people. But the more ye
strove to hinder, the more it took effect (to wit, the message that
they brought) and had place in their hearts; and the more cruel
you were, the deeper place it took, which in due time will come
forth and manifest itself. I say, your captain caused his drums to
beat when they sought to speak; and he would not cease beating
his drums whilst they were speaking. . . . And, as he led them to
the place of execution, your old and bloody priest [John] Wilson,
your high-priest of Boston, . . . was so old in blood that he . . .
said: "He would carry fire in one hand, and fagots in the other, to
burn all the Quakers in the world." And having some of those
people's books in his hand, when they were burning Friends'
books by your order, threw them into the fire, saying, "From the
devil they came, and to the devil let them go!"—a blasphemous
wretch! He who said to you, when you sat on the trial of these
men, "Hang them, or else—" drawing his finger athwart his
throat, and thus making signs for their throats to be cut if you
did not hang them,—I say, that this your bloody old high-priest,
with others of his brethren in iniquity and in persecuting the just,
met these sufferers in your train-field, and instead of having a
sense upon him suitable to such an occasion, and as is usual with

men of any tenderness, he fell a-taunting of W. Robinson, and
shaking his head in a light, scoffing manner, said, "Shall such
jacks as you come in before authority with your hats on?" with
many other taunting words. To which W. Robinson replied,
"Mind you! mind you! It is for the not putting off the hat that we
are put to death." And when W. Robinson went cheerfully up the
ladder, to the topmost round above the gallows, and spoke to the
people, "That they suffered not as evildoers, but as those who
testified and manifested the Truth; and that this was the day of
their visitation, and he therefore desired them to mind the Light
that was in them, the Light of Christ, of which he testified, and
was now going to seal it with his blood," this old priest, in much
wickedness, said, "Hold thy tongue! be silent! Thou art going to
die with a lie in thy mouth."

So being come to the place of execution hand in hand, as to a
wedding-day, all three of them with great cheerfulness of heart,
and having taken leave of each other with the dear embraces of
one another in the love of the Lord, your executioner put W. Robinson to death, and after him M. Stevenson, who died, both of
them, full of the joy of the Lord, and steadfast in Him, and have
received a crown of life; sealing their testimony with their blood,
their countenances not changing, though the priests had thought
to have found it otherwise, and some of them had spoken to this
purpose, that they should see whether they would change countenance when they had a halter about their necks; but they remained
as fresh, in a manner, even after they were dead as before, as was
observed by some. . . .

And because, when W. Robinson was bidden to speak, if he had
anything to say, wherefore you should not proceed to give sentence of death against him, he desired that his paper, giving the
cause of his coming and abiding in your jurisdiction, might be
read, fury rose up in your governor, and the form of his visage—
like Nebuchadnezzar's—was changed, and he said, "It should not
be read, and that the Court would not hear it," and so in effect
forbidding that which he bade him do, I shall set down the contents thereof, and of M. Stevenson's call into your parts,—for
which ye put him to death,—as a perpetual record to after ages of
that for which they suffered, and to your everlasting shame:—

William Robinson's Paper to the Court, before he was sen-

tenced to death, concerning the cause of their coming into those
parts, for which they were put to death, which the governor in a
great fury said "should not be read, and that the Court would not
hear it":

WHICH WAS IN THESE WORDS:—

*On the 8th day of the Eighth month, 1659, in the after part of the
day, in traveling betwixt Newport, in Rhode Island, and Daniel
Gould's house, with my dear brother, Christopher Holder, the Word
of the Lord came expressly to me, which did fill me immediately
with life and power, and heavenly love, by which He constrained me
and commanded me to pass to the town of Boston, my life to lay
down in His will, for the accomplishing of His service that He had
there to perform at the day appointed. To which Heavenly Voice I
presently yielded obedience, not questioning the Lord how He
would bring the thing to pass, being I was a child, and obedience
was demanded of me by the Lord, who filled me with living strength
and power from His heavenly presence, which at that time did
mightily overshadow me, and my life at that time did say Amen to
what the Lord required of me and had commanded me to do: and
willingly was I given up, from that time to this day, the will of
the Lord to do and perform, what ever became of my body. For the
Lord had said unto me, "Thy soul shall rest in everlasting peace,
and thy life shall enter into rest, for being obedient to the God of thy
life"; I being a child, and durst not question the Lord in the least,
but rather willing to lay down my life than to bring dishonour to the
Lord. . . . Oh, hear, ye rulers! and give ear and listen all ye that have
any hand herein, to put the innocent to death! For in the name, and
fear, and dread of the Lord God, I here declare the cause of my
staying here among you, and continuing in the jurisdiction after
there was a sentence of banishment upon death, as ye said, pronounced against me without a just cause, as ye all know, that we
that were banished committed nothing worthy of banishment, nor
of any punishment, much less banishment upon death. And now, ye
rulers, ye do intend to put me and my companion to death, unto
whom the word of the Lord God came, saying, "Go to Boston with
thy brother, W. Robinson.". . . . And will ye put us to death for
obeying the Lord, the God of the whole earth? Well, if ye do this act,
and put us to death, know this and be it known unto you all, ye*

*rulers and people within this jurisdiction,—that whosoever hath a
hand herein, will be guilty of innocent blood. And not only upon
yourselves will ye bring innocent blood, but upon the town and the
inhabitants thereof, and everywhere within your jurisdiction, that
had the least hand therein. Therefore be instructed, ye rulers of this
land, and take warning betimes, and learn wisdom before it be hid
from your eyes.*

*Written in the common jail, in Boston, the 19th of the Eighth
month, 1659, by one who feareth the Lord, who is called a Quaker
by ignorant people, and unto such am I known only by the name
of "WILLIAM ROBINSON," yet a new name have I received,
which such know not.*

Marmaduke Stevenson's Paper, on his Call to the Work and
Service of the Lord. Given forth by him a little while before he
was put to death, and after he had received his sentence:—

*In the beginning of the year 1655, I was at the plough in the east
part of Yorkshire, in Old England, near the place where my outward
being was; and as I walked after the plough, I was filled with the
love and the presence of the living God, which did ravish my heart
when I felt it; for it did increase and abound in me like a living
stream, so did the love and life of God run through me like precious
ointment, giving a pleasant smell which made me to stand still; and
as I stood a little still, with my heart and mind staid on the Lord,
the Word of the Lord came to me in a still small voice, which I did
hear perfectly, saying to me, in the secret of my heart and conscience,
"I have ordained thee a prophet unto the nations." And at the
hearing of the Word of the Lord, I was put to a stand, being that I
was but a child for such a weighty matter. So at the time appointed,
Barbados was set before me, unto which I was required of the Lord
to go, and leave my dear and loving wife and tender children. For
the Lord said unto me, immediately by His Spirit, that He would
be as a husband to my wife, and as a father to my children, and
they should not want in my absence, for He would provide for
them when I was gone. And I believed that the Lord would perform
what He had spoken, because I was made willing to give up myself
to His work and service, to leave all and follow Him, whose presence
and life is with me, where I rest in peace and quietness of spirit
with my dear brother, under the shadow of His wings, who hath*

made us willing to lay down our lives for His own name sake, if unmerciful men be suffered to take them from us; and if they do, we know we shall have peace and rest with the Lord forever in His holy habitation, when they shall have torment night and day. So, in obedience to the living God, I made preparation to pass to Barbados, in the Fourth month, 1658. So, after I had been for some time on the said island in the service of God, I heard that New England had made a law to put servants of the living God to death, if they returned after they were sentenced away,—which did come near me at that time; and as I considered the thing, and pondered it in my heart, immediately came the Word of the Lord unto me, saying, "Thou knowest not but that thou mayest go thither"; but I kept this word in my heart, and did not declare it to any until the time appointed. So after that, a vessel was made ready for Rhode Island, which I passed in. And after a little time that I had been there, visiting the Seed which the Lord hath blessed, the Word of the Lord came unto me, saying, "Go to Boston with thy brother, William Robinson"; and to His command I was obedient, and gave up myself to do His will, that so His work and service may be accomplished. For He had said unto me, that He had a great work for me to do; which is now come to pass. And for yielding obedience to, and obeying the voice and command of the everlasting God, who created heaven and earth, and the fountains of waters, do I, with my dear brother, suffer outward bonds near unto death. And this is given forth to be upon record, that all people may know, who hear it, that we came not in our own wills, but in the will of God. Given forth by me, who am known to men by the name of

"MARMADUKE STEVENSON," but have a new name given me, which the world knows not of, written in the Book of Life.

Written in Boston prison, in the Eighth month, 1659.

Thus they, and thus you; but as for Mary Dyer, when she had parted with her friends, between whom she came joyfully hand in hand to the place of execution, though Michaelson, your marshal, was troubled thereat, and asked, "Whether she was not ashamed to walk hand in hand between two young men?" not knowing her joy in the Lord; to whom she answered, "It is an hour of the greatest joy I can know in this world," adding these words, "No eye can see, no ear can hear, no tongue can speak, no heart can understand the sweet increase and refreshment of the Spirit of the Lord which I now enjoy,"—I say, after she had parted joyfully from her friends at the foot of the ladder, expecting to die, and seeing her two friends hanging dead before her, her arms and legs tied, the halter about her neck, and her face covered with a handkerchief which your priest Wilson lent the hangman, and was with the Lord in joy and peace, an order came for her reprieve, upon the petition of her son, and unknown to her; which being read, and the halter loosened and taken off her neck, she was desired to come down. But, not answering, and waiting on the Lord to know His pleasure in so sudden a change, having given herself up to die, as aforesaid, the people cried, "Pull her down." Nor could she prevail with them to stay a little, so earnest were they, whilst she might consider and know of the Lord what to do. But her and the ladder they were pulling down together, and were stopped, and your chief marshal and others took her down by the arms, and had her to prison; from whence she wrote to you, when she understood upon what account she was reprieved, denying your reprieve, and the ground of it; and the next morning tendered her life again, for the abrogating of your law; but some came presently and took her in their arms, and sat her on horseback, and conveyed her fifteen miles toward Rhode Island, and then left her with a horse and man, to be conveyed further; which she soon sent back, when she saw she might do it freely. For she was sensible how that her sudden reprieve had served your end, in turning the people to you, who were turning from you by the deaths of the others. But the Lord otherwise ordered it, in suffering you to put her to death after a reprieve: . . . Therefore He suffered this to be, and gave her liberty to go from those parts to Newport in Rhode Island, from whence she came.

But the people returned from the execution of the other two sad and with heavy hearts, as W. Robinson had foretold them; and the one end of a drawbridge rose up, and fell upon many, and some were hurt, especially a wicked woman, who was observed to have reviled those servants of the Lord at their death; whom it greatly bruised, and her flesh rotted from her bones, and her stink was so noisome, that people could hardly come near her; in which miserable condition she remained until she died, a sad example of the vengeance of the Lord, who renders to every man according to his work. Three also of priest Wilson's grandchildren died

within a short time after ye had put these two servants of the Lord
to death, as something upon his head,—who cared not how he
bereaved the mother of her son, and the children of their father,
and the wife of her husband. The judgment of the Lord in both of
which cases is to be taken notice of.

PART II

MATURING

1661–1690

WOMEN'S MINISTRY JUSTIFIED

MARGARET FELL

The active, visible ministry of Quaker women continued to be one of the most controversial aspects of the Quaker movement. In 1666, Margaret Fell published what would be for Quakers the definitive defense of women's ministry.

Margaret Fell, *Women's Speaking Justified,
Proved, and Allowed by the Scriptures*
(London, 1666).

Where it hath been an objection in the minds of many, and several times hath been objected by the clergy, or ministers, and others, against women's speaking in the church; and so consequently may be taken, that they are condemned for meddling in the things of God; the ground of which objection, is taken from the Apostle's words, which he writ in his first Epistle to the Corinthians, chap. 14, verses 34, 35. And also what he wrote to Timothy in the first Epistle, chap. 2, verses 11, 12. But how far they wrong the Apostle's intentions in these Scriptures, we shall show clearly when we come to them in their course and order. But first let me lay down how God himself hath manifested his will and mind concerning women, and unto women.

And first, when God created man in his own image; in the image of God he created them, male and female; and God blessed them; and God said unto them, be fruitful and multiply; and God said, behold, I have given you of every herb etc. Gen. 1. Here God joins them together in his own image, and makes no such distinctions and differences as men do; for though they be weak, he is strong; and as he said to the Apostle, His Grace is sufficient, and his strength is made manifest in weakness, 2 Cor. 12.9. And such hath the Lord chosen, even the weak things of the world, to confound the things which are mighty; and things which are despised, hath God chosen, to bring to naught things that are, 1 Cor. 1. And God hath put no such difference between the male and female as men would make.

It is true, the Serpent that was more subtle than any other beast of the field, came unto the woman, with his temptations, and with a lie; his subtlety discerning her to be more inclinable to hearken to him, when he said, "If ye eat, your eyes shall be opened"; and the woman saw that the fruit was good to make one wise; there the temptation got into her, and she did eat, and gave to her husband, and he did eat also, and so they were both tempted into the transgression and disobedience; and therefore God said unto Adam, when that he hid himself when he heard his voice, "Hast thou eaten of the tree which I commanded thee that thou shouldst not eat?" And Adam said, "The woman which thou gavest me, she gave me of the tree, and I did eat." And the Lord said unto the woman, "What is this that thou hast done?" and the woman said, "The Serpent beguiled me, and I did eat." Here the woman spoke the truth unto the Lord. See what the Lord saith, verse 15, after he had pronounced sentence on the Serpent: "I will put enmity between thee and the woman, and between thy seed and her seed; it shall bruise thy head, and thou shalt bruise his heel." Gen. 3.

Let this word of the Lord, which was from the beginning, stop the mouths of all that oppose women's speaking in the power of the Lord; for he hath put enmity between the woman and the Serpent; and if the seed of the woman speak not, the seed of the Serpent speaks; for God hath put enmity between the two seeds, and it is manifest, that those that speak against the woman and her seed's speaking, speak out of the enmity of the old Serpent's seed; and God hath fulfilled his word and his promise, "When the fullness of time was come, he hath sent forth his Son, made of a woman, made under the Law, that we might receive the adoption of Sons." Gal. 4.4.5.

Moreover, the Lord is pleased, when he mentions his Church, to call her by the name of Woman, by his prophets, saying, "I have called thee as a woman forsaken, and grieved in spirit, and as a wife of youth." Isa 54. Again, "How long wilt thou go about, thou back-sliding daughter? For the Lord hath created a new thing in the earth, a woman shall compass a man." Jer. 31.22. And David, when he was speaking of Christ and his Church, he saith, "The king's daughter is all glorious within, her clothing is of wrought gold; she shall be brought unto the king; with gladness and rejoicing shall they be brought; they shall enter into the king's palace." Psalm 45. And also King Solomon in his Song, where he speaks of Christ and his Church, where she is complaining and calling for Christ, he saith, "If thou knowest not, O thou fairest among women, go thy way by the footsteps of the flock." Cant. 1.8.c.5.9. And John, when he saw the wonder that was in heaven, he saw "a woman clothed with the sun, and the moon under her feet, and upon her head a crown of twelve stars; and there appeared another wonder in heaven, a great red dragon stood ready to devour her child." Here the enmity appears that God put between the woman and the dragon. Rev. 12.

Thus much may prove that the Church of Christ is a woman, and those that speak against the woman's speaking, speak against the Church of Christ, and the seed of the woman, which seed is Christ; that is to say, those that speak against the power of the Lord, and the spirit of the Lord speaking in a woman, simply, by reason of her sex, or because she is a woman, not regarding the seed, and the spirit, and the power that speaks in her; such speak against Christ, and his church, and are of the seed of the Serpent, wherein lodgeth the enmity. And as God the Father made no such difference in the first creation, nor never since between the male and the female, but always out of his mercy and loving kindness, had regard unto the weak. So also, his son, Christ Jesus, confirms the same thing; when the Pharisees came to him, and asked him if it were lawful for a man to put away his wife, he answered and said unto them, "Have you not read, that he that made them in the beginning, made them male and female," and said, "For this cause shall a man leave father and mother, and shall cleave unto his wife, and they twain shall be one flesh, wherefore they are no more twain but one flesh. What therefore God hath joined together, let no man put asunder." Matt. 19.

Again, Christ Jesus, when he came to the city of Samaria, where Jacob's well was, where the woman of Samaria was; you may read in John 4 how he was pleased to preach the Everlasting Gospel to her; and when the woman said unto him, "I know that when the Messiah cometh (which is called Christ) when he cometh, he will tell us all things." Jesus saith unto her, "I that speak unto thee am he." This is more than ever he said in plain words to man or woman (that we read of) before he suffered. Also he said unto Martha, when she said she knew that her brother should rise again in the last day, Jesus said unto her, "I am the Resurrection and the Life; he that believeth on me, though he were dead, yet shall he live; and whosoever liveth and believeth shall never die. Believest thou this?" She answered, "Yea Lord, I believe thou art the Christ, the Son of God." Here she manifested her true and saving faith, which few at that day believed so on him. John 11.25, 26.

Also that woman that came unto Jesus with an alabaster box of very precious ointment, and poured it on his head as he sat at meat; it's manifested that this woman knew more of the secret power and wisdom of God, than his Disciples did, that were filled with indignation against her; and therefore Jesus said, "Why do ye trouble the woman? For she hath wrought a good work upon me. Verily I say unto you, wheresoever this Gospel shall be preached in the whole world, there shall also this that this woman hath done, be told for a memorial of her." Matt. 26, Mark 14.3. Luke saith further, "She was a sinner," and that "she stood at his feet behind him weeping, and began to wash his feet with her tears, and did wipe them with the hair of her head, and kissed his feet, and anointed them with ointment." And when Jesus saw the heart of the Pharisee that had bidden him to his house, he took occasion to speak unto Simon, as you may read in Luke 7, and he turned to the woman, and said, "Simon, seest thou this woman? Thou gavest me no water to my feet; but she hath washed my feet with tears, and wiped them with the hair of her head. Thou gavest me no kiss; but this woman, since I came in, hath not ceased to kiss my feet. My head with oil thou didst not anoint, but this woman hath anointed my feet with ointment. Wherefore I say unto thee, her sins, which are many, are forgiven her, for she hath loved much." Luke 7.37 to the end.

Also there was many women which followed Jesus from Galilee, ministering unto him, and stood afar off when he was crucified. Matt. 28.55, Mark 15. Yea even the women of Jerusalem wept for him, insomuch that he said unto them, "Weep not for me, ye daughters of Jerusalem, but weep for yourselves, and for your children." Luke 23.28.

"And certain woman which had been healed of evil spirits and infirmities," Mary Magdalene; and Joanna the wife of Chuza, Herod's steward's wife, "and many others which ministered unto them of their substance." Luke 8.2.3.

Thus we see that Jesus owned the love and grace that appeared in women, and did not despise it; and by what is recorded in the Scriptures, he received as much love, kindness, compassion, and tender dealing towards him from women, as he did from any others, both in his lifetime, and also after they had exercised their cruelty upon him; for Mary Magdalene, and Mary the mother of Joses, beheld where he was laid; "And when the Sabbath was past, Mary Magdalene, and Mary the mother of James, and Salome, had brought sweet spices that they might anoint him. And very early in the morning, the first day of the week, they came unto the sepulcher at the rising of the sun; and they said among themselves, "Who shall roll us away the stone from the door of the sepulcher? And when they looked, the stone was rolled away, for it was very great." Mark 16.1, 2, 3, 4. Luke 24.1, 2, "And they went down into the sepulcher"; and as Matthew saith, "The angel rolled away the stone; and he said unto the women, fear not, I know whom ye seek, Jesus which was crucified; he is not here, he is risen." Matt. 28. Now Luke saith thus, that "there stood two men by them in shining apparel, and as they were perplexed and afraid, the men said unto them, He is not here; remember he said unto you when he was in Galilee, that the Son of Man must be delivered into the hands of sinful men, and be crucified, and the third day rise again; and they remembered his words, and returned from the sepulcher, and told all these things to the eleven, and to the rest."

It was Mary Magdalene, and Joanna, and Mary the mother of James, and the other women that were with them, which told these things to the Apostles. "And their words seemed unto them as idle tales, and they believed them not." Mark this, ye despisers of the weakness of women, and look upon yourselves to be so wise; but Christ Jesus doth not so, for he makes use of the weak: for when he met the women after he was risen, he said unto them, "All hail," and they came and held him by the feet, and worshiped him; then Jesus said unto them, "Be not afraid; go tell my brethren that they go into Galilee, and there they shall see me." Matt.

28.10, Mark 16.9. And John saith, when Mary was weeping at the sepulcher, that Jesus said unto her, "Woman, why weepest thou? And when she supposed him to be the gardener, Jesus saith unto her, 'Mary'; she turned herself, and saith unto him, 'Rabboni,' which is to say Master; Jesus saith unto her, 'Touch me not, for I am not yet ascended to my Father; but go to my brethren, and say unto them, I ascend unto my Father, and your Father, and to my God, and your God.'" John 20.16, 17.

Mark this, you that despise and oppose the message of the Lord God that he sends by women; what had become of the redemption of the whole body of mankind, if they had not believed the message that the Lord Jesus sent by these women, of and concerning his Resurrection? And if these women had not thus, out of their tenderness and bowels of love, who had received mercy, and grace, and forgiveness of sins, and virtue, and healing from him; which many men also had received the like, if their hearts had not been so united and knit unto him in love, that they could not depart as the men did, but sat watching, and waiting, and weeping about the sepulcher until the time of his Resurrection, and so were ready to carry his message, as is manifested; else how should his Disciples have known, who were not there?

Oh! blessed and glorified be the Glorious Lord; for this may all the whole body of mankind say, though the wisdom of man, that never knew God, is always ready to except against the weak; but the weakness of God is stronger than men, and the foolishness of God is wiser than men.

And in Acts 18 you may read how Aquila and Priscilla took unto them Apollos, and expounded unto him the way of God more perfectly; who was an eloquent man, and mighty in the Scriptures; yet we do not read that he despised what Priscilla said, because she was a woman, as many now do.

And now to the Apostle's words, which is the ground of the great objection against women's speaking; and first, 1 Cor. 14, let the reader seriously read that chapter, and see the end and drift of the Apostle in speaking these words: for the Apostle is there exhorting the Corinthians unto charity, and to desire spiritual gifts, and not to speak in an unknown tongue; and not to be children in understanding, but to be children in malice, but in understanding to be men; and that the spirits of the Prophets should be subject to the Prophets; for God is not the author of confusion, but of peace. And then he saith, "Let your women keep silence in the church," etc.

Where it doth plainly appear that the women, as well as others, that were among them were in confusion; for he saith, "How is it brethren, when ye come together, every one of you hath a Psalm, hath a doctrine, hath a tongue, hath a revelation, hath an interpretation? Let all things be done to edifying." Here was no edifying, but all was in confusion speaking together. Therefore he saith, "If any man speak in an unknown tongue, let it be by two, or at most by three, and that by course; and let one interpret; but if there be no interpreter, let him keep silence in the church." Here the man is commanded to keep silence as well as the woman, when they are in confusion, and out of order.

But the Apostle saith further, "They are commanded to be in obedience," as also saith the Law; and "If they will learn anything, let them ask their husbands at home; for it is a shame for a woman to speak in the church."

Here the Apostle clearly manifests his intent; for he speaks of women that were under the Law, and in that transgression as Eve was, and such as were to learn, and not to speak publicly, but they must first ask their husbands at home; and it was a shame for such to speak in the church. And it appears clearly, that such women were speaking among the Corinthians, by the Apostles exhorting them from malice and strife, and confusion, and he preacheth the Law unto them, and he saith, in the law it is written "With men of other tongues, and other lips, will I speak unto this people," verse 2.

And what is all this to women's speaking, that have the Everlasting Gospel to preach, and upon whom the Promise of the Lord is fulfilled, and his Spirit poured upon them according to his Word, Acts 2.16, 17, 18? And if the Apostle would have stopped such as had the Spirit of the Lord poured upon them, why did he say just before, "If anything be revealed to another that sitteth by, let the first hold his peace"? and, "You may all prophesy one by one." Here he did not say that such women should not prophesy as had the Revelation and Spirit of God poured upon them; but their women were under the Law, and in the transgression, and were in strife, confusion and malice in their speaking; for if he had stopped women's praying or prophesying, why doth he say, "every man praying or prophesying, having his head covered, dishonoureth his head; but every woman that prayeth or prophesyeth with her head uncovered, dishonoureth her head"? "For the woman is not without the man, neither is the man without the woman, in the Lord." 1 Cor. 11.3, 4, 13.

Also that other Scripture, in 1 Tim. 2. where he is exhorting that prayer and supplication be made everywhere, lifting up holy hands without wrath and doubting; he saith in like manner also, that "Women must adorn themselves in modest apparel, with shame-fastness and sobriety, not with broidered hair, or gold, or pearl, or costly array." He saith, "Let women learn in silence with all subjection, but I suffer not a woman to teach, nor to usurp authority over the man, but to be in silence; for Adam was first formed, then Eve; and Adam was not deceived, but the woman being deceived was in the transgression."

Here the Apostle speaks particularly to a woman in relation to her husband, to be in subjection to him, and not to teach, nor usurp authority over him, and therefore he mentions Adam and Eve. But let it be strained to the utmost, as the opposers of women's speaking would have it, that is, that they should not preach nor speak in the church, of which there is nothing here. Yet the Apostle is speaking to such as he is teaching to wear their apparel, what to wear, and what not to wear; such as were not come to wear modest apparel, and such as were not come to shamefastness and sobriety, but he was exhorting them from broidered hair, gold, and pearls, and costly array; and such are not to usurp authority over the man, but to learn in silence with all subjection, as it becometh women professing godliness with good works.

And what is all this to such as have the power and Spirit of the Lord Jesus poured upon them, and have the message of the Lord Jesus given unto them? Must not they speak the Word of the Lord because of these undecent and unreverent women that the Apostle speaks of, and to, in these two Scriptures? And how are the men of the generation blinded, that bring these Scriptures, and prevent the Apostle's words, and corrupt his intent in speaking of them, and by these Scriptures, endeavour to stop the message and Word of the Lord in women, by condemning and despising of them? If the Apostle would have had women's speaking stopped, and did not allow of them, why did he entreat his true yokefellow to help those women who laboured with him in the Gospel? Phil. 4.3. And why did the Apostles join in prayer and supplication with the women, and Mary the mother of Jesus, and with his brethren, Acts 1.14, if they had not allowed, and had union and fellowship with the Spirit of God, wherever it was revealed in women as well as others? But all this opposing and gainsaying of women's speaking, hath arisen out of the bottomless pit, and spirit of darkness that hath spoken for these many hundred years together in this night of apostacy, since the Revelations have ceased and been hid. And so that spirit hath limited and bound all up within its bond and compass, and so would suffer none to speak, but such as that spirit of darkness approved, man or woman.

And so here hath been the misery of these last ages past, in the time of the reign of the Beast, that John saw when he stood upon the sand of the sea, rising out of the sea, and out of the earth, having seven heads and ten horns. Rev. 13. In this great city of Babylon, which is that Woman that hath sitten so long upon the scarlet-coloured Beast, full of names of blasphemy, having seven heads and ten horns; and this woman hath been arrayed and decked with gold, and pearls, and precious stones; and she hath made a golden cup in her hand, full of abominations, and hath made all nations drunk with the cup of her fornication; and all the world hath wondered after the Beast, and hath worshiped the Dragon that gave power to the Beast; and this woman hath been drunk with the blood of the Saints, and with the blood of the Martyrs of Jesus; and this hath seen the woman that hath been speaking and usurping authority for many hundred years together. And let the times and ages past testify how many have been murdered and slain, in ages and generations past; every religion and profession (as it hath been called) killing and murdering one another, that would not join with another. And thus the Spirit of Truth, and the power of the Lord Jesus Christ hath been quite lost among them that have done this; and this Mother of Harlots hath sitten as a queen, and said, "She should see no sorrow"; but though her days have been long, many hundred of years, for there was power given unto the Beast, to continue forty and two months, and to make war with the Saints, and to overcome them; and all that have dwelt upon the earth have worshiped him, whose names are not written in the Book of Life of the Lamb, slain from the foundation of the world.

But blessed be the Lord, his time is over, which was above twelve hundred years, and the darkness is past, and the night of Apostacy draws to an end, and the true Light now shines, the morning Light, the bright morning star, the Root and Offspring of David, he is risen he is risen, glory to the highest for evermore; and the joy of the morning is come, and the Bride, the Lamb's Wife, is making herself ready, as a Bride that is adorning for her Husband, and to her is granted that she shall be arrayed in fine linen, clean and white, and the fine linen is the righteousness of the saints. The Holy Jerusalem is descending out of the heaven from God, having the glory of God, and her light is like a jasper stone, clear as crystal.

And this is that free woman that all the children of the promise are born of; not the children of the bond-woman, which is Hagar, which genders to strife and to bondage, and which answers to Jerusalem which is in bondage with her children; but this is the Jerusalem which is free, which is the mother of us all. And so this bond-woman and her children, that are born after the flesh, have persecuted them that are born after the Spirit, even until now; but now the bond-woman and her Seed is to be cast out, that hath kept so long in bondage and in slavery, and under limits; this bondwoman and her brood is to be cast out, and our Holy City, the New Jerusalem, is coming down from heaven, and her Light will shine throughout the whole earth, even as a jasper stone, clear as crystal, which brings freedom and liberty, and perfect redemption to her whole seed; and this is that woman and image of the Eternal God, that God hath owned, and doth own, and will own for evermore.

More might be added to this purpose, both out of the Old Testament and the New, where it is evident that God made no difference, but gave his good Spirit, as it pleased him both to man and woman, as Deborah, Huldah, & Sarah. The Lord calls by his prophet Isaiah, "Harken unto me, ye that follow after righteousness, ye that seek the Lord, look unto the Rock from whence ye were hewn, and to the hole of the Pit from whence ye were digged; look unto Abraham your father, and to Sarah that bare you; for the Lord will comfort Zion, etc." Isa. 5. And Anna the Prophetess, who was a widow of fourscore and four years of age, which departed not from the Temple, but served God with fastings and prayers night and day, she coming in at that instant (when old Simeon took the child Jesus in his arms, and) "she gave thanks unto the Lord, and spake of him to all them who look for redemption in Jerusalem." Luke 2.36, 37, 38. And Philip the Evangelist, into whose house the Apostle Paul, entered, who was one of the Seven, Acts, 6.3. He had four daughters who were virgins, that did prophesy. Acts 21.

And so let this serve to stop that opposing spirit that would limit the power and Spirit of the Lord Jesus, whose Spirit is poured upon all flesh, both sons and daughters, now in his Resurrection; and since that the Lord God in the creation, when he made man in his own image, he made them male and female; and since that Christ Jesus, as the Apostle saith, was made of a woman, and the power of the Highest overshadowed her, and the Holy Ghost came upon her, and the holy thing that was born of her, was called the Son of God, and when he was upon the Earth, he manifested his love, and his will, and his mind, both to the woman of Samaria, and Martha, and Mary her sister, and several others, as hath been shewed; and after his Resurrection also manifested himself unto them first of all, even before he ascended unto his Father. "Now when Jesus was risen, the first day of the week, he appeared first unto Mary Magdalene," Mark 16.9. And thus the Lord Jesus hath manifested himself and his Power, without respect of persons; and so let all mouths be stopt that would limit him, whose power and Spirit is infinite, that is pouring it upon all flesh.

And thus much in answer to these two Scriptures, which have been such a stumbling block, that the ministers of Darkness have made such a mountain of. But the Lord is removing all this, and taking it out of the way.

QUAKERISM DEFENDED

WILLIAM PENN

*Unquestionably the two most important converts to Quaker-
ism in the 1660s were William Penn and Robert Barclay. Penn
(1644–1718), the son of an admiral, is best remembered today
for founding the colony of Pennsylvania. After becoming a
Friend in 1666, however, he quickly emerged as a favorite
coworker of Fox, an able preacher and a prolific writer. Robert Barclay (1648–1690) was an unlikely Friend. One of the
handful of Scottish converts to Quakerism, he had been partially educated by Jesuits in France. He brought a university
education (at Aberdeen) and a keen mind to presenting a theological defense of Quaker beliefs.*

William Penn's The Sandy Foundation Shaken *would be
controversial, not just in its day but also among later generations of Friends, for its seeming challenge of the Trinity. Robert Barclay's* An Apology for the True Christian Divinity, *first
published in Latin in 1676, in contrast, is widely regarded as
the single most important Quaker theological work. Its pa-
rade of propositions and close argument reflects Barclay's
academic bent.*

The Sandy Foundation Shaken (1668), from *The
Select Works of William Penn* (London, 1825).

To the Unprejudiced Reader.

It was the fault of some in ancient times, that they made void
God's law by men's traditions, and certainly I may now assume the

same complaint; for whilst I take a serious prospect of the spiritual
nature and tendency of the second covenant, which God Almighty,
in the fulness of time, by his prophets, prophesied to make and
perfect; and also the accomplishment thereof by Jesus Christ, and
what was brought to pass amongst the primitive believers; methinks I do not only see an utter abolishment of ceremonial worships, but the inscribing that spiritual law on the heart, and
infusion of holy fear to the inward parts, whereby each person
became capacitated to know so much of God, as suited with his
present state, from an infallible demonstration in himself, and not
on the slender grounds of men's lo-here interpretations, or lo-
there; for the kingdom of God is within, where himself must be the
teacher of his people: but on the other hand, when from the noise
of every party's pretensions to and contentions for their own way,
as most infallible, I am induced to an impartial examination of
them, alas! how have all adulterated from the purity both of scripture record, and primitive example! receiving for unquestionable
doctrines, the fallible apprehensions, and uncertain determinations
of such councils, whose faction, prejudice, and cruelty, soon paral-
lelled the foregoing heathenish persecutions; and yet that the results of persons so incompetently qualified, should at this day in
their authority remain unquestioned by the nations, is matter both
of astonishment and pity; but an implicit faith has ever been the
consequence of ignorance, idleness, and fear, being strong impediments to a judicious enquiry how far professed and imposed opinions have their consistency with reason, and the true religion. But
that which most of all deserves a lamentation is, that Protestants,
whose better arguments have confuted the plea of such as made
tradition and men's prescriptions unquestionable in circumstan-
tials, should themselves, by print and practice, so openly declare
and contend for its authority in essentials; as must be obvious to
any that observe their zealous anathemas against whomsoever refuse a compliance with them in doctrines, manifestly bottomed
upon men's nice inventions.

This is the right state of the controversy that is maintained by
us (contemptibly called Quakers) against the world, and the un-
doubted reason of our severe treatment at its hands; the end of
God Almighty's raising us, being for no other purpose than to declare, that which our eyes have seen, our ears heard, and which
our hands have handled of the Eternal Word, in opposition to

private opinions, conjectures, and interpretations of men concerning God and religion, that all people might thereby be reduced to faith in and obedience to the universal grace which brings salvation; which as it only can restore sound judgment concerning God, and effect redemption from iniquity, so its being relinquished by men, was the very ground both of their division in judgment, and corruption in manners.

The Trinity of Distinct and Separate Persons, in the Unity of Essence, Refuted from Scripture.

"And he said, Lord God, there is no god like unto thee, to whom then will ye liken me? or shall I be equal? saith the Holy One.*— I am the Lord, and there is none else, there is no God besides me. Thus saith the Lord thy redeemer, the Holy One of Israel, I will also praise thee, O my God; unto thee will I sing, O Holy One of Israel, Jehovah shall be One, and his name One."† Which with a cloud of other testimonies that might be urged, evidently demonstrate, that in the days of the first covenant, and prophets, but One was the Holy God, and God but that Holy One.—Again, "And Jesus said unto him, why callest thou me good? there is none good but One, and that is God. And this is life eternal, that they might know Thee (father) the Only true God. Seeing it is One God that shall justify. There be gods many,—but unto us there is but One God, the father, of whom are all things. One God and father, who is above all things. For there is One God. To the Only-wise God be glory now and for ever."‡ From all which I shall lay down this one assertion, that the testimonies of scripture, both under the law, and since the gospel dispensation, declare One to be God, and God to be One, on which I shall raise this argument:

If God, as the scriptures testify, hath never been declared or believed, but as the Holy One, then will it follow, that God is not an Holy Three, nor doth subsist in Three distinct and separate Holy Ones: but the before-cited scriptures undeniably prove that One is

* 1 Kings viii. 23. Isa. xl. 25. Chap. xlv. 5, 6.

† Isa. xlviii. 17. Psal. xxi. 23. Zac. xiv. 9.

‡ Matt. xix. 17. John xvii. 3. Rom. iii. 30. 1 Cor. viii. 6, Eph. iv. 6. 1 Tim. ii. 5. Jude, ver. 25.

God, and God only is that Holy One; therefore he cannot be divided into, or subsist in an Holy Three, or Three distinct and separate Holy Ones.—Neither can this receive the least prejudice from that frequent but impertinent distinction, that he is One in substance, but Three in persons or subsistences; since God was not declared or believed incompletely, or without his subsistences: nor did he require homage from his creatures, as an incomplete or abstracted being, but as God the Holy One, for so he should be manifested and worshipped without that which was absolutely necessary to himself:—so that either the testimonies of the aforementioned scriptures are to be believed concerning God, that he is entirely and completely, not abstractly and distinctly, the Holy One, or else their authority to be denied by these trinitarians: and on the contrary, if they pretend to credit those holy testimonies, they must necessarily conclude their kind of trinity a fiction.

Refuted from Right Reason.

1. If there be three distinct and separate persons, then three distinct and separate substances, because every person is inseparable from its own substance; and as there is no person that is not a substance in common acceptation among men, so do the scriptures plentifully agree herein: and since the father is God, the son is God, and the spirit is God (which their opinion necessitates them to confess) then unless the father, son, and spirit, are three distinct nothings, they must be three distinct substances, and consequently three distinct gods.

2. It is farther proved, if it be considered, that either the divine persons are finite or infinite; if the first, then something finite is inseparable to the infinite substance, whereby something finite is in God; if the last, then three distinct infinites, three omnipotents, three eternals, and so three gods.

3. If each person be God, and that God subsists in three persons, then in each person are three persons or gods, and from three, they will increase to nine, and so ad infinitum.

4. But if they shall deny the three persons, or subsistences to be infinite, (for so there would unavoidably be three gods) it will fol-

low that they must be finite, and so the absurdity is not abated from
what it was; for that of one substance having three subsistences, is
not greater, than that an infinite being should have three finite
modes of subsisting. But though that mode which is finite cannot
answer to a substance that is infinite; yet to try if we can make their
principle to consist, let us conceive that three persons, which may
be finite separately, make up an infinite conjunctly; however this
will follow, that they are no more incommunicable or separate, nor
properly subsistences, but a subsistence; for the infinite substance
cannot find a bottom or subsistence in any one or two, therefore
jointly. And here I am also willing to overlook finiteness in th Father, Son, and Spirit, which this doctrine must suppose.

5. Again, if these three distinct persons are one, with some one
thing, as they say they are with the God-head, then are not they
incommunicable among themselves; but so much the contrary,
as to be one in the place of another: for if that the only God is the
father, and Christ be that only God, then is Christ the father. So
if that one God be the son, and the spirit that one God, then is the
spirit the son, and so round. Nor is it possible to stop, or that it
should be otherwise, since if the divine nature be inseparable
from the three persons, or communicated to each, and each person have the whole divine nature, then is the son in the father, and
the spirit in the son, unless that the God-head be as incommunicable to the persons, as they are reported to be amongst themselves; or that the three persons have distinctly allotted them such
a proportion of the divine nature, as is not communicable to each
other; which is alike absurd. Much more might be said to manifest the gross contradiction of this trinitarian doctrine, as vulgarly received; but I must be brief.

Information and Caution.

Before I shall conclude this head, it is requisite I should inform
thee, reader, concerning its original; thou mayest assure thyself, it
is not from the scriptures, nor reason, since so expressly repugnant; although all broachers of their own inventions strongly endeavour to reconcile them with that holy record. Know then, my
friend, it was born above three hundred years after the ancient

gospel was declared; and that through the nice distinctions, and too daring curiosity of the bishop of Alexandria, who being as hotly opposed by Arius, their zeal so reciprocally blew the fire of contention, animosity, and persecution, till at last they sacrificed each other to their mutual revenge.

Thus it was conceived in ignorance, brought forth and maintained by cruelty; for though he that was strongest imposed his opinion, persecuting the contrary, yet the scale turning on the trinitarian side, it has there continued through all the Romish generations: and notwithstanding it hath obtained the name of Athanasian from Athanasius, (a stiff man, witness his carriage towards Constantine the emperor) because supposed to have been most concerned in the framing that creed in which this doctrine is asserted; yet have I never seen one copy void of a suspicion, rather, to have been the results of popish school-men; which I could render more perspicuous, did not brevity necessitate me to an omission.

Be therefore cautioned, reader, not to embrace the determination of prejudiced councils, for evangelical doctrine; which the scriptures bear no certain testimony to, neither was believed by the primitive saints, or thus stated by any I have read of in the first, second, or third centuries; particularly Ireneus, Justin Martyr, Tertullian, Origen, with many others who appear wholly foreign to the matter in controversy.—But seeing that private spirits, and those none of the most ingenious, have been the parents and guardians of this so generally received doctrine; let the time past suffice, and be admonished to apply thy mind unto that light and grace which brings salvation; that by obedience thereunto, those mists tradition hath cast before thy eyes may be expelled, and thou receive a certain knowledge of that God, whom to know is life eternal, not to be divided, but One pure entire and eternal being; who in the fulness of time sent forth his Son, as the true light which enlighteneth every man; that whosoever followed him (the light) might be translated from the dark notions, and vain conversations of men, to this holy light, in which only sound judgment and eternal life are obtainable: who so many hundred years since, in person, testified the virtue of it, and has communicated unto all such proportion as may enable them to follow his example.

The Vulgar Doctrine, of Satisfaction Being
Dependent on the Second Person of the Trinity,
Refuted from Scripture.

That man having transgressed the righteous law of God, and so exposed to the penalty of eternal wrath, it is altogether impossible for God to remit or forgive without a plenary satisfaction; and that there was no other way by which God could obtain satisfaction, or save men, than by inflicting the penalty of infinite wrath and vengeance on Jesus Christ the second person of the trinity, who for sins past, present, and to come, hath wholly borne and paid it, (whether for all, or but some) to the offended justice of his father.

1. "And the Lord passed by before him, (Moses) and proclaimed, the Lord, the Lord God, merciful and gracious, keeping mercy for thousands, forgiving iniquity, transgression and sin."* [From whence I shall draw this position, that since God has proclaimed himself a gracious, merciful, and forgiving God, it is not inconsistent with his nature to remit, without any other consideration than his own love: otherwise he could not justly come under the imputation of so many gracious attributes, with whom it is impossible to pardon, and necessary to exact the payment of the utmost farthing.]

2. "For if ye turn again to the Lord, the Lord your God is gracious and merciful, and will not turn away his face from you."† [Where, how natural is it to observe, that God's remission is grounded on their repentance; and not that it is impossible for God to pardon, without plenary satisfaction, since the possibility, nay, certainty of the contrary, viz. his grace and mercy, is the great motive or reason, of that loving invitation to return!]

3. "They hardened their necks, and hearkened not to thy commandments; but thou art a God ready to pardon, gracious and merciful."‡ [Can the honest-hearted reader conceive, that God

* Exod. xxxiv. 6, 7.

† 2 Chron. xxx. 9.

‡ Neh. ix. 16, 17.

should thus be mercifully qualified, whilst executing the rigour of the law transgressed, or not acquitting without the debt be paid him by another? I suppose not.]

4. "Let the wicked forsake his way, and the unrighteous man his thoughts, and let him return unto the Lord, and he will have mercy upon him, and to our God, for he will abundantly pardon."* [Come let the unprejudiced judge, if this scripture doctrine is not very remote from saying, his nature cannot forgive sin, therefore let Christ pay him full satisfaction, or he will certainly be avenged; which is the substance of that strange opinion.]

5. "Behold the days come, saith the Lord, that I will make a new covenant with the house of Israel; I will put my law in their inward parts; I will forgive their iniquity, and I will remember their sin no more."† [Here is God's mere grace asserted, against the pretended necessity of a satisfaction to procure his remission; and this Paul acknowledgeth to be the dispensation of the gospel, in his eighth chapter to the Hebrews: so that this new doctrine doth not only contradict the nature and design of the second covenant, but seems, in short, to discharge God, both from his mercy and omnipotence.]

6. "Who is a God like unto thee, that pardoneth iniquity, and passeth by the transgression of the remnant of his heritage? he retaineth not his anger for ever, because he delighteth in mercy."‡ [Can there be a more express passage to clear, not only the possibility, but real inclinations in God to pardon sin, and "not retain his anger for ever?" since the prophet seems to challenge all other gods, to try their excellency by his God: herein describing the supremacy of his power, and superexcellency of his nature, "that he pardoneth iniquity, and retaineth not his anger for ever": so that if the satisfactionists should ask the question, who is a God like unto ours, that cannot pardon iniquity, nor pass by transgression, but retaineth his anger until some body make him satisfaction? I answer, many amongst the harsh and severe rulers of the

---

* Isa. lv. 7.

† Jer. xxxi. 31, 33, 34.

‡ Micah vii. 18.

nation; but as for my God, he is exalted above them all, upon the
throne of his mercy, "who pardoneth iniquity, and retaineth not
his anger for ever, but will have compassion upon us."]

7. "And forgive us our debts, as we forgive our debtors."* [Where
nothing can be more obvious, than that that which is forgiven, is
not paid: and if it is our duty to forgive our debtors, without a
satisfaction received, and that God is to forgive us, as we forgive
them, then is a satisfaction totally excluded: Christ farther para-
phrases upon that part of his prayer, ver. 14. "For if ye forgive
their trespasses, your heavenly Father will also forgive you." Where
he as well argues the equity of God's forgiving them, from their
forgiving others, as he encourages them to forgive others, from
the example of God's mercy, in forgiving them: which is more
amply expressed, chap. xviii. where the kingdom of heaven (that
consists in righteousness) is represented by a king; "who upon his
debtor's petition, had compassion, and forgave him; but the same
treating his fellow-servant without the least forbearance, the king
condemned his unrighteousness, and delivered him over to the
tormentors." But how had this been a fault in the servant, if his
king's mercy had not been proposed for his example? how most
unworthy therefore is it of God, and blasphemous, may I justly
term it, for any to assert that forgiveness impossible to God,
which is not only possible, but enjoined to men!]

8. "For God so loved the world, that he gave his only-begotten
Son, that whosoever believeth in him should not perish, but have
everlasting life."† [By which it appears, that God's love is not the
effect of Christ's satisfaction, but Christ is the proper gift and effect of God's love.]

9. "To him give all the prophets witness, that through his name,
whosoever believeth in him, shall receive remission of sins."‡ [So
that remission came by believing his testimony, and obeying his
precepts, and not by a strict satisfaction.]

* Matt. vi. 12.

† John iii. 16.

‡ Acts x. 43.

10. "If God be for us, who can be against us? he that spared not his own Son, but delivered him up for us all."* [Which evidently declares it to be God's act of love, otherwise, if he must be paid, he should be at the charge of his own satisfaction, for he delivered up the Son.]

11. "And all things are of God, who hath reconciled us to himself by Jesus Christ, and hath given to us the ministry of reconciliation, to wit, that God was in Christ, reconciling the world to himself, not imputing their trespasses unto them."† [How undeniably apparent is it, that God is so far from standing off in high displeasure, and upon his own terms, contracting with his Son for a satisfaction, as being otherwise uncapable to be reconciled, that he became himself the reconciler by Christ, and afterwards by the apostles, his ambassadors, to whom was committed the ministry of reconciliation.]

12. "In whom we have redemption through his blood, the forgiveness of sins, according to the riches of his grace."‡ [Now what relation satisfaction has to forgiveness of sins, or how any can construe grace to be strict justice, the meanest understanding may determine.]

13. "But the God of all grace, who hath called us unto his eternal glory, by Christ Jesus."§ [He does not say that God's justice, in consideration of Christ's satisfaction, acquitted us from sins past, present, and to come, and therefore hath called us to his eternal glory; but from his grace.]

14. "In this was manifest the love of God towards us, because that God sent his only-begotten Son into the world, that we might live through him."** [Which plainly attributes Christ, in his doctrine, life, miracles, death, and sufferings, to God, as the gift and expression of his eternal love, for the salvation of men.]

* Rom. viii. 31, 32.

† 2 Cor. v. 18, 19.

‡ Eph. i. 7.

§ 1 Peter v. 10.

** 1 John iv. 9.

1. In abolishing that other covenant, which consisted in external and shadowy ordinances, and that made none clean as concerning the conscience.

2. In promulgating his message, of a most free and universal tender of life and salvation, unto all that believed and followed him, (the light) in all his righteousness, the very end of his appearance being to destroy the works of the devil, and which every man only comes to experience, as he walks in an holy subjection to that measure of light and grace, wherewith the fulness hath enlightened him.

3. In seconding his doctrines with signs, miracles, and a most innocent self-denying life.

4. In ratifying and confirming all (with great love and holy resignation) by the offering up of his body, to be crucified by wicked hands: who is now ascended far above all heavens, and is thereby become a most complete captain, and perfect example.

So that I can by no means conclude, but openly declare, that the scriptures of truth are not only silent in reference to this doctrine of rigid satisfaction, but that it is altogether inconsistent with the dignity of God, and very repugnant to the conditions, nature, and tendency of that second covenant, concerning which their testimony is so clear.

The Absurdities That Unavoidably Follow the Comparison of This Doctrine with the Sense of Scripture.

1. That God is gracious to forgive, and yet it is impossible for him, unless the debt be fully satisfied.

2. That the finite and impotent creature is more capable of extending mercy and forgiveness, than the infinite and omnipotent Creator.

3. "That God so loved the world, he gave his only Son to save it"; and yet that God stood off in high displeasure, and Christ gave

himself to God as a complete satisfaction to his offended justice: with many more such like gross consequences that might be drawn.

Refuted from Right Reason.

But if we should grant a scripture silence, as to the necessity of Christ's so satisfying his Father's justice; yet so manifest would be the contradictions, and foul the repugnancies to right to reason, that who had not veiled his understanding with the dark suggestions of unwarrantable tradition, or contracted his judgment to the implicit apprehensions of some over-valued acquaintance, might with great facility discriminate to a full resolution in this point: for admitting God to be a creditor, or he to whom the debt should be paid, and Christ, he that satisfies or pays it on the behalf of man, the debtor, this question will arise, Whether he paid that debt, as God, or man, or both? (to use their own terms.)

Not as God.

1. In that it divides the unity of the God-head, by two distinct acts, of being offended, and not offended; of condemning justice and redeeming mercy; of requiring a satisfaction, and then making of it.

2. Because if Christ pays the debt as God, then the Father and the Spirit being God, they also pay the debt.

3. Since God is to be satisfied, and that Christ is God, he consequently is to be satisfied; and who shall satisfy his infinite justice?

4. But if Christ has satisfied God the Father, Christ being also God, it will follow then that he has satisfied himself, (which cannot be.)

5. But since God the Father was once to be satisfied, and that it is impossible he should do it himself, nor yet the Son or Spirit, because the same God; it naturally follows, that the debt remains unpaid, and these satisfactionists thus far are still at a loss.

Not as Man.

6. The justice offended being infinite, his satisfaction ought to bear a proportion therewith, which Jesus Christ, as man, could never pay, he being finite, and from a finite cause could not proceed an infinite effect; for so man may be said to bring forth God, since nothing below the divinity itself can rightly be stiled infinite.

Not as God and Man.

7. For where two mediums, or middle propositions, are singly inconsistent with the nature of the end, for which they were at first propounded, their conjunction does rather augment than lessen the difficulty of its accomplishment; and this I am persuaded must be obvious to every unbiassed understanding.

But admitting one of these three mediums possible for the payment of an infinite debt; yet, pray observe the most unworthy and ridiculous consequences, that will unavoidably attend the impossibility, of God's pardoning sinners without a satisfaction.

Consequences Irreligious and Irrational.

1. That it is unlawful and impossible for God Almighty to be gracious and merciful, or to pardon transgressors than which, what is more unworthy of God?

2. That God was inevitably compelled to this way of saving men; the highest affront to his incontroulable nature.

3. That it was unworthy of God to pardon but not inflict punishment on the innocent, or require a satisfaction where there was nothing due.

4. It doth not only dis-acknowledge the true virtue and real intent of Christ's life and death, but entirely deprive God of that praise which is owing to his greatest love and goodness.

5. It represents the Son more kind and compassionate than the Father; whereas if both be the same God, then either the Father is as loving as the Son, or the Son as angry as the Father.

6. It robs God of the gift of his Son for our redemption (which the scriptures attribute to the unmerited love he had for the world) in affirming the Son purchased that redemption from the Father, by the gift of himself to God as our complete satisfaction.

7. Since Christ could not pay what was not his own, it follows, that in the payment of his own, the case still remains equally grievous; since the debt is not hereby absolved or forgiven, but transferred only; and by consequence we are no better provided for salvation than before owing that now to the Son, which was once owing to the Father.

8. It no way renders man beholding, or in the least obliged to God; since by their doctrine he would not have abated us, nor did he Christ the last farthing; so that the acknowledgements are peculiarly the Son's; which destroys the whole current of scripture-testimony, for his good-will towards men.—O the infamous portraiture this doctrine draws of the infinite goodness! Is this your retribution, O injurious satisfactionists?

9. That God's justice is satisfied for sins past, present, and to come; whereby God and Christ have lost both their power of enjoining godliness, and prerogative of punishing disobedience; for what is once paid is not revokeable; and if punishment should arrest any for their debts, it either argues a breach on God's or Christ's part, or else that it has not been sufficiently solved, and the penalty completely sustained by another; forgetting, "that every one must appear before the judgment-seat of Christ, to receive according to the things done in the body; yea, every one must give an account of himself to God."* But many more are the gross absurdities and blasphemies that are the genuine fruits of this so-confidently believed doctrine of satisfaction.

A Caution.

Let me advise, nay warn thee, reader, by no means to admit an entertainment of this principle, by whomsoever recommended; since it does not only divest the glorious God of his sovereign

* Rom. xiv. 12. 2 Cor. xv. 10.

power, both to pardon and punish, but as certainly insinuates a licentiousness, at least a liberty, that unbecomes the nature of that ancient gospel once preached amongst the primitive saints, and that from an apprehension of a satisfaction once paid for all. Whereas I must tell thee, that unless thou seriously repent, and no more grieve God's holy Spirit place in thy inmost parts, but art thereby taught to deny all ungodliness, and led into all righteousness; at the tribunal of the great Judge, thy plea shall prove invalid, and thou receive thy reward without respect to any other thing than the deeds done in the body: "Be not deceived, God will not be mocked; such as thou sowest, such shalt thou reap:"* which leads me to the consideration of my third head, viz. Justification by an imputative righteousness.

The Justification of Impure Persons, by an Imputative Righteousness, Refuted from Scripture.

That there is no other way for sinners to be justified in the sight of God, than by the imputation of that righteousness of Christ, long since performed personally; and that sanctification is consequential, not antecedent.

1. "Keep thee far from a false matter; and the innocent and righteous slay thou not; for I will not justify the wicked."† [Whereon I ground this argument, that since God has prescribed an inoffensive life, as that which can only give acceptance with him, and on the contrary hath determined never to justify the wicked, then will it necessarily follow, that unless this so-much-believed imputative righteousness had that effectual influence, as to regenerate and redeem the soul from sin, on which the malediction lies, he is as far to seek for justification as before; for whilst a person is really guilty of a false matter, I positively assert, from the authority and force of this scripture, he cannot be in a state of justification; and as God will not justify the wicked, so, by the

* Gal. vi. 7.

† Exod. xxiii. 7.

acknowledged reason of contraries, the just he will never condemn, but they, and they only, are the justified of God.]

2. "He that justifieth the wicked, and he that condemneth the just, even they both are an abomination to the Lord."* [It would very opportunely be observed, that if it is so great an abomination in men to justify the wicked, and condemn the just, how much greater would it be in God, which this doctrine of imputative righteousness necessarily does imply, that so far disengages God from the person justified, as that his guilt shall not condemn him, nor his innocency justify him? But will not the abomination appear greatest of all, when God shall be found condemning of the just, on purpose to justify the wicked, and that he is thereto compelled, or else no salvation, which is the tendency of their doctrine, who imagine the righteous and merciful God, to condemn and punish his innocent Son, that he having satisfied for our sins, we might be justified (whilst unsanctified) by the imputation of his perfect righteousness. O! why should this horrible thing be contended for by Christians?]

3. "The son shall not bear the iniquity of his father; the righteousness of the righteous shall be upon him, and the wickedness of the wicked shall be upon him. When a righteous man turneth away from his righteousness, for his iniquity that he hath done shall he die. Again, when the wicked man turneth away from his wickedness, and doth that which is lawful and right, he shall save his soul alive; yet saith the house of Israel, the ways of the Lord are not equal: are not my ways equal?"† [If this was once equal, it is so still, for God is unchangeable; and therefore I shall draw this argument, that the condemnation or justification of persons is not from the imputation of another's righteousness, but the actual performance and keeping of God's righteous statutes or commandments, otherwise God should forget to be equal: therefore how wickedly unequal are those, who, not from scripture evidences, but their own dark conjectures and interpretations of obscure passages,

* Prov. xvii. 15.

† Ezek. xviii. 20, 26, 27, 28.

would frame a doctrine so manifestly inconsistent with God's most pure and equal nature; making him to condemn the righteous to death, and justify the wicked to life, from the imputation of another's righteousness:—a most unequal way indeed!]

4. "Not every one that saith unto me, Lord, Lord, shall enter into the kingdom of heaven, but he that doth the will of my Father. Whosoever heareth these sayings of mine, and doth them, I will liken him unto a wise man, which built his house upon a rock,"* &c. [How very fruitful are the scriptures of truth, in testimonies against this absurd and dangerous doctrine! these words seem to import a twofold righteousness; the first consists in sacrifice, the last in obedience; the one makes talking, the other a doing Christian. I in short argue thus: If none can enter into the kingdom of heaven, but they that do the Father's will, then none are justified, but they who do the Father's will, because none can enter into the kingdom but such as are justified; since therefore there can be no admittance had without performing that righteous will, and doing those holy and perfect saying; alas! To what value will an imputative righteousness amount, when a poor soul shall awake polluted in his sin, by the hasty calls of death, to make its appearance before the judgment-seat, where it is impossible to justify the wicked, or that any should escape uncondemned, but such as do the will of God?]

5. "If ye keep my commandments, ye shall abide in my love, even as I have kept my Father's commandments, and abide in his love."† [From whence this argument doth naturally arise; If none are truly justified that abide not in Christ's love, and that none abide in his love who keep not his commandments; then consequently none are justified, but such as keep his commandments. Besides, here is the most palpable opposition to an imputative righteousness that may be; for Christ is so far from telling them of such a way of being justified, as that he informs them the reason why he abode in his Father's love was, his obedience; and is so far from telling them of their being justified, whilst not abiding in

* Matt. vii. 21, 24, 25.

† John xv. 10.

his love, by virtue of his obedience imputed unto them, that unless they keep his commands, and obey for themselves, they shall be so remote from an acceptance, as wholly to be cast out; in all which Christ is our example.]

6. "Ye are my friends, if you do whatsoever I command you."* [We have almost here the very words, but altogether the same matter, which affords us thus much, that without being Christ's friends there is no being justified, but unless we keep his commandments, it is impossible we should be his friends: it therefore necessarily follows, that except we keep his commandments, there is no being justified: or, in short thus; if the way to be a friend is to keep the commandments; then the way to be justified is, to keep the commandments, because none can obtain the quality of a friend, and remain unjustified, or be truly justified whilst an enemy; which he certainly is that keeps not the commandments.]

7. "For not the hearers of the law are just before God, but the doers of the law shall be justified."† [From whence how unanswerably may I observe, unless we become doers of that law, which Christ came not to destroy, but, as our example, to fulfil, we can never be justified before God; wherefore obedience is so absolutely necessary, that short of it there can be no acceptance: nor let any fancy that Christ hath so fulfilled it for them, as to exclude their obedience from being requisite to their acceptance, but as their pattern: "for unless ye follow me; saith Christ, ye cannot be my disciples"; and it is not only repugnant to reason, but in this place particularly refuted; for if Christ had fulfilled it on our behalf, and we not enabled to follow his example, there would not be doers, but one doer only of the law justified before God. In short, if without obedience to the righteous law none can be justified, then all our hearing of the law, with but the mere imputation of another's righteousness, whilst we are actually breakers of it, is excluded, as not justifying before God. "If you fulfil the royal law, ye do well; so speak ye, and so do ye, as they that shall be judged thereby."]

* John xv. 14.
† Rom. ii. 13.

8. "If ye live after the flesh, ye shall die; but if ye through the spirit, do mortify the deeds of the body, ye shall live."* [No man can be dead, and justified before God, for so he may be justified that lives after the flesh; therefore they only can be justified that are alive; from whence this follows, If the living are justified and not the dead, and that none can live to God, but such as have mortified the deeds of the body through the spirit, then none can be justified but they who have mortified the deeds of the body through the spirit; so that justification does not go before, but is subsequential to the mortification of lusts, and sanctification of the soul, through the spirit's operation.]

9. "For as many as are led by the Spirit of God, are the sons of God."† [How clearly will it appear to any but a cavilling and tenacious spirit, that man can be no farther justified, than as he becomes obedient to the Spirit's leadings; for if none can be a son of God, but he that is led by the Spirit of God, then none can be justified but he that is a son of God: so that the way to justification and sonship, is through the obedience to the Spirit's leadings, that is, manifesting the holy fruits thereof by an innocent life and conversation.]

10. "But let every man prove his own work, and then shall he have rejoicing in himself alone, and not in another. Be not deceived, for whatsoever a man soweth that shall he reap."‡ [If rejoicing and acceptance with God, or the contrary, are to be reaped from the work that a man soweth, either to the flesh, or to the spirit, then is the doctrine of acceptance, and ground of rejoicing, from the works of another, utterly excluded, every man reaping according to what he hath sown, and bearing his own burden.]

11. "Was not Abraham our father justified by works, when he had offered Isaac his son upon the altar? Ye see then how that by works a man is justified, and not by faith only."§ [He that will seriously

* Rom. viii. 13.

† Rom. viii. 14.

‡ Gal. vi. 4, 7.

§ 1 Jam. ii. 21, 24.

peruse this chapter, shall doubtless find some, to whom this epistle was wrote, of the same spirit with the satisfactionists and imputarians of our time, they fain would have found out a justification from faith in the imputation of another's righteousness; but James, an apostle of the most high God, who experimentally knew what true faith and justification meant, gave them to understand from Abraham's self-denying example, that unless their faith, in the purity and power of God's grace, had that effectual operation to subdue every beloved lust, wean from every Delilah, and entirely to resign and sacrifice Isaac himself, their faith was a fable, or as a body without a spirit: and as righteousness therefore in one person cannot justify another from unrighteousness; so whoever now pretend to be justified by faith, whilst not led and guided by the Spirit into all the ways of truth, and works of righteousness, their faith they will find at last a fiction.]

12. "Little children, let no man deceive you, he that doth righteousness is righteous, as God is righteous, (but) he that committeth sin is of the devil."* [From whence it may be very clearly argued, that none can be in a state of justification, from the righteousness performed by another imputed unto them, but as they are actually redeemed from the commission of sin: for "if he that committeth sin is of the devil," then cannot any be justified completely before God, who is so incompletely redeemed, as yet to be under the captivity of lust, since then the devil's seed or offspring may be justified; but that is impossible: it therefore follows, that as he who doth righteousness is righteous, as God is righteous, so no farther is he like God, or justifiable; for in whatsoever he derogates from the works of that faith, which is held in a pure conscience, he is no longer righteous or justified, but under condemnation as a transgressor, or disobedient person to the righteous commandment; and if any would obtain the true state of justification, let them circumspectly observe the holy guidings and instructions of that unction, to which the apostle recommended the ancient churches, that thereby they may be led out of all ungodliness, into truth and holiness; so shall they find acceptance with the Lord, who has determined never to justify the wicked.]

* 1 John ii. 7, 8.

Refuted from Right Reason.

1. Because it is impossible for God to justify that which is both opposite and destructive to the purity of his own nature, as this doctrine necessarily obliges him to do, in accepting the wicked, as not such, from the imputation of another's righteousness.

2. Since man was justified before God, whilst in his native innocency, and never condemned till he had erred from that pure state; he never can be justified, whilst in the frequent commission of that for which the condemnation came; therefore, to be justified, his redemption must be as entire as his fall.

3. Because sin came not by imputation, but actual transgression; for God did not condemn his creature for what he did not, but what he did; therefore must the righteousness be as personal for acceptance, otherwise these two things will necessarily follow: first, that he may be actually a sinner, and yet not under the curse. Secondly, that the power of the first Adam to death, was more prevalent than the power of the Second Adam unto life.

4. It is therefore contrary to sound reason, that if actual sinning brought death and condemnation, any thing besides actual obedience unto righteousness, should bring life and justification; for death and life, condemnation and justification, being vastly opposite, no man can be actually dead and imputatively alive; therefore this doctrine, so much contended for, carries this gross absurdity with it, that a man may be actually sinful, yet imputatively righteous; actually judged and condemned, yet imputatively justified and glorified. In short, he may be actually damned, and yet imputatively saved; otherwise it must be acknowledged, that obedience to justification ought to be as personally extensive, as was disobedience to condemnation: in which real, not imputative sense, those various terms of sanctification, righteousness, resurrection, life, redemption, justification, &c. are most infallibly to be understood.

5. Nor are those words, impute, imputed imputeth, imputing, used in scripture by way of opposition to that which is actual and inherent, as the assertors of an imputative righteousness do by their

doctrine plainly intimate; but so much the contrary, as that they are never mentioned, but to express men really and personally to be that which is imputed to them, whether as guilty, as remitted, or as righteous: for instance: "What man soever of the house of Israel, that killeth an ox, and bringeth it not to the door of the tabernacle, to offer unto the Lord, blood shall be imputed unto that man,"* or charged upon him as guilty thereof. "And Shimei said unto the king, let not my lord impute iniquity unto me, for thy servant doth not know that I have sinned."†

6. "But sin is not imputed where there is no law."‡ From whence it is apparent that there could be no imputation, or charging of guilt upon any, but such as really were guilty. Next, it is used about remission: "Blessed is the man unto whom the Lord imputeth not iniquity,"§ or, as the foregoing words have it, "whose transgression is forgiven." Where the non-imputation doth not argue a non-reality of sin, but the reality of God's pardon; for otherwise there would be nothing to forgive, nor yet a real pardon, but only imputative, which, according to the sense of this doctrine, I call imaginary. Again, "God was in Christ reconciling the world unto himself, not imputing their trespasses unto them."** Where also non-imputation, being a real discharge for actual trespasses, argues an imputation, by the reason of contraries, to be a real charging of actual guilt. Lastly, it is used in relation to righteousness, "Was not Abraham justified by works, when he offered Isaac? and by works was faith made perfect, and the scripture was fulfilled, which saith, Abraham believed God, and it was imputed unto him for righteousness."†† By which we must not conceive, as do the dark imputarians of this age, that Abraham's offering personally was not a justifying righteousness, but that God was pleased to

* Lev. xvii. 4.

† 2 Sam. xix. 18, 19. 20.

‡ Rom. v. 13.

§ Ps. xxxii. 2.

** 2 Cor. v. 19.

†† Jam. ii. 21, 22, 23.

account it so; since God never accounts a thing that which it is not; nor was there any imputation of another's righteousness to Abraham, but on the contrary, his personal obedience was the ground of that just imputation; and therefore, that any should be justified from the imputation of another's righteousness, not inherent, or actually possessed by them, is both ridiculous and dangerous—Ridiculous, since it is to say a man is rich to the value of a thousand pounds, whilst he is not really or personally worth a groat, from the imputation of another, who has it all in his possession. Dangerous, because it begets a confident persuasion in many people of their being justified, whilst in captivity to those lusts, whose reward is condemnation; whence came that usual saying amongst many professors of religion, "that God looks not on them as they are in themselves, but as they are in Christ"; not considering that none can be in Christ, who are not new creatures, which those cannot be reputed, who have not disrobed themselves of their old garments, but are still in-mantled with the corruptions of the old man.

Consequences Irreligious and Irrational.

1. It makes God guilty of what the scriptures say is an abomination, to wit, that he justifieth the wicked.

2. It makes him look upon persons as they are not, or with respect, which is unworthy of his most equal nature.

3. He is hereby at peace with the wicked, (if justified whilst sinners) who said "there is no peace to the wicked."

4. It does not only imply communion with them here, in an imperfect state, but so to all eternity, "for whom he justified, them he also glorified."* Therefore whom he justified, whilst sinners, them he also glorified, whilst sinners.

5. It only secures from the wages, not the dominion of sin, whereby something that is sinful comes to be justified, and that which defileth, to enter God's kingdom.

* Rom. viii. 30.

6. It renders a man justified and condemned, dead and alive, redeemed and not redeemed, at the same time, the one by an imputative righteousness, the other a personal unrighteousness.

7. It flatters men, whilst subject to the world's lust, with a state of justification, and thereby invalidates the very end of Christ's appearance, which was to destroy the works of the devil, and take away the sins of the world; a quite contrary purpose than what the satisfactionists, and imputarians of our times have imagined, viz. to satisfy for their sins, and by his imputed righteousness, to represent them holy in him, whilst unholy in themselves; therefore since it was to take away sin, and destroy the devil's works, which were not in himself, for that Holy One saw no corruption, consequently in mankind; what can therefore be concluded more evidently true, than that such in whom sin is not taken away, and the devil's works undestroyed, are strangers (notwithstanding their conceits) to the very end and purpose of Christ's manifestation.

Conclusion, by Way of Caution.

Thus, reader, have I led thee through those three so generally applauded doctrines, whose confutation I hope though thou hast run, thou hast read; and now I call the righteous God of heaven to bear me record, that I have herein sought nothing below the defence of his unity, mercy, and purity, against the rude and impetuous assaults of tradition, press and pulpit, from whence I daily hear, what rationally induceth me to believe a conspiracy is held by counter-plots, to obstruct the exaltation of truth, and to betray evangelical doctrines, to idle traditions: but God will rebuke the winds, and destruction shall attend the enemies of his anointed.—Mistake me not, we never have disowned a Father, Word, and Spirit, which are One, but men's inventions: for, 1. Their trinity has not so much as a foundation in the scriptures. 2. Its original was three hundred years after Christianity was in the world. 3. It having cost much blood; in the council of Sirmium, anno 335, it was decreed, "that thenceforth the controversy should not be remembered, because the scriptures of God made no mention thereof."* Why then should it be mentioned now,

* Socrat. Schol. An. 355. Conc. Sirm. cap. xxv. pag. 275.

with a maranatha on all that will not bow to this abstruse opinion. 4. And it doubtless hath occasioned idolatry, witness the popish images of Father, Son, and Holy Ghost. 5. It scandalizeth Turks, Jews, and Infidels and palpably obstructs their reception of the Christian doctrine.—Nor there more to be said on the behalf of the other two; for I can boldly challenge any person to give me one scripture phrase which does approach the doctrine of satisfaction, (much less the name) considering to what degree it is stretched; not that we do deny, but really confess, that Jesus Christ, in life, doctrine, and death, fulfilled his Father's will, and offered up a most satisfactory sacrifice, but not to pay God, or help him, (as otherwise being unable) to save men; and for a justification by an imputative righteousness, whilst not real, it is merely an imagination, not a reality, and therefore rejected; otherwise confessed and known to be justifying before God, because "there is no abiding in Christ's love without keeping his commandments." I therefore caution thee in love, of whatsoever tribe, or family of religion thou mayest be, not longer to deceive thyself, by the over-fond embraces of human apprehensions, for divine mysteries; but rather be informed that God hath bestowed "a measure of his grace on thee and me, to shew us what is good, that we may obey and do it"; which if thou diligently wilt observe, thou shalt be led out of all unrighteousness, and in thy obedience shalt thou "receive power to become a son of God;" in which happy estate God only can be known by men, and they know themselves to be justified before him, whom experimentally to know, by Jesus Christ, is life eternal.

ROBERT BARCLAY

"Concerning the Universal Redemption by Christ, and also the Saving and Universal Light, wherewith Every Man Is Enlightened," in *An Apology for the True Christian Divinity, as the Same Is Held Forth and Preached by the People Called in Scorn Quakers* (Cincinnati, 1831).

Prop. 1. That God, who out of his infinite love sent his Son, the Lord Jesus Christ, into the world, who tasted death for every man, hath given to every man, whether Jew or Gentile, Turk or Scythian, Indian or Barbarian, of whatsoever nation, country, or place, a certain day or time of visitation; during which day or time it is possible for them to be saved, and to partake of the fruit of Christ's death.

Prop. 2. That for this end God hath communicated and given unto every man a measure of the light a measure of his own Son, a measure of grace, or a measure of the Spirit, which the scripture expresses by several names, as sometimes of the seed of the kingdom, Matt. xiii. 18, 19, the light that makes all things manifest, Eph. v. 13. the Word of God, Rom. x. 17. or manifestation of the Spirit given to profit withal, 1 Cor. xii. 7. a talent, Matt. xxv. 15. a little leaven, Matt. xiii. 33. the gospel preached in every creature, Col. i. 23.

Prop. 3. Thirdly, That God, in and by this Light and Seed, invites, calls, exhorts, and strives with every man, in order to save him, which, as it is received, and not wrought resisted, works the salvation of all, even of those who are ignorant of the death and sufferings of Christ, and of Adam's fall, both by bringing them to a sense of their own misery, and to be sharers in the sufferings of Christ inwardly, and by making them partakers of his resurrection, in becoming holy, pure, and righteous, and recovered out of their sins. By which also are saved they that have the knowledge of Christ outwardly, in that it opens their understanding rightly to use and apply the things delivered in the scriptures, and to receive the saving use of them: but that this may be resisted and rejected in both, in which then God is said to be resisted and pressed down, and Christ to be again crucified, and put to open shame in and among men. And to those who thus resist and refuse him, he becomes their condemnation.

First then, according to this doctrine the mercy of God is excellently well exhibited, in that none are necessarily shut out from salvation; and his Justice is demonstrated, in that he condemns none but such to whom he really made offer of salvation, affording them the means sufficient thereunto.

Secondly, this doctrine, if well weighed, will be found to be the foundation of Christianity, salvation, and assurance.

Thirdly, it agrees and answers with the whole tenor of the gospel promises and threats, and with the nature of the ministry of Christ; according to which, the gospel, salvation, and repentance are commanded to be preached to every creature, without respect of nations, kindred, families, or tongues.

Fourthly, it magnifies and commends the merits and death of Christ, in that it not only accounts them sufficient to save all, but declares them to be brought so nigh unto all, as thereby to be put into the nearest capacity of salvation.

Fifthly, it exalts above all the grace of God, to which it attributeth all good, even the least and smallest actions that are so; ascribing thereunto not only the first beginnings and motions of good, but also the whole conversion and salvation of the soul.

Sixthly, it contradicts, overturns, and enervates the false doctrine of [those] who exalt the light of nature, the liberty of man's will, in that it wholly excludes the natural man from having any place or portion in his own salvation, by any acting, moving, or working of his own, until he be first quickened, raised up, and actuated by God's Spirit.

Seventhly, as it makes the whole salvation of man solely and alone to depend upon God, so it makes his condemnation wholly and in every respect to be of himself, in that he refused and resisted somewhat that from God wrestled and strove in his heart, and forces him to acknowledge God's just judgment in rejecting and forsaking of him.

Eighthly, it takes away all ground of despair, in that it gives every one cause of hope and certain assurance that they may be saved; neither doth feed any in security, in that none are certain how soon their day may expire: and therefore it is a constant incitement and provocation, and lively encouragement to every man, to forsake evil, and close with that which is good.

Ninthly, it wonderfully commends as well the certainty of the Christian religion among infidels, as it manifests its own verity to all, in that it is confirmed and established by the experience of all men; seeing there never was yet a man found in any place of the earth, however barbarous and wild, but hath acknowledged, that at some time or other, less or more, he hath found somewhat in his heart reproving him for some things evil which he hath done, threatening a certain horror if he continued in them, as also promising and communicating a certain peace and sweetness, as he has given way to it, and not resisted it.

Tenthly, it wonderfully showeth the excellent wisdom of God, by which he hath made the means of salvation so universal and comprehensive, that it is not needful to recur to those miraculous and strange ways; seeing, according to this most true doctrine, the gospel reacheth all, of whatsoever condition, age, or nation.

Eleventhly, it is really and effectively, though not in so many words, yet by deeds, established and confirmed by all the preachers, promulgators, and doctors of the Christian religion, that ever were, or now are, even by those that otherwise in their judgment oppose this doctrine, in that they all, whatever they have been or are, or whatsoever people, place, or country they come to, do preach to the people, and to every individual among them, that they may be saved; entreating and desiring them to believe in Christ, who hath died for them. So that what they deny in the general, they acknowledge of every particular; there being no man to whom they do not preach in order to salvation, telling him Jesus Christ calls and wills him to believe and be saved; and that if he refuse, he shall therefore be condemned, and that his condemnation is of himself. Such is the evidence and virtue of Truth, that it constrains its adversaries even against their wills to plead for it.

Lastly, According to this doctrine the former argument used by the Arminians, and evited by the Calvinists, concerning every man's being bound to believe that Christ died for him, is, by altering the assumption, rendered invincible; thus, that which every man is bound to believe, is true: but every man is bound to believe that God is merciful unto him. . . .

This assumption no man can deny, seeing his mercies are said to be over all his works. And herein the scripture every way declares the mercy of God to be, in that he invites and calls sinners to repentance, and hath opened a way of salvation for them: so that though those men be not bound to believe the history of Christ's death and passion who never came to know of it, yet they are bound to believe that God will be merciful to them, if they follow his ways; and that he is merciful unto them, in that he reproves them for evil, and encourages them to good. Neither ought any man to believe that God is unmerciful to him, or that he hath from the beginning ordained him to come into the world that he might be left to his own evil inclinations, and so do wickedly, as a means appointed by God to bring him to eternal damnation;

which, were it true, as our adversaries affirm it to be of many thousands, I see no reason why a man might not believe; for certainly a man may believe the truth.

As it manifestly appears from the thing itself that these good and excellent consequences follow from the belief of this doctrine, so from the proof of them it will yet more evidently appear; to which before I come, it is requisite to speak somewhat concerning the state of the controversy, which will bring great light to the matter: for from the not right understanding of a matter under debate, sometimes both arguments on the one hand, and objections on the other, are brought, which do no way hit the case; and hereby also our sense and judgment therein will be more fully understood and opened.

First then, by this day and time of visitation, which we say God gives unto all, during which they may be saved, we do not understand the whole time of every man's life; though to some it may be extended even to the very hour of death, as we see in the example of the thief converted upon the cross: but such a season at least as sufficiently exonerateth God of every man's condemnation, which to some may be sooner, and to others later, according as the Lord in his wisdom sees meet. So that many men may outlive this day, after which there may be no possibility of salvation to them, and God justly suffers them to be hardened, as a just punishment of their unbelief, and even raises them up as instruments of wrath, and makes them a scourge one against another. Whence to men in this condition may be fitly applied those scriptures which are abused to prove that God incites men necessarily to sin. This is notably expressed by the apostle, Rom. i. from verse 17. to the end, but especially verse 28. And even as they did not like to retain God in their knowledge, God gave them over to a reprobate mind, to do those things which are not convenient. That many may outlive this day of God's gracious visitation unto them, is shown by the example of Esau, Heb. xii. 16, 17. who sold his birthright: so he had it once, and was capable to have kept it; but afterwards, when he would have inherited the blessing, he was rejected. This appears also by Christ's weeping over Jerusalem, Luke xix. 42. saying, If thou hadst known in this thy day the things that belong unto thy peace; but now they are hid from thine eyes. Which plainly imports a time when they might have known them, which now was removed from them, though they were yet alive; but of this more shall be said hereafter.

Secondly, By this seed, grace, and word of God, and light where-with we say every one is enlightened, and hath a measure of it, which strives with him in order to save him, and which may, by the stubbornness and wickedness of man's will, be quenched, bruised, wounded, pressed down, slain and crucified, we understand not the proper essence and nature of God precisely taken, which is not divisible into parts and measures, as being a most pure, simple being, void of all composition or division, and therefore can nei-ther be resisted, hurt, wounded, crucified, or slain by all the efforts and strength of men; but we understand a spiritual, heavenly, and invisible principle, in which God, as Father, Son, and Spirit, dwells; a measure of which divine and glorious life is in all men as a seed which of its own nature draws, invites, and inclines to God; and this some call *vehiculum Dei*, or the spiritual body of Christ, the flesh and blood of Christ, which came down from heaven, of which all the saints do feed, and are thereby nourished unto eter-nal life. And as every unrighteous action is witnessed against and reproved by this light and seed, so by such actions it is hurt, wounded, and slain, and flees from them; even as the flesh of man flees from that which is of a contrary nature to it. Now because it is never separated from God nor Christ, but wherever it is God and Christ are as wrapped up therein, therefore and in that respect as it is resisted, God is said to be resisted; and where it is borne down, God is said to be pressed as a cart under sheaves, and Christ is said to be slain and crucified. And on the contrary, as this seed is received in the heart, and suffered to bring forth its natural and proper effect, Christ comes to be formed and raised, of which the scripture makes so much mention, calling it the new man, Christ within, the hope of glory. This is that Christ within, which we are heard so much to speak and declare of, every where preaching him up, and exhorting people to believe in the light, and obey it, that they may come to know Christ in them, to deliver them from all sin.

But by this, as we do not at all intend to equal ourselves to that holy man the Lord Jesus Christ, who was born of the Virgin Mary, in whom all the fullness of the Godhead dwelt bodily, so neither do we destroy the reality of his present existence, as some have falsely calumniated us. For though we affirm that Christ dwells in us, yet not immediately, but mediately, as he is in that seed, which is in us; whereas he, to wit, the Eternal Word, which was with God, and was God, dwelt immediately in that holy man. He then is as the head, and we as the members; he the vine, and we the branches. Now as the soul of man dwells otherwise and in a far more immediate manner in the head and in the heart, than in the hands or legs; and as the sap, virtue, and life of the vine lodgeth far otherwise in the stock and root than in the branches; so God dwelleth otherwise in the man Jesus than in us. . . .

Thirdly, we understand not this seed, light, or grace to be an accident, as most men ignorantly do, but a real spiritual substance, which the soul of man is capable to feel and apprehend, from which that real, spiritual, inward birth in believers arises, maybe called the new creature, the new man in the heart. This seems strange to carnal-minded men, because they are not acquainted with it; but we know it, and are sensible of it, by a true and certain experience. Though it be hard for a man in his natural wisdom to comprehend it, until he come to feel it in himself; and if he should, holding it in the mere notion, it would avail him little; yet we are able to make it appear to be true, and that our faith concerning it is not without a solid ground: for it is in and by this inward and substantial seed in our hearts as it comes to receive nourishment, and to have a birth or geniture in us, that we come to have those spiritual senses raised by which we are made capable of tasting, smelling, seeing, and handling the things of God; for a man cannot reach unto those things by his natural spirit and senses, as is above declared.

Next, we know it to be a substance, because it subsists in the hearts of wicked men, even while they are in their wickedness, as shall be hereafter proved more at large. Now no accident can be in a subject without it give the subject its own denomination; as where whiteness is in a subject, there the subject is called white. So we distinguish betwixt holiness, as it is an accident, which denominates man so, as the seed receives a place in him, and betwixt the holy substantial seed, which many times lies in man's heart as a naked grain in the stony ground. So also as we may distinguish betwixt health and medicine; health cannot be in a body without the body be called healthful, because health is an accident; but medicine may be in a body that is most unhealthful, for that it is a substance. And as when a medicine begins to work, the body may in some respect be called healthful, and in some respect unhealthful, so we acknowledge as this divine medicine receives place in man's heart, it may denominate him in some part holy and good, though there remain yet a corrupted unmortified part, or some part of the evil humours unpurged out; for where two contrary accidents are in one subject, as health and sickness in a body, the subject receives its denomination from the accident which prevails most. So many men are called saints, good and holy men, and that truly, when this holy seed hath wrought in them in a good measure, and hath somewhat leavened them into its nature, though they may be yet liable to many infirmities and weaknesses, yea and to some iniquities: for as the seed of sin and ground of corruption, yea and the capacity of yielding thereunto, and sometimes actually falling, doth not denominate a good and holy man impious; so neither doth the seed of righteousness in evil men, and the possibility of their becoming one with it, denominate them good or holy.

Fourthly, we do not hereby intend any ways to lessen or derogate from the atonement and sacrifice of Jesus Christ; but on the contrary do magnify and exalt it. For as we believe all those things to have been certainly transacted which are recorded in the holy scriptures concerning the birth, life, miracles, sufferings, resurrection, and ascension of Christ; so we do also believe that it is the duty of every one to believe it to whom it pleases God to reveal the same, and to bring to them the knowledge of it; yea, we believe it were damnable unbelief not to believe it, when so declared; but to resist that holy seed, which as minded would lead and incline every one to believe it as it is offered unto them, though it revealeth not in every one the outward and explicit knowledge of it, nevertheless it always assenteth to it, . . . where it is declared. Nevertheless as we firmly believe it was necessary that Christ should come, that by his death and sufferings he might offer up himself a sacrifice to God for our sins, who his own self bare our sins in his own body on the tree; so we believe that the remission of sins which any partake of, is only in and by virtue of that most satisfactory sacrifice, and no otherwise. For it is by the obedience of that one that the free gift is come upon all to justification. For we affirm, that as all men partake of the fruit of Adam's fall, in that by, reason of that evil seed, which through

him is communicated unto them, they are prone and inclined unto
evil, though thousands of thousands be ignorant of Adam's fall,
neither ever knew of the eating of the forbidden fruit; so also
many may come to feel the influence of this holy and divine seed
and light, and be turned from evil to good by it, though they
knew nothing of Christ's coining in the flesh, through whose obedience and sufferings it is purchased unto them. And as we affirm
it is absolutely needful that those do believe the history of Christ's
outward appearance, whom it pleased God to bring to the knowledge of it; so we do freely confess, that even that outward knowledge is very comfortable to such as are subject to and led by the
inward seed and light. For not only doth the sense of Christ's love
and sufferings tend to humble them, but they are thereby also
strengthened in their faith, and encouraged to follow that excellent pattern which he hath left us, who suffered for us, as saith the
apostle Peter, 1 Pet. ii. 21. leaving us an example that we should
follow his steps: and many times we are greatly edified and refreshed with the gracious sayings which proceed out of his mouth.
The history then is profitable and comfortable and never without
it; but the mystery is and may be profitable without the explicit
and outward knowledge of the history.

But fifthly, this brings us to another question, . . . whether
Christ be in all men or no? Which sometimes hath been asked us,
and arguments brought against it; because indeed it is to be found
in some of our writings that Christ is in all men; and we often are
heard, in our public meetings and declarations, to desire every
man to know and be acquainted with Christ in them, telling them
that Christ is in them; it is fit therefore, for removing of all mis-
takes, to say something in this place concerning this matter. We
have said before how that a divine, spiritual, and supernatural
light is in all men; how that that divine supernatural light or seed
is *vehiculum Dei;* how that God and Christ dwelleth in it, and is
never separated from it; also how that as it is received and closed
with in the heart, Christ comes to be formed and brought forth:
but we are far from ever having said, that Christ is thus formed in
all men, or in the wicked: for that is a great attainment, which the
apostle travailed that it might be brought forth in the Galatians.
Neither is Christ in all men by way of union, or indeed to speak
strictly, by way of inhabitation; because this inhabitation, as it is
generally taken, imports union, or the manner of Christ's being

in the saints: as it is written, "I will dwell in them, and walk in them," 2 Cor. vi. 16. But in regard Christ is in all men as in a seed, yea, and that he never is nor can be separate from that holy pure seed and light which is in all men; therefore may it be said in a larger sense, that he is in all, even as we observed before. The scripture saith, Amos ii. 13. God "is pressed down as a cart under sheaves," and Christ crucified in the ungodly; though to speak properly and strictly, neither can God be pressed down nor Christ, as God, be crucified. In this respect then, as he is in the seed which is in all men, we have said Christ is in all men, and have preached and directed all men to Christ in them, who lies crucified in them by their sins and iniquities, that they may look upon him whom they have pierced, and repent: whereby he that now lies as it were slain and buried in them, may come to be raised, and have dominion in their hearts over all. . . . And forasmuch as Christ is called that light that enlightens every man, the light of the world, therefore the light is taken for Christ, who truly is the fountain of light, and hath his habitation in it for ever. Thus the light of Christ is sometimes called Christ, i.e. that in which Christ is, and from which he is never separated.

Sixthly, It will manifestly appear by what is above said, that we understand not this divine principle to be any part of man's nature, nor yet to be any relics of any good which Adam lost by his fall, in that we make it a distinct separate thing from man's soul, and all the faculties of it: yet such is the malice of our adversaries, that they cease not sometimes to calumniate us, as if we preached up a natural light, or the light of man's natural conscience. . . . We certainly know that this light of which we speak is not only distinct, but of a different nature from the soul of man, and its faculties. Indeed that man, as he is a rational creature, hath reason as a natural faculty of his soul, by which he can discern things that are rational, we deny not; for this is a property natural and essential to him, by which he can know and learn many arts and sciences, beyond what any other animal can do by the mere animal principle. Neither do we deny but by this rational principle man may apprehend in his brain, and in the notion, a knowledge of God and spiritual things; yet that not being the right organ, as in the second proposition hath more at length been signified, it cannot profit him towards salvation, but rather hindereth; and indeed the great cause of the apostacy hath been, that man hath

sought to fathom the things of God in and by this natural and
rational principle, and to build up a religion in it, neglecting and
overlooking this principle and seed of God in the heart; so that
herein, in the most universal and catholic sense, hath Anti-Christ
in every man set up himself, and sitteth in the temple of God as
God, and above everything that is called God. For men being the
temple of the Holy Ghost, as saith the apostle, 1 Cor. iii. 16, when
the rational principle sets up itself there above the seed of God, to
reign and rule as a prince in spiritual things, while the holy seed
is wounded and bruised, there is Anti-Christ in every man, or
somewhat exalted above and against Christ. Nevertheless we do
not hereby affirm as if man had received his reason to no purpose,
or to be of no service unto him, in no wise: we look upon reason as fit to order and rule man in things natural. For as God gave
two great lights to rule the outward world, the sun and moon, the
greater light to rule the day, and the lesser light to rule the night;
so hath he given man the light of his Son, a spiritual divine light,
to rule him in things spiritual, and the light of reason to rule him
in things natural. And even as the moon borrows her light from
the sun, so ought men, if they would be rightly and comfortably
ordered in natural things, to have their reason enlightened by this
divine and pure light. Which enlightened reason, in those that
obey and follow this true light, we confess may be useful to man
even in spiritual things, as it is still subservient and subject to the
other; even as the animal life in man, regulated and ordered by his
reason, helps him in going about things that are rational. We do
further rightly . . . distinguish this from man's natural conscience;
for conscience being that in man which ariseth from the natural
faculties of man's soul, may be defiled and corrupted. It is said
expressly of the impure, Titus. i. 15. that even their mind and
conscience is defiled; but this light can never be corrupted nor
defiled; neither did it ever consent to evil or wickedness in any: for
it is said expressly, that it makes all things manifest that are re-
proveable, Eph. v. 13, and so is a faithful witness for God against
every unrighteousness in man. Now conscience, . . . is that knowledge which ariseth in man's heart, from what agreeth, contra-
dicteth, or is contrary to any thing believed by him, whereby he
becomes conscious to himself that he transgresseth by doing that
which he is persuaded he ought not to do. So that the mind being
once blinded or defiled with a wrong belief, there ariseth a con-

science from that belief, which troubles him when he goes against it. As for example: A Turk who hath possessed himself with false belief that it is unlawful for him to drink wine, if he do it, his conscience smites him for it; but though he keep many concubines, his conscience troubles him not, because his judgment is already defiled with a false opinion that it is lawful for him to do the one, and unlawful to do the other. Whereas, if the light of Christ in him were minded, it would reprove him, not only for committing fornication, but also, as he became obedient thereunto, inform him that Mahomet was an impostor; as well as Socrates was informed by it, in his day, of the falsity of the heathen's gods.

So if a Papist eat flesh in Lent, or be not diligent enough in adoration of saints and images, or if he should condemn images, his conscience would smite him for it, because his judgment is already blinded with a false belief concerning these things: whereas the light of Christ never consented to any of these abominations. Thus then man's natural conscience is sufficiently distinguished from it; for conscience followeth the judgment, doth not inform it; but this light, as it is received, removes the blindness of the judgment, opens the understanding, and rectifies both the judgment and conscience. So we confess also, that conscience is an excellent thing, where it is rightly informed and enlightened: wherefore some of us have fitly compared it to the lantern, and the light of Christ to a candle: a lantern is useful, compared when a clear candle burns and shines in it; but otherwise of no use. To the light of Christ then in the conscience, and not to man's natural conscience, it is that we continually commend men; that, not this, is it which we preach up, and direct people to, as a most certain guide unto life eternal.

Lastly, this light, seed, etc. appears to be no power or natural faculty of man's mind; because a man that is in his health can, when he pleases, stir up, move, and exercise the faculties of his soul; he is absolute master of them; and except there be some natural cause or impediment in the way, he can use them at his pleasure: but this light and seed of God in man he cannot move and stir up when he pleaseth; but it moves, blows, and strives with man, as the Lord seeth meet. For though there be a possibility of salvation to every man during the day of his visitation, yet cannot a man, at any time when he pleaseth, or hath some sense of his misery, stir up that light and grace, so as to procure to himself tenderness of heart; but he must wait for it: which comes upon all at certain times and seasons, wherein it works powerfully upon the soul, mightily tenders it, and breaks it; at which time, if man resist it not, but close with it, he comes to know salvation by it. Even as the lake of Bethesda did not cure all those that washed in it, but such only as washed first after the angel had moved upon the waters; so God moves in love to mankind, in his seed in his heart, at some singular time, setting his sins in order before him, and seriously inviting him to repentance, offering to him remission of sins and salvation; which if man accept of, he may be saved. Now there is no man alive, and I am confident there shall be none to whom this paper shall come, who, if they will deal faithfully and honestly with their own hearts, will not be forced to acknowledge that they have been sensible of this in some measure, less or more; which is a thing that man cannot bring upon himself with all his pains and industry. This then, O man or woman, is the day of God's gracious visitation to thy soul, which, if thou resist not, thou shalt be happy forever. This is the day of the Lord, which, as Christ saith, is like the lightning, which shineth from the east unto the west; and wind or spirit, which blows upon the heart, and no man knows whither it goes, nor whence it comes.

GEORGE FOX

One of George Fox's most controversial works was a letter that he composed to the governor of Barbados in 1671, in answer to some accusations that Quakers there faced. Contemporary liberal Friends often find it troubling and argue that it is inconsistent with Fox's other statements. Evangelical Friends, in contrast, often point to it as a definitive statement of Quaker faith.

A Confession of Faith, . . . To Which Is Added an Extract from the Letter of George Fox and Others to the Governor and Council of Barbadoes, In the year 1671 (Philadelphia, 1827).

For the governor of Barbadoes, with his council and assembly, and all others in power, both civil and military, in this island; from the people called Quakers.

Whereas many scandalous lies and slanders have been cast upon us, to render us odious; as that "We deny God, Christ Jesus, and the scriptures of truth," &c. This is to inform you, That all our books and declarations, which for these many years have been published to the world, clearly testify the contrary. Yet, for your satisfaction, we now plainly and sincerely declare, That we own and believe in the only Wise, Omnipotent, and Everlasting God, the Creator of all things in heaven and earth, and the Preserver of all that he hath made; who is God over all, blessed forever; to whom be all honour, glory, dominion, praise and thanksgiving, both now and for evermore! And we own and believe in Jesus Christ, his beloved and only begotten Son, in whom he is well pleased; who was conceived by the Holy Ghost, and born of the Virgin Mary; in whom we have redemption through his blood, even the forgiveness of sins, who is the express image of the Invisible God, the first-born of every creature, by whom were all things created that are in heaven and in earth, visible and invisible, whether they be thrones, dominions, principalities, or powers; all things were created by him. And we own and believe that he was made a sacrifice for sin, who knew no sin, neither was guile found in his mouth; that he was crucified for us in the flesh, without the gates of Jerusalem; and that he was buried, and rose again the third day by the power of his Father, for our justification; and that he ascended up into heaven, and now sitteth at the right hand of God. This Jesus, who was the foundation of the holy prophets and apostles, is our foundation; and we believe there is no other foundation to be laid but that which is laid, even Christ Jesus: who tasted death for every man, shed his blood for all men, is the propitiation for our sins, and not for ours only, but also for the sins of the whole world: according as John the Baptist testified of him when he said, "Behold the Lamb of God, that taketh away the sins of the world," John i. 29. We believe that he alone is our Redeemer and Saviour, the captain of our salvation, who saves us from sin, as well as from hell and the wrath to come and destroys the devil and his works; he is the Seed of the woman that bruises the Serpent's head, to wit, Christ Jesus, the Alpha and Omega, the First and the

Last. He is, (as the scriptures of truth say of him,) our wisdom, righteousness, justification, and redemption; neither is there salvation in any other, for there is no other name under heaven given among men, whereby we may be saved. He alone is the Shepherd and Bishop of our souls; he is our Prophet, whom Moses long since testified of, saying, "A prophet shall the Lord your God raise up unto you of your brethren, like unto me; him shall ye hear in all things, whatsoever he shall say unto you: and it shall come to pass, that every soul that will not hear that prophet shall be destroyed from among the people," Acts ii. 22, 23. He is now come in Spirit, "and hath given us an understanding, that we know him that is true." He rules in our hearts by his law of love and life, and makes us free from the law of sin and death. We have no life, but by him; for he is the quickening Spirit, the second Adam, the Lord from heaven, by whose blood we are cleansed, and our consciences sprinkled from dead works, to serve the living God. He is our Mediator, who makes peace and reconciliation between God offended and us offending; he being the Oath of God, the new covenant of light, life, grace, and peace, the author and finisher of our faith. This Lord Jesus Christ, the heavenly man, the Emanuel, God with us, we all own and believe in; he whom the high-priest raged against, and said, he had spoken blasphemy; whom the priests and elders of the Jews took counsel together against, and put to death; the same whom Judas betrayed for thirty pieces of silver, which the priests gave him as a reward for his treason; who also gave large money to the soldiers to broach a horrible lie, namely, "That his disciples came and stole him away by night whilst they slept." After he was risen from the dead, the history of the Acts of the apostles sets forth how the chief priests and elders persecuted the disciples of this Jesus, for preaching Christ and his resurrection. This, we say, is that Lord Jesus Christ, whom we own to be our life and salvation.

Concerning the holy scriptures, we believe they were given forth by the holy Spirit of God, through the holy men of God, who, (as the Scripture itself declares, 2 Pet. i. 21,) "spoke as they were moved by the Holy Ghost." We believe they are to be read, believed, and fulfilled, (he that fulfils them is Christ;) and they are "profitable for reproof, for correction, and for instruction in righteousness, that the man of God may be perfect, thoroughly furnished unto all good works," 2 Tim. iii. 19, and are able to "make

wise unto salvation, through faith in Christ Jesus." We believe
the holy scriptures are the words of God; for it is said in Exodus
xx. 1. "God spake all these words, saying," &c. meaning the ten
commandments given forth upon mount Sinai. And in Rev. xxii.
18, saith John, "I testify to every man that heareth the words of
the prophecy of this book, if any man addeth unto these, and if
any man shall take away from the words of the book of this
prophecy," (not the Word,) &c. So in Luke i. 20. "Because thou
believest not my words." And in John v. 47. xv. 7. xiv. 23. xii. 47.
So that we call the holy scriptures, as Christ, the apostles, and
holy men of God called them, viz. the words of God.

EXPERIENCE

MARY PENINGTON

Mary (Proud) Springett Penington (1625–1683) was the wife of Isaac Penington, one of the most important Quaker writers of the 1660s, and the mother-in-law of William Penn. She was an articulate, deeply spiritual Friend, as this excerpt from her writings shows.

Norman Penney, ed., *Experiences in the Life of Mary Penington (Written by Herself)* (London, 1911).

I now come to relate a dream that I had at Worminghurst, between twenty and thirty years after the dream before-mentioned. I insert it here, because, at the close, I dreamed that I related a part of the foregoing one.

Being at Worminghurst, at my son Penn's, 30th of the Seventh month, 1676, at night, in bed and asleep, I dreamed I was with two other persons in an upper room; (who the persons were I do not perfectly remember); I looking out of the window, saw the sky very black and dismal, yea, the appearance of it to me, and the rest that beheld it, was very dreadful; but keeping cool and low in our spirits, to see what would follow, at length the sky grew thinner, and began to clear; not by the descending of rain, in the usual way, but by one great vent of water, issuing out of the midst of these thick clouds, which seemed quite driven way, divided into heaps, and a great clearness left in the midst; out of which clearness appeared a very bright head, breast, and arms, the complete upper part of a man, very beautiful (like pictures I have seen to represent an angel form), holding in his hand a long, green bough; not so green as a laurel, but of a sea, or willow-green color, resembling a palm. This palm or bough He held over his head, which to us was such a signification of good, that both by voice and action we made acclamations of joy; uttering forth, through fulness of joy and sense, indistinct sounds, expressive of being overcome with the greatness of our sense, which we could not set forth in words: sounds something like, oh! oh! ah! ah! in an astonished manner; spreading our hands, and running swiftly about the room, with constant acclamations of admiration and joy; signifying, by our manner, a being likely to burst with astonishment and joy, and our tongues or voices unable to deliver us of what we were so big with. After a little while there appeared lower in the element, nearer the earth, in an oval, transparent glass, a man and a woman (not in resemblance, but real persons), the man wore a greater majesty and sweetness than I ever saw with mortal: his hair was brown, his eyes black and sparkling, his complexion ruddy; piercing dominion in his countenance, splendid with affability, great gentleness, and kindness. The woman resembled him in features and complexion; but appeared tender and bashful, yet quick-sighted.

After having beheld these heavenly forms awhile, we, in a sense of their majesty and dominion, did reverence to them, falling on our faces in a solemn, not in a disturbed, confused manner, crying glory! glory! glory! glory! glory! at which the man ascended, but the woman came down to us, and spoke to us with great gravity and sweetness; the words I have forgotten, but the purport of them was, that we should not be formal, nor fall out. Then she disappeared, and we looked one at another, after a melted, serious manner; and I said to them: "This is a vision, to signify to us some great matter and glorious appearance; more glorious than the Quakers at their first coming forth." I added, that I had a distinct vision and sight of such state in a dream, before ever I heard of a Quaker; but it was in a more simple, plain manner than this. For I then saw Christ like a fresh, sweet, innocent youth, clad in light gray, neat, but plain; and so, likewise, was the bride, the Lamb's wife, in the same manner; but under this plain appearance, there was deep wisdom and discernment; for I saw Him own and embrace, such as I could not see any acceptable thing in; such as I thought Christ would not own, being old, poor, and contemptible women. "But now," said I, "his countenance and garb are altered: in the former was united to sweetness, majesty; in the latter, to plainness and neatness is joined resplendence." Without any further conversation I awoke.

A PRISON LETTER

JOHN BOWETER

Friends continued to fall afoul of the English justice system until the Act of Toleration in 1689. The authorities harried them for worshiping outside the established church and for refusing to take oaths and pay tithes. John Boweter (1630– 1705) was a Public Friend from Bromsgrove, Worcestershire, who in 1681 found himself clapped into the Fleet Prison in London.

Christian Epistles, Travels and Sufferings, of That Ancient Servant of Christ, John Boweter (London, 1705).

Something concerning the proceedings of Thomas Willmate, vicar of the parish of Bromsgrove, in the county of Worcester, against me, John Boweter, (who am a prisoner for the Testimony of Jesus Christ) with a salutation of Love to my loving and kind neighbours.

Many have been the troubles of the righteous, but the Lord hath been their deliverer, who said, "I will not leave you comfortless." He hath been a comfort unto us in the time of our affliction, who hath made a prison like a place unto us, as in faithfulness we have given up all for his name sake, and suffered the spoiling of our goods cheerfully, we have not lost our reward, we have had peace in the Lord (when our adversaries have been tormented) and the promise of Christ in the world to come, which is life everlasting. And the Apostle Paul, who had a part in sufferings, said, "I reckon the sufferings of this present life, is not to be compared to the glory that shall be revealed." This is that which makes our sufferings comfortable unto us; this recompence Moses had an eye unto, who refused to the glory of Egypt, choosing rather to suffer affliction with the people of God, than to enjoy the pleasures of sin for a season, counting the reproach of Christ greater riches than all the treasures of Egypt.

But some may say, Ye Quakers thrust yourselves into sufferings. What matter of conscience is it to detain your tithe from a minister?

To this I answer: Some years ago, Thomas Willmate, vicar of the parish of Bromsgrove (a professed minister of the Gospel; but not in the practice of the true Gospel-ministers in the primitive times; in which parish, I have had my abode from my childhood) he sending to me to demand tithe. I not being satisfied in my spirit concerning tithe in these Gospel times; I went unto him, expecting he might have satisfied me, or he have been satisfied with my proposal, which was this: if he could prove himself a minister of the Gospel, and tithe a Gospel maintenance, I would pay him tithe. But being he neither did, nor could make out to me by the Scripture, I refused to pay him, because Christ (who is a priest unto God, and hath put an end to that priesthood that tithe was to be paid unto) said, "Every plant that my heavenly father hath not planted, shall be rooted up." Matt. 15:13. I never read in the Scripture of the New Testament, that Christ ever ordained tithe to be a maintenance for his ministers, neither was tithe established by his Holy Apostles for a maintenance of ministers, but rather in the time of popery, when that apostacizing spirit was entered, of which Jude spoke. Jude 11: "Who run greedily after the error of Balaam, for reward," who were not content with such things as were set before them; stirred up the rulers to make laws to compel a maintenance, being departed from that purity that was in the primitive church; and so not content to receive freely of the Lord, and so to administer freely, but in the steps of those Christ spoke of, "That should come in sheep's clothing, but inwardly ravening wolves." Tithe was not a maintenance appointed by Christ nor his apostles for ministers, for it belonged to the tribe of Levi in the time of the Law, who were for the offering up of sacrifices; they were to set open their gates, that the widow, fatherless and strangers might be relieved. But Christ being come, and offered up became the complete sacrifice to God for us, and a reconciler between betwixt God and man, and so no need of that priesthood now: "The priesthood being changed, there is made of necessity change of the Law, also." Heb. 7.

But some may say, did not Christ say, at Luke 11:42: "Ye tithe mint, rue, and all manners of herbs"; these things ye ought to do.

Answer. This was not spoke to his ministers, nor to Christians, to establish tithe amongst them, but to those that were under the Law, and were boasting of their righteousness under the Law, for Christ said, "Woe unto you scribes, Pharisees, and hypocrites, for you pay tithes of mint, annis, etc., and omit or neglect the weightier matters of the Law." Matt. 23:23. These were not Christians, but were under the Law, which Law Christ came to fulfill, and did fulfill the Law, which was a shadow of the good things to come. Now Christ, who is the substance, being come, the shadows were to pass away. And so, Christ being "the end of the Law, for righteousness sake to everyone who believes," Rom. 10:4. "Who being nailed to the cross became a sacrifice acceptable with the Father." And so, this acceptable sacrifice being once offered up for all, there is no need now of those former shadows nor ceremonies that were in the time of the Law. No need now of those priests to offer sacrifices. No need now of offering as formerly; for Christ is the offering acceptable with God, whom God hath raised up from the dead; he hath led captivity captive, and given gifts unto men, by which gifts of his Holy Spirit many were furnished for the work of the ministry, and were faithful labourers in the work and service of the Lord, not seeking their own honour, but the honour of God, and the good of souls; not coveting any man's silver, or gold, or apparel, but labouring to bring them into the Lord. These freely received of the Lord, and as good stewards of the manifold grace of God, administered freely; these did not see after the fleece, but to gather the flock, and to feed the flock of God, taking the oversight thereof not by constraint, but willingly; not for filthy lucre, but of a ready mind; not as lords over God's heritage, but examples to the flock. But there were some in those days began to creep in amongst the Apostles, such as Christ spoke of, "That should come in sheep's clothing, but inwardly were ravening wolves," whom the Apostle said, were enemies to the cross of Christ, whose end was destruction, whose God was their belly, whose glory is their shame, who mind earthly things. And the Apostle Peter (in 2 Pet. 2:23) said, "There were false prophets among the people, even as there shall be false teachers amongst

you, who privily shall bring in damnable heresies, even denying
the Lord that bought them; who with feigned words, and fair
speeches, and through covetousness, make merchandise of you";
as the said Thomas Willmate hath of me, in hunting after me,
with writ upon writ, and hurrying me from prison to prison; who
contented not himself with keeping me a prisoner in Worcester
County Gaol about a year and a half, because of conscience towards the Lord, could not pay tithe and offerings, to the value of
six shillings, and could not so far deny my Lord and Master to be
come in the flesh, as to pay tithe and offerings now in these Gospel times; Christ being come, who is a priest forever, and the offering acceptable with the Father. But this merciless man hath
removed me to London, to the Fleet Prison, (that my children
might be, as it were, fatherless, who had need of a father to counsel them) though I never eat of his bread, nor employed him in any
business, neither received anything from him; but he appeared
like the false prophets, described in Micah 3:5. "He that putteth
not into their mouths, they even prepare war against him." And
as Ezekiel said, Chap. 34:2–3: "Woe be the shepherds, that do
feed themselves. Should not the shepherds feed the flocks? Ye eat
the fat, and clothe you with the wool, but the diseased strengthened they not, neither have ye healed them which were sick; but
with force and with cruelty have ye ruled them." The Lord said,
he was against the shepherds that did feed themselves; and he will
deliver his sheep from their mouths, that they may not be a prey
unto them any longer. And I may say, out of the hands of such
unreasonable men, the Lord deliver me; yet I can truly say, Father,
forgive him; Lord, lay not this sin to his charge.

I am a prisoner at the Fleet Prison, and am one that loves the
good of Zion, and desireth the prosperity of Israel; and prayeth,
that truth and righteousness may be set up in the earth.

LONDON, THE 26TH OF THE 10TH MONTH, 1681
                                                    JOHN BOWETER

LAST WORDS

MARGARET FELL FOX

Margaret Fell Fox outlived her husband, George, by more than a decade. In her last years, she saw much about Quakerism that troubled her, as the following epistle shows.

A Brief Collection of Remarkable Passages and Occurrences Relating to the Birth, Education, Life, Conversion, Travels, Services, and Deep Sufferings of That Ancient, Eminent, and Faithful Servant of the Lord, Margaret Fell (London, 1710).

4TH MONTH 1698

Dear Friends, Brethren, and Sisters:

God the Father of our blessed Lord and Savior Jesus Christ is a universal God of mercy and love to all people. And in that blessed love he visited us, "in an acceptable time and in a day of salvation, etc." And he that early brought unto us the glad tidings of the gospel of peace [George Fox] continued in the body among God's plantations up and down forty years; and we had from him certain directions and instructions upon many weighty accounts and occasions. He hath left us several writings and records, to be practiced according to the Gospel which he preached amongst us; and we have lived under the teaching of that blessed eternal Spirit of the eternal God, which he directed us to, unto this day. And now it is good for us all to go on and continue hand in hand in the unity and fellowship of this eternal Spirit, in humility and lowliness of mind, each esteeming others better than ourselves; and this is well-pleasing unto God.

And let us all take heed of touching anything like the ceremonies of the Jews; for that was displeasing to Christ, for he came to bear witness against them, and testified against their outside practices, who told him of their long robes and of their broad phylacteries. . . . So let us keep to the rule and leading of the eternal Spirit, that God hath given us to be our teacher; and let that put on and off as is meet and serviceable for every one's state and condition. And let us take heed of limiting in such practices; for we are under the Gospel leading and guiding and teaching, which is a free spirit, which leads into unity and lowliness of mind the saints and servants of Christ, desiring to be established in the free Spirit, not bound or limited. Legal ceremonies are far from gospel freedom; let us beware of being guilty or having a hand in ordering or contriving what is contrary to Gospel freedom; for the Apostle would not have dominion over their faith in Corinth, but to be helpers of their faith. It's a dangerous thing to lead young Friends much into the observation of outward things, which may be easily done; for they can soon get into an outward garb, to be all alike outwardly, but this will not make them true Christians: it's the Spirit that gives life; I would be loth to have a hand in these things. The Lord preserve us, that we do no hurt to God's work; but let him work whose work it is. We have lived quietly and peaceably thus far, and it's not for God's service to make breaches.

MARGARET FOX
2ND MONTH 1700

PART III

QUIETISM
1690–1820

TRAVELS AND TRAVAILS

ELIZABETH WEBB

Traveling ministers were central to Quaker life in the eighteenth century. They exhorted, carried news, and reinforced a sense of shared identity on both sides of the Atlantic. Here follow passages from the writings of three. The first, Elizabeth Webb (1663–1726), was a convinced Friend, born in Gloucestershire, who immigrated to Pennsylvania, where she became well known as a minister. In a letter to a chaplain at the court of Queen Anne of England, she described her life and experiences.

"A Letter from Elizabeth Webb to Anthony William Boehm," in *The Friends Library*, vol. 13 (Philadelphia, 1849).

Worthy Friend,

I will give thee a short account of the dealings of the Lord with me in my young years; how he brought my soul through fire and water. For what end this has lived in my mind I know not, except it be for our spiritual communion; but when my soul is lowest and nearest to the Lord in the simplicity of truth, then is my heart opened and my mind filled with divine love respecting this matter. I desire thee to peruse it inwardly, when thou art retired, and not to judge of it before thou hast gone through it; and then judge as freely as thou pleasest:—

I was baptized and educated in the way of the Church of England; and went to school to a minister thereof, whom I loved and honoured greatly; he showed great kindness and tenderness to me. In those days I looked on the ministers to be like angels, that brought glad tidings to the children of men. When I was about fourteen years of age, I went to live at a knight's house, who kept a chaplain: I observed his conversation, and saw it was vain, and I thought it ought not to be so, and was troubled in my mind; for I then began to think on my latter end and also on eternity, and I had no assurance of salvation or a state of happiness, if it should please the Lord to send the messenger of death to call me away.

So the fear of the Lord laid hold on my mind, and I began to search the Scriptures, and found they testified that "the wicked should be turned into hell, and all those that forget God." And I saw that both priests and people did too generally "forget God," as soon as they came off their knees, or from their devotion. I was much afraid of hell, and wanted an assurance of a place in the kingdom of heaven. Then I began to think on the great promises that were made for me in my baptism, as they called it, (whereby they said I was made a member of Christ, a child of God, &c.), that I should renounce the devil and all his works, the pomps and vanities of this wicked world, and all the sinful lusts of the flesh, and should keep God's holy will and commandments. I thought indeed this was the way to obtain a place in the kingdom of heaven; but I had no power to do what I ought to do, nor to forsake what I ought to forsake, for I was very proud, vain and airy. But as I was thus inwardly exercised, and outwardly searching the Scriptures, my understanding was more and more opened. I read and took notice that the ministers of Christ, whom he qualified, and sent forth to preach, were to do it freely; for Christ said, "Freely ye have received, freely give," and that those who run when the Lord never sent them, "should not profit the people at all." Many such things opened in my mind, and I used to ponder them in my heart; also the promises to the flock in the 34th of Ezekiel, where the Lord promised to bind up that which was sick. These and similar portions of the Scriptures were very comfortable to me, for I was sick of my sins, and my heart was broken many times before the Lord. I thought, Oh! that I had lived in the days of Christ, I would surely have been one of those that followed him; and I grieved because the Jews crucified him. Thus I loved Christ in the outward appearance, and could have said, (as Peter said), far be it from thee Lord to suffer: yet I did not know he was so near me by his Holy Spirit. But I was convinced that the hireling shepherds, who teach for hire and divine for money, were not the ministers of Christ, by the testimony of the prophets and of Christ himself, who said, "By their fruits ye shall know them." So I left going to hear them, and walked alone: for I had gone till a fear followed me into the worship-house, and I thought it would be just upon me, if I was made an example for my inattention to the Spirit of truth. When I was about fifteen years old, it pleased God to send the spirit of grace and supplication into my heart, by which I prayed fervently unto the Lord: there was a divine breathing in my soul; I had no life in my forms of prayer, except that one which Christ taught his disciples, for which I have always had a reverent esteem: but when I was in a state to pray, I found that the Spirit made intercession in me and for me, according to the present want and necessity of my soul. I remember the expressions that used to run through my mind were—"O Lord! preserve me in thy fear and in thy truth— O Lord! shew me thy way, and make known thy mind and will unto me"—and I thought I was ready to obey it, and much desired to know the people of God; for my soul cried, "O Lord! where dost thou feed thy flock; why should I be as one that is turned aside from the flocks of thy companions!"

I was convinced that the Quakers held the principles of truth, and that their ministry was the true ministry: but I dwelt then far from any of them, only thus it had happened:—When I was about twelve years old, I was at a meeting or two of theirs, and the doctrine of one man that preached there, proved to me, (as the wise man terms it), like bread cast upon the waters, for it was found after many days: the sound of his voice seemed to be in my mind when I was alone, and some of his words came fresh into my remembrance; and the voice and the words suited with the exercise of the mind. At that time I met also with a little book of theirs, [and finding] the doctrine it contained agreed with the doctrine of the apostles, I was confirmed in my judgment, that their profession agreed with the truth: but I did not join with them; for by that time flesh and blood began to be very uneasy under the yoke of retirement, and to groan for liberty. I was about sixteen years old; and the subtle enemy lay near, and did not want instruments: so I was persuaded by reasoning with flesh and blood, that I was young, and might take a little more pleasure, and might serve God when I was older. I let go my exercise of watching and praying, left off retirement, and let out my love to visible objects. Pride and

vanity grew up again; the divine, sweet, meek, loving Spirit with-
drew, and I could not find it again when I pleased, although I did
seek it sometimes; for I could have been pleased with the sweet
comforts of his love, yet I did not like to bear the daily cross. And
being convinced that was [required by] the Quakers' principles,
and believing they did enjoy the sweetness of divine love in their
meetings, I went sometimes a great way to a meeting to seek for
divine refreshment there; but to no purpose; for I was like some
dry stick that had no sap nor virtue, unto which rain and sunshine, summer and winter are all alike.—Thus it was with me for
about three years.

Oh, the remembrance of that misspent time! Oh, the tribulation
that came on me for my disobedience is never to be forgotten! But
when I was about nineteen years of age, it pleased the Almighty
to send his quickening Spirit again into my heart, and his light
shined into my mind; all my transgressions were set in order
before me, and I was made deeply sensible of my great loss. And
then, oh then! the vials of the wrath of an angry Father, were
poured out on the transgressing nature. Oh, then I cried, "woe is
me! woe is me! I am undone—I have slain the babe of grace—I
have crucified the Lord of life and glory to myself afresh, although
I have not put him to open shame." For I had been preserved in
moral honesty in all respects, to that degree, that I durst not tell
a lie, or speak an evil word, and could be trusted in any place, and
in any thing; for this would be in my mind many times, that if
I was not faithful in the unrighteous mammon I should not
be trusted with heavenly treasure. But notwithstanding my righteousness, He whose eye penetrates all hearts, found me so guilty,
that I thought there was no mercy for me. . . . But after many days
and nights of sorrow and great anguish, having no soul to speak
to, it came into my mind to give myself up into the hands of God;
and I said, "O Lord! if I perish, it shall be at the gate of thy mercy;
for if thou cast me into hell, I cannot help myself; therefore I will
give up my soul, my life, and all into thy holy hand: do thy pleasure by me; thy judgments are just, for I have slighted thy sweet
love and have slain the babe of grace." And as I sunk down into
death, and owned and submitted to the judgments of God, my
heart was broken, which before was hard; and it pleased my merciful Father to cause his divine, sweet love to spring again in my
hard, dry, and barren soul, as a spring of living water; the fire of

the wrath of God was mightily abated, and the compassionate bowels of a tender Saviour my soul felt. I had living hope raised in my mind: yet greater afflictions came afterwards; so that I may say by experience, "Strait is the gate and narrow is the way," indeed, "that leadeth unto life." And I have cause to believe, none but such as are made willing to be stript of all that belongs to self or the old man, and do become as little children, can rightly or truly enter in at the strait gate. And I do find by experience, that no vulture's eye, no venomous beast, nor lofty lion's whelp, can look into or tread in this holy, narrow way.

I thought all was well, [and said in my heart,] "The worst is now over, and I am again taken into the favour of God": so I was led into an elevation of joy, though inwardly in silence. But in a few days my soul was led into a wilderness where there was no way, no guide, no light that I could see, but darkness such as might be felt indeed: for the horrors of it were such, that when it was night I wished for morning, and when it was morning I wished for evening. The Lord was near, but I knew it not: he had brought my soul into the wilderness, and there he pleaded with me by his fiery law and righteous judgments. The day of the Lord came upon me, which burnt as an oven in my bosom, till all pride and vanity were burnt up, my former delights were gone, my old heavens were passed away within me, as with fire, and I had as much exercise in my mind of anguish and sorrow as I could bear, day and night for several months, and not a drop of divine comfort. I could compare my heart to nothing, unless it were a coal of fire, or a hot iron; no brokenness of heart or tenderness of spirit; although I cried to God continually in the deep distress of my soul, yet not one tear could issue from my eyes. Oh! the days of sorrow and nights of anguish that I went through, no tongue can utter, nor heart conceive which hath not gone through the like. . . . But my troubles were aggravated by the strong oppression and temptation of Satan, who was very unwilling to lose his subject: so he raised all his forces, and made use of all his armour which he had in the house: and I found him to be like a strong man armed indeed; for he would not suffer me to enter into resignation, but would have me look into mysteries that appertain to salvation, with an eye of carnal reason. And because I could not so comprehend, he caused me to question the truth of all things that are left upon record in the Holy Scriptures, and would have persuaded me

into the Jews' opinion concerning Christ; and many other baits
and resting places he laid before me. But my soul hungered after
the true bread, the bread of life, which came from God out of
heaven, which Christ testified of, (see John vi. beginning at the
27th verse, to the end), which I had felt near, and my soul had
tasted of. And although the devil prompted me with his temptations, my soul could not feed on them, but cried continually, "Thy
presence, O Lord! or else I die—Oh! let me feel thy saving arm,
or else I perish—O Lord! give me faith." . . .

So, in the Lord's due and appointed time, when he had seen my
suffering of that fiery kind to be sufficient, he was pleased to cause
his divine love to flow in my bosom in an extraordinary manner;
and the Holy Spirit of divine light and life did overcome my soul.
Then a divine sense and understanding was given me by which to
know the power and also the love of God, in sending his only Son
out of his bosom into the world, to take upon him a body of flesh,
wherein he did go through the whole process of suffering for the
salvation of mankind; and so did break through and break open
the gates of death, and repaired the breach that old Adam had
made between God and man, and restored the path for souls to
come to God. . . .

I was between nineteen and twenty years of age when these
great conflicts were on my mind: by them I was brought very
humble; and I entered into solemn covenant with God Almighty,
that I would answer his requirings, if it were to the laying down
my natural life. But when it was showed me that I ought to take
up the cross in a little thing, I had like to have hearkened to the
reasoner again, and been disobedient in the day of small things:
for although I had gone through so much inward exercise, yet I
was afraid of displeasing my superiors, being then a servant to
great persons. It was shewn me, that I should not give flattering
titles to man; and I was threatened inwardly, that if I would not
be obedient to the Lord's requirings, he would take away his good
Spirit from me again. So I was in a strait; I was afraid of displeasing God, and afraid of displeasing man; till at last I was charged
by the Spirit, with honouring man more than God: for in my address to God I did use the plain language, but when I spoke to
man or woman I must speak otherwise, or else they would be offended. Some would argue, that God Almighty being that only
One, therefore the singular language was proper to him alone;

and man being made up of compound matter, the plural language was more proper to him. Oh! the subtle twistings of proud Lucifer that I have seen, would be too large to insert; but although God Almighty is that only One, yet is he the Being of all beings, for in him we live, move, and have our being. But let the cover be what it would, I had Scripture on my side, which they called their rule; and I knew proud man disdained to receive that language from an inferior, which he gave to the Almighty. So it became a great cross to me: but it was certainly a letting thing in the way of the progress of my soul, until I gave up to the Lord's requirings in this small thing. . . .

And now I shew thee this in truth and sincerity, because I would not be misunderstood by thee, viz. I am a single soul, wholly devoted to the Lord, and so do not plead for a form for form's sake; neither do I plead for a people as a people; for we are grown to be a mixed multitude, much like the children of Israel, when they were in the wilderness. But this I may say to the praise and glory of God, the principle that we make profession of, is the very Truth, viz. Christ in the male and in the female, the hope of glory: and Christ, thou knowest, is the Way, the Truth, and the Life, and none comes to God but by him. So there is a remnant, who, like Joshua and Caleb of old, are true to the Lord their spiritual Leader, and follow him faithfully; and they stand clear in their testimonies against all dead formalities, which are but as images, when the vital principle, viz. the divine love is withdrawn. And yet as the spirit of Jesus leads out of all vain customs and traditions which are in the world, and into the plain, humble, meek, self-denying life and conversation which Christ walked in while he was visible among men, I could wish all to follow the leadings of his Spirit herein, that thereby they may confess him before men. But if it please the Almighty to accept of souls, without leading them through such fiery trials as he brought me through, or without requiring such, things of them as he required of me, far be it from me to judge that such have not known the Lord, or the indwellings of his love, if the fruits of the spirit of Jesus be plain upon them. . . . But dear friend, as thou well observedst, purification is a gradual work—I may say so by experience: for when the old adversary could no longer draw me out into vain talking and foolish jesting, then he perplexed me with vain thoughts; some of which were according to my natural disposition, and some of them quite contrary. Oh! I cried mightily unto the Lord for power over vain thoughts; for they were a great trouble to me; and I stood in great fear lest one day or other I should fall by the hand of the enemy. But the Lord spake comfortably to my soul in his own words left upon record, "Fear not, little flock, it is your Father's good pleasure to give you the kingdom"; and the Lord gave me an evidence along with it, that my soul was one of that little flock. . . . For then, when I went to meetings, I did not sit in darkness, dryness and barrenness, as I used to do in the times of my disobedience. . . . And I was constrained, under a sense of duty, to kneel down in the congregation, and confess to the goodness of God, also to pray to him for the continuation of it, and for power whereby I might be enabled to walk worthy of so great a favour, benefit and mercy, that I had received at his bountiful hand. And I remember after I had made public confession to the goodness of God, my soul was as if it had been in another world: it was so enlightened and enlivened by the divine love, that I was in love with the whole creation of God, and I saw everything to be good in its place. I was shewed things ought to be kept in their proper places, that the swine ought not to come into the garden, and the clean beasts ought not to be taken into the bedchamber; that as it was in the outward, so it ought to be in the inward and new creation. So everything began to preach to me; the very fragrant herbs, and beautiful, innocent flowers had a speaking voice in them to my soul, and things seemed to have another relish with them than before. The judgments of God were sweet to my soul, and I was made to call to others sometimes, to come taste and see how good the Lord is, and to exhort them to prove the Lord, by an obedient, humble, innocent walking before him, and then they would see that he would pour out of his spiritual blessings in so plentiful a manner, that there would not be room enough to contain them; but the overflowings would return to him who is the Fountain, with thanksgivings, &c. And I was made to warn people, that they should not provoke the Lord by disobedience: for although he bears and suffers long, as he did with the rebellious Israelites in the wilderness, yet such shall know him to be a God of justice and judgment, and shall be made so to confess one day.

Thus, dear friend, I have given thee a plain, but true account of my qualification and call to the service of the ministry. But it was several years before I came to a freed state, or even temper of mind; for sometimes clouds would arise and interpose between my soul and the rising Sun, and I was brought down into the furnace often, and found by experience that every time my soul was brought down as into the furnace of affliction, that it did still come up more clean and bright; and although the cloud did interpose between me and the rising Sun, yet when the Sun of Righteousness did appear again, he brought healing as under his wings, and was nearer than before. Thus dear friend, I express things in simplicity, as they were represented to me in the manifestation of them in the morning of my days. I came to love to dwell with judgment, and used often to pray, saying, "O Lord! search me and try me, for thou knowest my heart better than I know it; and I pray thee let no deceitfulness of unrighteousness lodge therein; but let thy judgments pass upon every thing that is contrary to thy pure, divine nature." Thus my soul used to breathe to the Lord continually, and hunger and thirst after a more full enjoyment of his presence. Although he is a consuming fire to the corrupt nature of the old man, yet my soul loved to dwell with him. I found many sorts of corruptions would be endeavouring to spring up again; but I resigned up my mind to the Lord, with desires that he would feed me with food convenient for me. . . .

After my inward tribulation was abated, then outward trials began; for there were some of no small account, that endeavoured with all their might and cunning, to hinder the work from prospering in me: and as Saul hunted David, and sought to take away his natural life, so these hunted my soul to take away its life, which it had in God: but all wrought together for my good. I have often seen, and therefore may say, the Lord knoweth what is best for his children, better than we know for ourselves: and so my enemies, instead of driving my soul away from God, drove it nearer to him. This trial caused me to prove the spirit which had the exercise of my mind, and I found it to be the Spirit of Truth, which the worldly and self-minded cannot receive; for I found the nature of it to be harmless and holy, and to lead me to love mine enemies, to pity them and pray for them. This love was my preservation; and as I gave up in obedience to the operation and requiring of this meek Spirit, it ministered such peace to my soul, as the world cannot give. But there was a disposition in me to please all, which I found very hard for me to be weaned from, so as to stand single to God: for when I did fear man, I had nothing but anguish and sorrow; and I used often to walk alone and pour out my complaint to the Lord. But after a long time, when the Lord had tried my fidelity to him as he saw meet, one day as I was sitting in a meeting in silence, waiting upon the Lord, to know my strength renewed in him and by him, this portion of Scripture was given to me, viz. "Comfort ye my people, saith your God: speak comfortably to Jerusalem, and cry unto her, that her warfare is accomplished, that her iniquity is pardoned; for she hath received of the Lord's hand double for all her sins." This brought great comfort to my soul; . . . my mind was brought into more stillness, and troublesome thoughts were in a good degree expelled; my outward enemies grew weary of their work and failed of their hope. . . .

So after I had [been favoured with] peace at home every way, I was drawn by the Spirit of love, to travel into the north of England. On my journey my soul had many combats with the evil spirit: when I was asleep he tormented me as long as he could. I have, indeed, had a long war with the devil many ways; abundance of courage was given to me to make war with him; and I always gained the victory when cowardly, fearful nature was asleep, which was comfortable to my mind: and I did hope that the Lord would give me perfect victory over the devil when I was awake, as he had let me see it to be so when I was asleep. The Spirit which led me forth, was to me like a needle of a compass, touched with a loadstone; for so it pointed where I ought to go, and when I came to the far end of the journey.

In those days I had certain manifestations of many things in dreams, which did come to pass according to their significations; I was many times forewarned of enemies, and so was better able to guard against them. I traveled in great fear and humility, and the Lord was with me to his glory and my comfort, and brought me home again in peace.

In the year 1697, in the Sixth Month, as I was sitting in the meeting in Gloucester, which was then the place of my abode, my mind was gathered into perfect stillness for some time, and my spirit was as if it had been carried away into America; and after it returned, my heart was as if it had been dissolved with the love of God, which flowed over the great ocean, and I was constrained to kneel down and pray for the seed of God in America. The concern never went out of my mind day nor night, until I went to

travel there in the love of God, which is so universal that it reaches
over sea and land. But when I looked at my concern with an eye
of human reason, it seemed to be very strange and hard to me;
for I knew not the country, nor any that dwelt therein. I reasoned much concerning my own unfitness, and when I let in such
reasonings, I had nothing but death and darkness; and trouble
attended my mind; but when I resigned up my all to the Lord,
and gave up in my mind to go, then the divine love sprang up in
my heart, and my soul was at liberty to worship the Lord as in
the land of the living. Thus I tried and proved the concern in my
own heart, till at last these words ran through my mind with
authority,—"The fearful and unbelieving shall have their portion
with the hypocrite, in the lake that burns with fire and brimstone;
which is the second death." This brought a dread; I then told my
husband that I had a concern to go to America; and asked him if
he could give me up. He said he hoped it would not be required of
me; but I told him it was; and that I should not go without his free
consent, which seemed a little hard to him at first. A little while
after, I was taken with a violent fever, which brought me so weak,
that all who saw me thought I should not recover. But I thought
my day's work was not done, and my chief concern in my sickness
was about going to America. Some were troubled that I had made
it public, because they thought I should die, and people would
speak reproachfully of me; and said, if I did recover, the ship would
be ready to sail before I should be fit to go, &c. But I thought if
they would only carry me and lay me down in the ship, I should
be well: for the Lord was very gracious to my soul in the time of
my sickness, and gave me a promise that his presence should go
with me. And then my husband was made very willing to give me
up; he said, if it were for seven years, rather than to have me taken
from him forever. So at last all those difficulties passed over, and
I sailed from Bristol in the Ninth Month, 1697, with my companion Mary Rogers. The dangers we were in at sea, and the faith
and courage the Lord gave to my soul, would be too large here to
relate; for I had such an evidence of my being in my proper place,
that the fear of death was taken away. . . .

About the middle of the Twelfth Month, 1697, through the good
providence of the Almighty, we arrived in Virginia. As I traveled
along the country from one meeting to another, I observed great
numbers of black people that were in slavery. They were a strange

people to me; I wanted to know whether the visitation of God was to their souls or not; and I observed their conversation, to see if I could discern any good in them. After I had traveled about four weeks, as I was in bed one morning in a house in Maryland, after the sun was up I fell into a slumber, and dreamed I was a servant in a great man's house, and that I was drawing water at a well to wash the uppermost rooms of the house. When I was at the well, a voice came to me, which bid me go and call other servants to help me, and I went presently. But as I was going along in a very pleasant green meadow, a great light shined about me, which exceeded the light of the sun, and I walked in the midst. As I went on in the way, I saw a chariot drawn with horses coming to meet me, and I was in care lest the light that shone about me should frighten the horses, and cause them to throw down the people whom I saw in the chariot. When I came to them, I looked on them, and I knew they were the servants I was sent to call: I saw they were both white and black people, and I said unto them, "Why have you staid so long?" They said, "The buckets were frozen, we could come no sooner"—So I was satisfied the call of the Lord was unto the black people as well as the white; and I saw the fulfilling of it in part, before I returned out of America, with many more remarkable things, which would be too tedious here to mention. But O how great is the condescension and goodness of God to poor mankind! It is a good observation on the tender dealings of our Heavenly Father, to set up our Ebenezer, and say, "Hitherto hath the Lord helped us"—and indeed I may say to his praise, it hath been [so with me] through many straits and difficulties, more than I can number; and they have all wrought together for the good of my soul. And I have cause to believe, that every son or daughter whom he receives, he chastens, tries, and proves; and those who do not bear the chastisements of God, do prove bastards and not sons. But I may say, as one did of old, "It is good for me that I have been afflicted," &c., and that it is good to follow the leadings of the Spirit of God, as faithful Abraham did, who was called the friend of God, and who did not withhold his only son when the Lord called for him. And it is my belief the Lord will try his chosen ones as gold is tried, and will yet refine them as gold is refined. And what if he bring us yet down again into the furnace, which way it shall please him, until we are seven times refined; we shall be the better able to bear the impression of his image upon us in all our conversation. . . .

Dear friend, excuse my freedom with thee, for the love of God constraineth me: and I do believe the Lord will shew thee yet further, what testimony thou must bear for his name, and what thou must suffer for his sake, if faithful. For trying times will come, and offences will be given and taken; but there is nothing will offend those that love the Lord Jesus above all. Many murmured and were offended at Jesus when he told them the truth, and that which was of absolute necessity for all to know and witness in themselves; as we read in the 6th of John, beginning at the 32nd verse. By that time he had done, many of his disciples went from him: then said he to the twelve, "Will ye also go away?" but Peter said, "Lord, to whom shall we go? Thou hast the words of eternal life. And we believe and are sure that thou art that Christ, the Son of the living God." So God hath given the faithful to believe; yea, and we are sure that the Spirit of Truth is come, that leads the followers of it into all truth; and that Christ who is one with his Spirit, and who was once offered to bear the sins of many, has appeared again the second time without sin unto salvation. Oh! surely the goodness of God hath been very great to the children of men from age to age, and from one generation to another, ever since the fall of our first parents. The more my mind penetrates into it, the more I am like to be swallowed up in admiration of his condescension and goodness through all his dispensations, but above all in the manifestation of Jesus Christ, our holy Pattern and heavenly Leader. O my soul! praise him for the knowledge of his holy footsteps, whom God gave for a light to us Gentiles, and to be his salvation unto the ends of the earth; and hath given his Spirit to dwell in us, and accepted our souls to dwell in him. O admirable goodness! Shall we leave him? He is the Word of eternal life, and whither shall we go. So far as any are followers of Jesus, so far I desire to follow them or to be one with them, and no farther. Let these do what they will, if any will go back into the sea, out of which the beast ariseth, and receive his mark, our Leader is not to be blamed; He holds on his way, and causes his trumpet to be blown in Zion, and an alarm to be beaten in his holy mountain: and whosoever heareth the sound of the trumpet, and taketh not warning, if the sword of the Lord do

come, (in any kind), and take him away, his blood shall be upon
his own head; he heard the sound of the trumpet and took not
warning: but he that taketh warning shall deliver his own soul. . . .
Yet I know the wisdom of God appears to be foolishness in the
eyes of the wise men of this world, and we know that the wisdom
of this world is foolishness with God, and will prove so in the
latter end to those poor souls that so mightily esteem it. But the
souls of the righteous are in the hand of the Lord, and then shall
no torment touch them; although in the sight of the unwise, both
their life and their death are taken for misery—nevertheless, they
are in peace.
    Thy friend in true sincerity,

                                                    ELIZABETH WEBB

JOHN WOOLMAN

*If American Quakerism has ever produced a saint, it was
John Woolman (1720–1772). A tailor and storekeeper from
New Jersey, Woolman traveled widely in the ministry from
the 1740s until his death on a visit to England. He was one
of the group of Friends who in the 1750s moved Friends to
question slavery through their writings. Even more influential
was his journal, which has never gone out of print since it
was first published in 1774. In this passage, Woolman describes his travels in the South in 1757.*

John Greenleaf Whittier, ed., *The Journal of John Woolman* (Boston, 1871).

Thirteenth of fifth month, 1757.—Being in good health, and abroad
with Friends visiting families, I lodged at a Friend's house in Burlington. Going to bed about the time usual with me, I awoke in
the night, and my meditations, as I lay, were on the goodness and
mercy of the Lord, in a sense whereof my heart was contrited.
After this I went to sleep again; in a short time I awoke. It was yet
dark, and no appearance of day or moonshine, and as I opened
mine eyes I saw a light in my chamber, at the apparent distance of
five feet, about nine inches in diameter, of a clear, easy brightness,
and near its centre the most radiant. As I lay still looking upon it

without any surprise, words were spoken to my inward ear, which filled my whole inward man. They were not the effect of thought, nor any conclusion in relation to the appearance, but as the language of the Holy One spoken in my mind. The words were, Certain Evidence Of Divine Truth. They were again repeated exactly in the same manner, and then the light disappeared.

Feeling the exercise in relation to a visit to the Southern Provinces to increase upon me, I acquainted our Monthly Meeting therewith, and obtained their certificate. Expecting to go alone, one of my brothers who lived in Philadelphia, having some business in North Carolina, proposed going with me part of the way; but as he had a view of some outward affairs, to accept of him as a companion was some difficulty with me, whereupon I had conversation with him at sundry times. At length feeling easy in my mind, I had conversation with several elderly Friends of Philadelphia on the subject, and he obtaining a certificate suitable to the occasion, we set off in the fifth month, 1757. Coming to Nottingham weekday meeting, we lodged at John Churchman's, where I met with our friend, Benjamin Buffington, from New England, who was returning from a visit to the Southern Provinces. Thence we crossed the river Susquehanna, and lodged at William Cox's in Maryland.

Soon after I entered this province a deep and painful exercise came upon me, which I often had some feeling of, since my mind was drawn toward these parts, and with which I had acquainted my brother before we agreed to join as companions. As the people in this and the Southern Provinces live much on the labor of slaves, many of whom are used hardly, my concern was that I might attend with singleness of heart to the voice of the true Shepherd, and be so supported as to remain unmoved at the faces of men.

As it is common for Friends on such a visit to have entertainment free of cost, a difficulty arose in my mind with respect to saving my money by kindness received from what appeared to me to be the gain of oppression. Receiving a gift, considered as a gift, brings the receiver under obligations to the benefactor, and has a natural tendency to draw the obliged into a party with the giver. To prevent difficulties of this kind, and to preserve the minds of judges from any bias, was that Divine prohibition: "Thou shalt not receive any gift; for a gift blindeth the wise, and perverteth the words of the righteous." (Exod. xxiii. 8.) As the disciples were sent forth without any provision for their journey, and our Lord said the workman is worthy of his meat, their labor in the gospel was considered as a reward for their entertainment, and therefore not received as a gift; yet, in regard to my present journey, I could not see my way clear in that respect. The difference appeared thus: the entertainment the disciples met with was from them whose hearts God had opened to receive them, from a love to them and the truth they published; but we, considered as members of the same religious society, look upon it as a piece of civility to receive each other in such visits; and such reception, at times, is partly in regard to reputation, and not from an inward unity of heart and spirit. Conduct is more convincing than language, and where people, by their actions, manifest that the slave trade is not so disagreeable to their principles but that it may be encouraged, there is not a sound uniting with some Friends who visit them.

The prospect of so weighty a work, and of being so distinguished from many whom I esteemed before myself, brought me very low, and such were the conflicts of my soul that I had a near sympathy with the Prophet, in the time of his weakness, when he said: "If thou deal thus with me, kill me, I pray thee, if I have found favor in thy sight." (Num. xi. 15.) But I soon saw that this proceeded from the want of a full resignation to the Divine will. Many were the afflictions which attended me, and in great abasement, with many tears, my cries were to the Almighty for his gracious and fatherly assistance, and after a time of deep trial I was favored to understand the state mentioned by the Psalmist more clearly than ever I had done before; to wit: "My soul is even as a weaned child." (Psalm cxxxi. 2.) Being thus helped to sink down into resignation, I felt a deliverance from that tempest in which I had been sorely exercised, and in calmness of mind went forward, trusting that the Lord Jesus Christ, as I faithfully attended to him, would be a counselor to me in all difficulties, and that by his strength I should be enabled even to leave money with the members of society where I had entertainment, when I found that omitting it would obstruct that work to which I believed he had called me. As I copy this after my return, I may here add, that oftentimes I did so under a sense of duty. The way in which I did it was thus: when I expected soon to leave a Friend's house where I had entertainment, if I believed that I should not keep clear from the gain of oppression without leaving money, I spoke to one of the heads of the family privately, and desired them to accept of those pieces of silver, and give them to such of their negroes as they believed would make the best use of them; and at other times I gave them to the negroes myself, as the way looked clearest to me. Before I came out, I had provided a large number of small pieces for this purpose and thus offering them to some who appeared to be wealthy people was a trial both to me and them. But the fear of the Lord so covered me at times that my way was made easier than I expected; and few, if any, manifested any resentment at the offer, and most of them, after some conversation, accepted of them.

Ninth of fifth month.—A Friend at whose house we breakfasted setting us a little on our way, I had conversation with him, in the fear of the Lord, concerning his slaves, in which my heart was tender; I used much plainness of speech with him, and he appeared to take it kindly. We pursued our journey without appointing meetings, being pressed in my mind to be at the Yearly Meeting in Virginia. In my traveling on the road, I often felt a cry rise from the center of my mind, thus: "O Lord, I am a stranger on the earth, hide not thy face from me." On the 11th, we crossed the rivers Potomac and Rappahannock, and lodged at Port Royal. On the way we had the company of a colonel of the militia, who appeared to be a thoughtful man. I took occasion to remark on the difference in general betwixt a people used to labor moderately for their living, training up their children in frugality and business, and those who live on the labor of slaves; the former, in my view, being the most happy life. He concurred in the remark, and mentioned the trouble arising from the untoward, slothful disposition of the negroes, adding that one of our laborers would do as much in a day as two of their slaves. I replied, that free men, whose minds were properly on their business, found a satisfaction in improving, cultivating, and providing for their families; but negroes, laboring to support others who claim them as their property, and expecting nothing but slavery during life, had not the like inducement to be industrious.

After some further conversation I said, that men having power too often misapplied it; that though we made slaves of the negroes, and the Turks made slaves of the Christians, I believed that liberty was the natural right of all men equally. This he did not deny, but said the lives of the negroes were so wretched in their

own country that many of them lived better here than there. I
replied, "There is great odds in regard to us on what principle
we act"; and so the conversation on that subject ended. I may here
add that another person, some time afterwards, mentioned the
wretchedness of the negroes, occasioned by their intestine wars,
as an argument in favor of our fetching them away for slaves. To
which I replied, if compassion for the Africans, on account of their
domestic troubles, was the real motive of our purchasing them,
that spirit of tenderness being attended to, would incite us to use
them kindly, that, as strangers brought out of affliction, their lives
might be happy among us. And as they are human creatures,
whose souls are as precious as ours, and who may receive the same
help and comfort from the Holy Scriptures as we do, we could not
omit suitable endeavors to instruct them therein; but that while
we manifest by our conduct that our views in purchasing them are
to advance ourselves, and while our buying captives taken in war
animates those parties to push on the war, and increase desolation amongst them, to say they live unhappily in Africa is far from
being an argument in our favor. I further said, the present circumstances of these provinces to me appear difficult; the slaves look
like a burdensome stone to such as burden themselves with them;
and that if the white people retain a resolution to prefer their
outward prospects of gain to all other considerations, and do not
act conscientiously toward them as fellow-creatures, I believe that
burden will grow heavier and heavier, until times change in a way
disagreeable to us. The person appeared very serious, and owned
that in considering their condition and the manner of their treatment in these provinces he had sometimes thought it might be just
in the Almighty so to order it.

Having traveled through Maryland, we came amongst Friends
at Cedar Creek in Virginia, on the 12th; and the next day rode,
in company with several of them, a day's journey to Camp Creek.
As I was riding along in the morning, my mind was deeply affected in a sense I had of the need of Divine aid to support me in
the various difficulties which attended me, and in uncommon distress of mind I cried in secret to the Most High, "O Lord be merciful, I beseech thee, to thy poor afflicted creature!" After some
time, I felt inward relief, and, soon after, a Friend in company
began to talk in support of the slave-trade, and said the negroes
were understood to be the offspring of Cain, their blackness being

the mark which God set upon him after he murdered Abel his brother; that it was the design of Providence they should be slaves, as a condition proper to the race of so wicked a man as Cain was. Then another spake in support of what had been said. To all which I replied in substance as follows: that Noah and his family were all who survived the flood, according to Scripture; and as Noah was of Seth's race, the family of Cain was wholly destroyed. One of them said that after the flood Ham went to the land of Nod and took a wife; that Nod was a land far distant, inhabited by Cain's race, and that the flood did not reach it; and as Ham was sentenced to be a servant of servants to his brethren, these two families, being thus joined, were undoubtedly fit only for slaves. I replied, the flood was a judgment upon the world for their abominations, and it was granted that Cain's stock was the most wicked, and therefore unreasonable to suppose that they were spared. As to Ham's going to the land of Nod for a wife, no time being fixed, Nod might be inhabited by some of Noah's family before Ham married a second time; moreover the text saith: "That all flesh died that moved upon the earth." (Gen. vii. 21.) I further reminded them how the prophets repeatedly declare "that the son shall not suffer for the iniquity of the father, but every one be answerable for his own sins." I was troubled to perceive the darkness of their imaginations, and in some pressure of spirit said, "The love of ease and gain are the motives in general of keeping slaves, and men are wont to take hold of weak arguments to support a cause which is unreasonable. I have no interest on either side, save only the interest which I desire to have in the truth. I believe liberty is their right, and as I see they are not only deprived of it, but treated in other respects with inhumanity in many places, I believe He who is a refuge for the oppressed will, in his own time, plead their cause, and happy will it be for such as walk in uprightness before him." And thus our conversation ended.

Fourteenth of fifth month.—I was this day at Camp Creek Monthly Meeting, and then rode to the mountains up James River, and had a meeting at a Friend's house, in both of which I felt sorrow of heart, and my tears were poured out before the Lord, who was pleased to afford a degree of strength by which way was opened to clear my mind amongst Friends in those places. From thence I went to Fork Creek, and so to Cedar Creek again, at which place I now had a meeting. Here I found a tender seed, and as I was preserved in the ministry to keep low with the truth, the same truth in their hearts answered it, that it was a time of mutual refreshment from the presence of the Lord. I lodged at James Stanley's, father of William Stanley, one of the young men who suffered imprisonment at Winchester last summer on account of their testimony against fighting, and I had some satisfactory conversation with him concerning it. Hence I went to the Swamp Meeting, and to Wayanoke Meeting, and then crossed James River, and lodged near Burleigh. From the time of my entering Maryland I have been much under sorrow, which of late so increased upon me that my mind was almost overwhelmed, and I may say with the Psalmist, "In my distress I called upon the Lord, and cried to my God," who, in infinite goodness, looked upon my affliction, and in my private retirement sent the Comforter for my relief, for which I humbly bless his holy name.

The sense I had of the state of the churches brought a weight of distress upon me. The gold to me appeared dim, and the fine gold changed, and though this is the case too generally, yet the sense of it in these parts hath in a particular manner borne heavy upon me. It appeared to me that through the prevailing of the spirit of this world the minds of many were brought to an inward desolation, and instead of the spirit of meekness, gentleness, and heavenly wisdom, which are the necessary companions of the true sheep of Christ, a spirit of fierceness and the love of dominion too generally prevailed. From small beginnings in error great buildings by degrees are raised, and from one age to another are more and more strengthened by the general concurrence of the people; and as men obtain reputation by their profession of the truth, their virtues are mentioned as arguments in favor of general error; and those of less note, to justify themselves, say, such and such good men did the like. By what other steps could the people of Judah arise to that height in wickedness as to give just ground for the Prophet Isaiah to declare, in the name of the Lord, "that none calleth for justice, nor any pleadeth for truth" (Isa. lix. 4), or for the Almighty to call upon the great city of Jerusalem just before the Babylonish captivity, "If ye can find a man, if there be any who executeth judgment, that seeketh the truth, and I will pardon it"? (Jer. v. 1.)

The prospect of a way being open to the same degeneracy, in some parts of this newly settled land of America, in respect to our conduct towards the negroes, hath deeply bowed my mind in this journey, and though briefly to relate how these people are treated is no agreeable work, yet, after often reading over the notes I made as I traveled, I find my mind engaged to preserve them. Many of the white people in those provinces take little or no care of negro marriages; and when negroes marry after their own way, some make so little account of those marriages that with views of outward interest they often part men from their wives by selling them far asunder, which is common when estates are sold by executors at vendue. Many whose labor is heavy being followed at their business in the field by a man with a whip, hired for that purpose, have in common little else allowed but one peck of Indian corn and some salt, for one week, with a few potatoes; the potatoes they commonly raise by their labor on the first day of the week. The correction ensuing on their disobedience to overseers, or slothfulness in business, is often very severe, and sometimes desperate.

Men and women have many times scarcely clothes sufficient to hide their nakedness, and boys and girls ten and twelve years old are often quite naked amongst their master's children. Some of our Society, and some of the society called Newlights, use some endeavors to instruct those they have in reading; but in common this is not only neglected, but disapproved. These are the people by whose labor the other inhabitants are in a great measure supported, and many of them in the luxuries of life. These are the people who have made no agreement to serve us, and who have not forfeited their liberty that we know of. These are the souls for whom Christ died, and for our conduct towards them we must answer before Him who is no respecter of persons. They who know the only true God, and Jesus Christ whom he hath sent, and are thus acquainted with the merciful, benevolent, gospel spirit, will therein perceive that the indignation of God is kindled against oppression and cruelty, and in beholding the great distress of so numerous a people will find cause for mourning.

From my lodgings I went to Burleigh Meeting, where I felt my mind drawn in a quiet, resigned state. After long silence I felt an engagement to stand up, and through the powerful operation of Divine love we were favored with an edifying meeting. The next meeting we had was at Black Water, and from thence went to the Yearly Meeting at the Western Branch. When business began, some queries were introduced by some of their members for consideration, and, if approved, they were to be answered hereafter by their respective Monthly Meetings. They were the Pennsylvania queries, which had been examined by a committee of Virginia Yearly Meeting appointed the last year, who made some alterations in them, one of which alterations was made in favor of a custom which troubled me. The query was, "Are there any concerned in the importation of negroes, or in buying them after imported?" which was thus altered, "Are there any concerned in the importation of negroes, or buying them to trade in?" As one query admitted with unanimity was, "Are any concerned in buying or vending goods unlawfully imported, or prize goods?" I found my mind engaged to say that as we profess the truth, and were there assembled to support the testimony of it, it was necessary for us to dwell deep and act in that wisdom which is pure, or otherwise we could not prosper. I then mentioned their alteration, and referring to the last-mentioned query, added, that as purchasing any merchandise taken by the sword was always allowed to be inconsistent with our principles, so negroes being captives of war, or taken by stealth, it was inconsistent with our testimony to buy them; and their being our fellow creatures, and sold as slaves, added greatly to the iniquity. Friends appeared attentive to what was said; some expressed a care and concern about their negroes; none made any objection, by way of reply to what I said, but the query was admitted as they had altered it.

As some of their members have heretofore traded in negroes, as in other merchandise, this query being admitted will be one step further than they have hitherto gone, and I did not see it my duty to press for an alteration, but felt easy to leave it all to Him who alone is able to turn the hearts of the mighty, and make way for the spreading of truth on the earth, by means agreeable to his infinite wisdom. In regard to those they already had, I felt my mind engaged to labor with them, and said that as we believe the Scriptures were given forth by holy men, as they were moved by the Holy Ghost, and many of us know by experience that they are often helpful and comfortable, and believe ourselves bound in duty to teach our children to read them; I believed that if we were divested of all selfish views, the same good spirit that gave them forth would engage us to teach the negroes to read, that they

might have the benefit of them. Some present manifested a concern to take more care in the education of their negroes.

Twenty-ninth of fifth month.—At the house where I lodged was
a meeting of ministers and elders. I found an engagement to speak
freely and plainly to them concerning their slaves; mentioning how
they as the first rank in the society, whose conduct in that case
was much noticed by others, were under the stronger obligations
to look carefully to themselves. Expressing how needful it was
for them in that situation to be thoroughly divested of all selfish
views; that, living in the pure truth, and acting conscientiously
towards those people in their education and otherwise, they might
be instrumental in helping forward a work so exceedingly necessary, and so much neglected amongst them. At the twelfth hour
the meeting of worship began, which was a solid meeting.

The next day, about the tenth hour, Friends met to finish their
business, and then the meeting for worship ensued, which to me
was a laborious time; but through the goodness of the Lord, truth,
I believed, gained some ground, and it was a strengthening opportunity to the honest-hearted.

About this time I wrote an epistle to Friends in the back settlements of North Carolina, as follows:—

To Friends at Their Monthly Meeting at New Garden and Cane
Creek, in North Carolina:

Dear Friends,—It having pleased the Lord to draw me forth on a
visit to some parts of Virginia and Carolina, you have often been
in my mind; and though my way is not clear to come in person to
visit you, yet I feel it in my heart to communicate a few things, as
they arise in the love of truth. First, my dear friends, dwell in humility; and take heed that no views of outward gain get too deep
hold of you, that so your eyes being single to the Lord, you may be
preserved in the way of safety. Where people let loose their minds
after the love of outward things, and are more engaged in pursuing
the profits and seeking the friendships of this world than to be
inwardly acquainted with the way of true peace, they walk in a
vain shadow, while the true comfort of life is wanting. Their examples are often hurtful to others; and their treasures thus collected do many times prove dangerous snares to their children.

But where people are sincerely devoted to follow Christ, and
dwell under the influence of his Holy Spirit, their stability and

firmness, through a Divine blessing, is at times like dew on the tender plants round about them, and the weightiness of their spirits secretly works on the minds of others. In this condition, through the spreading influence of Divine love, they feel a care over the flock, and the way is opened for maintaining good order in the Society. And though we may meet with opposition from another spirit, yet, as there is a dwelling in meekness, feeling our spirits subject, and moving only in the gentle, peaceable wisdom, the inward reward of quietness will be greater than all our difficulties. Where the pure life is kept to, and meetings of discipline are held in the authority of it, we find by experience that they are comfortable, and tend to the health of the body.

While I write, the youth come fresh in my way. Dear young people, choose God for your portion; love his truth, and be not ashamed of it; choose for your company such as serve him in uprightness; and shun as most dangerous the conversation of those whose lives are of an ill savor; for by frequenting such company some hopeful young people have come to great loss, and been drawn from less evils to greater, to their utter ruin. In the bloom of youth no ornament is so lovely as that of virtue, nor any enjoyments equal to those which we partake of in fully resigning ourselves to the Divine will. These enjoyments add sweetness to all other comforts, and give true satisfaction in company and conversation, where people are mutually acquainted with it; and as your minds are thus seasoned with the truth, you will find strength to abide steadfast to the testimony of it, and be prepared for services in the church.

And now, dear friends and brethren, as you are improving a wilderness, and may be numbered amongst the first planters in one part of a province, I beseech you, in the love of Jesus Christ, wisely to consider the force of your examples, and think how much your successors may be thereby affected. It is a help in a country, yea, and a great favor and blessing, when customs first settled are agreeable to sound wisdom; but when they are otherwise the effect of them is grievous; and children feel themselves encompassed with difficulties prepared for them by their predecessors.

As moderate care and exercise, under the direction of true wisdom, are useful both to mind and body, so by these means in general the real wants of life are easily supplied, our gracious Father having so proportioned one to the other that keeping in the medium we may pass on quietly. Where slaves are purchased to do our labor numerous difficulties attend it. To rational creatures bondage is uneasy, and frequently occasions sourness and discontent in them; which affects the family and such as claim the mastery over them. Thus people and their children are many times encompassed with vexations, which arise from their applying to wrong methods to get a living.

I have been informed that there is a large number of Friends in your parts who have no slaves; and in tender and most affectionate love I beseech you to keep clear from purchasing any. Look, my dear friends, to Divine Providence, and follow in simplicity that exercise of body, that plainness and frugality, which true wisdom leads to; so may you be preserved from those dangers which attend such as are aiming at outward ease and greatness.

Treasures, though small, attained on a true principle of virtue, are sweet; and while we walk in the light of the Lord there is true comfort and satisfaction in the possession; neither the murmurs of an oppressed people, nor a throbbing, uneasy conscience, nor anxious thoughts about the events of things, hinder the enjoyment of them.

When we look towards the end of life, and think on the division of our substance among our successors, if we know that it was collected in the fear of the Lord, in honesty, in equity, and in uprightness of heart before him, we may consider it as his gift to us, and, with a single eye to his blessing, bestow it on those we leave behind us. Such is the happiness of the plain ways of true virtue. "The work of righteousness shall be peace; and the effect of righteousness, quietness and assurance forever." (Isa. xxxii. 17.)

Dwell here, my dear friends; and then in remote and solitary deserts you may find true peace and satisfaction. If the Lord be our God, in truth and reality, there is safety for us; for he is a stronghold in the day of trouble, and knoweth them that trust in him.

Isle of Wight County, in Virginia, 20th of the 5th month, 1757.

From the Yearly Meeting in Virginia I went to [North] Carolina, and on the 1st of sixth month was at Wells Monthly Meeting, where the spring of the gospel ministry was opened, and the love of Jesus Christ experienced among us; to his name be the praise.

Here my brother joined with some Friends from New Garden who were going homeward; and I went next to Symons Creek Monthly Meeting, where I was silent during the meeting for worship. When business came on, my mind was exercised concerning the poor slaves, but I did not feel my way clear to speak. In this condition I was bowed in spirit before the Lord, and with tears and inward supplication besought him so to open my understanding that I might know his will concerning me; and, at length, my mind was settled in silence. Near the end of their business a member of their meeting expressed a concern that had some time lain upon him, on account of Friends so much neglecting their duty in the education of their slaves, and proposed having meetings sometimes appointed for them on a week-day, to be attended only by some Friends to be named in their Monthly Meetings. Many present appeared to unite with the proposal. One said he had often wondered that they, being our fellow creatures, and capable of religious understanding, had been so exceedingly neglected; another expressed the like concern, and appeared zealous that in future it might be more closely considered. At length a minute was made, and the further consideration of it referred to their next Monthly Meeting. The Friend who made this proposal hath negroes; he told me that he was at New Garden, about two hundred and fifty miles from home, and came back alone; that in this solitary journey this exercise, in regard to the education of their negroes, was from time to time renewed in his mind. A Friend of some note in Virginia, who hath slaves, told me that he being far from home on a lonesome journey had many serious thoughts about them; and his mind was so impressed therewith that he believed he saw a time coming when Divine Providence would alter the circumstance of these people, respecting their condition as slaves.

From hence I went to a meeting at Newbegun Creek, and sat a considerable time in much weakness; then I felt truth open the way to speak a little in much plainness and simplicity, till at length, through the increase of Divine love amongst us, we had a seasoning opportunity. This was also the case at the head of Little River, where we had a crowded meeting on a first-day. I went thence to the Old Neck, where I was led into a careful searching out of the secret workings of the mystery of iniquity, which, under a cover of religion, exalts itself against that pure spirit which leads in the way of meekness and self-denial. Piney Woods was the last meeting I was at in Carolina; it was large, and my heart being deeply engaged, I was drawn forth into a fervent labor amongst them.

When I was at Newbegun Creek a Friend was there who labored for his living, having no negroes, and who had been a min-

ister many years. He came to me the next day, and as we rode
together, he signified that he wanted to talk with me concerning
a difficulty he had been under, which he related nearly as follows.
That as moneys had of late years been raised by a tax to carry on
the wars, he had a scruple in his mind in regard to paying it, and
chose rather to suffer distraint of his goods; but as he was the only
person who refused it in those parts, and knew not that any one
else was in the like circumstances, he signified that it had been a
heavy trial to him, especially as some of his brethren had been
uneasy with his conduct in that case. He added, that from a sympathy he felt with me yesterday in meeting, he found freedom thus
to open the matter in the way of querying concerning Friends in
our parts; I told him the state of Friends amongst us as well as I
was able, and also that I had for some time been under the like
scruple. I believed him to be one who was concerned to walk up-
rightly before the Lord, and esteemed it my duty to preserve this
note concerning him, Samuel Newby.

From hence I went back into Virginia, and had a meeting near
James Copeland's; it was a time of inward suffering, but through
the goodness of the Lord I was made content; at another meeting,
through the renewings of pure love, we had a very comfortable
season.

Traveling up and down of late, I have had renewed evidences
that to be faithful to the Lord, and content with his will concerning me, is a most necessary and useful lesson for me to be learning; looking less at the effects of my labor than at the pure motion
and reality of the concern, as it arises from heavenly love. In the
Lord Jehovah is everlasting strength; and as the mind, by humble
resignation, is united to Him, and we utter words from an inward
knowledge that they arise from the heavenly spring, though our
way may be difficult, and it may require close attention to keep in
it, and though the manner in which we may be led may tend to
our own abasement; yet, if we continue in patience and meekness,
heavenly peace will be the reward of our labors.

I attended Curles Meeting, which, though small, was reviving
to the honest-hearted. Afterwards I went to Black Creek and Car-
oline Meetings, from whence, accompanied by William Stanley
before mentioned, I rode to Goose Creek, being much through the
woods, and about one hundred miles. We lodged the first night
at a public house; the second in the woods; and the next day we

reached a Friend's house at Goose Creek. In the woods we were under some disadvantage, having no fire-works nor bells for our horses, but we stopped a little before night and let them feed on the wild grass, which was plentiful, in the mean time cutting with our knives a store against night. We then secured our horses, and gathering some bushes under an oak we lay down; but the mosquitoes being numerous and the ground damp I slept but little. Thus lying in the wilderness, and looking at the stars, I was led to contemplate on the condition of our first parents when they were sent forth from the garden; how the Almighty, though they had been disobedient, continued to be a father to them, and showed them what tended to their felicity as intelligent creatures, and was acceptable to him. To provide things relative to our outward living, in the way of true wisdom, is good, and the gift of improving in things useful is a good gift, and comes from the Father of Lights. Many have had this gift; and from age to age there have been improvements of this kind made in the world. But some, not keeping to the pure gift, have in the creaturely cunning and self-exaltation sought out many inventions. As the first motive to these inventions of men, as distinct from that uprightness in which man was created, was evil, so the effects have been and are evil. It is, therefore, as necessary for us at this day constantly to attend on the heavenly gift, to be qualified to use rightly the good things in this life amidst great improvements, as it was for our first parents when they were without any improvements, without any friend or father but God only.

I was at a meeting at Goose Creek, and next at a Monthly Meeting at Fairfax, where, through the gracious dealing of the Almighty with us, his power prevailed over many hearts. From thence I went to Monoquacy and Pipe Creek in Maryland; at both places I had cause humbly to adore Him who had supported me through many exercises, and by whose help I was enabled to reach the true witness in the hearts of others. There were some hopeful young people in those parts. I had meetings afterwards at John Everett's, in Monalen, and at Huntingdon, and I was made humbly thankful to the Lord, who opened my heart amongst the people in these new settlements, so that it was a time of encouragement to the honest-minded.

At Monalen a Friend gave me some account of a religious society among the Dutch, called Mennonites, and amongst other things related a passage in substance as follows: One of the Mennonites having acquaintance with a man of another society at a considerable distance, and being with his wagon on business near the house of his said acquaintance, and night coming on, he had thoughts of putting up with him, but passing by his fields, and observing the distressed appearance of his slaves, he kindled a fire in the woods hard by, and lay there that night. His said acquaintance hearing where he lodged, and afterward meeting the Mennonite, told him of it, adding he should have been heartily welcome at his house, and from their acquaintance in former time wondered at his conduct in that case. The Mennonite replied, "Ever since I lodged by thy field I have wanted an opportunity to speak with thee. I had intended to come to thy house for entertainment, but seeing thy slaves at their work, and observing the manner of their dress, I had no liking to come to partake with thee." He then admonished him to use them with more humanity, and added, "As I lay by the fire that night, I thought that as I was a man of substance thou wouldst have received me freely; but if I had been as poor as one of thy slaves, and had no power to help myself, I should have received from thy hand no kinder usage than they."

In this journey I was out about two months, and traveled about eleven hundred and fifty miles. I returned home under an humbling sense of the gracious dealings of the Lord with me, in preserving me through many trials and afflictions.

SARAH GRUBB

One of the most admired ministers of this era, based on the reprinting of her Journal, *was Sarah (Tuke) Grubb (1756–1790), a Yorkshire Friend. In this passage, she describes her travels in 1786, exemplifying the Quietist concern that she never act in her own will.*

Some Account of the Life and Religious Labours of Sarah Grubb
(Wilmington, Del., 1795).

After my return from Ireland, my beloved companion R[ebecca]. J[ones], being detained in Yorkshire, on divers accounts, for three months, I was thereby set at liberty to adjust some family concerns at home, and pay some visits to neighbouring meetings, as Truth appeared to open the way; especially to Whitby, Scarborough, Bridlington, Hornsea, and Hull; in the course of which my mind was, in the needful time, mercifully supported with renewed supplies of holy help, though, in general, in a low and stripped state; fearing lest, in the exercise of the gift, a zeal which is not according to true knowledge, nor originating in that baptism of spirit wherein the creature is humbled, should so mix with the Divine openings, as to carry away the feet of the mind from that safe standing in the deeps, which is justly compared to the bottom of Jordan. Here it is necessary for true Gospel ministers, steadily to abide with the weight of the service they are engaged in upon their shoulders, till the spirits of the assembled are in some degree attracted to the promised land, the new heaven and the new earth, wherein dwelleth the righteousness of faith, and where spiritual worship is rightly performed, in the beauty of holiness and newness of life. To be instrumental in the Divine hand of thus, in any measure, converting the spirits of those to whom we may be led to minister, requires an unction altogether unmixed; but when revolt, backsliding, and a superficial spirit, have been necessarily unveiled, I have sometimes distressingly found, that some of my armour was carnal; and O! how hath all that was within me been humbled at the discovery, that the Lord's righteous controversy with the works of darkness, had not been righteously upheld, nor the door of escape therefrom wisely opened. An increase of experience convinces me that preaching is a mystery which every one exercised therein, has need to be often industriously and impartially learning, as far as concerns themselves; and where this is the case, I am abundantly persuaded that our dependence must be drawn from the sentiments of those friends to whose judgment we are most attached, in order rightly to distinguish betwixt the unity of the one infallible spirit, and their partiality to us, and to be weighed in the just balance of the sanctuary, where we are sometimes found defective, even when all around us speak peace.

My dear husband accompanied me in this little round; his sympathizing mind and care for my preservation every way, was truly strengthening, and afforded frequent occasions of humble thankfulness to the Author of all good, who had so bountifully provided for me, both in spiritual and temporal things. After our return home we gave up housekeeping, not with a conclusion that we should remove from England, but under an apprehension that it was right to take that step, as the way opened for my being again united in service with my beloved companion R. J., and my husband had no prospect of being settled during my absence. We therefore removed our furniture, and ourselves to York, the quarterly meeting there being at hand; after which, the 1st of 4th month, 1786, I went to Ackworth [School]* to meet my companion who had gone there the day before. We staid there on first day, and found some close and necessary labour, not only in public but in private opportunities amongst the masters, mistresses, and servants, severally; for the Enemy of all good hath proved himself busy, in endeavouring to sow his tares amongst the good seed in that institution and family; and unless those on whom the weight and care of it most devolves, keep in view the necessity of attending more to the holy Oracle in their movements, than to the strength of their own wisdom and understanding, it will lose the luster that Truth would put upon it and become the nursery of a worldly spirit, though disguised with an appearance of religious form. There is in that family a suffering, wrestling seed, an exercised remnant, which though small, is a means under the Divine blessing, of keeping open the spring of life; and if such keep their places, there is reason to hope that more will be added to their number, and through the influence of their example, the truth, in its own simplicity, gain ground, instead of the disguised spirit of error. A salutation of love flowed to such under a sense whereof we left them, save our worthy friend W. S. who went with us to Wakefield, where divers are under convincement, and some of them appear to be rightly so. Here we had an open, instructive opportunity; and from thence went to Bradford, and next day proceeded to Manchester, where we attended their weekday meeting; in which my companion was greatly favoured to dip into the state of the seed and profitably to visit it, and silence was, I believe rightly, my lot.

From Manchester we went to Stockport, Macclesfield, Morley, and so to Warrington, to the monthly meeting there; where again I thought my companion had eminent service, and close searching labour, wherewith I felt a spiritual travail, and sympathetic mourn-

---

* [Ackworth was a Quaker school, opened in 1779. —ed.]

ing over the great carnality, and departure from the way of peace, which greatly prevail in that, and the neighbouring places. Though there is a peculiar people, and a royal priesthood, in that monthly meeting, yet as the number in a very different spirit, is great, the pure life is prevented from circulating and purifying the temple. So that the prospect, amongst the youth especially, is exceedingly discouraging; dissipation, or the gilded corruptions of human nature, having possession, and, like the strong man armed, keeping the house and all the goods thereof in peace; and till a stronger than he, by the spirit of judgment and of burning, dislodges him of his hold, casts him out, and spoils all his goods, there is but little room to expect such to demonstrate unto others, by the liveliness of their spirits, the circumspection of their conduct, and a rightly seasoned conversation, that they are acquainted with the efficacious virtue of true religion. From Warrington, my husband returned to Yorkshire, in company with William Rotch, of Nantucket, and we back into Cheshire. It was rather a gloomy parting to me, being very unwell with a rheumatic complaint in my head, and more depressed in mind than I was free to express to any; which is often the case with me, when under a sense of the awfulness of the work I am embarked in, of the little effect it has on the minds of many, and of my own exceeding great weakness, and apparent unfitness for engaging with sacred things; so that my way oft seems to lie by the valley and shadow of death; where I feel myself subject to fearful apprehensions, and a deep and gloomy exercise. Nevertheless, to the praise of the Divine grace, my soul can thankfully and humbly acknowledge that, through what appeared the smallest grain of faith, preservation hath been experienced, and strength to ascend, in the Lord's time, that holy mountain where nothing can hurt or destroy; because the creature, and its attendant evils are subjected, and access to the feast of fat things, and of wine well refined, is graciously afforded, to the renewed support of the drooping mind, which was ready, but a little before, to cast away its confidence, and say, "the Lord hath forgotten me." Thus, as by a tender father, are we dealt with, under those proving dispensations, which are essentially necessary for carrying forward the work of sanctification in the soul, and a preparation to receive the inscription of "Holiness unto the Lord." When I consider the necessity hereof, a fear, on the other hand, often arises lest it should be partially or superficially effected; and a fervent craving of Spirit, that the refining operations of the Holy Ghost and fire, may so perform their assigned office, as that every specious appearance of self-love may be consumed, and the spring of action, in the performance of both religious and moral duties, rendered pure. Thus variously is the attention of the travailing soul turned; and if the pure discoveries of truth are but the object singly sought for, He who created light out of darkness, and hath sown it for the righteous, doth, in times of our greatest extremity, reveal himself to be the Lord Almighty. From Warrington we went to Sutton, Franley, Newton, Chester, Nantwich, and Middlewich, when our visit to Cheshire seemed ended, where, as in other places, we had to view, and mourn over the desolation which hath prevailed amongst the professors of Truth; so that the Heathen may query, "Where is their God?"

DREAMS AND VISIONS

SAMUEL FOTHERGILL

Eighteenth-century Friends gave considerable attention to dreams and visions, which they considered visitations of particular favor from God. Many Friends recorded such experiences. John Fothergill (1715–1772) was an English minister and one of the most influential members of London Yearly Meeting in the mid-eighteenth century. John Beals (1717–1796) was an otherwise obscure Friend, born in Pennsylvania, who joined the movement of Friends south into what would become Guilford County, North Carolina, in the 1750s. Joseph Hoag (1761–1846) was a minister of New York Yearly Meeting. His vision was widely circulated by Friends in the era of the Civil War.

George Crosfield, *Memoirs of the Life and Gospel Labours of Samuel Fothergill, with Selections from His Correspondence* (Liverpool, 1843).

Samuel Fothergill to Gilbert Thompson.

WARRINGTON, 6TH MO., 29TH, 1760.

Dear Cousin,

I believe I should be out of the way of my duty, if I did not impart to thee and thy sisters a dream or vision that was represented to me the last night, and perhaps the interpretation of it may be brought home to your own hearts.

I thought the great day of account was come, and all nations gathered to receive the irreversible sentence; I beheld a variety of states, and many clothed in different colours, many in white, which, nevertheless, was of different degrees of lustre and beauty. I saw many whom I knew, and amongst others thyself and sisters; I thought your garments appeared more white than many; and whilst I mused on the tremendous, yet glorious day, the trumpet sounded with a distinguishing energy, and seemed to say, Come, ye blessed. I beheld multitudes arise, as from the eminence of a mountain, and ascend triumphantly. My eye descended to the mountain whence many had risen, and in whose company I had seen thee and thy sisters. I thought I clearly saw you remain on the earth, clothed in garments measurably white. I queried in my heart, alas! how happens it that these are left behind? Immediately the white garments fell off, and each of you appeared in the common dress in which you usually appear. But I beheld chains which seemed fastened about your necks, and bound every limb and part of the body but the head, and these chains were fastened to great rings in the earth, and held you so fast as to prevent any of you ascending to those who had taken wing and risen on high. Here I awaked in great concern of mind, and found an engagement to impart it immediately to thyself and sisters; none other knows the least tittle of it, nor shall, from your most affectionate

S. F.

JOHN BEALS

"A Vision of John Beals," ca. 1796
(Friends Historical Collection, Guilford College, Greensboro, N.C.).

A remarkable account related by John Beals a little before his death to a friend at the close of a religious opportunity in the family to the following.

Impor't having had a fit of sickness but then on the recovery tho very weak he desired his family one evening to retire to rest sooner than usual all disposition to sleep being taken away his wife lying

beside him on a sudden the door of his room opening a person
drew to his bed side clothed in white raiment and bade him to arise
and follow him which he did they went out of the room together
and ascended up through the air and was brought by his guide to
heaven and placed before the greate being who was seated on a
bright throne of glory and his guide disappeared the divine being
looking upon him enquired how he came there to which he replied
that a person in white rament came to him and conducted him
thither and calling the guide who had conducted him to this glorious place he bade him to take him and show him the glory of the
saints which when he beheld his heart was over come with joy and
he was desirious of remaining there forever but was informed that
he must go back again to the world and remain for two days and
a half and if he spent his time in faithfulness he should return at
the accomplishment there of and have his inheritance amounge the
saints whom he beheld forever, then said he to the guide take him
where he may have a fragrent smell. He was accordingly conducted
to a place where a door opened out of which came the most de-
lightful odour he had ever before experienced and he was soon
filled there with and afterwords brought back by his guide to his
chamber and the bed where he lay and remarked that this fragrant
smell remained in his nostrells for many days and that he recovered very fast afterwards from his sichness and apprehended it
might not be long till the season was accomplished when even the
two days and a half which was alotted and if preserved to the end
he trusted what he had seen would be fulfilled

JOSEPH HOAG

*Journal of the Life of Joseph Hoag, an Eminent
Minister of the Gospel in the Society of Friends*
(Auburn, N.Y., 1861).

In the year 1803, probably in the eighth or ninth month, I was one
day alone in the fields, and observed that the sun shone clear, but
that a mist eclipsed the brightness of its shining.

As I reflected upon the singularity of the event, my mind was
struck into a silence, the most solemn I ever remember to have

witnessed, for it seemed as if all my faculties were laid low, and unusually brought into deep silence. I said to myself, "what can all this mean? I do not recollect ever before to have been sensible of such feelings." And I heard a voice from heaven say, "This that thou seest, which dims the brightness of the sun, is a sign of the present and coming times. I took the forefathers of this country from a land of oppression; I planted them here among the people of the forest. I sustained them, and while they were humble, I blessed them and fed them, and they became a numerous people: but they have now become proud and lifted up, and have forgotten Me, who nourished and protected them in the wilderness, and are running into every abomination and evil practice of which the old countries are guilty; and I have taken quietude from the land, and suffered a dividing spirit to come among them. Lift up thine eyes and behold." And I saw them dividing in great heat. This division began in the Church upon points of doctrine. It commenced in the Presbyterian Society, and went through the various religious denominations, and in its progress and close, the effect was nearly the same; those who dissented, went off with high heads and taunting language; and those who kept to their organized sentiments, appeared exercised and sorrowful. And when this dividing spirit entered the Society of Friends, it raged in as high a degree as any I had before discovered, and as before, those who separated, went with lofty looks and taunting, censuring language; those who kept to their ancient principles, retired by themselves.

It next appeared in the Lodges of the Free Masons, and it broke out in appearance like a volcano, inasmuch as it set the country in an uproar for a length of time. Then it entered politics throughout the United States, and did not stop, until it produced a civil war, and an abundance of human blood was shed in the course of the combat. The Southern States lost their power, and Slavery was annihilated from their borders. Then a Monarchical power arose—took the Government of the States—established a national religion, and made all Societies tributary to support its expenses. I saw them take property from Friends to a large amount. I was amazed at beholding all this, and heard a voice proclaim, "this Power shall not always stand, but with this Power I will chastise my Church until they return to the faithfulness of their forefathers. Thou seest what is coming on thy native land for their iniquity, and the blood of Africa; the remembrance of which has come up before me. This Vision is yet for many days."

I had no idea of writing it down for many years, until it became such a burden, that for my own relief I have written it.

JOSEPH HOAG.

A GOOD DEATH

MARY TURNER

Almost from the beginning of the Quaker movement, Friends recorded accounts of the deaths of pious Friends, giving particular attention to their last words and deathbed testimonies. To hope for a death that foretold everlasting bliss was common to all denominations, but Friends were unique in collecting and reading what amounted to collections of obituaries. This account of Mary Turner is longer than most, but typical in its themes.

John Tomkins and John Field, comps., *Piety Promoted, in a Collection of Dying Sayings of Many of the People Called Quakers. With Some Memorials of Their Virtuous Lives and Patient Sufferings* (Dublin, 1721).

Mary Turner, the wife of John Turner, at Tottenham High Cross, in the county of Middlesex, was the third daughter of that remarkable sufferer for the testimony of a good conscience, Richard Vickris, of Chew-Magna, in Somersetshire, deceased, and Elizabeth his wife, daughter to that ancient worthy, George Bishop, of Bristol. In her tender years, by the grace of God, through the care of her religious parents, she was instructed in, and seasoned with the principles of the holy truth, as professed by the people called Quakers; in which she continued faithful, and was an example of piety and virtue through the course of her life.

When a little child, our much esteemed friend William Penn coming in at her father's, where he was very conversant, and affected with her pretty innocent deportment, broke forth, extempore, thus:

Sweet soul! what makes thee stray
From the angelic way?
Was it to teach us how to love
The happy regions above?
If so, O! let thy wand'ring prove our gain,
And take us with thee back again.

She was naturally of a lively and cheerful temper, which remained when she came to years of discretion, yet took pleasure
in frequent retirement, and divine meditation, in meetings for worship, and religious conversation, and received worthy public Friends
with great comfort and satisfaction. When at home alone, she entertained herself chiefly in reading the Holy Scriptures, Friends'
writings, and the three first books of Thomas à Kempis, on the
Imitation of Christ; at other times with her pen and needle; for it
was rare to find her unemployed in something useful or necessary,
when her health permitted. In her dress and apparel she was very
neat and plain. The tenderness of her love and affection to her
husband, mother, brother and sisters, was more than common, and
very remarkable, and likewise so generally extended to her acquaintance, especially where truth had a prevalency, that it may be
said, love predominated in her.

A few years before her death, she was sensible of a gradual
decay of bodily strength, and when weakness and faintness prevailed, she bore it with much patience and resignation to God's
holy will. In a sense of the uncertainty of the comforts here below,
she wrote thus to a near friend:

"The enjoyments of this life appear very changeable, and we
are apt to seek them more than is good for us, which hinders our
inward comfort: so we have something to war against every day.
I desire thou mayest be directed by that divine hand which orders
all things for our good every way, as we have an eye to it."

And in another to a relation: "I am very sensible of my happiness, and desire to walk worthy of the mercies I enjoy; yet the want
of my health has been an affliction to me: but I do not repine at
that, since it is an advantage to us to have some alloy to the comforts of this life, which are mostly attended with disappointments
of one kind or other."

On her bed of sickness she said to her brother, she admired
people should so much place their affections on the things of this

world, which are but as dross, and like travelling in misery; and earnestly desired their family might, with Jacob, obtain a blessing; and as they had such worthy parents, who had educated them in the ways of truth, and enjoyed so many favours beyond many others, there ought to be a double thankfulness to the giver. She desired her brother to be a comfort to their tender mother, and to keep up their honourable father's name, as one of the branches of the family, and then there would be a blessing laid up for him.

Speaking to her sisters, she said, "We should be good examples in the plainness of our habits, as we make profession of the principle of truth, and should take up the cross daily; for we were not born to serve ourselves, but to honour the Lord. That pain and weakness were hard to bear; and when we are going out of the world, we had need to have nothing then to do: that she waited for the presence of the Lord, in which was more pleasure than in all the joys of this world." Then turning to one of them said, "The Lord hath done great things for thee, and may have a work for thee to do; there is good seed sown in thy heart, and I desire the Lord will bless thee."

Having been tendered in her spirit, some friends came to visit her, and prayed with her; whereupon she said, she saw the Lord had not forsaken her, but sent his servants to visit her, which was a great comfort to her.

Another time one of her sisters coming into the room, "O sister," said she, "the old accuser of the brethren lies very near, but the Lord's hand is underneath, and sweetly supports."

Some days after, the same sister being by her bedside, she had an extraordinary concern for her own welfare and her near relations, saying, "Dear sister, I have a steadfast hope, but not yet a full assurance. I desire thee, pray earnestly for me, lest there should be anything committed by me, that may have slipped out of my remembrance, and I not be earnest enough with the Lord for forgiveness. I also pray earnestly for you all, that you may come where I hope to be; and for my dear husband likewise": and expressed her great care, that not one of the family might be lost.

Another of her sisters, leaving her a little time, desired the Lord would support her under her weakness, she answered, "He hath, and I believe will"; and seemed comfortably resigned in her spirit.

A few hours before her departure she desired to be raised in her bed, on which she seemed as if she should pass away, and bade all farewell; but reviving, said, "I thought I had been going, but the Lord hath given me life from the pangs of death, praised be his name: oh! praises be to the Lord, he hath given me a little ease."

Her fear was so great of offending the Lord, that perceiving some disposition to slumber, she said to her mother, then near her, "Dost think he will be angry if I should drop asleep?"

Some time after, being moved again, she seemed refreshed, and lay in a sweet frame of mind, praising the Lord, saying, "Lord, thou art merciful, compassionate and true. Thou hast given me ease: oh! I will praise thy name at all times, from time to time; every hour, every minute while I live I will praise thee." Being in great pain, she said to some that were near her, "He will give me ease by and by"; and earnestly prayed to the Lord for it after this manner: "Dear Lord, give me ease: sweet Lord Jesus, give me ease"; and then said to her sister, he would. Her sister said, she did not doubt but the Lord would answer her desire, and give her a full assurance; to which she answered, "I believe he will." Then she desired those by her to pray for her.

Having slumbered a little, she awoke refreshed, and looking on one of her sisters, she said to her, "Dear sister, I shall do well, I shall do well." After which she was heard very sweetly in prayer to the Lord to receive her; and was sensible to the last.

Toward the conclusion of her days, her weakness was attended with such faintness and pain, sometimes, that it made her apprehensive it would be very hard to bear the struggles of her final dissolution, which she frequently begged of the Lord to make easy; and he was pleased to answer her desires accordingly; for she passed hence almost without sigh, groan, or any visible alteration of countenance.

She departed this life at Tottenham aforesaid, on the 31st of the Sixth month, 1711, and was decently interred in Friends' burying-ground in Bunhill-fields, at London, on the 5th day of the Seventh month following, about the thirty-third year of her age.

PART IV

CREATIVITY AND CONTROVERSY

1820–1870

THREE VISIONS OF
FAITH

ELIAS HICKS

*Between 1825 and 1850, Quakers split into three broad fac-
tions, each taking the name of the minister who was perceived
as its leader and chief advocate. Elias Hicks (1748–1830) was
a minister from Long Island whose views on the divinity
of Christ and authority of the Bible seemed to many Friends
simply to be restatements of historic Quaker doctrine. One
of Hicks's clearest articulations of such views came in a letter,
widely circulated, to fellow Long Island Friend Phebe Willis
in 1819. Many other Friends, in both North America and the
British Isles, found Hicks's views heterodox, indeed, smack-
ing of infidelity. These opponents became known as Orthodox Friends. Controversy became so heated that it brought
separations in most American yearly meetings in the 1820s.
Just why so many Friends found Hicks's views horrifying can
be seen in the writings of Joseph John Gurney (1788–1847),
from the 1820s until his death the best-known minister in
London Yearly Meeting. Gurney articulates a faith indistin-
guishable from that of other evangelicals. Gurney's teachings,
in turn, found critics among other Orthodox Friends. Of
these the best known was John Wilbur (1774–1856), a minister from Rhode Island. His letter to two fellow New England
Friends gives a clear sense of how uneasy some Orthodox
Friends were with the direction of Quakerism after 1840.*

Letters of Elias Hicks. Including Also a Few
Short Essays, Written on Several Occasions,
Mostly Illustrative of His Doctrinal Views
(New York, 1834).

To Phebe Willis.

JERICHO, 5TH MO. 19TH, 1818.

Dear Friend,

Thy acceptable epistle I have perused, and believing it to be the product of real friendship, it was gratefully received, and the language it utters would, not many years since, have been my own. But having for a considerable time past found from full conviction, that there is scarcely any thing so baneful to the present and future happiness and welfare of mankind, as a submission to tradition and popular opinion, I have therefore been led to see the necessity of investigating for myself all customs and doctrines, whether of a moral or of a religious nature, either verbally or historically communicated, by the greatest and best of men or angels, and not to sit down satisfied with any thing but the plain, clear, demonstrative testimony of the spirit and word of life and light in my own heart and conscience; and which has led me to see how very far all the professors of Christianity are from the real spirit and substance of the Gospel. And among other subjects, I have been led, I trust, carefully and candidly, to investigate the effects produced by the book called the Scriptures since it has borne that appellation; and it appears, from a comparative view, to have been the cause of four-fold more harm than good to Christendom, since the apostles' days, and which, I think, must be indubitably plain to every faithful, honest mind, that has investigated her history free from the undue bias of education and tradition. Mark the beginning of the apostacy. When the professors of Christianity began to quarrel with and separate from each other, it all sprang from their different views and different interpretations of passages of Scripture, and to such a pitch did their quarrels arise, as that a recurrence to the sword was soon deemed necessary to settle those disputes. And the strongest party in that line, finding that as long as the people were at liberty, and had the privilege of searching the Scriptures and putting their own interpretations upon them, and making them their rule, diversity of opinion and differences would increase, this led the strongest party to that disagreeable and unchristian alternative of wresting them out of their hands and forbidding their being read by the people at large. And this state of things continued for many years, until the beginning of reformation by Martin Luther.

It will be now necessary to consider, whether the Scriptures were in any wise accessary to this infant beginning of reformation? I think it is clear they were not; but as Luther and his adherents gained strength, they began to shake off the yoke of papal oppression, and, among other things, the restriction on the Scriptures was taken off, and every citizen that joined Luther's party, had the privilege of reading the Scriptures at his pleasure. And what was the result? A diversity of sentiment, respecting what they taught, which soon set the reformers one against another, and produced such divisions and animosities among them, that recourse was again had to the sword to settle disputes. In this condition things continued until George Fox was raised up to bear testimony to the light and spirit of truth in the hearts and consciences of men and women, as the only sure rule of faith and practice, both in relation to religious and moral things, and which was complete and sufficient, without the aid of books or men, as his doctrine and example clearly evinces; as his reformation was begun and carried on without the necessary aid of either. But, as the professors of Christianity then held the Scriptures, or their interpretations of them, as their chief idol, and [as] such was their veneration for them, that for anyone to hold up any thing else as a rule, he was immediately pronounced a heretic or schismatic, and not fit to company or associate with in any way, this led George and his friends to show, that their doctrines were in nowise derogatory to those written by those who were inspired by the same spirit in former days. And all goes to prove, that every step of reformation from the fall, in every age of the world, has been begun and best carried on when the reformers kept close to the leading and inspiration of the spirit of truth, and suffered nothing, whether books or men, to turn them aside from their ever-present and ever-blessed sure guide; seeing they have the Anointing to be their teacher, and the Spiritual Lamb to be their light.

And, I conceive, every man and woman, who has a right understanding and correct ideas of the Divine character, must have the same views; for otherwise they must contradict their own professions, as every one who believes in the existence of God, attributes to him justice, mercy, and love, and that he is unchangeable in his nature, and incapable of partiality; hence he must, and no doubt has, given to every man and woman, a complete and sufficient rule of faith and practice, without the aid of books or men; and hath so ordered in the course of events, that the more strictly and faithfully every man and woman lives up to the guidance and teaching of this inward anointing, and never turns aside to the right hand or to the left, for the precepts and traditions of men, the more instruction and help they afford one another. And to suppose a written rule to be necessary, or much useful, is to impeach the Divine character, and charge the infinite Jehovah with partiality and injustice, as the greater part of his rational creation have never been furnished with those means. And had they been needful, he certainly would, in order to deal with an even hand of justice, have furnished all his rational creatures with them; as it was equally in his power so to have done from the beginning. But as man's fall principally consists in his turning from his inward spiritual guide, to the direction of his outward senses and animal passions and affections, so [man having so far departed] that he lost almost all right knowledge of this inward guide, the Lord in mercy dispensed to him divers outward manifestations, as a means to lead his attention back to his spiritual guide; and these means have always been suited to the states of those to whom they were dispensed, and therefore often very different to different nations and people. To the family of Abraham he dispensed a very peculiar system of rituals and outward shadows, to which he required obedience, in order to bring them back to a submission to his will, as manifested by his Spirit in their hearts. But he dispensed them to no other people but to Israel, and those that came of their own accord and joined them; and as soon as the effect was produced by bringing them back to their inward guide, all those outward means became obsolete and useless. So likewise he made use of the ministry of Jesus Christ and his apostles for the same end, to turn from darkness to the inward light, and when that was effected, their ministry had done all it could do, and to such, as they continued to walk in the light, their doctrine became obsolete and useless. And so in every age where any real reformation has been produced, it has always been by instruments newly raised up, by the immediate operation of the spirit. And where any people have depended upon what has been written to former generations, such make no advancement, but just sit down in the labours of their forefathers, and soon become dry and formal, and fall behind those they are copying after or propose to follow.

This is very manifestly the case with our Society, although so highly favoured with almost every possible means to gather them from all outwards, to their true inward teacher, who teaches as never man taught—nothing but the truth. And this is the cause why many turn from him, to the teachings of men or books, because they can mostly turn their teachings to suit their own ends; hence plain truth is disagreeable to them, but teachings that they can interpret to suit their own inclinations, as most men do the Scriptures, these they cry up and speak highly of. And such as these cause all the animosities and divisions in Christendom, and from hence most of their quarrels and wars have arisen. And there is great cause to fear, that if those in our Society, who are united with those among others, in very improperly setting up the Scriptures above their true value, are adhered to, they will finally divide and scatter us, as they have all other professors of Christianity. For considerable disputes have already arisen concerning passages of the first importance. I will mention one wherein the very leaders are divided. And surely if it is so wrapt up in mystery that we cannot understand it alike, how much better should we be without it. It is Peter's testimony concerning the more sure word of prophecy, which many of those considered as the most wise and learned amongst us, tell us is the Scriptures. And should I be by these convinced that Peter really meant the Scriptures, it would, to me, render all his writings as unworthy much attention. And I have no kind of doubt if Friends generally, of the foremost ranks, should honestly and plainly speak their sentiments on the Scriptures in general, so great would be their diversity of prospects, that little help or edification, in a society capacity, could be derived from them, and it is altogether reasonable it should be so in the dispensings of a wise Providence, seeing, as we have the Scriptures at our command, that if there was sufficiency in them to point the way to Heaven, we might then by our own strength and labour arrive at that happy place and outstrip the sons of Noah. But the all-wise Jehovah, who hath declared that he will not give his glory to another, nor his praise to graven images, hath also decreed, that should all the various professors of Christianity associate and bind themselves together, by the strongest ties that lie within the reach of human contrivance, to circulate the Scriptures in their own will and wisdom, or pursue any other means or method to promote the spiritual interest of immortal souls, it will all prove abortive, and confusion of language, if not in a natural, yet in a spiritual sense, will be their portion: for, in my view, there has no event transpired since the building of the Babel Tower, on Shinar's plain, that is so fully representative thereof, as the multiplied Bible societies of the present day.

But my views respecting the Scriptures are not altered, although thus abused by others, and trust I shall, as I heretofore have done, as my mind is opened to it, call upon them as evidence to the truth of inspiration; and to show that the upright and faithful in former ages, were led and instructed by the same spirit as those in the present day; and that the Lord is graciously willing to reveal himself as fully to the children of men in this day as in any day of the world, without respect of persons, as each is attentive to his inward and spiritual manifestations. And how much more reasonable it is to suppose, that an inspired teacher in the present day, should be led to speak more truly and plainly to the states of the people, to whom he is led to communicate, than any doctrines that were delivered one thousand seven hundred years ago to a people very differently circumstanced to those in this day, I leave to every rational mind to judge. And that the doctrines of George Fox and our primitive Friends, should be easier understood, and plainer, being written in our own language, than the doctrines of the primitive Christians, appears very reasonable. But we are all, or have been, so bound down by tradition, being taught from the cradle to venerate the Scriptures, and people generally considering them so sacred as not to be investigated, but bound to receive them as we have been taught; hence we have all been more or less, dupes to tradition and error. I well remember how oft my conscience has smitten me when I have been endeavouring to support the society's belief of the Scriptures, that they so very far excelled all other writings, that the fear of man had too great a share in leading me to adopt the sentiment, and custom rendered it more easy, but I never was clear in my own mind as to that point; and had I carefully attended to my own feelings, I should have been preserved, I believe, in a line of more consistency in that respect.

And I may now acknowledge to thee, that I never expressed my own genuine feelings and prospects so clearly, and so much to the peace of my own mind, as in our last quarterly meeting; and indeed such was the view I had, and the clearness of the opening, that I apprehended there could not have been a rational mind present, acquainted with the subjects of my communication, but would have assented thereto. Much more might be said in proof of the foregoing, but my time and leisure will not reasonably admit me to proceed further. *And what I have written has been done in scraps of time, that I have as it were stolen from my other many avocations, without any time to copy it, or give it much examination; therefore, I hope thou wilt excuse the improprieties that may have escaped my notice, believing that thou wilt be able to apprehend the main drift of the arguments, and be willing to put the best construction on such parts as may, to thee, appear erroneous.* Thy assured friend.

ELIAS HICKS

JOSEPH JOHN GURNEY

Joseph John Gurney, *A Letter to a Friend on the Authority, Purpose, and Effects of Christianity, and Especially on the Doctrine of Redemption* (London, 1835).

The mercy of God in Christ Jesus is a subject which I have long been accustomed to regard as superior to all others, in point of interest and importance. Conscious, in some degree, of the perfect purity of an omnipresent Deity, as well as of the corruption of my own heart, I rejoice in the assurance that means are provided through which the stain of my sins may be washed out, and through which I may be accepted with favour by the Author of all true happiness. Nor is it wonderful that I should entertain, for others whom I love, an earnest, and even painful solicitude, that they also may be brought to the discovery of this way of escape, and may come to acknowledge Jesus Christ, the Lord of glory, to be "the propitiation for their sins"—their "resurrection" and their "life." . . .

Let it be observed, in the first place, that Christianity is to be received, not as a moral science of human invention, but as a religion revealed to mankind by the Creator himself, and promulgated upon his authority. In reference to this primary position, there are a few particulars of evidence, to which it may be desirable for us shortly to advert.

I. That the principal writings of which the New Testament consists are genuine—that they were written in the apostolic age, and by the individuals with whose names they are inscribed—is a point evinced to be true by a greater variety and quantity of evidence, than has probably ever been brought to bear on a similar subject. . . . Nor can we with any reason question the general correctness of the text of the New Testament; for although the early multiplication of copies naturally gave rise to many unimportant various readings, it obviously afforded an ample check upon any willful alteration of the common record. In the numerous manuscripts of the Greek Testament now existing, some of which are of very considerable antiquity, in the early versions, and in the quotations made by the ancient fathers, modern critics have found sufficient criteria for the settlement of the sacred text; and the result of their indefatigable enquiries is this—that the New Testament, as Christians for several centuries past have been accustomed to read it, continues unimpaired—that it has not been deprived of a single article of faith, a single historical narration, or a single moral precept.

II. It being a well-established point, that the writings, of which the New Testament consists, are the genuine work of the evangelists and apostles, we may, in the next place, observe that the history, related in those writings, is credible and true. In support of this proposition, it might be almost sufficient to remark, that the gospels were composed by four honest, simple, and independent writers; two of whom were apostles, and eye-witnesses of the facts which they relate, and the other two, companions of apostles, and in full possession of the sources of exact information. With regard to the book of Acts, the truth of the history contained in it is evinced in a highly satisfactory manner, . . . by a variety of incidental accordances between that book and the epistles of Paul. . . .

III. It appears, in the third place, to be a clear and undeniable position, that the actual knowledge of the future is an attribute peculiar to the Divine Being. No one, who admits the existence of the one God, will refuse to allow that, in point of both knowledge and power, he is placed at an infinite distance above all his creatures—that, while he regulates the course of events according to his own will, none of those creatures are his counselors, and none of them are capable of penetrating his secret designs and intentions. From these premises, it follows that all prophecies, which, by their exact fulfillment, are proved to have proceeded, not from intellectual sagacity and human conjecture, but from actual fore-knowledge, must have been inspired, or dictated by the Almighty himself; and further, that the religion, which is attested by such prophecies, is a divinely authorized religion.

That Christianity is attested by true prophecies, is a fact capable of easy proof. Jesus Christ was a prophet, and during his conversation among men accurately predicted a variety of events, which were then future; especially his own death and resurrection, and the circumstances by which they were to be attended; the outpouring of the Holy Ghost; and the approaching sufferings of the Jews, with the destruction of their city and temple. But, perhaps, the most striking prophecies, which attest the truth of Christianity, are those contained in the Old Testament, and relating to our Saviour himself. The writings of the Hebrew prophets are replete with the promises of a great spiritual deliverer, denominated the Messiah, who was appointed to appear in the world at a certain period declared by the prophet Daniel. In various parts of these writings (composed as they were by a number of unconnected persons, living at different periods) it is predicted that this long-expected deliverer should arise, according to the flesh, out of the seed of Abraham, Gen. xxii. 18; and from the family of David, Isa. xi. 1, Jer. xxiii. 5; that he should be born miraculously of a virgin, Isa. vii. 14; that his birthplace should be Bethlehem, Micah, v. 2; that his outward situation should be of a very humble description, Isa. liii. 2; that he should be engaged in proclaiming glad tidings, and in relieving the sufferings of mortality, Isa. Ixi. 1; that his character should be distinguished for gentleness, kindness, faithfulness, and all righteousness, Isa. xi. 4, 5, 6, xliii. 1-3; that nevertheless the Jews would refuse to believe in him, Isa. liii. 1; that he should be despised, rejected, and persecuted, of men, Isa. liii. 3, 4, Ps.

xxii; that he should be betrayed by one of his familiar friends, and that his followers should be scattered from him, Ps. xli. 9, Zech. xiii. 7; that he should be led as a lamb to the slaughter, and be as a sheep dumb before her shearers, Isa. liii. 7; that he should be cut off, yet not for himself, Dan. ix. 26; that his body should not see corruption, nor his life be left in the grave, Ps. xvi. 10; finally, that he should ascend into heaven, Ps. lxviii. 18; and that he should exercise an universal and never-ending government over mankind, Ps. lxxii. 8, Isa. ix. 7, Dan. vii. 14. Zech. ii. 10-13. . . .

At the time appointed for the appearance of the Messiah, Jesus was born, of the seed of Abraham, of the family of David, at Bethlehem, of a virgin. We find him living in a humble outward condition—engaged in preaching the gospel, in healing the sick, and in relieving every species of bodily and mental distress—meek, gentle, kind, faithful, and fulfilling all righteousness—not believed by the Jews—despised, rejected, and persecuted of men—betrayed by his familiar friend—forsaken in the hour of trial by all his followers—led as a lamb to the slaughter—dumb in the presence of his persecutors—cut off, but not for himself—rising from the dead—ascending into heaven, and assuming a spiritual government over men—fulfilling in his own character and circumstances a variety of minor particulars—and all these things in precise accordance with the predictions of the Old Testament. More particularly, in the midst of his humiliations and distresses, and notwithstanding the lowliness and piety of his human character, we find him, in agreement with those predictions, receiving the homage, asserting the character, displaying the powers, and described by the titles, which appertain to Jehovah himself. . . .

IV. It is generally allowed by all persons who confess the existence and unity of God, (whether they are believers in the Christian revelation or otherwise), that he is a Being not only of infinite power and knowledge, but of the highest moral perfection. A comprehensive view even of natural religion leads to an easy admission of the declarations of the sacred writers that God is just, holy, true, bounteous, and merciful. Such being the moral attributes of our heavenly father, we cannot refuse to allow, that it is our reasonable service to walk in his fear, to worship him with devotion of spirit, to obey his law, to promote his glory, and more especially to set our love upon him with the whole heart. And yet it is a fact, to which the history of past ages and present observation bear alike the most decisive testimony, that, by mankind in their unregenerate condition, this reasonable service is set aside and neglected. Now Christianity, considered as a religious system consisting of both doctrines and precepts, and applied by faith to the heart—that is to say, comprehensive and vital Christianity—is unquestionably the means of so transforming men, that in the dispositions of the soul, and in the regulation of the conduct, they come to "render unto God the things that are God's."

But further—when the true Christian is thus introduced to a peaceful communion with the Father of spirits, he is gradually weaned from his evil passions, and becomes conformed, in his own person, to the moral attributes of the Deity. As the face of a man is seen reflected in the mirror, so are those attributes seen reflected in his life and conversation. Pretenders to religion—the mere professors of the Christian name—form no exception to this observation, because they have no real connection with our argument; but of those persons who place a full reliance upon Christ as their Saviour, and who have yielded themselves without reserve to his guidance and government, it may with truth be asserted, that they are created anew in the image of their Maker. Undoubtedly they have still to contend with innumerable infirmities, and with many corrupt inclinations; and they can readily acknowledge, that, in the sight of the Most High, they are less than nothing and vanity. Nevertheless, in the integrity of their words and actions, in the purity of their intentions and conduct, in their kindness, charity, and long-suffering, towards all around them, they shew forth the truth, the holiness, and the love, of that Being from whom alone all their virtue is derived.

Lastly, Christianity procures for mankind a pure and substantial happiness. The true Christian is happy far above all other persons, for various reasons:—because, though his sins have been many, he is reconciled to the Father, through the mediation of the Son; because, notwithstanding his natural weakness, he is enabled to walk in the way of righteousness, by the power of the Holy Spirit; because a sense of the divine love and approbation dwells in his heart; because he is taught to regard every tribulation as a moral discipline directed to greater good; and, lastly, because he is animated by the expectation of a future joy, perfectly unsullied in its nature, and eternal in its duration.

Now the several excellent results which have formed the subject of these observations, have never been adequately produced in men by any principles, except those of Christianity; but by the principles of Christianity, when cordially embraced and fully submitted to, they are produced without fail. Experience may convince us that the contrivance of so comprehensive, so extraordinary, and so operative, a moral system, was placed far beyond the reach of human invention: like the works of nature, it can be traced to nothing less efficacious than the wisdom, the power, and the love of God. . . .

V. Christianity, then, being the religion of God—the true, and only true religion—where are we to find an authorized record of the doctrines of which it consists? I answer, not in the scholastic productions of polemical divines; not in the treatises of modern and uninspired theologians; not in the declarations of any particular church: but in the genuine compositions of inspired men; in the Holy Scriptures of the Old and New Testament. . . .

It being admitted that the Scriptures of the Old and New Testament are genuine, that the gospel history is true, and that Christ was a divinely commissioned teacher; we are placed at once in possession of satisfactory evidence that these writings were given by inspiration of God. . . . Inspiration, it may be remarked, operates under various circumstances, and is bestowed in various measures. Now that the inspiration of the apostles and of some of their companions was of a very high and plenary description, may be inferred from a most important fact already noticed, viz. that they were endued with the power of working miracles. The work of God confirmed the word of God. The signs and wonders which the Lord displayed through the agency of those gifted men, afforded a specific and irresistible evidence, that he was also the author of their doctrine, in whatsoever form that doctrine was delivered. . . .

The Scriptures, then, are a divinely authorized record of religious truth. If I am told that there is much in the Bible which even the learned cannot understand, and some things, perhaps, which the wicked have perverted to evil purposes, I would observe in reply, that in this respect there is an obvious analogy between the written word and the works of God; for there is much also in the science of nature itself, which the wise cannot comprehend, and which the vicious have misapplied to evil. And I would further remark, that the Scriptures are not intended to gratify the curiosity, or to illuminate the speculations, of worldly wisdom; but to instruct the humble and devotional reader, and to teach the simple and the meek the way to heaven. To such as these, whatsoever be their condition in life, or their measure of mental cultivation, the Bible, as to every main doctrine and every practical principle, is explicit and intelligible. While the divine law is so accordant with the conclusions of profound reasoning, that the most enlightened philosophers have yielded to it their willing homage, it is also so plain, that when it is received with simplicity and godly sincerity, "the wayfaring man, though a fool, cannot err therein."

VI. Having thus briefly surveyed some of the principal evidences, from which the conclusion is safely deduced that Christianity is true, and that the Bible contains a genuine and divinely authorized record of all its truths,—we may now proceed to enquire what things that sacred volume declares respecting God, ourselves, and Jesus Christ.

There is nothing by which the Scriptures are more eminently distinguished,—nothing by which their importance and divine origin are more clearly evinced,—than by the information which they impart respecting the nature and character of God. Much light indeed, on this great subject, may be derived from the works of the Deity which surround us on every side, and which proclaim, in intelligible language, his wisdom, power, and goodness; and also from that moral sense of his own existence and authority, which (however it may, in numberless instances, be depraved and perverted,) he appears to have impressed universally on the mind of man. But the knowledge which we derive from natural religion respecting God is, in a wonderful manner, augmented and completed in the records of his revealed will. We learn from the Scriptures that there is no other God but Jehovah—that he exists from eternity to eternity—that he is the creator, governor, and preserver of the universe—that he is omnipresent, omnipotent, omniscient, and perfectly wise—that in him we live, and move, and have our being—that he is the author of the moral law—that he is the source of every good and perfect gift, and more especially of everlasting life—that he is holy, just, true, faithful, righteous, long-suffering, and merciful—that he is love; a tender and compassionate Father to those who walk in his fear and obey his law—that, eternal and infinite as he is, he graciously extends his immediate care to the most minute interests of his creatures—that not a sparrow falleth to the ground without him, and that he numbers the very hairs of our heads. It is more particularly to our present purpose to observe, that the Deity is ever described in the Bible as a Being of absolute purity; so that in his sight every species of iniquity, whether in thought, word, or deed, is abominable. Hence it follows; that he will by no means acquit his guilty creatures while they continue in sin; and it is plainly declared, that without holiness none shall see God. . . .

Respecting ourselves, the scriptures reveal many truths of the highest importance to us. From various declarations contained in them, we plainly learn, that man is endued not only with a frail body, but with a soul; and that when the body perishes, the soul continues to exist, Matt. x. 28, xvi. 26. 1 Thess. v. 23. Heb. x. 39. Luke xvi. 19-31, xx. 38, xxiii. 42, 43. 2 Cor. v. 1-8; that moreover, in a day to come the dead will be raised in a body incorruptible and spiritual, John v. 28, 29. 1 Cor. xv; that this short life is the only time appointed for our probation; and that, in another world, we shall all stand before the judgment-seat of Christ, and shall then be rewarded with everlasting happiness, or punished with everlasting misery—according to our works; Matt. xxv. 31-46. Rom. ii. 6-11, xiv. 10, Rev. xx. 12–15. The scriptures, moreover, declare that man was created in the moral similitude of God—that, yielding to the temptations of the devil, he fell from that image—that now, being a fallen and depraved creature, he is, in his unregenerate nature, prone to wickedness—that his heart is "deceitful above all things, and desperately wicked" (or diseased)—that "all have sinned and come short of the Glory of God"—that "they are together become unprofitable; that there is none that doeth good, no not one," and that thus "all the world" is "become guilty before God"; Jer. xvii. 9. Rom. iii. 1–19, 23. comp. Isa. liii. 6. Matt. xv. 19.

Such are the awful statements contained in the sacred volume respecting ourselves. Where, then, is there any hope for us who are fallen, corrupt, inclined to sin, and, in so great a multitude of particulars, sinners; and who are therefore separated in our natural state from a just and holy God, and are plainly liable to eternal separation from him in the world to come? Truly our hope is only in the mercy of God, through the Saviour of men. A Saviour, or I die—a Redeemer, or I perish forever!

Lastly, therefore, we may enquire, what is the doctrine of the Bible respecting our Lord and Saviour Jesus Christ? We read in Scripture, that he is the Word—the Son of God the Father Almighty—that in the beginning, before the world was created, and from everlasting, he was with God, John i. 1, xvii. 5. comp. Mic. v. 2—that by him all things were created that are in heaven and that are in earth, Col. i. 16. Heb. i. 2, 10—that without him was not any one thing made that was made, John i. 3—that he was the light and life of men, John i. 4, 9—that he and the Father are one, John x. 30—that he is therefore God, John i. 1; Jehovah our righteousness, Jer. xxiii. 5; the mighty God, Isa. ix. 6; the true God, 1 John v. 20; the great God, Tit. ii. 13; God over all, Rom. ix. 5—that he is the searcher of the reins and the hearts, knows what is in man, and bestows upon his servants all their spiritual gifts and graces, Rev. ii. 23. Acts ii. 33. 2 Cor. xii. 9. Eph. iv. 11—the object of faith, prayer, glorification, and all worship, John iii. 16. Acts vii. 59, 60. 2 Cor. xii. 8. Heb. i. 6, xiii. 21. Rev. v. 13—that he "filleth all in all," Eph. i. 23—that he is "the same yesterday, and today, and for ever"; "the Alpha and Omega, the beginning and the ending, the first and the last," Heb. xiii. 8. Rev. xxii. 13. The Bible further declares, that when the fullness of time was come, "God sent forth his Son, made of a woman, made under the law," Gal. iv. 4—that the Word became flesh, John i. 14—that he was born a child into the world, and really took our frail nature upon him, being made in all points "like unto his brethren, yet without sin," Heb. ii. 14—that he went about doing good, healing the sick, giving sight to the blind and hearing to the deaf, raising the dead to life, and preaching the gospel to the poor—that he was betrayed into the hands of wicked men, and died on the cross—that on the third day he rose from the dead, and that he ascended to the right hand of the Majesty on high, being restored to that state of infinite and unsearchable glory, which he possessed in the Father's presence before the world began, John xvii. 5. Heb. i. 3—that now he is exalted of the Father, far above all principality, and power, and might, and dominion, and every name that is named not only in this world, but also in that which is to come, Eph. i. 21—finally, that he will bring to a termination the whole economy or dispensation of which he is the Mediator, by coming again with all his holy angels, for the final and universal judgment of quick and dead, Matt. xiii. 40-42, xxiv. 30, 31. 1 Cor. xv. 25–28. . . .

VII. Having thus adduced some of the principal declarations of Scripture respecting the nature and history of our Lord Jesus Christ, I may proceed, without further delay, to the consideration of that doctrine of redemption, for the elucidation of which, this Letter is principally intended; and I may commence by putting a very simple question, What could be the mighty and equivalent purpose for which this infinitely glorious Person, the Son of God, who is one with the Father, and is therefore himself the everlasting Jehovah—should so marvelously condescend and humble himself as to take our nature upon him, in that nature to undergo every species of contumely and contradiction of sinners, and finally to die on the cross a cruel and shameful death? . . .

Christ did indeed come in order to bestow upon us, not only information and precept, but indemnity and cure. But happily this is a subject on which we are not left to any conclusions of our own formation. It is one on which the declarations of Holy Writ are equally abundant and explicit.

The very first passage of Scripture in which the Messiah is alluded to, proclaims the great purpose of his mission. "I will put enmity," said Jehovah to the serpent, "between thee and the woman, and between thy seed and her seed; it shall bruise thy head, and thou shalt bruise his heel"; Gen. iii. 15. Christian commentators generally allow, that by the seed of the woman is here intended the Messiah, and that by the serpent is represented the devil, the author of all moral evil. We therefore learn from the prophecy, that Christ was to bruise the serpent's head; or, in other words, to destroy the devil and his works. Comp. Heb. ii. 14. "For as much, then, as the children are partakers of flesh and blood, he also himself took part of the same; that through death he might destroy him that had the power of death, even the devil"—and 1 John iii. 8—"He that committeth sin is of the devil, for the devil sinneth from the beginning. For this purpose the Son of God was manifested, that he might destroy the works of the devil." It was by means of his death, that the Messiah was to obtain a complete victory over our spiritual adversary; a doctrine which perfectly accords with Isaiah's celebrated prophecy respecting his vicarious and propitiatory sufferings: "Surely he hath borne our griefs, and carried our sorrows; yet we did esteem him stricken, smitten of God, and afflicted. But he was wounded for our transgressions; he was bruised for our iniquities; the chastisement of our peace (or whereby our peace is procured) was upon him; and with his stripes we are healed. All we like sheep have gone astray: we have turned every one to his own way: and the Lord hath laid on him the iniquity of us all. He was oppressed, and he was afflicted: he is brought as a lamb to the slaughter, and as a sheep before her shearers is dumb, so he opened not his mouth. Therefore will I divide him a portion with the great, and he shall divide the spoil with the strong; because he hath poured out his soul unto death: and he was numbered with the transgressors, and he bare the sin of many, and made intercession for the transgressors"; Isa. liii. 4–12. . . .

But in order to that destruction of the works of the devil which was to be effected by the Messiah, there was need, not only of a propitiatory sacrifice, but of a powerful purifying influence. Accordingly, in those prophecies of the Old Testament which are acknowledged by both Jews and Christians to relate to the times of the Messiah, we find many clear promises of the more abundant effusion of such an influence on the Lord's people, and of its practical and internal operation. . . .

Let us now direct our attention to the New Testament. When the angel Gabriel predicted to the virgin Mary the approaching birth of her son, he added, "Thou shalt call his name Jesus (or the Saviour), for he shall save his people from their sins"; Matt. i. 21. By John the Baptist, also, the approaching Saviour of men was announced in the same character—"Behold the Lamb of God," said he, "which taketh away the sin of the world"; John i. 29.

By our blessed Lord himself, the great object of his coming, was frequently and explicitly declared: "The Son of man is come to seek and to save that which was lost," Luke xix. 10; "The Son of man came not to be ministered unto, but to minister, and to give his life a ransom for many," Matt. xx. 28; "This is my blood of the New Testament which is shed for many, for the remission of sins," Matt. xxvi. 28: "As Moses lifted up the serpent in the wilderness, even so must the Son of man be lifted up; that whosoever believeth in him should not perish, but have eternal life.—God sent not his Son into the world to condemn the world, but that the world through him might be saved," John iii. 14, 17. "I am the living bread which came down from heaven: if any man eat of this bread, he shall live forever: and the bread that I will give is my flesh which I will give for the life of the world," John vi. 51. After his ascension, also, when he delivered to the converted Paul an apostolic commission, he said, "I have appeared unto thee for this purpose, to make thee a minister and a witness—delivering thee from the people and from the Gentiles, to whom now I send thee, to open their eyes, and to turn them from darkness to light, and from the power of Satan unto God, that they may receive forgiveness of sins, and inheritance among them which are sanctified, by faith that is in me," Acts xxvi. 16-18. . . .

Justification through the blood of Christ, and sanctification by his Spirit, are very usually treated on as distinct doctrines; but different as they are in one point of view, it is nevertheless evident, from the tenor of these extracts, that they are inseparably connected. Both are essential to the work of salvation; both originate in the same divine mercy, and both are described, by the sacred writers, as arising out of the sacrifice of the Son of God. Was Christ "set forth" of the Father, to be "a propitiation through faith in his blood"? Did he bear "our sins in his own body on the tree"? Did he thus give himself for us? It was not only for the "remission of sins that are past," and for the justification of penitent believers, but also, that "he might sanctify and cleanse" his church—"that he might redeem us from all iniquity"—that our consciences might be "purified from dead works, to serve the living God"—"that we, being dead to sin, should live. . . ."

Lastly, we learn from the inspired writers that the same Mediator of the New Covenant, who was a propitiation for our sins, and who sheds forth on mankind the gifts and graces of the Holy Spirit, is mercifully engaged in pleading for his people before the throne of his Father. "My little children," said the apostle John, "these things write I unto you, that ye sin not. And if any man sin, we have an advocate with the Father, Jesus Christ the righteous"; 1 John ii. 1, 2. "Who is he that condemneth?" writes another apostle: "It is Christ that died, yea rather that it is risen again, who also maketh intercession for us"; Rom. viii. 34. "But this (man), because he continueth ever, hath an unchangeable priesthood. Wherefore he is able also to save them to the uttermost that come unto God by him, seeing he ever liveth to make intercession for them"; Heb. vii. 24, 25.

Now to the enquiry already suggested,—for what mighty and equivalent purpose the Son of God, by whom all things both in heaven and in earth were created, condescended to take our frail nature upon him, to dwell amongst us, and to die on the cross,— these statements afford an intelligible and perfectly satisfactory answer. In his adorable mercy, in his almighty power, he came to deliver mankind; to recover them from their lost condition; to save them from the dominion of Satan, and from everlasting destruction; to supply all their spiritual need: to reconcile them through his own blood-shedding and mediation to the Father Almighty; to regenerate and sanctify them by his Holy Spirit; to provide for them both indemnity and cure; and thus to secure for them a boundless eternity of perfect happiness. Here are unfolded purposes worthy of the Son of God, and worthy of that peculiar display of his love and condescension revealed to us in the Bible—purposes fully adequate to his divine dignity, and capable of being carried into effect, only by him who, while he suffered in our suffering nature, was One with Jehovah—personally participating in the wisdom, power, and nature, of the only true God. Whether, indeed, we regard the human nature of Christ—in which he died for us, and is still "touched with the feeling of our infirmities,"—or his divine nature, which imparts a mighty efficacy to the whole plan of our redemption;—we cannot but acknowledge, that between the spiritual wants of mankind, on the one hand, and the sure mercies of the Messiah of God, on the other, there is a nice, an accurate, a perfect adaptation.

VIII. In order to avail ourselves of the means which God in his unsearchable wisdom has thus ordained for our salvation, it is plainly necessary that we should believe in Jesus Christ. "These are written," says the apostle John, "that ye might believe that Jesus is the Christ, the Son of God; and that believing ye might have life through his name," John xx. 81. "God so loved the world," said Jesus himself, "that he gave his only begotten Son, that whosoever believeth in him should not perish, but have everlasting life," John iii. 16. "I am the resurrection and the life: he that believeth in me, though he were dead, yet shall he live; and whosoever liveth and believeth in me shall never die," John xi. 25, 26. Paul has declared, that "a man is not justified by the works of the law, but by the faith of Jesus Christ," Gal. ii. 16; and John the

Baptist, when he bore witness to the power and excellency of the Lord Jesus, plainly stated the consequences both of believing and of not believing on the Son of God: "He that believeth on the Son, hath everlasting life: and he that believeth not the Son, shall not see life; but the wrath of God abideth on him." John iii. 86.

Now, the faith in Christ, which is thus frequently declared to be the means of our salvation, is not only an assent of the understanding to the history and doctrines of the gospel. Such a faith is of itself a "dead faith," and we read that the "devils also believe and tremble"; Jas. ii. 19. Saving faith is that living and active principle in our minds, by which, under the softening impressions of the love of God, we accept the Lord Jesus Christ as our only Saviour; spiritually feed upon him as upon the bread of life; place a humble yet sure reliance upon his mercy and power; and, with full purpose and devotion of heart, submit our whole selves to his spiritual government. This is "the faith which worketh by love," Gal. v. 6; this is the faith which enables us to bring forth the pure and lovely fruits of holiness, charity, gentleness, patience, joy, and peace. And thus "if any man be in Christ, he is a new creature: old things are passed away: behold, all things are become new"; 2 Cor. v. 17.

Mortally diseased as we are,—the fatal malady of sin rankling within us,—how are we to experience recovery, if we refuse to accept the appointed remedy? Then let us endeavour to lay aside the "evil heart of unbelief"; let us no longer amuse ourselves with skeptical speculations on the theory of religion: but rather let us lay hold of its substance, and flee from the wrath to come. Let us listen to the words of love and tenderness with which our compassionate Redeemer continues to invite us; "Come unto me, all ye that labour and are heavy laden, and I will give you rest: take my yoke upon you and learn of me; for I am meek and lowly in heart, and ye shall find rest unto your souls; for my yoke is easy, and my burden is light," Matt. xi. 28-30. Yes, we must take upon us the yoke of Christ. "To obey is better than sacrifice, and to hearken than the fat of rams," 1 Sam. xv. 22. As we obtain reconciliation with the Father, through the sacrifice of Christ, let us ever remember that we can be brought into a state of true holiness, and avail ourselves of that reconciliation, only by a full submission to the influence and guidance of his Spirit. It is by his Spirit that our all-sufficient Redeemer changes our vile hearts, mortifies our sinful affections, imparts to us his own holy nature, enables us to walk before him in purity and love, and thus prepares us for the enjoyment of that heavenly inheritance, which he has meritoriously procured for us, by his own perfect obedience and by the sacrifice of himself. "If we walk in the light, as (God) is in the light," says the apostle John, "we have fellowship one with another, and the blood of Jesus Christ his Son cleanseth us from all sin," 1 John i. 7. . . .

Trusting, my dear friend, (and reader of every description,) that thou hast acceded, step by step, to all the essential points detailed in the present argument, I will now venture to add the words of persuasion and exhortation. . . .

Since it is through faith and obedience alone that we can any of us escape the just judgments of God, and become the heirs of a blessed immortality, mayest thou be enabled to believe and obey! Thy understanding is convinced of the truth of our holy religion, but rest not in a mere notional faith. Lay aside the evil heart of unbelief. Venture not to amuse thyself with mere speculation on the theory of Christianity, but lay firm hold of its substance, and flee from the wrath to come. Remember that thou art a sinner unworthy of the love of God—wretched, and miserable, and blind, and poor, and naked. Confess thy transgressions unto the Lord; be broken down under the sense of them; and, well knowing that there is nothing in the fleeting scenes of this present life, which can satisfy the aspirations of an immortal spirit, seek a sure refuge for a wounded and weary soul, in the bosom of Jesus. Cast thyself, just such as thou art, on the Mediator between God and man, "in whom are hid all the treasures," not only of "wisdom and knowledge," but of mercy, compassion, and love. . . .

And now a single additional observation will bring this letter to its conclusion. If we are taught to mourn over our sins, we shall mourn also over the sins of mankind: we shall be humbled before God with deep sorrow of heart, when we reflect on the forgetfulness of their Creator, the falsehood, lasciviousness, malice, cruelty, and bloodshed, which are still so fearfully prevalent among the sons of Adam. But everyone who is brought to a right understanding of the gospel of Christ knows, that in its doctrines, as they are humbly accepted and practically applied, there is a powerful remedial principle, by which moral evil of every description may be counteracted and subdued. Let us then pray for the hastening of that day when the dominion of Jesus shall extend "from

sea to sea, and from the river unto the ends of the earth," Ps. lxxii.
8: for under its blessed influence, a mighty change shall still be
wrought in the character and condition of men. "They shall beat
their swords into ploughshares and their spears into pruning
hooks: nation shall not lift up sword against nation, neither shall
they learn war any more," Isa. ii. 4. "The wolf also shall dwell
with the lamb, and the leopard shall lie down with the kid, and
the calf, and the young lion, and the fading, together, and a little
child shall lead them. They shall not hurt nor destroy in all my
holy mountain, (saith the Lord), for the earth shall be full of the
knowledge of the Lord, as the waters cover the sea," Isa. xi. 6–9.
Then shall this moral wilderness become a fruitful field. "The
wilderness and the solitary place shall be glad for them; and the
desert shall rejoice, and blossom as the rose. It shall blossom
abundantly, and rejoice, even with joy and singing; the glory of
Lebanon shall be given unto it, the excellency of Carmel and Sha-
ron; they shall see the glory of the Lord, and the excellency of our
God. And an highway shall be there, and a way, and it shall be
called the way of holiness: the unclean shall not pass over it, but
it shall be for those; the wayfaring men, though fools, shall not
err therein. No lion shall be there, nor any ravenous beast shall go
up thereon; it shall not be found there; but the redeemed shall
walk there. And the ransomed of the Lord shall return and come
to Zion, with songs and everlasting joy upon their heads: they
shall obtain joy and gladness, and sorrow and sighing shall flee
away," Isa. xxxv. 1, 2, 8-10. . . .

JOHN WILBUR

*Journal of the Life of John Wilbur, a Minister of
the Gospel in the Society of Friends; with
Selections from His Correspondence, &c.*
(Providence, 1859).

My Dear Friends Eli and Sybil Jones,
  I have not heard from you since you left Fall River, but many
times have I thought of you, and more especially of late, and as I

believe in that which revives a living evidence of the unity of the one Spirit, as well as the fellowship of the gospel of Christ in the bonds whereof his messengers can greet each other—can greet those that are in bonds as being bound with them; and how truly great is their work of withstanding that which is evil, and of furthering that which is good, of pulling down the kingdom of Satan, and of building up the kingdom of Christ the Redeemer. To be bound to such a work as this, is a solemn, and a high and holy calling, of which I am sure you are well aware, as also that the anointing of the savor of life, in and by that gospel, which is the power of God unto salvation, is the appointed and only means of the exaltation of God's kingdom and power successfully among men. Wherever that is raised up, it is and must necessarily be upon the ruins of Satan's empire in their hearts, and accomplished only through contention and strife, even to making war in righteousness against the mighty foe wherever he may have encamped himself, and in whatever form, or under whatever name he may be seen and detected, even by that true light of Christ, without which you know that his warriors and messengers will run in vain, and instead of saving the lives of others will jeopard their own. The stronghold and kingdom of the enemy is in the minds of men; and although he is a distinct being, his dominion is only known in the hearts of men, that is, in this world—in the hearts of those who receive him and serve him. Hence when the poor warrior of Christ's banner makes war against him (otherwise than in his own heart) he necessarily has a twofold contention and combat, namely, with the enemy combined with his servants. And more especially arduous must be the contest, when his servants are many and leagued together; and most of all under the dominion of a spurious religion. The popular prevalence of such a state of things combined with power, has undoubtedly been the hardest thing which the Lord's messengers have ever had to contend with in this lower world; a stronghold of which Satan has been wont proudly to possess himself; and however little by little were his strides in the primitive Christian church, yet alas how lamentably he finally succeeded in apostatizing and corrupting that once best of all bodies, which instead of continuing to be the spouse, the Lamb's wife, degenerated into a horde of sordid, cruel oppressors, and even murderers of the faithful.

How easily might that apostasy have been arrested at first

whilst yet it had gained but little ground, by a united stand of the church at large. But alas! what inexpressible suffering and rivers of blood it cost, to obtain but a partial reformation after the consummation of the lapse of the church into formality and idolatry. Again how the fear of man, the love of ease, and the dread of conflict and controversy, unhappily induced the primitive Christians to jeopard the standing and safety of the church. Satan who had striven in vain to destroy them from without, now resorts to a different stratagem. Men of influence, talent and learning, having got above the pure witness in themselves, introduced innovations by degrees within her pale, upon her pure doctrines and practices, until at length her principles were subverted and her destiny sealed. Is it not wonderful as well as sorrowful that the cry of these innovators of peace, of safety and security, should have deterred the faithful from sounding the alarm at the insidious approach of an enemy, and of unflinchingly making a stand against him; for it is not altogether unlikely that there were some if not many who from time to time saw the danger which awaited them and gave warning of it, but were decried and made unpopular by the leaders in those innovations, and their credulous adherents. Herein the plausibility of the snare consisted, and the great subtlety and power of the enemy was successful, the cry being peace, peace, no detraction, no controversy, &c.

Now in this view and mirror of former times, we clearly see the face of things in these our days. The Hicksites at the West, whilst they were persistently undermining Quakerism, were plausibly avowing their integrity, and at the same time striving to avoid all inquiry, and to stop the mouths of the honest by crying peace, peace, love and unity, no detraction, no controversy. The very same course was taken by Isaac Crewdson and his party in England, as also by Elisha Bates, striving to impress the minds, even of honest Friends, (and sometimes successfully,) that it was improper to speak of any apprehended danger, lest, as they said, the peace and quiet of the Society should be disturbed, and the good order broken. It was seen, however, that those plausible pretensions were but the seductions of the enemy, because the principal movers of them had evidently departed from Friends' doctrine and only resorted to this artful policy to avoid detection. Time was as above hinted, when the grand enemy warred against the true church by his ministers *from without*. This was the case both in the primitive times and in the days of George Fox and his contemporaries; causing great contention and controversy, at each of those periods, though we know most in relation to the latter. And our early Friends, honestly and manfully met and rebutted every attack upon the true doctrines of the gospel, in due season, and without fear of consequences. And how are we to suppose that God's tender image of purity and uprightness was preserved in them and kept alive, amid the strife of tongues, and such a mighty controversy? Was it not because they were covered with the armor of God? Was it not because they accounted not their own lives dear in coming up to the help of the Lord against the mighty? Was it not because they walked in the light, and dwelt in the life, and were endowed with the temper and spirit of heaven? Was it not because the Captain of their salvation led them out and brought them in and covered them with his unfailing power in the day of battle? Was it not because their plaindealing with those who committed wrong upon the Truth, was in the love of Christ, and therein extended, as well for their recovery as for the defence of his doctrines and testimonies? And now, my dear friends, if such resisting of that which is evil from an enemy without the camp, was in the will and ordering of the blessed Head of the church, what may we suppose is his will in relation to resisting that which is evil and dangerous within our walls? Men, women and children were then united in making a stand against the opposers of Truth's doctrines. And inasmuch as those doctrines are as eminently valuable, both to us and to the world now, as they were then, is it not as needful that all of every class, should unite heart and hand in withstanding and repelling everything which tends to lead off and scatter from the blessed standard of *life* and *power*, in all that is worth the name of religion. Is the danger less to the flock, when the wolf has attired himself with the sheep's clothing, and made his way into the fold? Is less effort requisite expelling and getting him out than to prevent his coming in? And if God's testimonies and doctrines are as dear to himself now as they were in former times, when he gave the lives of many of his faithful children for them, will he not extend the arm of his power for the spiritual preservation of those who walk in his fear and trust in him in fulfilling his command, in their allotment of watching over the flock now, as well as formerly? We read in Acts xx. 28th, "Take heed therefore unto yourselves and to all the flock over which the Holy Ghost hath made you overseers, to feed the church of God, which he hath purchased with his own blood; for I know this, that after my departure shall grievous wolves enter in among you, not sparing the flock," &c. And the solemn charge to Ezekiel, iii. 20th, "When a righteous man doth turn from his righteousness, because thou hast not given him warning, he shall die, but his blood will I require at thy hand." This passage has divers times been brought home to my mind; and if the church were substituted for the righteous man, how vastly greater the responsibility upon him who neglecteth or refuseth to give warning. But this warning we know must be in the spirit and temper of the gospel, in that love and meekness which entertaineth no personal animosity, in that wisdom described by the apostle as being first pure, then peaceable, &c. Why did William Penn advise Joseph Pike to read *controversy* on the doctrines of Friends, if it were not for his confirmation in them—he knew that J. P. was no superficial man, and that he had no life in the faults and failings of others; but he knew that to see the deformity and tendency of bad doctrines, would be likely to enhance and confirm the excellency of the good in that sincere and upright man. At this day there seems to be no safety without it—to compare all doctrines now introduced to our reading with the standard; and for those who cannot test them with a standard within themselves—to test them by a comparison with Barclay and other sound writers. This letter has been written to you in the liberty of gospel freedom, and if you have any remarks to make upon it, let them come as freely. In the full feeling of gospel love to you both I must now say farewell, and am your friend,

JOHN WILBUR.

REFORM

ELIZABETH FRY

*In the nineteenth century, Friends became increasingly iden-
tified with humanitarian and reform work. Some reformers
believed that an organization was incomplete if it lacked a
Quaker among its leaders. Friends also were widely identified with prison reform. Historians today debate some of
their methods. Some view Friends as more interested in im-
posing Quaker morality on unruly lower classes than in justice. Others argue that the Quaker reformers brought real
improvements to jails and prisons that had been brutal and
often deadly. Perhaps the best known of Quaker reformers
was Elizabeth Gurney Fry (1780–1845), a sister of Joseph
John Gurney, who worked with female prisoners at London's
notorious Newgate Prison.*

Susanna Corder, ed., *Life of Elizabeth Fry.
Compiled from Her Journal.* (Philadelphia, 1884).

Account of a visit to Newgate, June 2d, 1820, written by the late
Hon. Mrs. Waldegrave, for her mother, lady Elizabeth Whit-
bread, on whose death, in 1846, it was sent to me.

ELIZABETH WALDEGRAVE, JUN.

4, HARLEY STREET, LONDON,

MARCH 2D, 1852.
June 2nd, 1820.—We reached Newgate at half-past ten, and
waited with the rest of the company in a small room up stairs; in

the way to it we passed through several wards, in which the most perfect stillness prevailed; these were the former scenes of all the riot and confusion of which we had heard so much.

After waiting a short time, Mrs. Fry entered, saluting everybody in the most dignified manner. The female convicts, forty in number, came in upon a bell being rung, and took their seats at one end of the room with perfect order—the monitors sitting on the first bench, and the others in classes behind; each had her work, at which she employed herself till Mrs. Pry began reading. They had ivory tickets round their necks with numbers on them.

Mrs. Fry arranged a large old Bible on her desk, and sat down—her voice was so gentle that we wondered we could hear what she said, but remarkably mild and sweet. She began by requesting their *attention.*—"I am desirous that your attention should be, as much as possible, undivided—notwithstanding our being subject to-day to the interruptions of company, it is equally important that your minds should be fixed on what I say—praying that the Holy Spirit may enlighten your understanding. I am going to read the 4th chapter of Paul's Epistle to the Ephesians." They all laid aside their work, most of them fixed their eyes on the ground, and we could not observe that more than two or three looked about afterwards till she had done reading. She read the chapter slowly and impressively—the 6th, 28th, and 32nd verses appeared to affect them deeply—every word that she uttered seemed to be written in her own heart. She then turned to the book of Psalms. After a moment's pause, she turned back to the chapter which she had been reading, and said, I was going to read a Psalm, but I thought I should be best satisfied to say a word on the chapter I have been reading; the greater part of it is so simple and clear, that a very little endeavour on your part will enable you to understand it; but there is one expression which perhaps may be obscure: "One Lord, one Faith, one Baptism." If you look only at the external, you might say, so many different opinions prevail, people are so divided as to what they think ought to be believed, how can they be said to have one faith? I have always viewed it very differently: "One Lord,"—yea, and have not all Christians the same Lord, which is Christ? and while we acknowledge him our Master, look to him for our justification, follow his precepts, obey his commandments, love him, serve him,—he is our Lord—he is the "one Lord" of all who *thus* acknowledge him their *head.*—Again, "one Faith"—there is a diversity of opinions, but only one true, and saving Faith, the Faith which lives in the heart; and becomes evident by its fruits, which lays hold of the promises, which actuates to all godliness, and produces the blessed effects of a holy life. This one true, saving faith, is common to *all* Christians—how exceedingly soever they may seem to differ. So also, "one Baptism": Christians may differ as to the manner of administering the Baptism of water, nay, though some even dispense with *that* altogether, yet there is one spiritual baptism of the heart,—the Spirit of God, sanctifying and renewing the heart, and creating it after God, in righteousness and true holiness. In this manner we have all "one Lord, one Faith, one Baptism; one God and Father of all, who is above all, and through all, and in you all. What a sweet bond of unity is this, where we are not only brethren in this world, but may hope to meet in Heaven, there to give glory to Him with one accord, for ever and for evermore."

Mrs. Fry then read the 86th Psalm, at the end of which, a brother Quaker said a few words of exhortation to all present, to join in Prayer on behalf of the poor sufferers contained in these walls, and not to be unmindful that all were sinners, all under one condemnation.

She then knelt down, and prayed so beautiful a Prayer,—with such fervency, so rich a flow of ideas, and such perfect command of Scripture language to clothe them in, that it is impossible to convey an idea of its beauty—the *chaunt*, in which the Quakers recite their prayers, gave it a very singular, but very impressive effect; for her voice is good, and when exerted, very strong and clear. This, after a few words from one of the company, concluded the service—the women retired in perfect order, each class separately, with its monitor from the front row; all making courtesies as they left the room. Mrs. Fry, in the course of some conversation with Lord Albemarle, said, that she believed the coolness she had experienced from Lord Sidmouth, to have originated in too anxious a desire on her part to save the life of a condemned woman; which had induced her to speak to the Duke of Gloucester on the subject, after Lord Sidmouth had refused to interfere; by which she believed that she had given offence, that she thought they had been wrong and had urged it too far; that at first they had free communication with the Secretary of State's office, but that it had been closed for some time.

She said that her success surprised herself as much as it did others—that a very remarkable Providence had attended all her efforts—she had never seen the Bible received as it had been there. "Ten years ago," said she, "when it occurred to me to make trial, I went with a young Friend into one of the wards, in which the greatest riot and confusion prevailed. I went in with my Bible in my hand, and told them I was come to read the Scriptures; they all flocked round me, and I am convinced many had never heard them before—it seemed to be glad tidings to them—all were attentive. I had been warned to take off such things as could possibly be stolen, but no attempt of the kind was made; if I dropped anything, it was picked up and brought to me. I felt rather alarmed at first, at the idea of being shut up with these poor creatures, but I was preserved through it."

She said that some remarkable things had happened for her encouragement: one, which occurred lately she related,—"A woman, who was one of the lowest of the low—a thief, a drunkard, and in every way as bad as possible, was committed to Newgate. On the first day that she attended (the reading) I happened to read the parable of the prodigal son; she was much affected by it, and the next day, I received from her a letter, (she could write,) in which she expressed her thankfulness to God that, through our instrumentality, a new way had been opened before her—that she was like the prodigal son, and it seemed as if God had seen her afar off—that she prayed to be enabled to hold fast the hope she felt— all in this strain. We made her our school-mistress, and during the whole term of her imprisonment, I never knew her break one rule, or be guilty of the smallest impropriety of speech or behaviour. When they quit Newgate, we support them from our fund, till they are otherwise provided for—in consequence of illness, *she* remained for some time dependent on us. We received a message from her, requesting that we would, if possible, obtain her admittance into some workhouse, where, if we could furnish her with a little tea and sugar, she should be much happier than now, for that she was miserable at the idea of diminishing *that fund*, which might be the means of rescuing other poor creatures from the state she had herself been in. We got her into a workhouse, where she lately died, one of the most peaceful, happy deaths; the only pain she experienced was, from none of us being present, that she might have expressed to us her gratitude for the benefit she had derived through our means. Another young woman, too, of the same character, is lately dead; she lived well, and died well."

We went afterwards through part of the prison, but in a very unsatisfactory manner, owing to the number of persons present. She said that one proof of essential good being done, was, that, whereas the returns used to be 30 per cent., they are now less than 4.

PHILADELPHIA YEARLY MEETING
INDIAN COMMITTEE

Another Quaker concern lay with Native Americans. Friends, as they had earlier, tried to hold their governments to fair dealing during treaty negotiations, and to be sure that when Friends moved west, they settled on lands that had been fairly purchased from Native peoples. More controversial today are the efforts of Friends to persuade Native Americans to give up traditional ways and become farmers. Early in the nineteenth century, Philadelphia Friends began work in up-state New York among the Seneca people.

A Brief Account of the Proceedings of the Committee, Appointed in the Year 1795 by the Yearly Meeting of Friends of Pennsylvania, New-Jersey, &c. for Promoting the Improvement and Gradual Civilization of the Indian Natives (Philadelphia, 1805).

The beneficial effects of the labours at Oneida, having been observed by the Seneca Indians, it opened the way for an introduction among them, and Friends were invited into their country. Three Friends, who offered their services to go and instruct them being accompanied by two of the Committee, arrived, in the Fifth month, 1798, at the Indian towns on the Alleghany River, where they met with a friendly reception.

A general council was called, and the motives of the visit were explained. The Indians expressed their thankfulness to the great Spirit, for Friends safe arrival amongst them; but queried how Indians could learn to plough, and do what was proposed, seeing they had no horses or oxen, and were poor, living in cabins covered with bark. Friends told them, great matters were not expected at once, but it was wished they would make a beginning; that they had two horses, which perhaps might be taught to draw a plough; and as they had an annuity paid them by the United States, they might save some of it to buy oxen: and then allusion was made to their great intemperance, many both men and women having been seen intoxicated.

At another council, Cornplanter, their chief, made a speech, of which the following is an extract:

> *Brothers the Quakers. Listen now to what I am going to say to you. You know, brothers, the red people are poor. They are not like the white people. The Great Spirit has made them of another language; so that is very hard for us to understand one another plainly.*
>
> *Brothers, we suppose the reason you came here was to help poor Indians some way or other; and you wish the chiefs to tell their warriors not to go on so bad as they have done; and you wish us to take up work like the white people. Now, brothers, some of our sober men will take up work and do as you say; and if they do well, then your young men will stay longer; but some others will not mind what you say.*
>
> *Brothers, we can't say a word against you. It is the best way to call Quakers, brothers. You never wished any part of our lands, therefore we are determined to try to learn your ways; and these young men may stay here two years to try; and then if they like it, and we like it, your young men may stay longer.*

In reply, they were informed that our young Friends must have some place to live in, and a piece of land to work in order to set them an example, and raise bread for themselves to eat; but that the land should still be theirs; and all the improvements put upon it, should also be theirs, when it was left. Further, that a number of hoes, axes, scythes, several sets of plough irons and other farming implements; also carpenters', masons', and coopers' tools were coming up in a boat; which were intended for the general use of the settlement, and would be placed under the care of the young men, to lend to such Indians as wanted to use them, and although they would be left with them, and never taken away by us, yet we did not think it prudent to distribute them as a gift at present; for they knew some of their people were not very good, and such might pawn or sell them for whiskey, and then they would be as bad off as they were before.

After looking about the country, Friends fixed on an ancient village called Genesangohta, as the place of their residence. A few Indian families live there. It is situate near the line dividing New York from Pennsylvania, and nearly in the center of the Indian settlements on the Alleghany River; many living from five to ten miles above, and their largest town called Jeneshadago is nine miles below.

At a conference with the natives, previously to the two members of the Committee returning home, among other things, the oppressive labour required of their women, was laid before them; that it was not right to suffer their women to work all day in the fields and woods; either in cultivating with the hoe all that was raised for their subsistence, or getting firewood and bringing it home on their backs; whilst the men and boys were at the same time amusing themselves with shooting arrows from their bows, or some such diversions.

They were recommended to begin our way, and take their boys out to hoe, &c. reminding them, it was from the Good Spirit they and we received every good thing; that they were equally, with the white people, objects of his tender care and regard; and that the great disparity they so frequently spoke of, between themselves and the white people, with regard to poverty and plenty, was the natural result of the different plans pursued to obtain the blessings of this life; and as their ground was equally good with that possessed by the white people. It would also be equally productive, if the same industry and methods of farming were pursued. In a letter from the Friends residing among the Indians, dated First month, 1799, they mention that several of the young men manifest some willingness to labour; and that in the preceding fall, they had employed one to work a while with them. A school was kept this winter, which was attended by a few children.

In a letter from one of the Friends dated Third month 1799, he mentions that the Indians were very desirous to build themselves better houses, our Friends having then erected a good log house covered with shingles; and further, that three old Indian men, with their assistance and instruction, very soon learned to make shingles.

In the Ninth Month of this year, four of the Committee visited this settlement, one of whom had been there in the spring of last year, when Friends were first introduced into this country, and consequently was enabled to form a correct opinion of the improvements made. Several of the Indians were building good log houses, which were either roofed, or intended to be roofed, with shingles. Their crop of corn was much larger than they raised when Friends went there; and several small lots of land were under good fence. A council being convened, a speech was made to the Indians, of which the following is an extract:

Brothers, It has afforded us satisfaction, in passing through your town, to notice marks of industry taking place; that you are building better and warmer houses to live in; and that so much of your cleared land is planted with corn, beans, potatoes, &c. and to see these articles kept in good order.

Brothers, we observe where your new houses are building, that the timber is very much cut off a rich flat, which we wish you encouraged to clear and make fit for ploughing. We hope more of your men will assist in clearing and fencing land, and planting it with corn; also sowing it with wheat; you will then have a supply of provision, more certain to depend upon than hunting.

Brothers, we are pleased to see your stock of cattle increased. The rich bottoms on the river will be plenty for them to live on in the summer season; but, as your winters are long and cold, it will require something for them to live on in the winter. The white people keep their cattle on hay, on straw, and on corn fodder. Straw, you cannot get until you raise wheat or other grain; the rich bottoms if put in order would produce a great deal of hay. But for an immediate supply, we think, that as soon as you gather the corn, if you would cut the stalks close at the ground, bind them up in small bundles, and put them in stacks as our young men do, they would keep your cattle part of the cold weather.

Brothers, we are pleased to see a quantity of fence made this summer, and we would not have you discouraged at the labour it takes; for if you will clear a little more land every year, and fence it, you will soon get enough to raise what bread you want; as well as some for grass to make hay for your cattle in winter.

Brothers, we understand you are desirous to discourage whiskey from being brought among you, with which we are much pleased, and should be glad you could entirely keep it away. To get it, you give your money with which you should buy clothing, oxen, etc. . . .

Cornplanter, on behalf of the nation, made a reply, in substance, as follows:

That when our young Friends first settled among them, many of his chiefs were averse to it; but they had this summer several councils among themselves respecting the young men; and all the chiefs seeing their good conduct and readiness to assist Indians, were now well satisfied. He hoped several of his young men would do more at farming than heretofore; and Friends must not be discouraged because so little was done; but exercise patience towards them, as it was hard for them to make much change from their ancient customs. He regretted the loss of the Friend who expected to leave them soon; he said he had been useful to him in keeping whiskey, and other strong liquor, out of the town that they now drank much less than formerly, but feared when the Friend was gone he should not keep it away so well as he had lately done.

ELIZABETH HEYRICK

Friends continued the antislavery witness that John Woolman and others had begun in the eighteenth century. Among the most influential figures was an English Friend, Elizabeth Heyrick (1769–1831). Her 1824 pamphlet on the abolition of British colonial slavery is generally regarded as the first to call for an immediate end to human slavery.

Elizabeth Heyrick, *Immediate Not Gradual Abolition; or, an Inquiry into the Shortest, Safest, and Most Effectual Means of Getting Rid of West Indian Slavery* (London, 1824).

It is now seventeen years since the Slave Trade was abolished by the Government of this country—but Slavery is still perpetuated in our West India colonies, and the horrors of the Slave Trade are aggravated rather than mitigated. By making it felony for British subjects to be concerned in that inhuman traffic, England has only transferred her share of it to other countries. She has, indeed, by negotiation and remonstrance, endeavoured to persuade them to follow her example.—But has she succeeded?—How should she, whilst there is so little consistency in her conduct? Who will listen to her pathetic declamations on the injustice and cruelty of the Slave Trade—whilst she rivets the chains upon her own slaves, and subjects them to all the injustice and cruelty which she so eloquently deplores when her own interest is no longer at stake? Before we can have any rational hope of prevailing on our guilty neighbours to abandon this atrocious commerce—to relinquish the gain of oppression,—the wealth obtained by rapine and violence,—by the deep groans, the bitter anguish of our unoffending fellow creatures;—we must purge ourselves from these pollutions;—we must break the iron yoke from off the neck of our own slaves,—and let the wretched captives in our own islands go free. Then, and not till then, we shall speak to the surrounding nations with the all-commanding eloquence of sincerity and truth,—and our persuasions will be backed by the irresistible argument of consistent example. But to invite others to be just and merciful whilst we grasp in our own hands the rod of oppression,—to solicit others to relinquish the wages of iniquity whilst we are putting them into our own pockets—what is it but cant and hypocrisy? Do such preachers of justice and mercy ever make converts? On the contrary, do they not render themselves ridiculous and contemptible?

But let us, individually, bring this great question closely home to our own bosoms. We that hear, and read, and approve, and applaud the powerful appeals, the irrefragable arguments against the Slave Trade, and against slavery,—are we ourselves sincere, or hypocritical? Are we the true friends of justice, or do we only cant about it?—To which party do we really belong?—to the friends of emancipation, or of perpetual slavery? Every individual belongs to one party or the other; not speculatively, or professionally merely, but practically. The perpetuation of slavery in our West India colonies, is not an abstract question, to be settled between the Government and the Planters,—it is a question in which

we are all implicated;—we are all guilty,—(with shame and com-
punction let us admit the opprobrious truth) of supporting and
perpetuating slavery. The West Indian planter and the people of
this country, stand in the same moral relation to each other, as the
thief and the receiver of stolen goods. The planter refuses to set
his wretched captive at liberty,—treats him as a beast of burden,—
compels his reluctant unremunerated labour under the lash of
the cart whip,—why?—because we furnish the stimulant to all
this injustice, rapacity, and cruelty,—by PURCHASING ITS
PRODUCE. Heretofore, it may have been thoughtlessly and
unconsciously,—but now this palliative is removed;—the veil of
ignorance is rent aside;—the whole nation must now divide itself
into the active supporters, and the active opposers of slavery;—
there is no longer any ground for a neutral party to stand upon. . . .

But is all this knowledge to end in exclamations, in petitions,
and remonstrances?—Is there nothing to be done, as well as said?
Are there no tests to prove our sincerity,—no sacrifices to be offered in confirmation of our zeal?—Yes, there is one,—(but it is in
itself so small and insignificant that it seems almost burlesque to
dignify it with the name of sacrifice)—it is ABSTINENCE FROM
THE USE OF WEST INDIAN PRODUCTIONS, sugar, espe-
cially, in the cultivation of which slave labour is chiefly occupied.
Small, however, and insignificant as the sacrifice may appear,—it
would, at once, give the deathblow to West Indian slavery. When
there was no longer a market for the productions of slave labour,
then, and not till then, will the slaves be emancipated. . . .

But were such a measure to be ultimately injurious to the interest of the planter—that consideration ought not to weigh a feather
in the scale against emancipation. The slave has a right to his
liberty, a right which it is a crime to withhold—let the consequences to the planters be what they may. If I have been deprived
of my rightful inheritance, and the usurper, because he has long
kept possession, asserts his right to the property of which he has
defrauded me; are my just claims to it at all weakened by the boldness of his pretensions, or by the plea that restitution would im-
poverish and involve him in ruin? And to what inheritance, or
birthright, can any mortal have pretensions so just, (until forfeited by crime) as to liberty? What injustice and rapacity can
be compared to that which defrauds a man of his best earthly
inheritance,—tears him from his dearest connections, and con-

demns him and his posterity to the degradation and misery of interminable slavery?

In the great question of emancipation, the interests of two parties are said to be involved,—the interest of the slave and that of the planter. But it cannot for a moment be imagined that these two interests have an equal right to be consulted, without confounding all moral distinctions, all difference between real and pretended, between substantial and assumed claims. With the interest of the planters, the question of emancipation, has (properly speaking) nothing to do. The right of the slave, and the interest of the planter, are distinct questions; they belong to separate departments, to different provinces of consideration. If the liberty of the slave can be secured not only without injury but with advantage to the planter, so much the better, certainly;—but still the liberation of the slave ought ever to be regarded as an independent object; and if it be deferred till the planter is sufficiently alive to his own interest to cooperate in the measure, we may for ever despair of its accomplishment. The cause of emancipation has been long and ably advocated. Reason and eloquence, persuasion and argument have been powerfully exerted; experiments have been fairly made,—facts broadly stated in proof of the impolicy as well as iniquity of slavery,—to little purpose; even the hope of its extinction, with the concurrence of the planter, or by any enactment of the colonial, or British legislature's still seen in very remote perspective,—so remote, that the heart sickens at the cheerless prospect. All that zeal and talent could display in the way of argument, has been exerted in vain. All that an accumulated mass of indubitable evidence could effect in the way of conviction, has been brought to no effect.

It is high time, then, to resort to other measures,—to ways and means more summary and effectual. Too much time has already been lost in declamation and argument,—in petitions and remonstrances against British slavery. The cause of emancipation calls for something more decisive, more efficient than words. It calls upon the real friends of the poor degraded and oppressed African to bind themselves by a solemn engagement, an irrevocable vow, to participate no longer in the crime of keeping him in bondage. It calls upon them to "wash their own hands in innocency"—to abjure forever the miserable hypocrisy of pretending to commiserate the slave, whilst, by purchasing the productions of his labour they bribe his master to keep him in slavery. The great Apostle of the gentiles declared, that he would "eat no flesh whilst the world stood, rather than make his Brother to offend." Do you make a similar resolution respecting West Indian produce. Let your resolution be made conscientiously, and kept inviolably;—let no plausible arguments which may be urged against it from without,—no solicitations of appetite from within, move you from your purpose,—and in the course of a few months, slavery in the British dominions will be annihilated.

"Yes, (it may be said) if all would unite in such a resolution,—but what can the abstinence of a few individuals, or a few families do, towards the accomplishment of so vast an object?"—It can do wonders. Great effects often result from small beginnings. Your resolution will influence that of your friends and neighbours;—each of them will, in like manner, influence their friends and neighbours;—the example will spread from house to house,—from city to city,—till, among those who have any claim to humanity, there will be but one heart, and one mind,—one resolution,—one uniform practice. Thus, by means the most simple and easy, would West Indian slavery be most safely and speedily abolished.

"But, (it will be objected) it is not an immediate, but a gradual emancipation, which the most enlightened and judicious friends of humanity call for, as a measure best calculated, in their judgment, to promote the real interests of the slave, as well as his master; the former, not being in a condition to make a right use of his freedom, were it suddenly restored to him." This, it must be admitted, appears not only the general, but almost universal sentiment of the abolitionists;—to oppose it therefore, may seem a most presumptuous, as well as hopeless attempt. But truth and justice are stubborn and inflexible;—they yield neither to numbers or authority. . . .

In the face of such a body of evidence, the detaining our West Indian slaves in bondage, is a continued acting of the same atrocious injustice which first kidnapped and tore them from their kindred and native soil, and robbed them of that sacred unalienable right which no considerations, how plausible soever, can justify the withholding. We have no right, on any pretext of expediency or pretended humanity, to say—"because you have been made a slave, and thereby degraded and debased,—therefore, I will continue to hold you in bondage until you have acquired a capacity to make a right use of your liberty." As well might you say to a poor wretch, gasping and languishing in a pest house, "here will I keep you, till I have given you a capacity for the enjoyment of pure air." . . .

The enemies of slavery have hitherto ruined their cause by the senseless cry of gradual emancipation. It is marvelous that the wise and the good should have suffered themselves to have been imposed upon by this wily artifice of the slaveholder,—for with him must the project of gradual emancipation have first originated. The slaveholder knew very well, that his prey would be secure, so long as the abolitionists could be cajoled into a demand for gradual instead of immediate abolition. He knew very well, that the contemplation of a gradual emancipation, would beget a gradual indifference to emancipation itself. He knew very well, that even the wise and the good, may, by habit and familiarity, be brought to endure and tolerate almost anything. . . . He caught the idea, and knew how to turn it to advantage.—He knew very well, that the faithful delineation of the horrors of West Indian slavery, would produce such a general insurrection of sympathetic and indignant feeling; such abhorrence of the oppressor, such compassion for the oppressed, as must soon have been fatal to the whole system. He knew very well, that a strong moral fermentation had begun, which, had it gone forward, must soon have purified the nation from this foulest of its corruptions;—that the cries of the people for emancipation, would have been too unanimous, and too importunate for the Government to resist, and that slavery would, long ago, have been exterminated throughout the British dominions. Our example might have spread from kingdom to kingdom,—from continent to continent,—and the slave trade, and slavery, might, by this time, have been abolished—all the world over:—"A sacrifice of a sweet savour," might have ascended to the Great Parent of the Universe;—"His kingdom might have come, and his will (thus far) have been done on earth, as it is in Heaven."

But this GRADUAL Abolition, has been the grand marplot of human virtue and happiness;—the very masterpiece of satanic policy. By converting the cry for immediate, into gradual emancipation, the prince of slave holders, "transformed himself, with astonishing dexterity, into an angel of light,"—and thereby— "deceived the very elect."—He saw very clearly, that if public justice and humanity, especially, if Christian justice and humanity, could be brought to demand only a gradual extermination of the enormities of the slave system;—if they could be brought to acquiesce, but for one year, or for one month, in the slavery of our African brother,—in robbing him of all the rights of humanity,—and degrading him to a level with the brutes;—that then, they could imperceptibly be brought to acquiesce in all this for an unlimited duration. . . .

The father of lies, the grand artificer of fraud and imposture, transformed himself therefore, on this occasion, preeminently, "into an angel of light"—and deceived, not the unwary only, the unsuspecting multitude,—but the wise and the good, by the plausibility, the apparent force, the justice, and above all, by the humanity of the arguments propounded for gradual emancipation. He is the subtlest of all reasoners, the most ingenious of all sophists, the most eloquent of all declaimers.—He, above all other advocates, "can make the worst appear the better argument"; can, most effectually pervert the judgment and blind the understanding,—whilst they seem to be most enlightened and rectified. Thus, by a train of most exquisite reasoning, has he brought the abolitionists to the conclusion,—that the interest of the poor, degraded, and oppressed slave, as well as that of his master, will be best secured by his remaining in slavery. It has indeed, been proposed to mitigate, in some degree, the miseries of his interminable bondage, but the blessings of emancipation, according to the propositions of the abolitionists in the last session of Parliament, were to be reserved for his posterity alone,—and every idea of immediate emancipation is still represented, not only as impolitic, enthusiastic and visionary, but as highly injurious to the slave himself,—and a train of supposed apt illustrations is continually at hand, to expose the absurdity of such a project. Who (it is asked) would place a sumptuous banquet before a half-famished wretch, whilst his powers of digestion were so feeble that it would be fatal to partake of it?—Who would bring a body benumbed and half frozen with cold, into sudden contact with fervid heat? Who would take a poor captive from his dungeon, where he had been immured whole years, in total darkness, and bring him at once into the dazzling light of a meridian sun? No one, in his senses, certainly. All these transitions from famine to plenty,—from cold to heat,—from darkness to light, must be gradual in order to be salutary. But must it therefore follow, by any inductions of common sense, that emancipation out of the gripe of a robber or an assassin,—out of the jaws of a shark or a tiger, must be gradual? Must, it, therefore, follow, that the wretched victim of slavery must always remain in slavery?—that emancipation must be so gradual, that the blessings of freedom shall never be tasted by him who has endured all the curses of slavery, but be reserved for his posterity alone?

LEVI COFFIN

Between 1800 and 1860, thousands of Friends left the American South for Ohio and Indiana. Some were simply farmers looking for good land, but many were drawn to the states north of the Ohio River because slavery was banned there. Many in turn became active in antislavery work. Among the best known was Levi Coffin (1798–1877). Late in life, Coffin recorded his memories of his work aiding fugitive slaves.

Reminiscences of Levi Coffin, the Reputed President of the Underground Railroad: Being a Brief History of the Labors of a Lifetime in Behalf of the Slave (Cincinnati, 1880).

In the early part of the ninth month, 1826, we took a final leave of North Carolina. . . . We located at Newport, Wayne County, Indiana, where we lived for more than twenty years. This village was in the midst of a large settlement of Friends, and a Quarterly Meeting was then established at New Garden Meetinghouse, about a half mile from the village. I bought property in Newport, and finding that there was a good opening there for a mercantile business, I concluded to engage in it. . . . This venture was successful, and I increased my stock and varied my assortment of goods until a large retail business was established.

The next year I commenced cutting pork in a small way, besides carrying on my other business. This I continued to do, enlarging my operations every year, and kept it up as long as I remained in Newport.

In the year 1836, I built an oil mill and manufactured linseed oil. Notwithstanding all this multiplicity of business, I was never too busy to engage in Underground Railroad affairs. Soon after we located at Newport, I found that we were on a line of the U. G. R. R. Fugitives often passed through that place, and generally stopped among the colored people. There was in that neighborhood a number of families of free colored people, mostly from North Carolina, who were the descendants of slaves who had been liberated by Friends many years before, and sent to free states at the expense of North Carolina Yearly Meeting. I learned that the fugitive slaves who took refuge with these people were often pursued and captured, the colored people not being very skillful in concealing them, or shrewd in making arrangements to forward them to Canada. I was pained to hear of the capture of these fugitives, and inquired of some of the Friends in our village why they did not take them in and secret them, when they were pursued, and then aid them on their way to Canada? I found that they were afraid of the penalty of the law. I told them that I read in the Bible when I was a boy that it was right to take in the stranger and administer to those in distress, and that I thought it was always safe to do right. The Bible, in bidding us to feed the hungry and clothe the naked, said nothing about color, and I should try to follow out the teachings of that good book. I was willing to receive and aid as many fugitives as were disposed to come to my house. I knew that my wife's feelings and sympathies regarding this matter were the same as mine, and that she was willing to do her part. It soon became known to the colored people in our neighborhood and others, that our house was a depot where the hunted and harassed fugitive journeying northward, on the Underground Railroad, could find succor and sympathy. It also became known at other depots on the various lines that converged at Newport.

In the winter of 1826–27, fugitives began to come to our house and as it became more widely known on different routes that the slaves fleeing from bondage would find a welcome and shelter at our house, and be forwarded safely on their journey, the number increased. Friends in the neighborhood, who had formerly stood aloof from the work, fearful of the penalty of the law, were encouraged to engage in it when they saw the fearless manner in which I acted, and the success that attended my efforts. They

would contribute to clothe the fugitives, and would aid in forward-
ing them on their way, but were timid about sheltering them under
their roof; so that part of the work devolved on us. Some seemed
really glad to see the work go on, if somebody else would do it.
Others doubted the propriety of it, and tried to discourage me, and
dissuade me from running such risks. They manifested great concern for my safety and pecuniary interests, telling me that such a
course of action would injure my business and perhaps ruin me;
that I ought to consider the welfare of my family; and warning me
that my life was in danger, as there were many threats made
against me by the slave-hunters and those who sympathized with
them.

After listening quietly to these counselors, I told them that I felt
no condemnation for anything that I had ever done for the fugitive slaves. If by doing my duty and endeavoring to fulfill the in-
junctions of the Bible, I injured my business, then let my business
go. As to my safety, my life was in the hands of my Divine Master,
and I felt that I had his approval. I had no fear of the danger that
seemed to threaten my life or my business. If I was faithful to
duty, and honest and industrious, I felt that I would be preserved,
and that I could make enough to support my family. At one time
there came to see me a good old Friend, who was apparently very
deeply concerned for my welfare. He said he was as much opposed to slavery as I was, but thought it very wrong to harbor
fugitive slaves. No one there knew of what crimes they were
guilty; they might have killed their masters, or committed some
other atrocious deed, then those who sheltered them, and aided
them in their escape from justice would indirectly be accomplices.
He mentioned other objections which he wished me to consider,
and then talked for some time, trying to convince me of the errors of my ways. I heard him patiently until he had relieved his
mind of the burden upon it, and then asked if he thought the
Good Samaritan stopped to inquire whether the man who fell
among thieves was guilty of any crime before he attempted to help
him? I asked him if he were to see a stranger who had fallen into
the ditch would he not help him out until satisfied that he had
committed no atrocious deed? These, and many other questions
which I put to him, he did not seem able to answer satisfactorily.
He was so perplexed and confused that I really pitied the good old
man, and advised him to go home and read his Bible thoroughly,

and pray over it, and I thought his concern about my aiding fugitive slaves would be removed from his mind, and that he would feel like helping me in the work. We parted in good feeling, and he always manifested warm friendship toward me until the end of his days. . . .

The Underground Railroad business increased as time advanced, and it was attended with heavy expenses, which I could not have borne had not my affairs been prosperous. I found it necessary to keep a team and a wagon always at command, to convey the fugitive slaves on their journey. Sometimes, when we had large companies, one or two other teams and wagons were required. These journeys had to be made at night, often through deep mud and bad roads, and along by-ways that were seldom traveled. Every precaution to evade pursuit had to be used, as the hunters were often on the track, and sometimes ahead of the slaves. We had different routes for sending the fugitives to depots, ten, fifteen, or twenty miles distant, and when we heard of slavehunters having passed on one road, we forwarded our passengers by another.

In some instances where we learned that the pursuers were ahead of them, we sent a messenger and had the fugitives brought back to my house to remain in concealment until the bloodhounds in human shape had lost the trail and given up the pursuit.

I soon became extensively known to the friends of the slaves, at different points on the Ohio River, where fugitives generally crossed, and to those northward of us on the various routes leading to Canada. . . . We found it necessary to be always prepared to receive such company and properly care for them. We knew not what night or what hour of the night we would be roused from slumber by a gentle rap at the door. That was the signal announcing the arrival of a train of the Underground Railroad, for the locomotive did not whistle, nor make any unnecessary noise. I have often been awakened by this signal, and sprang out of bed in the dark and opened the door. Outside in the cold or rain, there would be a two-horse wagon loaded with fugitives, perhaps the greater part of them women and children. I would invite them, in a low tone, to come in, and they would follow me into the darkened house without a word, for we knew not who might be watching and listening. When they were all safely inside and the door fastened, I would cover the windows, strike a light and build a

good fire. By this time my wife would be up and preparing vict-
uals for them, and in a short time the cold and hungry fugitives
would be made comfortable. I would accompany the conductor
of the train to the stable, and care for the horses, that had, perhaps, been driven twenty-five or thirty miles that night, through
the cold and rain. The fugitives would rest on pallets before the
fire the rest of the night. Frequently, wagonloads of passengers
from the different lines have met at our house, having no previous
knowledge of each other. The companies varied in number, from
two or three fugitives to seventeen.

The care of so many necessitated much work and anxiety on
our part, but we assumed the burden of our own will and bore it
cheerfully. It was never too cold or stormy, or the hour of night
too late for my wife to rise from sleep, and provide food and comfortable lodging for the fugitives. Her sympathy for those in distress never tired, and her efforts in their behalf never abated. This
work was kept up during the time we lived at Newport, a period
of more than twenty years. The number of fugitives varied considerably in different years, but the annual average was more than
one hundred. They generally came to us destitute of clothing, and
were often barefooted. Clothing must be collected and kept on
hand, if possible, and money must be raised to buy shoes, and
purchase goods to make garments for women and children. The
young ladies in the neighborhood organized a sewing society, and
met at our house frequently, to make clothes for the fugitives.

Sometimes when the fugitives came to us destitute, we kept them
several days, until they could be provided with comfortable clothes.
This depended on the circumstances of danger. If they had come a
long distance and had been out several weeks or months—as was
sometimes the case—and it was not probable that hunters were on
their track, we thought it safe for them to remain with us until fitted for traveling through the thinly settled country to the North. . . .

Such as these we have kept until they were recruited in strength,
provided with clothes, and able to travel. When they first came to
us they were generally unwilling to tell their stories, or let us
know what part of the South they came from. They would not
give their names, or the names of their masters, correctly, fearing
that they would be betrayed. In several instances fugitives came
to our house sick from exhaustion and exposure, and lay several
weeks. One case was that of a woman and her two children—

little girls. Hearing that her children were to be sold away from her, she determined to take them with her and attempt to reach Canada. She had heard that Canada was a place where all were free, and that by traveling toward the north star she could reach it. She managed to get over the Ohio River with her two little girls, and then commenced her long and toilsome journey northward. Fearing to travel on the road, even at night, lest she should meet somebody, she made her way through the woods and across fields, living on fruits and green corn, when she could procure them, and sometimes suffering severely for lack of food. Thus she wandered on, and at last reached our neighborhood. Seeing a cabin where some colored people lived she made her way to it. The people received her kindly, and at once conducted her to our house. She was so exhausted by the hardships of her long journey, and so weakened by hunger, having denied herself to feed her children, that she soon became quite sick. Her children were very tired, but soon recovered their strength, and were in good health. They had no shoes nor clothing except what they had on, and that was in tatters. Dr. Henry H. Way was called in, and faithfully attended the sick woman, until her health was restored. Then the little party were provided with good clothing and other comforts, and were sent on their way to Canada.

Dr. Way was a warm friend to the fugitive slaves, and a hearty co-worker with me in anti-slavery matters. The number of those who were friendly to the fugitives increased in our neighborhood as time passed on. Many were willing to aid in clothing them and helping them on their way, and a few were willing to aid in secreting them, but the depot seemed to be established at my house.

Notwithstanding the many threats of slave hunters and the strong prejudices of proslavery men, I continued to prosper and gained a business influence in the community. Some of my customers, who had left me several years before on account of my antislavery sentiments, began to deal with me again. I had been elected a director in the Richmond branch of the State Bank, and was reelected annually for six or seven years, by the stockholders, to represent our district. When anyone wished accommodation from the bank, much depended on the director from the district where the applicant lived. His word or influence would generally decide the matter. The remembrance of this seemed to hold a check on some of the proslavery men of our neighborhood. They

wished to retain my friendship, and did not openly oppose my
U. G. R. R. work as they might otherwise have done. My business
influence no doubt operated in some degree to shield me from the
attacks of the slave hunters. These men often threatened to kill
me, and at various times offered a reward for my head. I often received anonymous letters warning me that my store, pork-house,
and dwelling would be burned to the ground, and one letter,
mailed in Kentucky, informed me that a body of armed men were
then on their way to Newport to destroy the town. The letter
named the night in which the work would be accomplished, and
warned me to flee from the place, for if I should be taken my life
would pay for my crimes against Southern slaveholders. I had become so accustomed to threats and warnings, that this made no
impression on me—struck no terror to my heart. The most of
the inhabitants of our village were Friends, and their principles
were those of peace and nonresistance. They were not alarmed at
the threat to destroy the town, and on the night appointed retired
to their beds as usual and slept peacefully. We placed no senti-
nels to give warning of danger, and had no extra company at our
house to guard our lives. We retired to rest at the usual hour, and
were not disturbed during the night. In the morning the buildings
were all there—there was no smell of fire, no sign of the terrible
destruction threatened. . . .

Slave hunters often passed through our town, and sometimes
had hired ruffians with them from Richmond, and other neighboring places. They knew me well, and knew that I harbored
slaves and aided them to escape, but they never ventured to search
my premises, or molest me in any way.

I had many employees about my place of business, and much
company about my house, and it seemed too public a place for
fugitives to hide. These slave hunters knew that if they committed
any trespass, or went beyond the letter of the law, I would have
them arrested, and they knew also that I had many friends who
would stand at my back and aid me in prosecuting them. Thus,
my business influence and large acquaintance afforded me protection in my labors for the oppressed fugitives. I expressed my antislavery sentiments with boldness on every occasion. I told the
sympathizers with slave-hunters that I intended to shelter as many
runaway slaves as came to my house, and aid them on their way;

and advised them to be careful how they interfered with my work. They might get themselves into difficulty if they undertook to capture slaves from my premises, and become involved in a legal prosecution, for most of the arrests of slaves were unlawful. The law required that a writ should be obtained and a proof that the slave was their property before they could take him away and if they proceeded contrary to these requirements, and attempted to enter my house, I would have them arrested as kidnappers. These expressions, uttered frequently, had, I thought, a tendency to intimidate the slave hunters and their friends, and to prevent them from entering my house to search for slaves.

The pursuit was often very close, and we had to resort to various stratagems in order to elude the pursuers. Sometimes a company of fugitives were scattered, and secreted in the neighborhood until the hunters had given up the chase. At other times their route was changed and they were hurried forward with all speed. It was a continual excitement and anxiety to us, but the work was its own reward. . . .

Many of the fugitives came long distances, from Alabama, Mississippi, Louisiana, in fact from all parts of the South. Sometimes the poor hunted creatures had been out so long, living in woods and thickets, that they were almost wild when they came in, and so fearful of being betrayed, that it was some time before their confidence could be gained and the true state of their case learned. Although the number of fugitives that I aided on their way was so large, not one, so far as I ever knew, was captured and taken back to slavery. Providence seemed to favor our efforts for the poor slaves, and to crown them with success.

LUCRETIA MOTT

One of the best-known Quaker reformers of the nineteenth century was Lucretia (Coffin) Mott (1793-1880), a Hicksite minister. Born on Nantucket, she spent most of her life in Philadelphia. An enthusiastic abolitionist, in 1848 she helped organize the first women's rights convention in the United States, held at Seneca Falls, New York. The following lecture was her most extended work on women and reform.

Lucretia Mott, *Discourse on Woman, Delivered
at the Assembly Buildings, December 17, 1849.*
(Philadelphia, 1850).

There is nothing of greater importance to the well-being of society
at large—of man as well as woman—than the true and proper position of woman. Much has been said, from time to time, upon
this subject. It has been a theme for ridicule, for satire and sarcasm. We might look for this from the ignorant and vulgar; but
from the intelligent and refined we have a right to expect that such
weapons shall not be resorted to,—that gross comparisons and
vulgar epithets shall not be applied, so as to place woman, in a
point of view, ridiculous to say the least.

This subject has claimed my earnest interest for many years. I
have long wished to see woman occupying a more elevated position than that which custom for ages has allotted to her. It was
with great regret, therefore, that I listened a few days ago to a
lecture upon this subject, which, though replete with intellectual beauty, and containing much that was true and excellent, was
yet fraught with sentiments calculated to retard the progress of
woman to the high elevation destined by her Creator. I regretted
the more that these sentiments should be presented with such intellectual vigor and beauty, because they would be likely to en-
snare the young.

The minds of young people generally, are open to the reception
of more exalted views upon this subject. The kind of homage that
has been paid to woman, the flattering appeals which have too
long satisfied her—appeals to her mere fancy and imagination,
are giving place to a more extended recognition of her rights, her
important duties and responsibilities in life. Woman is claiming
for herself stronger and more profitable food. Various are the in-
dications leading to this conclusion. The increasing attention to
female education, the improvement in the literature of the age,
especially in what is called the "Ladies' Department," in the pe-
riodicals of the day, are among the proofs of a higher estimate of
woman in society at large. Therefore we may hope that the intellectual and intelligent are being prepared for the discussion of this
question, in a manner which shall tend to ennoble woman and
dignify man.

Free discussion upon this, as upon all other subjects, is never to be feared; nor will be, except by such as prefer darkness to light. "Those only who are in the wrong dread discussion. The light alarms those only who feel the need of darkness." It was sound philosophy, uttered by Jesus, "He that doeth truth cometh to the light, that his deeds may be made manifest, that they are wrought in God."

I have not come here with a view of answering any particular parts of the lecture alluded to, in order to point out the fallacy of its reasoning. The speaker, however, did not profess to offer anything like argument on that occasion, but rather a sentiment. I have no prepared address to deliver to you, being unaccustomed to speak in that way; but I felt a wish to offer some views for your consideration, though in a desultory manner, which may lead to such reflection and discussion as will present the subject in a true light.

In the beginning, man and woman were created equal. "Male and female created he them, and blessed them, and called their name Adam." He gave dominion to both over the lower animals, but not to one over the other.

> Man o'er woman
> He made not lord, such title to himself
> Reserving, human left from human free.

The cause of the subjection of woman to man, was early ascribed to disobedience to the command of God. This would seem to show that she was then regarded as not occupying her true and rightful position in society.

The laws given on Mount Sinai for the government of man and woman were equal, the precepts of Jesus make no distinction. Those who read the Scriptures, and judge for themselves, not resting satisfied with the perverted application of the text, do not find the distinction, that theology and ecclesiastical authorities have made, in the condition of the sexes. In the early ages, Miriam and Deborah, conjointly with Aaron and Barak, enlisted themselves on the side which they regarded the right, unitedly going up to their battles, and singing their songs of victory. We regard these with veneration. Deborah judged Israel many years—she went up with Barak against their enemies, with an army of 10,000, assuring him that the honor of the battle should not be to him, but to a woman. Revolting as were the circumstances of their success, the acts of a semi-barbarous people, yet we read with reverence the song of Deborah: "Blessed above woman shall Jael, the wife of Heber, the Kenite be; blessed shall she be above women in the tent. . . . She put her hand to the nail, and her right hand to the workman's hammer; she smote Sisera through his temples. At her feet he bowed, he fell, he lay down dead." This circumstance, revolting to Christianity, is recognized as an act befitting woman in that day. Deborah, Huldah, and other honorable women, were looked up to and consulted in times of exigency, and their counsel was received. In that eastern country, with all the customs tending to degrade woman, some were called to fill great and important stations in society. There were also false prophetesses as well as true. The denunciations of Ezekiel were upon those women who would "prophesy out of their own heart, and sew pillows to all armholes."

Coming down to later times, we find Anna, a prophetess of four-score years, in the temple day and night, speaking of Christ to all them who looked for redemption in Jerusalem. Numbers of women were the companions of Jesus,—one going to the men of the city, saying, "Come, see a man who told me all things that ever I did; is not this the Christ?" Another, "Whatsoever he saith unto you, do it." Philip had four daughters who did prophesy. Tryphena and Tryphosa were coworkers with the apostles in their mission, to whom they sent special messages of regard and acknowledgment of their labors in the gospel. A learned Jew, mighty in the Scriptures, was by Priscilla instructed in the way of the Lord more perfectly. Phebe is mentioned as a servant of Christ, and commended as such to the brethren. It is worthy of note, that the word *servant*, when applied to Tychicus, is rendered *minister*. Women professing godliness, should be translated *preaching*.

The first announcement, on the day of Pentecost, was the fulfillment of ancient prophecy, that God's spirit should be poured out upon *daughters* as well as sons, and they should prophesy. It is important that we be familiar with these facts, because woman has been so long circumscribed in her influence by the perverted application of the text, rendering it improper for her to speak in the assemblies of the people, "to edification, to exhortation, and to comfort."

If these scriptures were read intelligently, we should not so learn Christ, as to exclude any from a position, where they might exert an influence for good to their fellow-beings. The epistle to the Corinthian church, where the supposed apostolic prohibition of women's preaching is found, contains express directions how woman shall appear, when she prayeth or prophesyeth. Judge then whether this admonition, relative to speaking and asking questions, in the excited state of that church, should be regarded as a standing injunction on woman's preaching, when that word was not used by the apostle. Where is the Scripture authority for the advice given to the early church, under peculiar circumstances, being binding on the church of the present day? Ecclesiastical history informs us, that for two or three hundred years, female ministers suffered martyrdom, in company with their brethren.

These things are too much lost sight of. They should be known, in order that we may be prepared to meet the assertion, so often made, that woman is stepping out of her appropriate sphere, when she shall attempt to instruct public assemblies. The present time particularly demands such investigation. It requires also, that "of yourselves ye should judge what is right," that you should know the ground whereon you stand. This age is notable for its works of mercy and benevolence—for the efforts that are made to reform the inebriate and the degraded, to relieve the oppressed and the suffering. Women as well as men are interested in these works of justice and mercy. They are efficient coworkers, their talents are called into profitable exercise, their labors are effective in each department of reform. The blessing to the merciful, to the peacemaker is equal to man and to woman. It is greatly to be deplored, now that she is increasingly qualified for usefulness, that any view should be presented, calculated to retard her labors of love.

Why should not woman seek to be a reformer? If she is to shrink from being such an iconoclast as shall "break the image of man's lower worship," as so long held up to view; if she is to fear to exercise her reason, and her noblest powers, lest she should be thought to "attempt to act the man," and not "acknowledge his supremacy"; if she is to be satisfied with the narrow sphere assigned her by man, nor aspire to a higher, lest she should transcend the bounds of female delicacy; truly it is a mournful prospect for woman. We would admit all the difference, that our great and beneficent Creator has made, in the relation of man and woman, nor would we seek to disturb this relation; but we deny that the present position of woman, is her true sphere of usefulness: nor will she attain to this sphere, until the disabilities and disadvantages, religious, civil, and social, which impede her progress, are removed out of her way. These restrictions have enervated her mind and paralyzed her powers. While man assumes, that the present is the original state designed for woman, that the existing "differences are not arbitrary nor the result of accident," but grounded in nature; she will not make the necessary effort to obtain her just rights, lest it should subject her to the kind of scorn and contemptuous manner in which she has been spoken of.

So far from her "ambition leading her to attempt to act the man," she needs all the encouragement she can receive, by the removal of obstacles from her path, in order that she may become a "true woman." As it is desirable that man should act a manly and generous part, not "mannish," so let woman be urged to exercise a dignified and womanly bearing, not womanish. Let her cultivate all the graces and proper accomplishments of her sex, but let not these degenerate into a kind of effeminacy, in which she is satisfied to be the mere plaything or toy of society, content with her outward adornings, and with the tone of flattery and fulsome adulation too often addressed to her. True, nature has made a difference in her configuration, her physical strength, her voice,—and we ask no change, we are satisfied with nature. But how has neglect and mismanagement increased this difference! It is our duty to develop these natural powers, by suitable exercise, so that they may be strengthened "by reason of use." In the ruder state of society, woman is made to bear heavy burdens, while her "lord and master" walks idly by her side. In the civilization to which we have attained, if cultivated and refined woman would bring all her powers into use, she might engage in pursuits which she now shrinks from as beneath her proper vocation. The energies of men need not then be wholly devoted to the counting house and common business of life, in order that women in fashionable society, may be supported in their daily promenades and nightly visits to the theatre and ball room. . . .

A new generation of women is now upon the stage, improving the increased opportunities furnished for the acquirement of knowledge. Public education is coming to be regarded the right of the children of a republic. The hill of science is not so difficult of ascent as formerly represented by poets and painters; but by fact and demonstration smoothed down, so as to be accessible to the assumed weak capacity of woman. She is rising in the scale of being through this, as well as other means, and finding heightened pleasure and profit on the right hand and on the left. The study of physiology, now introduced into our common schools, is engaging her attention, impressing the necessity of the observance of the laws of health. The intellectual lyceum and instructive lecture room are becoming, to many, more attractive than the theatre and the ballroom. The sickly and sentimental novel and pernicious romance are giving place to works, calculated to call forth the benevolent affections and higher nature. It is only by comparison that I would speak commendatory of these works of imagination. The frequent issue of them from the press is to be regretted. Their exciting contents, like stimulating drinks, when long indulged in, enervate the mind, unfitting it for the sober duties of life.

These duties are not to be limited by man. Nor will woman fulfill less her domestic relations, as the faithful companion of her chosen husband, and the fitting mother of her children, because she has a right estimate of her position and her responsibilities. Her self-respect will be increased; preserving the dignity of her being, she will not suffer herself to be degraded into a mere dependent. Nor will her feminine character be impaired. Instances are not few, of woman throwing off the encumbrances which bind her, and going forth in a manner worthy of herself, her creation, and her dignified calling. Did Elizabeth Fry lose any of her feminine qualities by the public walk into which she was called? Having performed the duties of a mother to a large family, feeling that she owed a labor of love to the poor prisoner, she was empowered by Him who sent her forth, to go to kings and crowned heads of the earth, and ask audience of these; and it was granted her. Did she lose the delicacy of woman by her acts? No. Her retiring modesty was characteristic of her to the latest period of her life. It was my privilege to enjoy her society some years ago, and I found all that belonged to the feminine in woman—to true nobility, in a refined and purified moral nature. Is Dorothea Dix* throwing

* [Dorothea Dix (1802–1887) advocated reform in American insane asylums.—ed.]

off her womanly nature and appearance in the course she is pursuing? In finding duties abroad, has any, "refined man felt that something of beauty has gone forth from her?" To use the contemptuous word applied in the lecture alluded to, is she becoming "mannish?" Is she compromising her womanly dignity in going forth to seek to better the condition of the insane and afflicted? Is not a beautiful mind and a retiring modesty still conspicuous in her? . . .

Woman was not wanting in courage, in the early ages. In war and bloodshed this trait was often displayed. Grecian and Roman history have lauded and honored her in this character. English history records her courageous women too, for unhappily we have little but the records of war handed down to us. The courage of Joan of Arc was made the subject of a popular lecture not long ago, by one of our intelligent citizens. But more noble, moral daring is marking the female character at the present time, and better worthy of imitation. As these characteristics come to be appreciated in man too, his warlike acts, with all the miseries and horrors of the battleground, will sink into their merited oblivion, or be remembered only to be condemned. The heroism displayed in the tented field, must yield to the moral and Christian heroism which is shadowed in the signs of our times. . . .

The question is often asked, "What does woman want, more than she enjoys? What is she seeking to obtain? Of what rights is she deprived? What privileges are withheld from her?" I answer, she asks nothing as favor, but as right, she wants to be acknowledged a moral, responsible being. She is seeking not to be governed by laws, in the making of which she has no voice. She is deprived of almost every right in civil society, and is a cypher in the nation, except in the right of presenting a petition. In religious society her disabilities, as already pointed out, have greatly retarded her progress. Her exclusion from the pulpit or ministry—her duties marked out for her by her equal brother man, subject to creeds, rules, and disciplines made for her by him—this is unworthy her true dignity. In marriage, there is assumed superiority, on the part of the husband, and admitted inferiority, with a promise of obedience, on the part of the wife. This subject calls loudly for examination, in order that the wrong may be redressed. Customs suited to darker ages in Eastern countries, are not binding upon enlightened society. The solemn covenant of marriage may be entered into without these lordly assumptions, and humiliating concessions and promises.

There are large Christian denominations who do not recognize such degrading relations of husband and wife. They ask no magisterial or ministerial aid to legalize or to sanctify this union. But acknowledging themselves in the presence of the Highest, and invoking his assistance, they come under reciprocal obligations of fidelity and affection, before suitable witnesses. Experience and observation go to prove, that there may be as much harmony, to say the least, in such a union, and as great purity and permanency of affection, as can exist where the more common custom or form is observed. The distinctive relations of husband and wife, of father and mother of a family are sacredly preserved, without the assumption of authority on the one part, or the promise of obedience on the other. There is nothing in such a marriage degrading to woman. She does not compromise her dignity or self-respect; but enters married life upon equal ground, by the side of her husband. By proper education, she understands her duties, physical, intellectual and moral; and fulfilling these, she is a helpmeet, in the true sense of the word.

I tread upon delicate ground in alluding to the institutions of religious associations; but the subject is of so much importance, that all which relates to the position of woman, should be examined, apart from the undue veneration which ancient usage receives.

> Such dupes are men to custom, and so prone
> To reverence what is ancient, and can plead
> A course of long observance for its use,
> That even servitude, the worst of ills,
> Because delivered down from sire to son,
> Is kept and guarded as a sacred thing.

So with woman. She has so long been subject to the disabilities and restrictions, with which her progress has been embarrassed, that she has become enervated, her mind to some extent paralyzed; and, like those still more degraded by personal bondage, she hugs her chains. Liberty is often presented in its true light, but it is liberty for man.

Whose freedom is by suffrance, and at will
Of a superior—he is never free.
Who lives, and is not weary of a life
Exposed to manacles, deserves them well.

I would not, however, go so far, either as regards the abject
slave or woman; for in both cases they may be so degraded by the
crushing influences around them, that they may not be sensible of
the blessing of Freedom. Liberty is not less a blessing, because
oppression has so long darkened the mind that it cannot appreci-
ate it. I would therefore urge, that woman be placed in such a
situation in society, by the yielding of her rights, and have such
opportunities for growth and development, as shall raise her from
this low, enervated and paralyzed condition, to a full appreciation
of the blessing of entire freedom of mind.

It is with reluctance that I make the demand for the political rights of woman, because this claim is so distasteful to the age.
Woman shrinks, in the present state of society, from taking any
interest in politics. The events of the French Revolution, and the
claim for woman's rights are held up to her as a warning. But let
us not look at the excesses of women alone, at that period; but
remember that the age was marked with extravagances and wickedness in men as well as women. Indeed, political life abounds
with these excesses, and with shameful outrage. Who knows, but
that if woman acted her part in governmental affairs, there might
be an entire change in the turmoil of political life. It becomes man
to speak modestly of his ability to act without her. If woman's
judgment were exercised, why might she not aid in making the
laws by which she is governed? Lord Brougham remarked that the
works of Harriet Martineau upon political economy were not
excelled by those of any political writer of the present time. The
first few chapters of her *Society in America*, her views of a republic, and of government generally, furnish evidence of woman's capacity to embrace subjects of universal interest.

Far be it from me to encourage woman to vote, or to take an
active part in politics, in the present state of our government. Her
right to the elective franchise, however, is the same, and should
be yielded to her, whether she exercise that right or not. Would that
man too, would have no participation in a government based
upon the life-taking principle—upon retaliation and the sword. It

is unworthy a Christian nation. But when, in the diffusion of light and intelligence, a convention shall be called to make regulations for self-government on Christian, nonresistant principles, I can see no good reason, why woman should not participate in such an assemblage, taking part equally with man.

[Timothy] Walker, of Cincinnati, in his *Introduction to American Law*, says: "With regard to political rights, females form a positive exception to the general doctrine of equality. They have no part or lot in the formation or administration of government. They cannot vote or hold office. We require them to contribute their share in the way of taxes, to the support of government, but allow them no voice in its direction. We hold them amenable to the laws when made, but allow them no share in making them. This language, applied to males, would be the exact definition of political slavery; applied to females, custom does not teach us so to regard it." Woman, however, is beginning so to regard it.

"The law of husband and wife, as you gather it from the books, is a disgrace to any civilized nation. The theory of the law degrades the wife almost to the level of slaves. When a woman marries, we call her condition coverture, and speak of her as a femme covert. The old writers call the husband baron, and sometimes, in plain English, lord. . . . The merging of her name in that of her husband is emblematic of the fate of all her legal rights. The torch of Hymen serves but to light the pile, on which these rights are offered up. The legal theory is, that marriage makes the husband and wife one person, and that person is the husband. On this subject, reform is loudly called for. There is no foundation in reason or expediency, for the absolute and slavish subjection of the wife to the husband, which forms the foundation of the present legal relations. Were woman, in point of fact, the abject thing which the law, in theory, considers her to be when married, she would not be worthy the companionship of man."

I would ask if such a code of laws does not require change? If such a condition of the wife in society does not claim redress? On no good ground can reform be delayed. Blackstone says, "The very being and legal existence of woman is suspended during marriage,—incorporated or consolidated into that of her husband, under whose protection and cover she performs every thing." [Elisha] Hurlbut, in his *Essays upon Human Rights*, says: "The laws touching the rights of woman are at variance with the laws of the Creator. Rights are human rights, and pertain to human beings, without distinction of sex. Laws should not be made for man or for woman, but for mankind. Man was not born to command, nor woman to obey. . . . The law of France, Spain, and Holland, and one of our own States, Louisiana, recognizes the wife's right to property, more than the common law of England. . . . The laws depriving woman of the right of property is handed down to us from dark and feudal times, and not consistent with the wiser, better, purer spirit of the age. The wife is a mere pensioner on the bounty of her husband. Her lost rights are appropriated to himself. But justice and benevolence are abroad in our land, awakening the spirit of inquiry and innovation; and the Gothic fabric of the British law will fall before it, save where it is based upon the foundation of truth and justice."

May these statements lead you to reflect upon this subject, that you may know what woman's condition is in society—what her restrictions are, and seek to remove them. In how many cases in our country, the husband and wife begin life together, and by equal industry and united effort accumulate to themselves a comfortable home. In the event of the death of the wife, the household remains undisturbed, his farm or his workshop is not broken up, or in any way molested. But when the husband dies, he either gives his wife a portion of their joint accumulation, or the law apportions to her a share; the homestead is broken up, and she is dispossessed of that which she earned equally with him; for what she lacked in physical strength, she made up in constancy of labor and toil, day and evening. The sons then coming into possession of the property, as has been the custom until of latter time, speak of having to keep their mother, when she in reality is aiding to keep them. Where is the justice of this state of things? The change in the law of this State and of New York, in relation to the property of the wife, go to a limited extent toward the redress of these wrongs; but they are far more extensive, and involve much more, than I have time this evening to point out.

On no good ground can the legal existence of the wife be suspended during marriage, and her property surrendered to her husband. In the intelligent ranks of society, the wife may not in point of fact, be so degraded as the law would degrade her; because public sentiment is above the law. Still, while the law stands, she is liable to the disabilities which it imposes. Among the ignorant classes of society, woman is made to bear heavy burdens, and is degraded almost to the level of the slave.

There are many instances now in our city, where the wife suffers much from the power of the husband to claim all that she can earn with her own hands. In my intercourse with the poorer class of people, I have known cases of extreme cruelty, from the hard earnings of the wife being thus robbed by the husband, and no redress at law.

An article in one of the daily papers lately, presented the condition of needlewomen in England. There might be a presentation of this class in our own country, which would make the heart bleed. Public attention should be turned to this subject, in order that avenues of more profitable employment may be opened to women. There are many kinds of business which women, equally with men, may follow with respectability and success. Their talents and energies should be called forth, and their powers brought into the highest exercise. The efforts of women in France are sometimes pointed to in ridicule and sarcasm, but depend upon it, the opening of profitable employment to women in that country, is doing much for the enfranchisement of the sex. In England also, it is not an uncommon thing for a wife to take up the business of her deceased husband and carry it on with success. . . .

In visiting the public school in London, a few years since, I noticed that the boys were employed in linear drawing, and instructed upon the black board, in the higher branches of arithmetic and mathematics; while the girls, after a short exercise in the mere elements of arithmetic, were seated, during the bright hours of the morning, stitching wristbands. I asked, Why there should be this difference made; why they too should not have the black board? The answer was, that they would not probably fill any station in society requiring such knowledge.

But the demand for a more extended education will not cease, until girls and boys have equal instruction, in all the departments of useful knowledge. We have as yet no high school for girls in this state. The normal school may be a preparation for such an establishment. In the late convention for general education, it was cheering to hear the testimony borne to woman's capabilities for head teachers of the public schools. . . . At the last examination of the public schools in this city, one of the alumni delivered an address on Woman, not as is too common, in eulogistic strains, but directing the attention to the injustice done to woman in her position in society, in a variety of ways. The unequal wages she receives for her constant toil, presenting facts calculated to arouse attention to the subject.

Women's property has been taxed, equally with that of men's, to sustain colleges endowed by the states; but they have not been permitted to enter those high seminaries of learning. Within a few years, however, some colleges have been instituted, where young women are admitted, nearly upon equal terms with young men; and numbers are availing themselves of their long denied rights. This is among the signs of the times, indicative of an advance for women. The book of knowledge is not opened to her in vain. Already is she aiming to occupy important posts of honor and profit in our country. We have three female editors in our state—some in other states of the Union. Numbers are entering the medical profession—one received a diploma last year; others are preparing for a like result.

Let woman then go on—not asking as favor, but claiming as right, the removal of all the hindrances to her elevation in the scale of being—let her receive encouragement for the proper cultivation of all her powers, so that she may enter profitably into the active business of life; employing her own hands, in ministering to her necessities, strengthening her physical being by proper exercise, and observance of the laws of health. Let her not be ambitious to display a fair hand, and to promenade the fashionable streets of our city, but rather, coveting earnestly the best gifts, let her strive to occupy such walks in society, as will befit her true dignity in all the relations of life. No fear that she will then transcend the proper limits of female delicacy. True modesty will be as fully preserved, in acting out those important vocations to which she may be called, as in the nursery or at the fireside, ministering to man's self-indulgence.

Then in the marriage union, the independence of the husband and wife will be equal, their dependence mutual, and their obligations reciprocal.

In conclusion, let me say, "Credit not the old fashioned absurdity, that woman's is a secondary lot, ministering to the necessities of her lord and master! It is a higher destiny I would award you. If your immortality is as complete, and your gift of mind as capable as ours, of increase and elevation, I would put no wisdom of mine against God's evident allotment. I would charge you to water the undying bud, and give it healthy culture, and open its beauty to the sun—and then you may hope, that when your life is bound up with another, you will go on equally, and in a fellowship that shall pervade every earthly interest."

CONTROVERSY

THE FRIEND

Not all Friends looked with favor on such activism. They worried that Quakers endangered their standing as a peculiar people by joining with non-Quakers, even in good causes. Typical of this outlook was this article, which appeared in The Friend, *a journal published by Orthodox Friends in Philadelphia.*

S. S., "Mixed Associations," *The Friend*, vol. 6 (7th Mo. 20, 1833).

The recommendation contained in the epistle of our last yearly meeting, to our young friends, to avoid an indiscriminate commingling in associations with others not in profession with us, has received an enhanced importance in the view of some, who have been led to look a little about them as to the *cause* of the concern then felt.

The practical effect of such intercourse, even upon minds no longer young, is sorrowfully apparent to those who cast enquiring glances over the Society, and seek for some who had at different periods become a little conspicuous and loved among their brethren, but who have gradually receded from view, and too many become aliens to the commonwealth of Israel. If then the devastating power of association with and conformity to the world, is apparent in those who have had strength to make some little advances in the way, and to declare on whose side they were; how much more powerful must such intercourse prove to the susceptible mind, tendered with desires after good, but with little stability of purpose or experience to guide it?

The writer of these remarks has often had occasion, in reflecting on this subject, to remember one, who in the earlier day of his existence had a "gift in the ministration of the word" committed to him; who stood conspicuously in the front rank of the battle; honoured among the elders, and beloved among the youth; persuading with apostolic energy the wanderer to return, the wicked to repent; and dwelling with the love of a disciple upon the attributes of his Lord, as he handed forth the provender which the Master had blessed to the multitude; and he has often to reflect on the downward path of this star of the firmament. "My mountain standeth firm, I shall never be moved," is a dangerous thought to admit into the human heart, opposed in its very nature to the alone safe ground, "Watch and pray, lest ye enter into temptation." Through unfaithfulness in this individual, weakness and uneasiness entered; instead of "communing with his own heart and being still," he strove to drown the voice of reproof in personal activity. In his immediate neighbourhood he became conspicuous in the formation and encouragement of associations for objects ostensibly praiseworthy; his strength thereby was dissipated, and he fearfully and lamentably fell, while his place in Society knows him no more.

There are many within the very limited knowledge of the writer, who have been visibly injured by such associations, who would have "found their safety to have consisted in stillness, and a deep indwelling with the seed of life in their own hearts." It requires firmness in the youthful mind, to resist the contagion of example where epithets of honour and courtesy are the current medium of conversation. Nor is it easy, when at meetings for benevolent purposes an individual is called upon by another for a prayer, to decline the customary observances of such occasions; we do not like to appear singular, and rather than bear the cross, we let the testimony of the Society fall to the ground.

"Lead us not into temptation," continues to be a necessary aspiration, fitted to our mutual condition, and peculiarly adapted to the season of youth. Continued intercourse presents a succession of temptations, and in some particular or other almost every individual thus commingling, through a very mistaken charity, contributes something of his convictions and peculiarities to the general stock of condescensions. "In this thing the Lord pardon thy servant, that when my master goeth into the house of Rimmon to worship there, and he leaneth on my hand, and I bow myself in the house of Rimmon; when I bow down myself in the house of Rimmon, the Lord pardon thy servant in this thing."

The compliances which a promiscuous intermixture with the world have a tendency to lead our young men into, are but the outward and visible signs of important transactions within; they are as the hands of the time-piece that show forth the secret revolutions of the machine. If personal activity is suffered to drown the still small voice, and the pattern shown upon the mount is forgotten in the glow of animal sensation produced by popular pursuits and associations, the change will be visible to the eyes of mourning friends, even though the unhappy individual may say "no eye seeth me."

S. S.

WATERLOO YEARLY MEETING OF CONGREGATIONAL FRIENDS

In some yearly meetings, conservative opponents of radical reform disowned Friends who disregarded the advice of the larger body of Friends to avoid antislavery societies. This led to separations in several. Among the most visionary reformers were Hicksite Friends in upstate New York who in 1848 formed the Waterloo Yearly Meeting of Congregational Friends.

Basis of Religious Association, Adopted by the Conference Held at Farmington, in the State of New York, on the 6th and 7th of Tenth month, 1848 (Waterloo, N.Y., 1848).

To All to Whom These May Come:

Beloved Brethren, and Sisters:—

Having, pursuant to adjournment, in the 6th month last, again met, to consider what measures it will be right to adopt, that the blessings of Religious Society may be placed within the reach of all, our minds have been led into an examination of religious association in general. In looking at this subject, melancholy evidences present on every hand, that societies or church-organizations, ostensibly for the promotion of religion, have been among the greatest impediments to its progress, and the most fruitful sources of tyranny and oppression. But, while we feel that these facts should lead to the utmost care in regard to the principles permitted to enter into their structure, we are abundantly assured that these results are their abuse, not their necessary attendants—the consequence of the admission into them of elements hostile to man's nature, his duties, and inalienable rights. Religious association has manifestly its foundation in the religious and social elements of the human mind—principles powerful and constant in our nature, and most beneficent in their legitimate action. We are made pre-eminently social beings. From the exercise of the social principles of our nature, flow all the reciprocal benefits, all the countless offices of love and kindness, which strew with blessings the path of life. Not only in the physical, but especially in the higher departments of man's nature—the moral and religious— we behold the working of this beautiful and beneficent economy;— in the mingling of sympathies and affections; in imparting to each other the treasures of the intellect, the conscience, the religious feelings; in united aspirations to, and reverence and adoration of the Supreme Being.

To attain these social religious benefits in the highest degree, assemblies are needed; these require arrangement, time, manner, as well as object; in short, organization, or understood modes of action. We need only that these be wise and right—not conflicting with man's prerogatives, nor God's.

The object of religious association may be defined in brief to be, the promotion of righteousness—of practical goodness—love to God and man—on the part of every member composing the association, and in the world at large. So far as it is instrumental to this end, it is Christian, a blessing to the community in which it exists. So far as it is not thus instrumental, its non-existence were desirable. To promote this object there must be a practical conformity to the Divine laws—the principles of the association must be in harmony with the principles of the Divine government. For righteousness is none other than the result of these laws—the exemplification of these principles in the actions of moral agents.

Man is made to sustain a relation of an intelligent and accountable agent under the Supreme Intelligence; has the law of

God written on the conscious powers of his soul; stands in such contiguity to Omnipresent God as to have immediately revealed to him God's will regarding him. This is the fundamental fact in religion; that which constitutes man a subject of God's moral government; the foundation of his hopes, of his accountability. This revelation of God's will to him he feels and knows to be personal— his accountability personal and not transferable, though connecting him in obligation, and binding him by kindred ties with the whole family of man. Yet, as absolutely personal and individual as though he and God were alone in the Universe. Hence his conscience must be kept sacred in its devotion and allegiance to God, from whom the law comes. No laws nor institutions of men, should restrict this individual exercise of conscience, of responsibility. The only restriction that can be Christian or lawful in this momentous matter, in the terms of association, is the admission of the obvious principle, that no pretext of conscience can be valid which violates the equal rights of others, or any of the unchangeable principles of moral obligation, which are primary to conscience, and by which, in the Divine order, it is to be governed.

Liberty of conscience, then—the recognition of the right of every member to act in obedience to the evidence of Divine Light, in its present and progressive unfoldings of truth and duty to the mind, must be a fundamental principle in every right organization. That this perfect liberty of conscience, is the right of every sane and accountable human being, appears from several other considerations. Mankind partake of the variety which every where marks the Creator's works. Though identical in the elements of their being, these elements exist in the race in infinitely diversified proportions. Hence their individuality, their peculiarities of character. Again: they are each subject to influences as diversified as their mental and physical peculiarities—all which affect their character, their views, their actions. This diversity furnishes occasion for a most profitable exercise of some of the finest feelings and affections of our nature—tenderness, kindness, tolerance. From the universality of the facts in the case, the practice of these virtues is obligatory on all, and no institution can be Christian—can exemplify love to God and man—(the substance of Christianity)—that is deficient in these virtues. "Christianity," says an enlightened writer, "respects this diversity in men—aiming not to undo but further God's will; not fashioning all men after one pattern—to think alike, act alike, be alike, even look alike. It is something far other than Christianity which demands that. A Christian church then should put no fetters on the man; it should have unity of purpose, but with the most entire freedom for the individual. When you sacrifice the man to the mass in church or state—church or state becomes an offence, a stumbling-block in the way of progress, and must end or mend. The greater the variety of individualities in church or state, the better is it—so long as all are really manly, humane, and accordant. A Church must needs be partial, not catholic, where all men think alike—narrow and little." It has been the want of this broad and Christian ground of toleration that has been the bane of every church, Catholic and Protestant. In proportion to its absence, despotic and oppressive measures have marred the harmony and painfully defeated the objects of religious society.

Another cause of the exercise of despotic power in professed Christian churches, has been the establishment of an ascending scale of authority of larger bodies over smaller, terminating in a Head or Supreme Controlling Power. This, we are persuaded, has been a prominent cause of the difficulties which have been experienced in the Society of Friends, at different periods of its history, and especially of the divisions which have occurred within the last quarter of a century.

In the establishment of Preparative, Monthly, Quarterly, and Yearly Meetings, it was, doubtless, not contemplated, in the early periods of the Society, that any despotic authority should be exercised by larger meetings over smaller. The only power intended to be exercised, appears to have been that of persuasion and love. But the history of the Society shows how easy it is to abuse power, when men have incautiously been vested with it, by the expressed or implied rules of a written code. And the experience of the past admonishes us to recur to original fundamental ground, in regard to the design of religious association, and remove from it an element demonstrably evil in its tendency and results—*the subordination of meetings*, or the vesting of larger meetings with authority over smaller. As in a right organization the man can not be sacrificed to the mass, the individual conscience to an assemblage of consciences; so neither can a number of individual consciences in a congregation rightfully be sacrificed to a larger assembly, or any assumed or established head. The order of independent congregations, therefore, has opened, with great unanimity and clearness, as most in harmony with man's nature and rights, and least liable to abuse.

Each congregation or meeting, will consequently attend to its own internal or disciplinary concerns. Larger meetings—Quarterly or Yearly—will be for *counsel and advice*, and for the consideration and promotion of the great interests of humanity—every thing that concerns man at large—including of consequence the existing evils of the day, War, Slavery, Intemperance, Licentiousness, or in whatever form cruelty, injustice, and other perverted principles may operate. Yearly meetings may suggest rules or regulations for the government of particular meetings or congregations, but shall have no power to enforce.

Another fruitful cause of difficulty and disaffection, has been the institution of Meetings of Ministers and Elders. Of these we propose the discontinuance, as also of the practice of recommending or ordaining ministers. Every meeting or congregation will attend to the regulation of the ministry among themselves: and if any one proposing to travel to a distance, wishes a certificate of moral character, it can be granted for the time being.

Not only will the equality of woman be recognized, but so perfectly, that in our meetings, larger and smaller, men and women will meet together and transact business jointly.

These principles, simply carried out, will, we apprehend, effectually prevent the abuses and evils of ecclesiastical organizations. And should they at any time fail to be exemplified in the practice of a meeting toward any of its members, the evil would be limited, and not very oppressive, as any member affected by it, would be at liberty to join another congregation, and still participate in the privileges of the general association.

Two evils at least, if not wholly excluded, would find but scanty soil to grow in—*Tyranny* and *Sectarianism*. And these will be the more effectually prevented by the recognition of the great principle, already adverted to, of perfect liberty of conscience—which, in our view, forbids the establishing of any thing as a barrier to religious fellowship, either as regards individuals or the inter-communication of congregations, but the violation of the great unchangeable principles of morals, revealed, as facts of consciousness, to the universal human mind—Reverence of God, Justice, Mercy, Benevolence, Veracity, Chastity, &c. In other words, nothing but what is plainly incompatible with *love to God*, and *love to man*—leaving each to the test: "By their fruits ye shall know them," independently of abstract opinions. Thus a brother or sister might hold the doctrine of the Trinity, or of a Vicarious Atonement—might practice Water Baptism, the ceremony of Bread and Wine, and kindred rituals, or he might believe none of these, and his right should be recognized to preach his conscientious convictions of these matters; in any of our meetings—each, in either case, conceding the right of every other brother and sister, who may deem that error has been promulgated, to endeavor, in the pure spirit of love and kindness, to make it apparent, either before the same congregation, or in any of our meetings where they apprehend themselves called upon to do so. Thus, by the recognition of equal rights, and the sacredness of conscience, and of the duty of reciprocal kindness, a narrow sectarianism and party feeling would vanish before the light of truth, and the minds of the sincere and pious be more and more united. Nothing would be found so potent to promote unanimity of sentiment and brotherly love, as action based on these Divine principles. Under their influence a censorious and contentious spirit would find no place, the governing desire would be the attainment of truth. And thus would be verified the words of the excellent Isaac Penington—"It is not the different practice from one another that breaks the peace and unity, but the judging one another because of differing practices."

We may advert to yet another great evil, which, in the church order we have defined, must receive an effectual check. We mean *Priestcraft*. This naturally grows out of a dependance on our fellow beings, as possessing superior means of Divine knowledge. In this dependance individual talents are neglected, and individual responsibility is sought to be transferred to the person or persons on whom the dependance rests. And this dependance gives POWER to those on whom it is placed, and makes those who place it easy subjects for its exercise. In this way a large proportion of the professors of religion become, to a greater or less extent, the dupes of priestcraft. The same effect takes place, to a certain extent, among Friends, as the consequence of *recommending ministers*, as it is called; that is, setting them apart, by a particular process, as ministers of the Society. By this practice—which is a virtual ordination—the idea naturally obtains, that those thus distinguished have nearer access to the Divine Mind—superior means of Divine knowledge, than others. This leads to an improper dependance on them, and a consequent neglect on the part of the other members of their own spiritual gifts. Here great injury is sustained, both by the preachers and those who thus defer to them; and by the non-employment of individual gifts, in the inculcation of moral and religious truth, the body and community at large suffer incalculable loss.

Intimately connected with the right use of the gifts of every member, is the mode of conducting assemblies for spiritual edification and improvement—of which we will here say a word. Agreeably to the facts before stated, and the objects of religious association, every accountable human being stands in such a relation to the Divine Mind, as to be privileged to receive, from the Fountain of Wisdom and Goodness, immediate instruction relative to all the duties of life, personal and social. The responsibility in respect to these duties being personal, and not transferable, no one can appoint another to act for him in their fulfillment. Fidelity to God can be maintained only by individual obedience to Divine requiring. No society arrangement can be right, which admits not of this obedience. No man has a right to absolve himself from it. In view of these important truths, we deem that a true church organization does not admit of placing one or more persons over a congregation as the stated spiritual teacher, or teachers. Consistently with individual rights and responsibilities, all must meet together as brethren, recognizing one Divine Teacher, and leaving the mind of each free, to speak or be silent, according to his highest perceptions of duty, and in agreement with a just estimate of each other's equal rights. Thus may the gifts of all be exercised in the promotion of truth and goodness, and, while they are improved "by reason of use," the body will "edify itself in love."

Associating on these principles, we have concluded to hold a Yearly Meeting, in Friends' Meeting-house, known as Junius, (now Waterloo,) Seneca County, New York, commencing on Second-day, the 4th of 6th month next, 1849, at 11 o'clock in the morning: and we recommend that Friends, in their different meetings, who may be prepared for the measure, appoint representatives accordingly. And we further invite all, of whatever name or wherever scattered, who unite in the principles of the foregoing basis of association, to be present and participate with us in the objects contemplated—to promote truth, piety, righteousness, and peace in the earth. That all may find in the endearments of Religious Society A HOME for their spirits, and that, by a union of effort, virtue and happiness may be diffused in the human family, and God be glorified, who is over all, blessed forever.

Signed on behalf of the Conference.

THOMAS M'CLINTOCK, \
RHODA DE GARMO, } CLERKS.

PART V

SEPARATE WAYS

1870–1920

A REVIVED QUAKERISM

DAVID B. UPDEGRAFF

After 1865, the largest body of American Friends, the Gurney-
ites, were largely transformed by a wave of revivalism. This
brought innovations such as music, revival meetings, and ul-
timately pastors into their worship. Most of the traditional
features of Quaker life, such as plain dress and plain life,
passed away. At the heart of this revival movement was the
preaching of holiness, or sanctification, as a second, instanta-
neous experience. The most enthusiastic leader in these
changes was a minister from Mount Pleasant, Ohio, David B.
Updegraff (1830–1894).

David B. Updegraff, *Old Corn; or, Sermons and*
Addresses on the Spiritual Life (Boston, 1892).

CHAPTER XXXVI.

Personal Testimony.

This poor man cried, and the Lord heard him, and saved him
out of all his troubles.

—PSALMS 34:6.

I have yielded to the impression that I ought not to close this book
without giving its readers as clear an insight as possible into my
own heart's experience in the "Way of Holiness." I have felt that
to hesitate to do so would be inconsistent with the teachings of
these chapters. It is of this blessed experience that this book has

been born. Whatever I may have said, or done, or written to the glory of God or for the good of men, has, in fact, been the outgrowth of an experimental knowledge of the truth set forth in these pages. I have seen so much debate and questioning arise on account of vagueness in personal testimony that I have felt that I ought to be definite. May it all be for the glory of God, and for the comfort and blessing of every beloved brother and sister who accepts this invitation into the sacred sanctuary of my secret audience with the King.

What I say will be the utterance of a grateful heart, and I trust it shall be spoken in true humility. My parents and grandparents were all of the highest type of religious people. Two of my grandparents were ministers, and one of them died in a foreign land, while on a religious mission. My father was an elder in the church, a man of devout and sterling piety, while my saintly mother was a preacher of the glorious gospel that she loved so much, and understood so well. They read and believed in President Finney, and he was their personal friend; but his Caleb-like spirit and *full gospel* was fully forty years in advance of our Israel; and, in consequence, "stoning with stones" (Num. 14:10) was a common occupation in those days, and not wholly a lost art in this.

Their greatest desire for their children was that they might glorify God in this life and enjoy Him forever. I cannot doubt that I was solemnly given to God from my birth. My infant lips were taught to pray, and when I said,

> Now I lay me down to sleep,
> I pray the Lord my soul to keep,

I really expected Him to do it. Precious is the memory of those days of childish innocence, and mother love, when home and heaven seemed almost interchangeable terms. My young heart was not a stranger to the gracious visitations of the Spirit of God, and was often melted under the power of His love. But as I grew up, I grew in sinfulness and in rebellion against God. Though mercifully preserved from many sins of a gross and disgraceful character, I was often in great distress of soul because of those I did commit. At such times I would earnestly repent in secret, and cry unto God for mercy. I deeply realized the wickedness of my heart, and the weakness of my efforts to withstand temptation. Many covenants were made with God, and often, though not always, broken. The prayers, restraints, and instructions of faithful parents were not lost upon me. God had respect unto their covenant for their children. I see it now as I could not then. I want to praise the Lord for His answer to prayers for guidance, even in my rebellious boyhood, and for His manifest direction in the most important undertakings of my life.

After being settled in life I renewed my covenants with God, and sought to do right, because it was right. I was a member of the church, and grew jealous of the peculiarities of my denomination. I was "zealous toward God, according to the perfect manner of the law of the fathers." For ten years or more I proved that this law "*gendereth to bondage.*" I certainly did "fear the Lord," but it is a poor service that is rendered by one who is only a servant, when he ought to be a *son.* And I had not "received the adoption of a son." I know now that I was simply a legalist, "kept under the law, shut up unto the faith, which should afterwards be revealed." In this dispensation of the Father, with the "bondwoman" for their mother, multitudes of professors that are in doubt as to their position, might properly locate themselves. "There is a remembrance again made of sins every year," since "the law makes nothing perfect," not even the conscience. In a Methodist meeting, when more than thirty years of age, God met me in wondrous power. And I met the test of public confession of sins and need of the Savior. It was a hard struggle, for I was proud and stubborn, but my dear wife joined me at the penitents' form, and we mingled our tears and prayers together. I thank God to this day for the depth and pungency of old-fashioned conviction. Rebellion against God was seen and felt to be the awful damning thing that it is. I was glad to submit to God, and agree to His terms — *any terms* in order to have peace with Him. But the witness of the Spirit did not come; and after all others had retired, I had it out with my Lord in the silent watches of the night, upon my library floor. And, as people sometimes say by way of emphasis, I was converted through and through. And I knew it! I was free as a bird. "Justified by faith," I had peace with God. His Spirit witnessed with my spirit that I was born again.

I was at once a glad and willing witness to the power of Jesus to save. For a time I was faithful and obedient, and then came waywardness, neglect and disobedience. This brought severe chas-

tening and suffering from the hand of the Lord, followed by restoration of soul. My consecration to His service was renewed
from time to time. I longed to see God glorified in the salvation of
souls and the liberation of the church. Several years had passed
since I had found the liberty of the sons of God; and yet I had seen
few brought into the kingdom. To be sure, I was only a business
man, and was utterly averse to the idea of being a minister. I
greatly desired to serve both God and men in a quiet and unob-
trusive way. The church began to lay some work upon me, but I
shrank from it with a deep sense of unfitness. And then I felt
within me a quenchless protest against the formalism and regular-
ity of *death* all about me. Irregularity is the most dreaded foe of
a legal, lifeless church. My nature instinctively shrank from the
conflict, I *felt* it far more than I could *understand* it. But I determined to have a meeting where the Lord should have right of way,
and the practical work of soul saving be done. Accordingly, my
house was opened to all who would come to evening meetings,
during our yearly meeting week in 1869. Our parlors were filled
with earnest people, and without were those who were watching
and waiting to see whereunto this would grow. The Scriptures
were read, prayers offered, hymns were sung, testimonies were
given and souls were blessed. But it was all unusual, and quite
irregular in those days. We had live meetings, and living things
are always irregular, while dead things *never* are. I began to learn
what real loyalty to God was to cost, and that if really led by the
Spirit of God, according to His word, reproaches and other like
blessings that Jesus had promised, would become a *reality*.

In conducting a few of these meetings, I learned a great deal of
myself. I was somewhat troubled by the people and the circumstances around me, but I discovered one "old man" who gave me
more trouble than all the others, and he was *within* me. "His
deeds" had been put off, and truly there was "no condemnation,"
but whenever I "would do good" he was present with me. His
omnipresence was something wonderful to my opening eyes. And
he was there, to "war against the law of my mind" with a resolute
purpose to "bring me into captivity to the law of sin." If he succeeded, even partially, I was humbled and grieved, and if he did
not succeed, I was in distress with fear lest he might. Some special
incidents were greatly blessed to me. I began to see quite clearly
that the "law was weak through the flesh." I hated pride, ambi-

tion, evil tempers and vain thoughts, but I *had* them, and they were a part of me. They were not acts to be repented of and forgiven at all, but dispositions lying behind the acts and prompting thereto, natural to the old man and inseparable from his presence in my being.

I began to cry to God to "cast him out." As I did this, there came a great "hunger and thirst after righteousness," that I might be "filled with all the fullness of God." My new nature speedily developed wonderful aptitudes for "holiness." I longed for a "clean heart and a right spirit," and this yearning increased until one memorable evening, after the close of the series of meetings referred to, when a few of us met at my sister's for prayer and conference. Up to this time I had never heard a straight sermon on holiness, nor read a treatise upon it, nor seen any one who claimed the experience for themselves. It had never occurred to me that I had not received the Holy Ghost since I believed. Knowing as much of the work of the blessed Spirit upon my heart as I undoubtedly had, I supposed, as a matter of course, that I had been "baptised with the Holy Ghost and with fire." His creative work in regeneration, and His destructive work in sanctification, are distinctions of great importance, but not clearly seen by me at that time. And I might have answered much as the Ephesians answered Paul in Acts 19:2, had I been asked the same question. I had not even heard of such an experience. But there was present with us a brother who had heard that grand and dauntless herald of the cross, John S. Inskip, and his noble band of compeers at Round Lake. And he earnestly told us of their wonderful meetings, and preaching of consecration and holiness. It was only a spark of God's fire that was needed to kindle into a flame the sacrifice that was placed upon His altar. As I went upon my knees, it was with the resolute purpose of "presenting my body a living sacrifice to God," and of proving His word that the "altar sanctifieth the gift." But I speedily found myself in the midst of a severe conflict. There passed quickly and clearly before me every obstacle to entire consecration, and "a life hid with Christ in God." How the "old man" plead for his life! The misapprehensions, suspicions, sneers and revilings of carnal professors were all pictured before me, and they were not exaggerations, either. Selfishness, pride and prejudice all rose in rebellion and did their utmost. But I could not, would not, draw back. Every "vile affection" was resolutely nailed to the cross. Denominational standing, family, business, reputation, friends, time, talent and earthly store, were quickly and irrevocably committed to the sovereign control and disposal of my Almighty Savior. It came to be easy to trust Him, and I had no sooner reckoned myself "dead indeed unto sin and alive unto God," than the "Holy Ghost fell" upon me, just as I suppose He did "at the beginning."

Instantly, I felt the melting and refining fire of God permeate my whole being. Conflict was a thing of the past. I had entered into "rest." I was nothing and nobody, and glad that it was settled that way. It was a luxury to get rid of ambitions. The glory of the Lord shone round about me, and, for a little season, I was "lost in wonder, love and praise." I was deeply conscious of the presence of God within me, and of His sanctifying work. Nothing seemed so sweet as His will, His law written in the heart after the chaff had been burned out. It was no effort to realize that I loved the Lord with all my heart, and mind, and strength, and my neighbor as myself. My calmness and absolute repose in God was a wonder to me. But I cannot describe it all. It was a "weight of glory."

> O matchless bliss of perfect love,
> It lifts me up to things above.

When I rose from my knees I was constrained to speak of what God had wrought, the best I knew how. The people looked so different! I had new eyes! I *felt* so different that I examined myself, to see if I was the same person. When the next day I rode out upon my farm, I felt that every acre belonged to God, and I was only a tenant at will. The hills and fields and flocks and trees were all more beautiful as they clapped their hands in praise. On the Sabbath following, I broke the silence of our meeting, by a testimony to the truth as I had found it in Jesus. I do not remember what I said, but I am sure that I preached about "perfect love," for I was in the enjoyment of that blessing, though perfectly innocent of terminology, and I have been at it ever since.

I record this narrative of the way in which I have been led by the good hand of my God, with the hope and earnest prayer that He may make it a comfort and a blessing to those who may read it. It is both a duty and a privilege to "show forth the praises" of the Lord Jesus. It is of Him and His work that I speak, and not of myself, or "frames of mind." It was Jesus that I found as a complete Savior. And it is Jesus that abides as my sanctification, wisdom and redemption. It is His blood that cleanses from all sin, and His Spirit alone that protects from the assaults of the devil. It is to the Holy Spirit that I look for the power that preserves from committing sin, and He is able to do it, and to "keep us from falling."

The special experience just related is now twenty-three years in the past, and might be a dead and forgotten thing, but that moment by moment the blood has cleansed, and the Spirit has indwelt in answer to a perpetuated faith and obedience to God. During all these years the mode of my life, which was inaugurated in that hour, when I received the "baptism with the Holy Ghost," has been totally different from that which preceded it. It began a new era in my Christian life. I have had abundant time and occasion to scrutinize the reality and nature of the work wrought then, and perpetuated ever since. I have often had such a sense of my own unworthiness and human imperfections as to be well nigh overwhelmed. But then I had settled it that Jesus was my worthiness, and as to *human* or legal perfection, David had seen the "end" of that long ago. In and of myself I am neither holier nor stronger than before.

> But this I do find
> We two are so joined,
> That He'll not be in glory
> And leave me behind.

What I am, I am by the grace of God. What I do, I do "through Christ who strengthened me." And if God cannot "work in us to will and to do of his own good pleasure," we cannot *retain* our experience. We *must* "work out our salvation." "The willing and obedient shall eat the fat of the land," and none others.

But entire sanctification, and the filling of the Spirit, means a quickened conscience, as tender as the apple of the eye. It means a keen sense of the revealed word of God. It means an obedience that does not stand to debate and reason, and wonder about results. It means the priestly service of a true Levite, who is bearing the ark of God some paces in advance of the rank and file of the slow marching church, that has much of its inheritance on the wilderness side of Jordan.

It is only when men are really "crucified with Christ" and "filled with the Holy Ghost" that they are fitted to act as the forerunners of the Lord Jesus. For all such must pass through their Gethsemanes alone, in a distant likeness to Christ. Too advanced for the multitude, they are even strange to the best of friends. Then there is the consciousness of unrequited toil, unacknowledged sacrifice and unappreciated service, that would be fearfully galling were it not for that sweet sense of *privilege*, which comes of "putting on Christ," and seeking "the reward that comes from God only." And self-devotion is the secret of all heroic life. Calling forth the very best there is in us, and always strengthened by a tonic of "bitter herbs." Oh! the blessedness of trusting God to keep all of our accounts, sure that He will see to it that we get our dues, without any jealous anxiety on our part.

All of this, and much more, is involved, if we continue to "walk in the light as He is in the light, and have fellowship with God."

And it is in this matter of obeying Him, of keeping His commandments, of "walking as he walked," that multitudes draw back and lapse into their old ways of thinking and acting. When "iniquity abounds the love of many shall wax cold," many "hearts are overcharged with surfeiting and cares of this life." And then the spirit of persecution is still rife in the church. The same generation carries it on, that "were filled with envy, and spake against those things which were spoken by Paul, contradicting and blaspheming." Paul's custom was to "reason and persuade" and "warn," though "all men forsook" him, which indeed they did. But he lived in the thirteenth of Corinthians, and "the Lord stood with him and strengthened him." The family of "Demas" (popular) is a very large one, and, true to the instincts of the old nature, "love this present world," and will always go back to it, rather than go forward with Christ, at the cost of being unpopular and suffering reproach. To "rejoice, inasmuch as ye are partakers of Christ's sufferings," is almost a lost art in our day. Oh! that we may believe that Jesus means what He says when He bids us "Rejoice and leap for joy, when men shall hate you and shall separate you from their company, and reproach you, and cast out your name as evil, for the Son of man's sake."

Now the secret of victory is in trusting God and holding still in quietness and assurance; allowing Satan to stretch the last link in his chain without quivering. And if thus kept in the love of God, and in sweetness and patience, while "fighting the fight of faith," we shall "always triumph through Christ." Glory be to Jesus! It takes a little time for Haman to build his gallows, and get things all fixed, but Mordecai has no concern about it, whether it takes a time longer or shorter, since the coming execution is not to be his, but Haman's. He simply did his duty without compromise.

> Oh for a faith that will not shrink,
> Though pressed by every foe,
> That will not tremble on the brink
> Of any earthly woe!

How the lives of the old saints who "quenched the violence of fire, escaped the edge of the sword, out of weakness were made strong, and waxed valiant in fight," inspire us with loyalty and courage! How much more such lives of faith in the Son of God, and victory through Him, when lived all about us! There are *some* such. May God increase the number! I pray that these utterances may be used of Him to assist some into the land of victorious warfare, and encourage others already there to push the battle to the gate. I have written for such as these and not for the "wise," or "the disputer of this world"; not for such as are "ever learning and never coming to a knowledge of the truth." For these I pray, and for myself, that I may more and more be enabled to publish this great salvation, and continually to "rejoice in hope of the glory of God." "Brethren, pray for us that the word of the Lord may have free course and be glorified, and that we may be delivered from unreasonable and wicked men." Glory to His name!

HANNAH WHITALL SMITH

A different vision of Quaker revivalism was that of Hannah Whitall Smith (1832–1911). She was a Philadelphia Ortho-dox Friend who spent much of her life in England, and who left the Friends for a time. Although her vision of Quaker holiness was not that of most Friends in the nineteenth cen-

tury, her works, especially The Christian's Secret of a Happy
Life, *remain widely read today.*

Hannah Whitall Smith, "Diversities of Gifts and the Unity of the Spirit," in *The Christian Worker* (New Vienna, Ohio), 6th Mo. 10, 1880.

*I therefore, the prisoner of the Lord, beseech you that ye walk
worthy of the vocation wherewith ye are called, with all lowliness and meekness, with long suffering, forbearing one another
in love: endeavoring to keep the unity of the spirit in the bond
of peace.*

The lesson contained in this passage is very much needed just now
among Friends, and I desire to say a little on the subject as it presents itself to me.

It can not be doubted that there is an awakening of religious life
among us, and almost every Christian heart is longing for a fresh
outpouring of the Holy Spirit upon the Society, and for a renewal
of the primitive zeal and success in Christian work. The need is felt
to be great. But the views of different workers as to how this revival is to be accomplished are so diverse, that in many places the
church, instead of presenting a common front against its enemies
without, is divided against itself without, and workers are using a
large part of their energies and zeal in combating one another, and
in opposing one another's efforts to advance the cause so dear to
both.

This has always been the case in the church but none the less is
it wrong, and contrary to the spirit of Christ. Our Lord himself
had to meet it when he was on the earth, and the way in which he
rebuked it then will teach us, if we have cars to hear, how we ought
to regard it now. In Mark ix: 38–41 we read that after he had been
trying to teach his disciples the wonderful lesson that in his kingdom that man only was greatest who gave up the most and endured
the most, John in apparent perplexity said, as though seeking for
a clearer understanding of the subject—"Master, we saw one casting out devils in thy name, and he followeth not us; and we forbade
him because he followeth not us."

The universal reason, "because he followeth not *us,*" because
his views and his ways differ from *ours!*

"But Jesus said, forbid him not: for there is no man which shall do a miracle in my name that can lightly speak evil of me. For he that is not against us is on our part." And then he added that which, if rightly understood, would forever settle the question as to our treatment of those who give even so much as a cup of cold water, however bunglingly, in the name of Christ. "And whosoever shall offend one of these little ones that believe in me, it is better for him that a millstone were hanged about his neck, and he were cast into the sea." Far rather let us endure anything from our brother, than come under such condemnation as this from our Lord!

Let us then see if it is not possible for us even in the midst of the multiplicity of views and opinions in the present day to obey the apostles' beseeching, and really to walk worthy of the vocation wherewith we are called, with all lowliness and meekness, with long suffering, forbearing one another in love; endeavoring to keep the unity of the spirit in the bond of peace.

That there are very great differences of views and methods among Friends in the present day, can not be questioned, and that each party should think their own especial views and ways the best is all right. But that any should reject a brother or a sister because he followeth not them, or should forbid such to exercise their gifts, can never be anything but all wrong, since it is entirely contrary to the spirit and teaching of the Master.

Let us consider for a little wherein those differences mainly consist, and whether they do not admit of such harmonizing as will permit all parties to preserve the unity of the spirit, while still each holding to their own views, and working in their own ways.

Alexander Knox says there are foundation truths and superstructure truths in our religion; and affirms that each have their needed place in the divine harmony. They are very different, of course, as different as the foundations of a building are from the superstructure that is reared upon them. But their difference is a difference of harmony, not of discord. Each one is necessary to the other, if we would have any completeness.

Foundation truths deal with the beginnings of things, superstructure truths deal with their development. The first show the entrance into the ways the last teach the life and walk after we are in. Without the superstructure truths, the foundations remain bare and crude; without the foundation truths the superstructure will be tottering and unsafe.

Our conservative Friends are essentially superstructure Christians; our modern revivalists are foundation Christians. The latter class labor to establish the right relationships between the soul and God, the former teach the duties and privileges of these relationships; the revivalist deals with the birth; the conservative deals with the life and walk.

It is very manifest that these different kinds of work are each necessary in the church; but the trouble lies in the interference of the one with the other. The man who lays the foundations says, "What I am doing is the only right work to do, all is contained in this; anything different is legality and unsoundness." While the man who is building the superstructure says on his part, "What I am doing is the only thing to be done. All the rest is superficial and dangerous, and will be fatal to any real depth of spiritual life." And in their narrow zeal each set of workmen finds fault with the other set, and denunciations and separations follow.

A right understanding of 1 Cor. xii would remedy all this. The Holy Spirit through the pen of the Apostle Paul is there telling us what the true church is, and he says concerning it, "Now there are diversities of gifts, but the same spirit. And there are differences of administrations, but the same Lord. And there are diversities of operations, but the same God which worketh all in all. . . . For the body is not one member, but many. . . . And if they were all one member where were the body? But now are they many members, yet but one body. And the eye can not say unto the hand, I have no need of thee: nor again the head to the feet, I have no need of you." Nothing could well be more utterly diverse than the operations of the eye and of the hand, or of the head and of the feet, and yet neither may question or despise the other. And just so it is in the church.

One teacher presents one phase of the truth, or one stage of the life, and another presents a phase or a stage that seems utterly different. Are they on this account either of them to say, "I present the whole truth, and my brother is all wrong?" Are they to forbid one another saying "because he followeth not us?" Surely this would not be to follow the Master nor to walk in his steps.

For a long time there were few but superstructure preachers among Friends. The most we heard was how to walk and live, how to be good, how to obey and please God. It was very valuable teaching for those who were already in the kingdom, but it failed to tell souls how to get in. It left the relationships between the soul and God uncertain, and put a trembling hope in the place of assured possession. It urged holiness of life, but failed to tell the secret by which this holiness could be realized. It emphasized the word "ought," but overlooked the word "how." And hungry souls reaching out after that beautiful ideal of a holy life which was set before them, were left without the definite teaching of the way to reach it. The one foundation need of all as to "How to do it," remained unanswered. I remember through all my young life how eagerly and hungrily I watched and waited to be told how, and how continually I was disappointed.

Then came the revival, and foundation preachers were raised up who told us how. They gave the principles of things, not their development; the beginnings, not the growth. They taught us our relations with Christ as our Savior and with God as our Father. They made us know that our sins were forgiven and our peace made with God. They revealed to us by the spirit the light of his reconciled countenance, and showed us the provision there was in Christ for all our need. Our souls were brought into a consciousness of the new birth, or were helped over Jordan into the land of promise. A sudden change seemed to take place in many experiences; definite steps of faith were taken, and definite points of surrender were reached. And in our delight at all this, both we and those who had been instrumental in bringing us into it, were naturally tempted to undervalue our previous teaching, and even to look upon it as entirely mistaken and false. While on the other hand those who had been our previous teachers could not understand the new ways of expression and of working, and were tempted to feel they were superficial and very dangerous. Both sides thus made the very serious mistake of saying to the other, "I have no need of thee," and of thereby creating a schism in the body.

Without that charity which can mutually bear and forbear, which can suffer long and be kind, which can believe all things, hope all things, endure all things; which is broad enough to see a possible good in the views and methods of others, even when they differ from our own, and which can feel the unity of the spirit in the midst of diversities of gifts; without in short the love of Christ thus shed abroad in our hearts and acted out in our lives, church fellowship is an impossibility, and schism is the inevitable result.

But with this divine and Christ like charity, each party will be broad enough to stand aside and let the other do its share of the work; the conservatives acknowledging that some other line of teaching than their own is needed to bring souls into a consciousness of their right relationships with God, and the revivalists acknowledging that some additional teaching to theirs is necessary to lead souls on into all the fulness of the blessing of conformity to Christ.

No doubt there are things in the methods of each that the others could not understand. It would naturally be hard for the eye to understand the way in which the hand performs its offices. But this broad Christian charity would prevent all harsh judgments, and would enable each to do their own work faithfully, and to leave their brother's work to their common Master.

Those of us who were in the full tide of the revival when it first began years ago can I believe verify all this in our own experience. We had been used to the superstructure preaching all our lives, and it had made us very hungry for a Christian experience, but it had not taught us either definitely or clearly how to enter into it. And when the foundation preaching of the revival came, it found us ready to embrace its lessons, and to enter into the doors it opened. Then we were so busy with the foundations that we lost for a time all interest in the superstructure, and even began to think the teachings concerning it were unsound. But as years have passed on, and the foundations of our Christian life have been as we believe securely laid, we have become more and more interested in the superstructure; and now to some of us the old preaching, which once we did not understand, has become marrow and fatness to our souls. This is not so much because the preaching has changed, as because we have changed. We have grown up to that stage in the Christian life to which their preaching ministers, or at least are growing.

It ought to be very easy therefore for us of this generation to exercise the broad charity I have been speaking of, and to recognize the different workers in God's great harvest field, as true fellow laborers with us and with our Master, even though in the "diversities of gifts" their service may differ greatly from our own.

And I can not but say just here, that so exalted are my views of the degree and sort of holiness required from all believers in the Lord Jesus Christ, that it is hard for me to believe any one is fully sanctified who fails in a complete Christ likeness of feeling and action towards those who differ from them.

I recall to mind as I write, one meeting of Friends where this spirit has to a great degree prevailed, and has produced the most blessed results. It has among its members some of the most conservative Friends to be found anywhere, and also some of the most liberal. But there has been throughout many years a spirit of mutual concession and forbearance on the part of both sides, and it is now one of the most united and living meetings I know of. The dear conservative Friends have been helped into more assured relationships with God through the teachings of the revival element in their midst, and the liberal part of the meeting have been stirred into an increasing hunger after true holiness, and have been greatly deepened in the divine life, by the teachings of their more conservative fellow members.

Andrew Jukes says the faith by which we buy a ticket and secure a berth on an ocean steamer for a voyage across the Atlantic, and feel that all is done, is a very different thing from the actual experience of crossing the ocean and enduring all the discomforts and privations of the voyage itself. Yet both are equally necessary, and it would be folly indeed for any one to conclude that either thing alone was enough.

To carry out this figure I would say that the revivalist teaching shows us how to secure our ticket and engage our berth, while the conservative teaching shows us how to make the voyage.

Let us then welcome both as equally necessary; and above all things and in all things obey the exhortation of the apostle. Let us not therefore judge one another any more; but judge this rather, "that no man put a stumbling block or an occasion to fall in his brother's way."

H. W. S.

MAHALAH JAY

One of the most lasting fruits of the revival movement among Gurneyite Friends was the development of interest in missionary work in all parts of the world. By 2000, a majority of the world's Quakers lived in East Africa, and thousands more

were found in Latin America, the Caribbean, and on Taiwan.
One of the central figures in the creation of a Quaker mis-
sionary movement was Mahalah (Pearson) Jay (1827–1916).
A teacher in Quaker schools and a professor at Earlham
College in Richmond, Indiana, she was one of the founders
of the Women's Foreign Missionary Union of Friends in
America. Her 1887 article shows both the goals of Quaker
missions and the central role that women played in them.

Mahalah Jay, "The Rise of W. F. M. Societies amongst Friends, Providential," *Friends' Missionary Advocate* (Chicago), 6th Month 1887.

Each age has its *methods* of working as well as its work. That government, society, business, or church accomplishes most that keeps abreast with its age in the methods and instruments it employs.

Look at a few common-place illustrations of this thought. Harvests once were reaped, and may still be reaped by the sickle in the hand of the individual laborer,—but not the vast acreage of grain now grown on our midland prairies. The mothers and daughters of our land once spun and wove in their several homes, the fabrics that clothed their households. And they did well. Shall we return to the hand-loom and the distaff? And if not, why not? Horses once drew the coaches that carried our mails,—they can still draw. Would we be willing now to give up the use of the railroad and telegraph? No; those methods belong to the past, or to an unadvanced state of society. The vanguard of civilization has left them behind. And not more in the industries of the world than in carrying forward philanthropic and Christian enterprises must we work by the methods and with the implements of our age. We shall fall to the rear if we do not.

Now, union of effort, *organization*, is the characteristic and effective method of to-day. Joint-stock companies, and other forms of combination are used to advance almost every manufacture, trade, or other business interest of civilization, and they are necessary to meet the requirements of the age, but not more necessary than are Bible Societies and Foreign Missionary Boards in hastening the carrying of the gospel to the heathen world. Some little may be done in nearly any direction by individual work, but vastly more by united action. "In union there is strength" is the working-day gospel for this century. The bad combine. Greed has its unions. The powers of darkness organize and so must "the children of light," or they will be less wise in their generation. Individual Christians here and there have had the courage to be faithful to those among whom they dwelt, but how many more have allowed their convictions to die out, in despair of doing the needed work single-handed, convictions which supported by contact with an organization like, for example, the Young Men's Christian Association, would have become stronger and have become a component part of a great aggregate of beneficent force. Wives and mothers have labored and prayed as earnestly to save their loved ones from the drink demon in the past as they do now. If a better public sentiment is forming in regard to the liquor traffic, if statutes favorable to temperance begin to appear, and if these things are forwarded by the Woman's Christian Temperance Union, it is because of the *union*, not because of their greater love. Union promotes intelligence, strengthens convictions, begets hope, increases courage, *becomes strength.* It is ours to avail ourselves of this principle in working out the last charge Christ gave to his church on earth, "Go, disciple all nations." A view of the breadth of this command would appall the individual worker, but organized Christendom feels no such sinking of the heart, but is ready to make answer, With Thy help we will.

The leading Protestant denominations have recognized these conditions of our age, have organized, and are moving forward in the work with a speed that is as the railroad to the slow teams of the past,—isolated "individual concern." It is not a century since the oldest of the modern foreign missionary societies was formed, only about one half of a century old is the oldest of these societies among women, yet they have already accomplished more for the spread of the gospel than all that Protestants had ever done previously. The single missionaries have become thousands, the dollars for the work are counted by the millions, and missionaries have touched the borders at least of almost all the heathen lands. Woman began to wake up to her *personal* responsibility in the discipling of all nations, when she comprehended that more than two hundred millions of her own sex, shut off by Eastern customs from the teaching of men, must receive the gospel, if at all, through her personal labor. In the last three decades women have, through their different foreign missionary

Boards, sent out some hundreds of female missionaries as teachers, zenana workers, Bible readers, medical missionaries, and evangelists. They have supported many pupils, schools, orphanages, and native workers. Their aggregate contributions to the cause have already reached several millions of dollars, and their churches at home, warmed by their zeal and labor of love, are also receiving a blessing from their works.

Our own branch of the church, possibly resting in its high profession and its supposed high record in the past, has been slow to take a part in these movements. The women at length have felt the impulse and caught the spirit of this century. No longer satisfied to use the methods and do the work of a past age, they have *organized* to some extent for foreign missionary work. It is well they did so before it was too late, for already had a sort of disintegration of their working forces set in, a drawing off of some earnest women into the organizations of other churches, not of preference, but because they would rather work for Christ in this way, outside of their own denomination, than not work at all. Their contributions may help foreign fields as much elsewhere as in their own religious home, but woe to that church that is thus shorn of its strength and "let alone" to sink into confirmed inactivity! It was observed by the great missionary, Dr. Duff, that the church that ceases to be evangelistic will soon cease to be evangelical. The rise at such a time, therefore, of Women's Foreign Missionary Societies amongst us seems in a degree providential, to save us from such a fate by helping to arouse the church to its duty toward the dying millions who have not heard of Christ, and by detaining within our midst the life and energy and motive power of those on whose spirits rests a burden for the souls of the heathen world. We need the stirring up from indifference and lethargy that these societies give, we need the *union of effort* that they represent, need it not only in our connected meetings, but as one bond of church fellowship among our independent Yearly Meetings. The strength derived from united work will be of cementing influence, will help to preserve us from falling asunder and teach us to value our denominational fellowship. For this end our little paper, *Friends' Missionary Advocate*, has claims upon us. It is a sweet monthly letter from the sisters of our American Yearly Meetings, written on a subject of mutual interest. Then how the "Uniform Lesson" would be missed by a large number of our local societies, as well as the carefully provided information and the earnest appeals! We can hardly do without an organ for our work, it is a part of the needful machinery of this age. Shall we gain by letting this paper go down and trying to start again? If we would keep it we must work for it.

Let us strengthen and extend the bonds of our union in every suitable way. Great results seldom proceed from isolated efforts. When the time comes that *all* of our Christian name can unite their labor, we shall accomplish more. May our present organizations be the stepping-stones to a more complete union yet to be. And if, besides, they shall sustain their part at present in the mission fields and train the children for the future work, if they shall foster Christian activity, and prove a means under God of bringing our church to see its duty on the subject of *Christian giving*, and of educating the next generation to practice it, their rise may rightfully be regarded as providential.

RICHMOND, IND.

LIBERAL QUAKERISM

JOHN WILLIAM GRAHAM

*In the late nineteenth century, the London Yearly Meeting
was transformed by the emergence of an articulate and aggressive group of young Friends who argued that Quakerism
must accommodate itself to advances in science and biblical
scholarship. Historians agree that a conference held in Manchester in 1895 marked a clear turning point in the decline of
Gurneyite evangelicalism and the embrace of a self-avowedly
liberal Quakerism. One of the leaders of this movement was
John William Graham (1859–1932).*

John William Graham, "The Attitude of the
Society of Friends Towards Modern Thought," in
*The Society of Friends: Report of the Proceedings
of the Conference of Members of the Society of
Friends, Held, by Direction of the Yearly Meeting,
in Manchester, from Eleventh to the Fifteenth of
Eleventh Month, 1895* (London, 1896).

John William Graham read a paper
as follows :—

Every man's religion begins and ends in God, and from our
thought of Him flows every religious belief we hold. This thought
is also the crowning conclusion of all our other thoughts, and so
grows with the growth of men and of Churches. Happy is the man
who is at home in God, whose thought of Him colours every deci-

sion and penetrates all conduct. A possession so valuable comes
only to those who, by dying to themselves, have "taken up their
freedom" in the Heavenly City.

But tradition, handed down in human words, clogs the feet of
the seeker after God. The whole vocabulary of religion is, primarily, earth-born metaphor. All words used for the Unseen are bor-
rowed from things seen; so that words hinder thought in this
supreme department. We forget that we are not talking plain prose
in speaking of the Lord's hand or His eye, or of the footstool of
His feet. Since the highest we know on earth is man, care is needed
not to limit Him to our own likeness. He can have none of the
limitation which attaches to the word "person" in every other
connection. To describe Him so is to ask for Him not too much,
but far too little.

The Greeks personified the wind and the springtime, and every
vehicle of the creative power. We are called to a higher generaliza-
tion; to conceive and to rest in the unity behind all differences,
and including all—the One in whom we live and move, and have
our being. We are to learn to see His tenderness in tender human
hearts, His grace in gracious intercourse, His love in all love.
There is not any enthusiasm for others, nor ever has been, which
is not God's very own. Of the Apostolic utterances there is one
startlingly modern, "God is Love"—not He *has* it, or feels it, but
that is what He is. And *that* is round our footsteps, from the home
of our infancy to the bedside of our departure.

> If thou wouldst hear the Nameless, and wilt dive
> Into the temple cave of thine own self,
> There, brooding by the central altar, thou
> Mayst haply learn the Nameless hath a voice.

Without a principle of unity between subject and object there
could be no inward perception of an outer world, the incomprehen-
sible link between the thinker and the object thought of would be
lacking—force could not touch matter nor life absorb its nutriment.

> And if the Nameless should withdraw from all
> Thy frailty counts most real, all thy world
> Might vanish like thy shadow in the dark.

We are in God as in an atmosphere. We may breathe grudgingly
and in rebellion, or, with loyal and hearty inhaling, we may pu-
rify the blood of our souls.

We have given up the idea that any organization can be the sole
vehicle of the Infinite Spirit. The clergy are judged just as other
men are. The age only plays with ritual, as in a kind of solemn
trifling. Every Church stands for what it is found to be worth.
Authorities are only respected with qualifications, and those who
most frequently appeal to an outward authority take such liberties
themselves with their authority that we see that they also are really
more free than they think. He that inhabiteth eternity, revealed in
the heart of man, "not known, but felt through what we feel
within ourselves is highest," is the sole authority. Men have got
down to the bed rock of faith, so that the religious world has come
round to the Indwelling Voice as its central conception, and so
essential Quakerism holds the future in the hollow of its hand.
Our little organisation may be too weak to rise to a great expan-
sion. We only understand Quakerism ourselves imperfectly, and
with much diversity of view;—intellectually, it must be confessed,
we are feeble;—many of our strongest men devote but little of their
strength to the work of the Church; our leaders are at times more
distinguished by caution and by policy than by courage; a timid
public opinion has been known to overrule conviction, just as it
does among other people. Our system almost excludes great popular preachers, and we have little provision for teaching religious
truth or Bible knowledge, except by importing it into ministry. But
to return:—

In contemplating Divine Providence, modern religion regards it
as constant, not as occasional. A certain editor, I see, ascribes the
bad opium crop since 1890 to God's interposition, to aid thereby
the revived agitation which began in that year. This, the Indian
officials, it was said, could not understand, having left God out of
account. Rather has the editor done so. He has forgotten the
teaching, that the Father maketh His sun to rise upon the evil and
upon the good. He does not see with the Psalmist, "Fire and hail,
snow and vapour, stormy wind fulfilling His word" in every harvest. The fatal result of claiming "Special" Providences, is to ban-
ish God from the other ninety-nine per cent, of causation, and
generally, alas, to glorify the creature, rather than the Creator.

Religion glories now, not only in the glitter and gold of a distant heaven, momentarily revealed by miraculous vision, but chiefly in the sunshine of the never-withdrawn presence, lighting up our humdrum drudgery with inscription of the Divine name thereon. When the Metaphysical Society was discussing Joshua's sun standing still upon Gibeon, John Ruskin is represented to have said that it would not surprise him at all to see the sun stop; the wonder to him was that it always went on. This reverence for the ordinary world-order, not craving for irregular marvels, is characteristic of our time. Thereby is fulfilled the essential purpose of all religion in binding man and God more closely together.

The same tendency has had the most beneficial effect upon practice. We now see that the words, "Inasmuch as ye have done it to the least of these, ye have done it unto Me"—and further—"unto Him that sent me," is one of the key texts of the New Testament. It could not be more plainly put that the service of humanity is the service of God, and that there really is no other. Hence the conspicuous devotion of religious effort now-a-days to defend the weak and redeem the sinner.

In the light of the above conception of the Divine Nature, the sonship of our Lord, as the Divine Spirit incarnated in a human life, becomes simplified. We cannot *account* for our Lord's character; we need not try. There are fountains of the grace of God which flow from mountain tops we have not climbed. But to conceive of it is more within our power.

To argue that Christ was or was not God, was or was not man, is profitless till we know what we mean by "God" and by "man." This is no verbal quibble: it is an essential preliminary thought. We must go deeper than these volcanic monosyllables can take us. A human life perfectly united to and identified with the Divine Spirit, in whom dwelt all the fulness of the Godhead bodily, can be nothing else than God manifest in the flesh. There can have been no conflict between the Humanity and the Divinity of our Lord. There were in His nature no jarring elements. His personality, we may be sure, was single and stable. His Humanity became glorified into Divinity, and Divinity thus became visible, where to us it alone could, in Humanity. The exact relation was expressed by Himself when He prayed for His disciples, that "As Thou, Father, art in Me, and I in Thee, that they also may be one in us." I desire to attempt no improvement on these words. For us it is enough that we fulfil them, and by the only way, Christ's own way,

enter into fellowship with the Father and the Son. His Via Dolo-
rosa will become to us also the Sacred Way of triumph. Thus the
Gospel becomes its own evidence, and is independent of the pre-
carious accuracy of historical records. We know that the kingdom
of God is among us. Our Lord is the best, indeed the only, authority here, and the fact that He chose "Son of Man" to be His title,
throws light upon His inner mind, as that of one from whom
no human temptation or sorrow is alien. "Son of God" and "Son
of Man," if we think about it, are bound to meet in their perfect
development. Around us are myriads of beings on the flat earth,
above us is the limitless heaven, and Christ is on the horizon line,
where heaven and earth bow and climb and meet.

All this, is, once more, in harmony with the careful line taken
on speculative matters by the founders of Quakerism. The Society
has never entered the lists in the great arithmetical controversy
embodied in the Athanasian Creed; and there are signs that after
fifteen hundred years that controversy is finally coming to an end.
No battlefield of human thought is everlasting.

Next:—What has modern thought to say of what is often called
the atonement, but less ambiguously, by its Scriptural synonym, the
Reconciliation. The answer is that our Lord is, first and last, the
reconciler of man to God, with an effectual reconciliation never
laid hold of so clearly as now.

Two conflicts rage round the imprisoned spirit—one with its
fleshly tabernacle, and one with sin and pain outside—fightings
within and fears without. Time forbids our touching on the second of these, but with regard to the former—man's reconciliation
to God within, by which he enters into harmony with his own
highest nature, is to be found in the uncompromising message of
the Master:—"Die to live again." Four times are we told in the
Gospels that we are to save our lives by losing them. And modern
thought finds in the surrender of the will the only satisfactory use
of the will. Otherwise it masters its possessor. Sanctification,
complete surrender to the will of God, stands out in undimmed
outline, as the plain message of Christ and the scientifically reasonable thing to do. "Our wills are ours, to make them Thine."
We are well within the region of experience here. Every saint
knows it, and to maintain it is the Christian's daily task.

Thus the scene of the work of salvation is the human heart. We
are saved through the washing of regeneration and the renewing

of the Holy Ghost, which He shed on us abundantly, through Jesus Christ our Saviour. Paul knew of no other salvation. How it was shed on us is told us beforehand by Christ. "If I be lifted up, I shall draw all men unto me," and again, "except a corn of wheat fall into the ground and die, it abideth alone, but if it die it bringeth forth much fruit." He implies that His teaching about self-consecration would have been futile, had it not been carried out by Himself to the bitterest of bitter ends, and so gained power to draw all men unto Him. Paul explains it very clearly: "Being found in fashion as a man, he humbled himself, becoming obedient even unto death, yea, the death of the Cross." Thus the climax of the Cross is led up to by the Apostle as a necessary consequence of "being found in fashion as a man." Indeed, a man not mortal is not a brother man, and the Son of Man could not have fulfilled His mission without meeting that death which is common to His brethren.

The author of the Epistle to the Hebrews is very emphatic about this: "Since then the children are sharers in flesh and blood, He also partook of the same, that through death He might . . . deliver them who, through fear of death, were all their lifetime subject to bondage. . . . It behoved Him in all things to be made like unto His brethren. . . . For in that He Himself hath suffered being tempted, He is able also to succour them that are tempted." (Heb. ii., 14–18.) Brotherhood with men, temptation with men, death with men; such is the clear teaching of Christ and His Apostles, and the most modern Christian thought joins hands with the most ancient.

There is much intermediate thought, modern in its day, which has been abandoned, such as the supposed spiritual value of shedding physical blood, and all attempts to buy the Grace of God. Such conceptions have reached us through men who wrote in the corners of cloisters, who, in monastic seclusion, could barely learn what human love means, were denied even the common insight which is the inheritance of every husband and every father, and so were the last men to expound either human nature or Divine love. They are dead; and unblest, on the whole, is their memory.

Our Society on the other hand has avoided systematic statements of the method of salvation. It has shunned any attempt to describe the eternal workings of love in the language of law, or in terms of business.

The Christian life is thus based on, and built entirely out of, unselfishness. Any teaching which appeals to the selfish instincts, even which attracts by a postponed reward the judicious egoist, has no purifying power, and brings no salvation, but slow ruin to the soul. The strength of every form of faith is the absorption of self in God. The call is clear—to put away all pride, selfwill and self-seeking, the desire for mansions here or in a new world, which will be a world of service hereafter, to live steadily and consciously as a part of the whole, as a vehicle of God. There is no easy Gospel in the air.

Over the *Bible* a change has come like the process of restoration of an ancient Church, covered formerly with a uniform coat of speckless and infallible whitewash, thickened and renewed by the devotion of generations, but obscuring the construction, concealing features of architectural interest, all its past vicissitudes, and the thoughts of its builders. The first effect of such a process is defacement, desecration and plentiful dust. We cannot just then worship there at all. That epoch is now over; the dust is cleared; the defacement is too complete to deface any longer, and it is found that nothing has been lost but late accretions. The old building, with all its rugged edges, its patched-up gaps, and its evident repairs, is before us now, in many styles of architecture, with the enemy's cannon-balls sticking here and there in its masonry, and with the gargoyles, past spirits of terror, gaping from its spouts. We love the pathos of it, and admire the richness. We really know it now partially, and for the first time. This knowledge has become part of the durable stock of mankind. It will never be lost or reversed. The clergy know it and their flocks soon will.

All this George Fox and Robert Barclay would have welcomed. The claim for the mechanical infallibility of the Scriptures rests on less than any other great intellectual position known to me. It has nothing to rest on but the ill-informed views of the bishops of the early centuries, and against the dicta of those bishops Friends are in revolt on every kind of question. When we cease to be afraid of the competition of other books with the Bible, we shall find out by how much it excels them all. As the record of the life of our Lord, if for no other reason, it must ever be to the Christian the Book of Books.

In conclusion, having attempted an outline synthesis of parts of the faith of the modern world, may I hold out the hand to any fearful one, with the words used by our Great Exemplar to the traditionalists of His day:—"Think not that I come to destroy the law or the prophets, I come not to destroy but to fulfil."

RUFUS M. JONES

Arguably the single most influential American Friend of the first half of the twentieth century was Rufus M. Jones (1863–1948). A native of Maine and a Gurneyite Friend by background, he spent forty years teaching at Haverford College. As editor of the weekly American Friend, *and as the author of dozens of books and hundreds of articles, he advocated a Quakerism that reclaimed doctrines that evangelicalism had minimized, particularly the inward light, and urged accommodation to modern scholarship and science.*

Rufus M. Jones, "The Message of Early Quakerism," in *A Dynamic Faith* (London, 1901).

Every great movement in the world embodies an idea. It often happens that those who are working out the idea are only dimly conscious of its full meaning, but yet it gives direction and form to the whole process, and if we wish to understand the movement, we must first hunt down the idea. The great religious movement of the seventeenth century, which is called Quakerism, is no exception. It has its fundamental principle which throws light upon, if it does not explain, all the peculiarities of this so-called revival of primitive Christianity.

In a certain rough and general way religions may be divided into two classes, those which have an aim and purpose to change the attitude and disposition of God toward men, and secondly, those which deal primarily with the disposition, the character, the inner nature of the human soul and its attitude toward God. In religions of the first class priests are essential and sacrifice and ritual become an elemental part of worship. In the second, the whole problem becomes a personal one: How to get a transformed and sanctified nature, how to realize the potential self, how to perfect the being. The supreme question for the first is, How can we get

God to account us righteous and how can we escape the consequences of wrongdoing? For the second it is, How can we become righteous and avoid sin? For the first, the church and its rites and ceremonies, its creeds and its prayers, are a good, as an end in themselves; for the second, nothing is a good in itself, except a glorified nature, a rightly fashioned will, and a pure and loving heart.

George Fox, who is the original exponent of Quakerism, could find no satisfaction for himself in the peculiar performances which in his day largely constituted religion. The whole system appeared foreign to his needs. It did not materially contribute to the end, which for him from very early life was the supreme one, the attainment of inward harmony and peace through deliverance from sin. He felt that there was no correspondence between the religious system of the church and the supreme purpose of life. No amount of faithfulness to the one produced the other. It was the clear conviction that the church of his day had no "open sesame" to the life which alone could satisfy his nature that drove him into a profound melancholy and made him a solitary seeker for another way, if peradventure there were any other way. The "hollow casks," as he called the ministers to whom he went for light, had no single word to give him. They could not understand in the first place what the young man really wanted. It was a new idea that anybody should want a real face back of the picture, when for them the picture was the face. Why should he plague his head over any other reality than this shadow which satisfied all ordinary men? But it was just that reality other than the shadow which the young man felt he must have. Shadow raised to the nth power was for him shadow still. He would have substance or nothing. The real difficulty was that he wanted to find God, and no person could give him any method which furthered his quest; all known trails merely led to where God had been once. Here was a book which told how God once expressed Himself directly to men, even took flesh and tabernacled among them. But the Book only told of divine historic facts, which were now glorious memories, that made the present silence all the harder to bear. Here was a church which had a divine origin. Far off at its source God had wrought and the first building stones had been laid by divine hands, but the link with that divine Personality was the shadowy touch of a succession of consecrated hands. Here was a system of theology which was supposed to express the divine thought and preserve it unchanged through the ages, but the very central feature of it was a dead Christ and nowhere in it could he find the present God he sought—only at the most some exact and careful language about Him. These are all things which a person might accept and assent to and still remain in sin and be as far from a soul's peace as ever. He has as yet found no reconstructive principle which puts the whole life on a new level. Such a principle does, however, come to him in a "revelation" as an "opening," like a flash out of the sky. This principle may be summed up in his discovery, that religion must begin as a divine life within a man. "All believers," he would say, "must be born of God, pass from death to life, and none others are true believers but such." It means, of course, that salvation is an actual change in the man's life. His next step is the discovery that Christ is no dead Christ but a living one, still present and able to "speak to one's condition." He saw now that this very restlessness and hunger for truth which he had experienced in the years of search were proof of the infinite goodness of God, who had never left him, who had disturbed his ease as the mother-bird disturbs the nest that the young may learn to fly. But there is more involved than this: Christ, and so God Himself, is found right here within and not somewhere else. It is no longer the old disappointing story that He was somewhere once, but disappeared. We have the glorious fact announced, "Behold He is here now and I have found Him," and this is the key to the whole Quaker message. The same God who said "Let there be light," who shaped the course of the Hebrew commonwealth, who led His prophets to the mount of vision, who dwelt among men in Jesus Christ and so manifested His glory and His love—that same God is so near that the heart that wants Him finds Him, the soul that listens for Him hears Him and the person who obeys Him and trusts Him becomes born into His life, and so begins a new life which at its source is divine, and may in time crowd the old life completely out. It will be seen at once that we are here dealing with a religion of, what we called, the second type. It begins in a purpose to find God, it ends with a conscious likeness to Him. "I was taken up," says George Fox, "in the love of God, so that I could not but admire the greatness of His love; and while I was in that condition it was opened unto me by the eternal light and power, and I therein clearly saw, that all was done and to be done, in and by Christ."

"Christ," he says again, "it was who had enlightened me, that gave me His light to believe in and gave me hope which is in Himself, revealed Himself in me and gave me His spirit."

George Fox variously calls his newly discovered principle "the Christ within," "the inner light" and the "seed." It means in any case that a man becomes truly religious when he becomes aware that there is a divine Being within the reach of his own consciousness, i.e., that the self and God are not wholly foreign to each other. It means that religion is fundamentally a life and a growth, and that this life, which produces a "new creature," is the divine Being taking root, so to speak, and growing within the human soul. This life becomes light, and the soul thereby becomes sensitive to good and evil and is made capable of free choices of the right. It is a veritable divine life forming within so that the old self yields place to a spiritual self. It becomes the Christian ideal to have the spirit and life of God in the heart—the Christ within. This is no new idea with George Fox, as everybody knows; it is the beginning and ending of the original Gospel—the "good news" that there is something so close and intimate between humanity and Divinity that God can express Himself in human terms—even in human form—and that man—any man—who receives Him can become like Him, and further, that life on its very highest level is nothing less than living a life in the flesh which reproduces in measure and degree that perfect typical God-man life. George Fox takes it all literally, and goes to work to realize it in himself and to call all other men to it. "I saw the blood of the new covenant, how it came into the heart." "The Lord opened to me how every man was enlightened by the divine light of Christ." "I knew God by revelation as He who hath the key did open, and as the Father of life drew me to His Son by His spirit." These words mean that religion, at least with this man, is first of all an inward, personal experience. The blood of the covenant is not merely a theological dogma, it is not a metaphysical theory to be held and preached about alone. Out from the heart the new life must spring and all that blood means or can mean must be grasped, not in a doctrine, but as a fact of the life. The very life-principle, which the blood symbolizes, which was in the Saviour of men, must become the principle of the Christian's life and must pulsate from his heart through every fiber of his being. So, too, with the light. It means hardly more or less than a self-demonstration through the spirit of a relationship with God, which, through obedience, becomes clearer and more expansive, until the things of the Spirit attest themselves and prove their reality, as to the experienced mathematician the figures and laws of empty space become more sure even than the temporal, tangible world.

As Kant finds the form of an eternal moral law written in the very structure of the being, which says to every man, "thou must," so the Quaker says that there is a law of the heart, a divine light in the soul, "that of God," as he calls it, which is absent from no sane man. It may, only too easily, be disobeyed, shut round with our own darkness and lost to use as the diamond in the dirt. Browning, who held substantially the same truth, says: "The child feels God a moment, ichors o'er the place, plays on and grows to be a man like us." But Fox believes still further that this so-called "light," this "voice," this "law," this "seed" is the living Christ, the Holy Spirit coming into immediate relations with us, and working out, as we cooperate, our salvation; as the principle of life works within the growing plant. The question at once arises, as it did in an earlier day, what place does this leave for the Scriptures and for the historic basis of Christianity, if every man may enjoy a light in his own soul, if every man may be taught directly, and if salvation is a work of the Divine Spirit bringing transformation and newness of life to all who cooperate with Him? This problem hardly presented itself to George Fox. Like the happy child who enjoys his mother's love too much to ask how such unselfish love is consistent with the law of individual struggle for existence, he is too sure of direct alliance with God to ask how this is to be reconciled with certain historical theories. It is possible, however, to suggest how he would answer the question: "God has always been talking to men," he would say, "as far as they have been ready and willing to listen to Him and capable of understanding Him. The very crudest religion of the untutored savage is indication of a light, however feeble and dim; the very distinction of right and wrong, however imperfect the standard, is evidence of a budding principle which could not originate in a mere clay image, a man of mere carnal nature. This vision, which is so dim and shadowy in most men, may become unclouded sight in those rare souls who have been purified and refined and made holy and spiritual by bringing their lives into complete parallelism with the divine purposes. Through such holy men God has

spoken. The messages which have come through them have a per-
manent value and are profitable for the spiritual life of all ages.
But these writings—called Scriptures—have a meaning and spiritual significance to us only because we partake of the same Spirit
as did those men who were moved to write them. They are not
to take the place of the Spirit, they only show us how the Spirit
manifests Himself when He has a perfectly responsive instrument;
and so they become the standard of revelation. In no sense do they
do away with the necessity for a present immediate communion
with God or for a personal revelation of God in the soul, or do
they preclude the search for further truth which God may reveal
in these or any other times. They simply stand as the high water
mark of God's revelation through men. The proper Christian
must see them as the master literature of the Spirit of God, but he
is not shut up to this Book alone—to spell out as with fingers of
the blind the words which God once wrote before He ceased to
speak to us. Each Christian must live in the Spirit which gave
forth these Scriptures, and so only can he authenticate them, understand them, and use them." Those who know their Fox's *Journal* and Barclay's *Apology* will recognize that I have summed up
the spirit of their teaching on this subject. In regard to the historic
basis of Christianity, it may be said that the early Friends took
practically the same position which the Apostle Paul took. The
earthly life of Christ was to them a fact of supreme importance.
It was the culmination of the manifestation of the self-revealing
God. It showed once for all what God was like and what He would
do to bring men to Him. The real purpose of His coming was to
make men like Himself, not to enact a divine drama as a specta-
cle. In order to make men like Himself, He had completely to reveal Himself, and then to give such a mighty motive and spiritual
impulse as should move men forever to Himself. Both Paul and
Fox find that in the Cross of Christ. "He loved me and gave Himself for me," therefore, "the life I now live in the flesh I live by the
faith of the Son of God." Fox takes the Incarnation literally, as
"God with us," but he finds in it the further fact that this same
Christ who became a sinless Personality is striving to win all lives
and to reproduce Himself in men. "They asked me," he says,
"whether I was sanctified. I answered, Yes; for I was in the paradise of God. Then they asked me if I had no sin. I answered that

Christ my Saviour had taken away my sin; and in Him is no sin. They asked how we knew that Christ did abide in us? I said by His spirit that He hath given us. They temptingly asked if any of us were Christ. I answered, Nay we were nothing. Christ was all. They said, If a man steal is it no sin? I answered, All unrighteousness is sin." This leads us to the phase of the Quaker message which is sometimes called perfectionism or sanctification. This idea of a victorious and triumphant life is involved in the very essence of the message and cannot be divorced from it. His great contemporary, Bunyan, expresses a type of religion which is in decided contrast to this idea. The "Christian" of the "Progress" is probably a correct picture of the ordinary Christian, but it is a type which Fox's whole life is bent on proving a false type. "Christian" wants to escape hell, he wishes to get rid of a burden on his back. But he is never sure of himself. He loses his roll and has to go back after it, he yields to Giant Despair and lies down in the dungeon of Doubting Castle. He just manages to get along over the difficulties by the constant help and stimulus of his valiant and courageous friends, but the real shout of victory is heard only when the last deep water has been passed and heaven's gate opens. The Quaker's whole struggle is to get freed from sin and to live a present life in the power of God. The "Holy Grail" of his quest is nothing short of a redeemed nature and a victorious spiritual life to be realized as a demonstrated fact. That he meant by perfection, or sanctification, incapacity or inability to sin, he nowhere says, and such a view is inconsistent with what he does say. He could not, furthermore, have meant that he had attained to the goal and limit of spiritual progress. He merely meant that he had been delivered from the power of sin and the love of it, and was living instead in the power of Christ. He believed that so long as he continued to live in this power of Christ, sin was foreign to him, impossible in fact for him, and that in this same power lay the possibility of apprehending the full measure of life in Christ. This, or something quite like it, is the seed principle of Quakerism. We have put it into the language of our own time, but we believe we have not distorted it.

It remains to see how the principle applies itself and how it explains some of the peculiarities which attach to our history. It must be recognized at once that it is a method of reformation, of reconstruction, of regeneration for individuals and for society. In fact, the apostles of Quakerism profoundly believed that they had a principle which would transform society and make "this world another world." They believed that their ideal would become a universal reality and would reconstruct human society as Newton's law of gravitation had reconstructed all conceptions of the universe. They went out to call men to strict obedience to the divine Voice wherever it spoke. There is no better illustration of the effect of faith. So long as this high faith lasted, no country was too remote, no labour too hard, no call too high, no prison too horrible to daunt the Quaker with his message. The greatest statesman, even Oliver himself, and the meanest politician with his paltry scheme, were called to govern according to the divine Voice. "I did admonish him [Oliver Cromwell] to harken to God's voice, that he might stand in his counsel and obey it." This same principle was to be applied to every conceivable business and profession of life. "Mind the leading of God." "Your teacher is within you, obey him." "Mind that in thee which doth convince thee." This was to be the rule and test for all actions however simple and unimportant until this law within should be obeyed as naturally as the law of gravitation now is. This of course made the Quaker a reformer of evil customs of every sort. He came into history during a great civil war, and he saw at once that war was a wicked custom, inconsistent at every point with the religion which he illustrated. He settled his position by saying that he lived "in virtue of that life and power which does away with the occasion for all war." It was his mission, not to cry against war in the abstract, but to live himself in "this life and power" and to bring, as far as it lay in his ability, all other men into it, and so to produce a society in which war would be impossible. He became an uncompromising opponent of injustice in the courts, of corruption and tyranny in the administration of law, of arbitrary methods in government, not simply because he himself suffered from such abuses, but really because his principle was at stake. According to this principle, every man is a man and has a man's rights. In other words, the divine right of man is superior to the divine right of kings. The judge and the king must be called back to observe "that of God within them" as much as the poorest peasant, and the man who rules or judges by a selfish or arbitrary method is out of accord with the divine nature of things and must be testified against at all costs, for this principle of the divine right of man is at stake.

It is his adherence to what I have called the divine right of man that constitutes the Quaker's sense of human equality. He was not a "leveler"—except as he wanted to level everybody up to the highest. He knew that men were differently endowed and equipped, and that they could not be reduced to a lot of equal atoms of human society. What he meant was that every man had a right to be a man, and to work out his manhood under the divine leading. That whether low or high each human being has a self to realize for which he is responsible to God, and that nothing must prevent him from exercising his functions as a free spiritual man. The man is more than raiment and he must not become a creature of fashion, a peg to hang clothes upon. The personality must govern dress, not dress the personality. This worth and dignity of man—of all men—must, the Quaker held, be everywhere emphasized, therefore hollow custom and sham manners in every walk of life must cease. A man is a man, and he shall be treated as one. There is much in the garb question and "hat honour" and "singular" address and absence of title—even of Mr.—which strikes us today as rather petty and foolish, an overdrawn distinction. That may be so, but it was occasioned by the Quaker's resolve to be absolutely honest, and to fight sham, as the mythical Hercules fought beasts, and overdrawn or not, this scrupulous determination to be as honest and straightforward before man as before God has done much to clear the air of sham and to crack the husk of the foolish customs.

But a much greater issue than this is involved in the Quaker's conception of man and his relation to God. Let it be remembered that our fundamental principle is, that each man has direct relation and dealings with God. If he is saved, it must be through his own choices, not by the act of another. Within the circle of his own life stands a sanctuary of which he alone is the priest. If God is met there, it is because he meets Him; if God's voice is heard and obeyed, he is the one who hears it; if sins are forgiven it is not through another that it is known, but by the forgiven soul itself. Therefore, all that is absolutely necessary for divine worship, or service, is a human being—any devout human being— with an open heart toward God. A man and God, met together, make a holy place, and this meeting constitutes worship. The

vocal expression is not the important thing—it is the real meeting
of the soul with God that is all-important. It is a fact that such
meeting is rendered easier where many kindred spirits meet with
one accord than where one individual sits alone, and this is one
reason for public meetings for worship. Another reason, and perhaps the main one, for public meetings, is the fact that some persons are more capable of appreciating and apprehending divine
truth than others are. It becomes thus the duty and privilege of
those who see, to interpret to those who do not see so clearly. This
ability to minister is a gift which consists first in the power to see,
and secondly in the power to impart the truth in its relation to the
spiritual needs of men. The minister, of course, can do nothing
for the congregation apart from their cooperation. He does not act
or speak or pray for them. He is merely one man among them who
is gifted with rare spiritual sight and whose sole function is to
help others see. Every office or position in the church rests on the
same principle, for the Quaker. No magical authority attaches to
any position. The weight of the official person rests solely on his
spiritual capacity and his ability to perform the functions which
devolve upon him. It is after all only a man, doing some particular
work for which the Lord has fitted him.

The Quaker needs to say little of the so-called ordinances, for
there is no more place for them in his conception of Christianity
than there is for horses on an electric car. They fall off as the old
leaves do when the new ones come. It is an essential feature of
Quakerism that the individual Christian communes with God
and feeds his spiritual life by partaking of the living Christ who
nourishes the whole inner being. If this is so in fact, what place is
left for bread and wine, which at best could only be a symbol of
what he already has in reality? If it is true that the believer enters
consciously into the divine life, i.e., is baptised into Christ and
puts on Christ, what place is left for the use of water, which at
best could only symbolise what he already has in fact. Furthermore, the use of material things to produce a spiritual effect seems
to him from the nature of the case unwarrantable. He fails further
to find any clear and unmistakeable command from the Master
for the institution of a system of things which seems to him incompatible with the whole spirit of the Gospel, and he concludes
that if they ever had a place in the church it could only have been

while it was in its Jewish swaddling clothes. In short, he finds no justification for any system or practice which becomes a substitute for the Spirit Himself, or which lessens the positive aspiration of the soul to find God Himself and to live in Him.

JOAN MARY FRY

By the early twentieth century, liberal Friends had reached consensus on the essence of Quakerism: equality, worship based on silence, opposition to ritualism, and peace. Joan Mary Fry (1862–1952), an English Friend, summarized these well in a pamphlet published shortly before World War I.

Joan Mary Fry, *For Fellowship and Freedom: Some Aspects of the Society of Friends* (York, England, n.d.).

Creeds pass, rites change, no altar standeth whole. Yet we her memory, as she prayed, will keep, Keep by this: Life in God, and union there!

MATTHEW ARNOLD

It will be generally admitted that the present is a time when the minds of men are deeply stirred by questions about the spiritual life. Not long ago the trend of thought seemed to be away from religion: it was but the receding swirl of a tide which we now know to be fast rising and like to reach heights but lately esteemed to be far beyond its limit. There is a drawing towards things spiritual, an interest—born of the age-long human need, and now, at last, nourished by science herself—in the unseen forces which play about us, a sense that our heritage in life is larger than we know, and that we want teaching how to use the powers of a higher consciousness which may yet be ours. And whilst we are aware, even if too dimly, of a quickening of individual aspirations and desires, we are urged, by much that is passing around us, to a growing sense of the realities of brotherhood, and the need for some more adequate expression of a common life. It becomes continually more evident that religion should help to create some form of fellowship which shall give free play to the individual whilst answering the demand for union with others. Fellowship and freedom are both essential.

Many religious bodies seek to create the bond of union by demanding adherence to some formulated belief, and excluding those who cannot adopt a certain creed or creeds. The idea that faith can be kept pure and true by drawing outlines round it makes it essential to preserve these defining boundary lines with great care. But "Creeds pass, rites change," and there are those whose conception of faith as a power which grows by use, rather than as a doctrine once for all defined, who will have to find some other bond than creeds, however beautiful, however hallowed by age. In theory, it can scarcely be said always in practice, Friends have sought another bond of fellowship—"Life in God and union there." This is one of their fundamental positions, and it has various results in their organisation and views.

Equality.

In the first place all the members of the Society, both men and women, are equal, as indeed all must be when they come into the oneness of a common worship of the one Father. All members have a voice in the regulation of the affairs of the Society, all are equally responsible for the right holding of meetings for worship, and the only source of outward authority is the consensus of opinion in the body as a whole. There is, and can be, no fundamental distinction between those who preach and those whose service lies in other directions; but for the right ordering of the body, special functions are allotted to some members according as they shew an aptitude for specialised service. Ministers, elders and overseers are recognised, in some cases for a time only: but with very insignificant exceptions, they have no different status from the humblest member. Each congregation regulates its own affairs: groups of congregations are united in Monthly, and these again in Quarterly Meetings, and finally, all in the Yearly Meeting of the whole Society, which is the ultimate authority, humanly speaking. This is said expressly, because Friends have dared to base their conception of a religious organisation upon the *fact* of union in God, and unity of purpose as directly led by His Spirit, and they have shewn for upwards of 200 years that it is possible to conduct the business of a religious body without appeal to any other authority than the spiritual discernment of its members. Questions are settled, not by voting, but by the Clerk (appointed by the gathering itself) taking the "sense of the meeting." This plan has never really failed.

Silence.

Out of this equality and oneness before God there arises the peculiar form of worship practised by Friends. There is no priest, there are no rites. How then shall men worship the Father? Surely by coming into consciousness of their actual relation to Him, by recognising that it is His Life which moves and stirs in them, and His Love which is ever redeeming and saving them. And so, as Friends gather to their hours of worship, they find that to wait upon the Lord, to re-adjust the harmony of the deeper self, too often jarred by outward events, they must first be silent before God. Silence is the basis of their worship—silence not merely of words, but that stilling of the whole being before the infinite majesty of the Divine, which sets man in his true place, and tunes his pulses to spiritual keys. Out of such a silence there may come words of prayer, of praise, of aspiration, or it may be of confession or warning: they may come from those recognised as Ministers, but just as truly may they fall from other lips: anyone may be called to vocal service. There is, and can be, no distinction where this deepest of communions is reached: all that is needful is that the human instruments should be in harmony with the guiding Spirit, and the experience of the overmastering of the Divine power—the tender, yet forcible, compulsion to give forth some message of the Father's love or wisdom for the uplifting of the whole gathering—is one that is too sacred to be described, too wonderful not to be desired.

Sacraments.

To those who have found the deepest kind of union with God and with one another, who have become conscious of some of the far-reaching meaning of the doctrine that God is our Father, Who made us in His own image, there can be no value in any merely external initiation into, or participation with, the body of the Church. If the Sacraments are outward signs of inward grace, then

the inward grace is the main factor, and it is scarcely well to re-
verse the process, and to act as if the sign were the cause of that
which it is said to express: to say that there must first be a cross
of water on an infant's forehead, before it can be truly a child of
God, or that a person must take particular bread and wine before
they can feed upon Christ, the Living Bread. Friends hold that
the Sacraments are real and spiritual, and not confined to certain
rare and stated acts or rites. The marks of the Holy Spirit's baptism are to be seen in the daily life of consecration, and His action
is continuous, not once for all in childhood, but needed ever more
and more as the soul yearns for larger experience of the Divine
cleansing and renewing. And, in like manner, of the Communion
it may be said that Friends find in our Lord's teaching, not the
institution of a rite, but the inculcation of that entire dependence
upon the love of God as manifested in Christ, which makes us
aware that our very life is sustained, not by material food in itself,
but by the power of the Life within each one of us. "This do in
remembrance of Me" does not, we believe, bid us receive heavenly
food only on certain set occasions, but it lifts the whole thought
of our necessary sustenance into the region of the Spirit, teaching us that, since in God "we live, and move, and have our being,"
therefore our daily eating—as oft as we do it—should be a
reminder to us that Christ is indeed the true Bread of Life, the Sus-
tainer of our very being. Into this mystical and non-ritualistic
interpretation many scholars of the present day find that they are
being led by the compulsion of a scientific study of texts, and the
position which Friends arrived at in the 17th century by other
means is likely to be held now by many whose studies have driven
them to it as the only valid explanation of the New Testament
documents.

Peace.

One more may be mentioned of the many results flowing from
Friends' endeavour to rule their lives and their community upon
the belief in the "Inner Light," the Christ within. The earthly life
and death of Jesus was a setting forth of the illimitable power of
the Divine Love, of its absolute supremacy in the places of sin and
death, which had before seemed to be given over to some alien and
antagonistic force. And since the Divine Son has redeemed man

by the way of the Cross rather than by the way of might, it is clear that the powers of evil are to be overcome by spiritual rather than by material means. Friends, therefore, hold it to be so surely the duty of Christians to enter into the living Spirit of their Master that it is inconsistent with their following of Him for them to take up arms against their fellows, and their history abounds in proofs of the success and surety of this method.

It would be impossible to condense into a few paragraphs the many forms in which the inner life may express itself; when our creed is a growing communion with God, our expression of it will be diverse and wide as His world, to be lived rather than written. Let no one, therefore, imagine that all Friends' doctrine and practice has been even outlined here.

To those who like the ease of a worship mellowed by the long usage of beautiful forms, the strenuous methods of the Society will scarcely appeal. With those who find support in creeds and outward sacraments, Quakerism has no quarrel; it merely stands as a reminder to them that the essentials of religion lie deeper than such things.

But to those who cannot make their spiritual home in the incense-laden air of ceremonial, who crave some fellowship where they shall still be able to welcome all of new truth that may be coming forth out of the Eternal fulness, Friends hold out the hand of welcome; they bid such add their power to the common stock, that so, in a fellowship founded upon the spiritual oneness of the sons of God, we may all come into the freedom wherewith the indwelling Christ makes all men free.

PART VI

PEACE

ORIGINS

A DECLARATION

Today, pacifism—a refusal to bear arms or use violence against fellow human beings even in self-defense—is one of the beliefs most closely associated with Friends. But historians have shown that what Friends call "the peace testimony" developed gradually. While George Fox had rejected offers of an army commission in the 1650s, other Friends well into the 1670s saw military service, under certain circumstances, as compatible with their faith. Most historians consider the following statement, issued by a group of Friends in London in the aftermath of a failed uprising against King Charles II, as the earliest articulation of Quaker pacifism.

A Declaration from the Harmless and Innocent people of God, Called Quakers, against All Plotters and Fighters in the World, for the Removing the Ground of Jealousy and Suspicion from Both Magistrates and People in the Kingdom, concerning Wars and Fightings (London, 1661).

Our principle is, and our practice have always been, to seek peace and ensue it and to follow after righteousness and the knowledge of God, seeking the good and welfare and doing that which tends to the peace of all. We know that wars and fightings proceed from the lusts of men (as Jas. iv. 1–3), out of which lusts the Lord hath redeemed us, and so out of the occasion of war. The occasion of which war, and war itself (wherein envious men, who are lovers of themselves more than lovers of God, lust, kill, and desire to have men's lives or estates) ariseth from the lust. All bloody principles and practices, we, as to our own particulars, do utterly deny, with all outward wars and strife and fightings with outward weapons, for any end or under any pretence whatsoever. And this is our testimony to the whole world.

And whereas it is objected:

"But although you now say that you cannot fight nor take up arms at all, yet if the spirit do move you, then you will change your principle, and then you will sell your coat and buy a sword and fight for the kingdom of Christ."

Answer:

As for this we say to you that Christ said to Peter, "Put up thy sword in his place"; though he had said before that he that had no sword might sell his coat and buy one (to the fulfilling of the scripture), yet after, when he had bid him put it up, he said, "He that taketh the sword shall perish with the sword." And further, Christ said to Peter, "Thinkest thou, that I cannot now pray to my Father, and he shall presently give me more than twelve legions of angels?" And this might satisfy Peter, after he had put up his sword, when he said to him that he took it, should perish by it, which satisfieth us. (Luke xxii, 36; Matt. xxvi. 51–53). And in the Revelation it's said, "He that kills with the sword shall perish with the sword: and here is the faith and the patience of the saints." (Rev. xiii. 10). And so Christ's kingdom is not of this world, therefore do not his servants fight, as he told Pilate, the magistrate who crucified him. And did they not look upon Christ as a raiser of sedition? And did not he say, "Forgive them"? But thus it is that we are numbered amongst fighters, that the Scriptures might be fulfilled.

That the spirit of Christ, by which we are guided, is not changeable, so as once to command us from a thing as evil and again to move unto it; and we do certainly know, and so testify to the world, that the spirit of Christ, which leads us into all Truth, will never move us to fight and war against any man with outward weapons, neither for the kingdom of Christ, nor for the kingdoms of this world.

First:

Because the kingdom of Christ God will exalt, according to the promise, and cause it to grow and flourish in righteousness. "Not by might, nor by power [of outward sword], but by my spirit, said the Lord." (Zech. iv. 6). So those that use any weapon to fight for Christ, or for the establishing of his kingdom or government, both the spirit, principle and practice in that we deny.

Secondly:

And as for the kingdoms of this world, we cannot covet them, much less can we fight for them, but we do earnestly desire and wait, that by the Word of God's power and its effectual operation in the hearts of men, the kingdoms of this world may become the kingdoms of the Lord, and of his Christ, that he may rule and reign in men by his spirit and truth, that thereby all people, out of all different judgments and professions may be brought into love and unity with God, and one with another, and that they may all come to witness the prophet's words who said, "Nation shall not lift up sword against nation, neither shall they learn war any more." (Isa. ii. 4; Mic. iv. 3).

So, we whom the Lord hath called into the obedience of his Truth have denied wars and fightings and cannot again any more learn it. This is a certain testimony unto all the world of the truth of our hearts in this particular, that as God persuadeth every man's heart to believe, so they may receive it. For we have not, as some others, gone about cunningly with devised fables, nor have we ever denied in practice what we have professed in principle, but in sincerity and truth and by the word of God have we laboured to be made manifest unto all men, that both we and our ways might be witnessed in the hearts of all people.

And whereas all manner of evil hath been falsely spoken of us, we hereby speak forth the plain truth of our hearts, to take away the occasion of that offence, that so we being innocent may not suffer for other men's offences, nor be made a prey upon by the wills of men for that of which we were never guilty; but in the uprightness of our hearts we may, under the power ordained of God for the punishment of evildoers and for the praise of them that do well, live a peaceable and godly life in all godliness and honesty. For although we have always suffered, and do now more abundantly suffer, yet we know that it's for righteousness' sake; "for all our rejoicing is this, the testimony of our consciences, that in simplicity and godly sincerity, not with fleshly wisdom but by the grace of God, we have had our conversation in the world" (2 Cor. i. 12), which for us is a witness for the convincing of our enemies. For this we can say to the whole world, we have wronged

no man's person or possessions, we have used no force nor violence against any man, we have been found in no plots, nor guilty
of sedition. When we have been wronged, we have not sought to
revenge ourselves, we have not made resistance against authority,
but wherein we could not obey for conscience' sake, we have suffered even the most of any people in the nation. We have been
accounted as sheep for the slaughter, persecuted and despised,
beaten, stoned, wounded, stocked, whipped, imprisoned, haled
out of synagogues, cast into dungeons and noisome vaults where
many have died in bonds, shut up from our friends, denied needful sustenance for many days together, with other like cruelties.

And the cause of all this our sufferings is not for any evil, but
for things relating to the worship of our God in obedience to his
requirings of us. For which cause we shall freely give up our bodies a sacrifice, rather than disobey the Lord. For we know, as the
Lord hath kept us innocent, so he will plead our cause, when there
is none in the earth to plead it. So we, in obedience to his truth,
do not love our lives unto the death, that we may do his will, and
wrong no man in our generation, but seek the good and peace of
all men. And he that hath commanded us that we shall not swear
at all (Matt. v. 34), hath also commanded us that we shall not kill
(Matt. v. 21), so that we can neither kill men, nor swear for or
against them. And this is both our principle and practice, and
hath been from the beginning, so that if we suffer, as suspected to
take up arms or make war against any, it is without ground from
us; for it neither is, nor ever was in our hearts, since we owned the
truth of God; neither shall we ever do it, because it is contrary to
the spirit of Christ, his doctrine, and the practice of his apostles,
even contrary to him for whom we suffer all things, and endure
all things.

And whereas men come against us with clubs, staves, drawn
swords, pistols cocked, and do beat, cut, and abuse us, yet we never
resisted them, but to them our hair, backs and cheeks have been
ready. It is not an honour to manhood nor to nobility to run upon
harmless people who lift not up a hand against them, with arms
and weapons.

Therefore consider these things ye men of understanding; for
plotters, raisers of insurrections, tumultuous ones, and fighters,
running with swords, clubs, staves and pistols one against another,
we say, these are of the world and hath its foundation from this

unrighteous world, from the foundation of which the Lamb hath been slain, which Lamb hath redeemed us from the unrighteous world, and we are not of it, but are heirs of a world in which there is no end and of a kingdom where no corruptible thing enters. And our weapons are spiritual and not carnal, yet mighty through God to the plucking down of the strongholds of Satan, who is author of wars, fighting, murder, and plots. And our swords are broken until ploughshares and spears into pruning hooks, as prophesied of in Micah iv. Therefore we cannot learn war any more, neither rise up against nation or kingdom with outward weapons, though you have numbered us among the transgressors and plotters. The Lord knows our innocency herein, and will plead our cause with all men and people upon earth at the day of their judgment, when all men shall have a reward according to their works. . . .

A VISION OF PEACE

WILLIAM PENN

Friends were not merely passive in their pacifism. William Penn, who had a profound interest in good government, in 1693 proposed a method for preventing and conciliating international disputes that may be seen as presaging the League of Nations and the United Nations in the twentieth century. In the early 1690s, as Penn wrote, Europe was in the first of a series of conflicts that would have France and England at war about half of the years between 1689 and 1815.

William Penn, *An Essay Towards the Present and Future Peace of Europe* (London, 1693).

To the Reader:

I have undertaken a subject that I am very sensible requires one of more sufficiency than I am master of to treat it, as, in truth, it deserves, and the groaning state of Europe calls for; but since bunglers may stumble upon the game, as well as masters, though it belongs to the skilful to hunt and catch it, I hope this essay will not be charged upon me for a fault, if it appear to be neither chimerical nor injurious, and may provoke abler pens to improve and perform the design with better success. I will say no more in excuse of myself, for this undertaking, but that it is the fruit of my solicitous thoughts, for the peace of Europe, and they must want charity as much as the world needs quiet, to be offended with me for so pacific a proposal. Let them censure my management, so they prosecute the advantage of the design; for till the millenary doctrine be accomplished, there is nothing appears to me so ben-

eficial an expedient to the peace and happiness of this quarter of
the world.

Section I:
Of Peace, and Its Advantages.

He must not be a man, but a statue of brass or stone, whose bowels
do not melt when he beholds the bloody tragedies of this war, in
Hungary, Germany, Flanders, Ireland, and at sea: the mortality of
sickly and languishing camps and navies, and the mighty prey the
devouring winds and waves have made upon ships and men since
[16]88. And as this with reason ought to affect human nature, and
deeply kindred, so there is something very moving that becomes
prudent men to consider, and that is the vast charge that has accompanied that blood, and which makes no mean part of these
tragedies; especially if they deliberate upon the uncertainty of the
war, that they know not how or when it will end, and that the expense cannot be less, and the hazard is as great as before. So that
in the contraries of peace we see the beauties and benefits of it;
which under it, such is the unhappiness of mankind, we are too apt
to nauseate, as the full stomach loathes the honeycomb; and like
that unfortunate gentleman, that having a fine and a good woman
to his wife, and searching his pleasure in forbidden and less agreeable company, said, when reproached with his neglect of better
enjoyments, that he could love his wife of all women, if she were
not his wife, though that increased his obligation to prefer her. It is
a great mark of the corruption of our natures, and what ought to
humble us extremely, and excite the exercise of our reason to a
nobler and juster sense, that we cannot see the use and pleasure of
our comforts but by the want of them. As if we could not taste the
benefit of health, but by the help of sickness; nor understand the
satisfaction of fullness without the instruction of want; nor, finally,
know the comfort of peace, but by the smart and penance of the
vices of war: and without dispute is not the least reason that God
is pleased to chastise us so frequently with it. What can we desire
better than peace, but the grace to use it? Peace preserves our possessions; we are in no danger of invasions; our trade is free and safe,
and we rise and lie down without anxiety. The rich bring out their
hoards, and employ the poor manufacturers; buildings and diverse

projections, for profit and pleasure, go on. It excites industry, which brings wealth, as that gives the means of charity and hospitality, not the lowest ornaments of a kingdom or commonwealth. But war, like the frost of [16]83, seizes all these comforts at once, and stops the civil channel of society. The rich draw in their stock, the poor turn soldiers, or thieves, or starve: no industry, no building, no manufactory, little hospitality or charity; but what the peace gave, the war devours. I need say no more upon this head, when the advantages of peace, and the mischiefs of war, are so many and sensible to every capacity under all governments, as either of them prevails. I shall proceed to the next point. What is the best means of peace; which will conduce very much to open my way to what I have to propose.

Section II:
Of the Means of Peace, Which Is Justice
Rather than War.

As justice is a preserver, so it is a better procurer of peace than war. Though *pax quaeritur bello* be an unusual saying, peace is the end of war, and as such it was taken up by O[liver] C[romwell] for his motto; yet the use generally made of that expression shows us, that properly and truly speaking, men seek their wills by war rather than by peace, and that as they will violate it to obtain them, so they will hardly be brought to think of peace, unless their appetites be some way gratified. If we look over the stories of all times, we shall find the aggressors generally moved by ambition; the pride of conquest and greatness of dominion more than right. But as those leviathans appear rarely in the world, so I shall anon endeavor to make it evident that they had never been able to devour to the peace of the world, and ingross whole countries as they have done, if the proposal I have to make for the benefit of our present age had been then in practice. The advantage that justice has upon war is seen by the success of embassies, that so often prevent war, by hearing the pleas and memorials of justice in the hands and mouths of the wronged party. Perhaps it may be in a good degree owing to reputation or poverty, or some particular interest or conveniency of princes and states, as much as justice; but it is certain, that as war cannot in any sense be justified, but upon wrongs received, and right, upon complaint, refused; so the generality of wars have their rise from such pretension. This is better seen and understood at home; for that which prevents a civil war in a nation, is that which may prevent it abroad, viz: justice, and we see where that is notably obstructed, war is kindled between the magistrates and people in particular kingdoms and states; which, however, it may be unlawful on the side of the people, we see never fails to follow, and ought to give the same caution to princes, as if it were the right of the people to do it. Though I must needs say, the remedy is almost ever worse than the disease: the aggressors seldom getting what they seek, or performing, if they prevail, what they promised. And the blood and poverty that usually attend the enterprise, weigh more on earth, as well as in heaven, than what they lost or suffered, or what they get by endeavouring to mend their condition, comes to. Which appointment seems to be the voice of Heaven, and judgment of God against those violent attempts. But to return, I say, justice is the means of peace, betwixt the government and the people, and one man and company and another. It prevents strife, and at last ends it. For besides shame or fear, to contend longer, he or they being under government, are constrained to bound their desires and resentment with the satisfaction the law gives. Thus peace is maintained by justice, which is a fruit of government, as government is from society, and society from consent.

Section III.
Government, Its Rise and End under All Models.

Government is an expedient against confusion; a restraint upon all disorder; just weights and an even balance: that one may not injure another, nor himself, by intemperance.

This was at first without controversy, patrimonial, and upon the death of the father or head of the family, the eldest son or male of kin succeeded. But time breaking in upon this way of governing, as the world multiplied, it fell under other claims and forms; and is as hard to trace to its original, as are the copies we have of the first writings of sacred or civil matters. It is certain the most natural and human is that of consent, for that binds freely, (as I may say) when men hold their liberty by true obedience to rules of their own making. No man is judge in his own cause, which ends the confusion and blood of so many judges and executioners. For out of society every man is his own king, does what he lists at his own peril. But when he comes to incorporate himself, he submits that royalty to the conveniency of the whole, from whom he receives the returns of protection. So that he is not now his own judge nor avenger, neither is his antagonist, but the law, in indifferent hands between both. And if he be servant to others that before was free, he is also served of others that formerly owed him no obligation. Thus while we are not our own, everybody is ours, and we get more than we lose, the safety of the society being the safety of the particulars that constitute it. So that while we seem to submit to, and hold all that we have from society, it is by society that we keep what we have.

Government then is the prevention or cure of disorder, and the means of justice, as that is of peace. For this cause they have sessions, terms, assizes, and parliaments, to overrule men's passions and resentments, that they may not be judges in their own cause, nor punishers of their own wrongs, which, as it is very incident to men in their corrupt state, so, for that reason they would observe no measure; nor on the other hand would any be easily reduced to their duty. Not that men know not what is right, their excesses, and wherein they are to blame, by no means; nothing is plainer to them. But so depraved is human nature, that without compulsion some way or other, too many would not readily be brought to do what they know is right and fit, or avoid what they are satisfied they should not do. Which brings me near to the point I have undertaken; and for the better understanding of which, I have thus briefly treated of peace, justice, and government, as a necessary introduction, because the ways and methods by which peace is preserved in particular governments, will help those readers most concerned in my proposal to conceive with what ease as well as advantage the peace of Europe might be procured and kept; which is the end designed by me, with all submission to those interested in this little treatise.

Section IV:
Of a General Peace, or the Peace of Europe, and the Means of It.

In my first section, I showed the desirableness of peace; in my next, the truest means of it; to wit, justice not war. And in my last, that this justice was the fruit of government, as government itself was the result of society which first came from a reasonable design in men of peace. Now if the sovereign princes of Europe, who represent that society, or independent state of men that was previous to the obligations of society, would, for the same reason that engaged men first into society, viz: love of peace and order, agree to meet by their stated deputies in a general diet, estates, or parliament, and there establish rules of justice for sovereign princes to observe one to another; and thus to meet yearly, or once in two or three years at farthest, or as they shall see cause, and to be styled, "The Sovereign or Imperial Diet, Parliament, or State of Europe," before which sovereign assembly, should be brought all differences depending between one sovereign and another, that cannot be made up by private embassies, before the sessions begin; and that if any of the sovereignties that constitute these imperial states, shall refuse to submit their claim or pretensions to them, or to abide and perform the judgment thereof, and seek their remedy by arms, or delay their compliance beyond the time prefixed in their resolutions, all the other sovereignties, united as one strength, shall compel the submission and performance of the sentence, with damages to the suffering party, and charges to the sovereignties that obliged their submission. To be sure, Europe would quietly obtain the so much desired and needed peace, to her harassed inhabitants; no sovereignty in Europe having the power and therefore cannot show the will to dispute the conclusion; and, consequently, peace would be procured, and continued in Europe.

Section V:
Of the Causes of Difference, and Motives
to Violate Peace.

There appears to be but three things upon which peace is broken, viz.: to keep, to recover, or to add. First, to keep what is one's right, from the invasion of an enemy, in which I am purely defensive. Secondly, to recover, when I think myself strongly enough, that which by violence, I, or my ancestors have lost by the arms of a stronger power; in which I am offensive; or, lastly, to increase my dominion by the acquisition of my neighbor's countries, as I find them weak, and myself strong. To gratify which passion, there will never want some accident or other for a pretense. And knowing my own strength, I will be my own judge and carver. This last will find no room in the imperial states. They are an impassable limit to that ambition. But the other two may come as soon as they please, and find justice in the sovereign court. And considering how few there are of those sons of prey, and how early they show themselves, it may be not once in an age or two, this expedition being established, the balance cannot well be broken.

Section VI:
Of Titles, upon Which These Differences May Arise.

But I easily foresee a question that may be answered in our way, and that is this: what is right? Or else we can never know what is wrong. It is very fit that this should be established. But that is fitter for the sovereign states to resolve than me. And yet that I may lead a way to the matter, I say that title is either by a long and un-doubted succession . . . ; or by election, . . . ; or by marriage, . . . ; or by purchase; or by conquest. . . . This last title is, morally speaking, only questionable. It has indeed obtained a place among the rolls of titles, but it was engrossed and recorded by the point of the sword, and in bloody characters. What cannot be controlled or resisted, must be submitted to; but all the world knows the date of the length of such empires, and that they expire with the power of the possessor to defend them. And yet there is a little allowed to conquest, too, when it has the sanction of articles of peace to con-firm it. Though that hath not always extinguished the fire, but it lies, like embers and ashes, ready to kindle so soon as there is fit matter prepared for it. Nevertheless, when conquest has been con-firmed by a treaty, and conclusion of peace, I must confess it is an adopted title; and if not so genuine and natural, yet being engrafted, it is fed by that which is the security of better titles, consent. . . .

[In sections 7 and 8, Penn suggests the composition of his "as-sembly of states," which will have ninety members proportional to population, and how it will conduct its debates, vote, choose officers, and keep its records.]

Section IX:
Of the Objections That May Be Advanced
against the Design.

The first of them is this, that the strongest and richest sovereignty will never agree to it, and if it should, there would be danger of corruption more than of force one time or other. I answer to the first part, he is not stronger than all the rest, and for that reason you should promote this, and compel him into it; especially before he be so, for then, it will be too late to deal with such an one. To the last part of the objection, I say the way is as open now as then; and it may be the number fewer, and as easily come at. However, if men of sense and honour, and substance, are chosen, they will either scorn the baseness, or have wherewith to pay for the knavery. At least they may be watched so, that one may be a check upon the other, and all prudently limited by the sovereignty they represent. In all great points, especially before a final resolve, they may be obliged to transmit to their principles, the merits of such important cases depending, and receive their last instructions; which may be done in four and twenty days at the most, as the place of their session may be appointed.

The second is, that it will endanger an effeminacy by such disuse of the trade of soldiery. . . .

There can be no danger of effeminacy, because each sovereignty may introduce as temperate or severe a discipline in the education of youth, as they please, by low living, and due labour. Instruct them in mechanical knowledge, and in natural philosophy, by operation, which is the honour of the German nobility. This would make them men, neither women nor lions. For soldiers are the other extreme to effeminacy. But the knowledge of nature, and the useful as well as agreeable operations of art, give men an understanding of themselves, of the world they are born into, how to be useful and serviceable, both to themselves and others, and how to save and help, not injure and destroy. The knowledge of government in general; the particular constitutions of Europe; and above all of his own country, are very recommending accomplishments. This fits him for the parliament, and council at home, and the courts of princes and services in the imperial states abroad. At least, he is a good commonwealth man, and can be useful to the public, or retire, as there may be occasion. . . .

The third objection is that there will be great want of employ-ment for younger brothers of families; and that the poor must either turn soldiers or thieves. I have answered that in my return to the second objection. We shall have the more merchants and husbandmen, or ingenious naturalists, if the government be but anything solicitous of the education of their youth: which, next to the present and immediate happiness of any country, ought of all things to be the care and skill of the government. For such as the youth of any country is bred, such is the next generation, and the government in good or bad hands.

I am come now to the last objection, that sovereign princes and states will hereby become not sovereign, a thing they will never endure. But this also, under correction, is a mistake, for they re-main as sovereign at home as ever they were. Neither their power over their people, not the usual revenue they pay them, is dimin-ished. It may be that the war establishment may be reduced, which will indeed of course follow, or be better employed to the advan-tage of the public. . . . And if this be called a lessening of their power, it can be only because the great fish can no longer eat up the little ones, and that each sovereignty is equally defended from injuries, and disabled from committing them. . . .

Section X:
Of the Real Benefits That Flow from This
Proposal about Peace.

Let it not, I pray, be the least, that it prevents the spilling of so much human and Christian blood. For a thing so offensive to God, and terrible and afflicting to men, as that has never been, must recommend our expedient beyond all objections. For what can a man give in exchange for his life, as well as soul? And though the chiefest in government are seldom personally exposed, yet it is a duty incumbent upon them to be tender of the lives of their people; since without all doubt, they are accountable to God for the blood that is spilt in their service. So that besides many the loss of so many lives, of importance to any government, both for labour and propagation, the cries of so many widows, parents and fatherless are prevented, that cannot be very pleasant in the ears of any gov-ernment, and is the natural consequence of war in all government.

There is another manifest benefit which redounds to Christendom, by this peaceable expedient: the reputation of Christianity will in some degree be recovered in the sight of infidels; which, by the many bloody and unjust wars of Christians, not only with them, but one with another, hath been greatly impaired. For, to the scandal of that holy profession, Christians, that glory in their saviour's name, have long devoted to the credit and dignity of it to their worldly passions, as often as they have been excited by the impulses of ambition or revenge. They have not always been in the right, nor has right been the reason of war. And not only Christians against Christians, but the same sort of Christians have embrewed their hands in one another's blood; invoking and interesting, all they could, the good and merciful God to prosper their arms to their brethren's destruction. Yet their Saviour has told them, that he came to save, and not to destroy the lives of men, to give and plan peace among men. And if in any sense he may be said to send war, it is the holy war against the devil, and not the persons of men. Of all his titles this seems the most glorious as well as comfortable for us, that he is the Prince of Peace. . . .

The third benefit is, that it saves money, both to the prince and people; and thereby prevents those grudgings and misunderstandings between them that are wont to follow the devouring expenses of wars; and enables both to perform public acts for learning, charity, manufactures, etc., the virtues of government and ornaments of countries. . . .

Our fourth advantage is, that the towns, cities, and countries, that might be laid waste by the rage of war, are thereby preserved: a blessing that would be very well understood in Flanders and Hungary, and indeed upon all the borders of sovereignties, which are almost ever the stages of spoil and misery. . . .

The fifth benefit of this peace, is the ease and security of travel and traffic, and happiness never understood since the Roman Empire has been broken into so many sovereignties. . . .

Another advantage is, the great security it will be to Christians against the inroads of the Turk, in their most prosperous fortune. For it had been impossible for the [Ottoman Empire] to have prevailed so often, and so far from Christendom, but by the carelessness, or willful connivance, if not aid, of some Christian princes. And for the same reason, why no Christian monarch will adventure to oppose, or break such a union, the [sultan] will find himself obliged to concur, for the security of what he holds in

Europe, where, with all his strength, he would feel it an over-match for him. The prayers, tears, treason, blood and devastation, that war has cost in Christendom, for these two last ages especially, must add to the credit of our proposal, and the blessing of the peace thereby humbly recommended.

The seventh advantage of an European, imperial diet, parliament, or estates, is, that it will beget and increase personal friendship between princes and states, which tends to the rooting up of wars, and planting peace in a deep and fruitful soil. For princes have the curiosity of seeing the courts and cities of other countries, as well as their private men, if they would as securely and familiarly gratify their inclinations. It were a great motive to the tranquility of the world, that they could freely converse face to face, and personally and reciprocally give and receive marks of civility and kindness. An hospitality that leaves these impressions behind it, will hardly let ordinary matters prevail, to mistake or quarrel one another. Their emulation would be in the instances of goodness, laws, customs, learning, arts, buildings, and in particular those that relate to charity, the true glory of some governments, where beggars are as much a rarity, as in other places it would be to see none.

Nor is this all the benefit that would come. . . . For natural affection would hereby be preserved, which we see little better than lost, from the time their children, or sisters, are married into other courts. For the present state and insincerity of princes forbid them the enjoyment of that natural comfort which is possessed by private families, insomuch, that from the time a daughter or sister is married to another crown, nature is submitted to interest, and that, for the most part, grounded not upon solid or commendable foundations, but ambition, or unjust avarice. I say, this freedom, that is the effect of our pacific proposal, restores nature to her just right and dignity in the families of princes, and them to the comfort she brings, wherever she is preserved in her proper station. . . .

To conclude this section, there is yet another manifest privilege that follows this intercourse and good understanding, which methinks should be very moving with princes, viz. that thereby they may choose wives for themselves, such as they love, and not by proxy merely to gratify interest; an ignoble motive; and that rarely begets, or continues that kindness which ought to be between men and their wives. A satisfaction very few princes ever knew, and to which all other pleasures ought to resign. Which has often obliged me to think, that the advantage of private men upon princes, by family comforts, is a sufficient balance against their greater power and glory: the one being more in imagination than real; and often unlawful; but the other, natural, solid, and commendable. Besides, it is certain, parents loving well before they are married, which very rarely happens to princes, has kind and generous influences upon their offspring: which, with their example, makes them better husbands, and wives, in their turn. This, in great measure, prevents, unlawful love, and the mischief of those intrigues that are wont to follow them: What hatred, feuds, wars, and desolations have, in divers ages, flown from unkindness between princes and their wives? What unnatural divisions among their children, and ruin to their families, if not loss of their countries by it? Behold an expedient to prevent it, a natural and efficacious one: happy to princes, and happy to their people also. . . .

The Conclusion.

I will conclude this my proposal . . . with that which I have touched on before, and which falls under the notice of everyone concerned, by coming home to their particular and respective experience within their own sovereignties. That by the same rules of justice and prudence, by which parents and masters govern their families, and magistrates their cities, and estates their republics, and princes and kings their principalities and kingdoms, Europe may obtain and preserve peace among her sovereignties. For wars are the duels of princes; and as government in kingdoms and states, prevents men being judges and executioners for themselves, overrules private passions as to injuries or revenge, and subjects the great as well as the small to the rule of justice, that power might not vanquish or oppress right, nor one neighbor act an independency and sovereignty upon another, while they have resigned that original claim to the benefit and comfort of society; so this being soberly weighed in the whole, and parts of it, it will not be heard to conceive or frame, nor yet to execute the design I have here proposed.

THE AMERICAN
REVOLUTION

ABEL THOMAS

The American Revolution was a difficult time for American Friends. Many were suspicious of the movement for independence, which was often spearheaded by Presbyterians and others at odds with Friends. Quaker refusal to bear arms or to take oaths of allegiance to new state governments also caused problems. Abel Thomas (1736/37–1816), a Friend from the Exeter Monthly Meeting in Pennsylvania, left a vivid account of his experiences.

A Brief Memoir concerning Abel Thomas, a Minister of the Gospel of Christ in the Society of Friends (Philadelphia, 1824).

After being some time in the vicinity of New Garden, North Carolina, Amos Lee, finding his mind released from further prosecution of the journey, it was their judgment, that it would be best for him to return homeward; but being closely united in the bonds of Gospel fellowship, and in that inward endearment which, through the love of Christ, connects the real members of his church, it was no easy matter for them to part: yet, seeing it necessary, with the tenderest desires for their mutual preservation, resigning each other into the hand of Him, who in great condescension, had hitherto preserved them in much tribulation, they separated. Abel, after this, not feeling easy to omit making a further essay towards the fulfilment of his prospects of religious duty, proceeded to South Carolina, where the trials of faith, and the remarkable deliverances vouchsafed to him, in this perilous travel, is in some degree set forth in the following relation.

In a thankful sense of preservation by a strong arm through many dangers and deep conflicts, both within and without, which I met with in my journey through South Carolina and Georgia, do I write these lines, in order to encourage the weak, the poor afflicted people of God, to trust in his powerful arm, which doth work salvation and deliverance, and by bringing strange and unexpected things to pass. He is greatly to be feared, and loved, and adored, by his afflicted children. They who know him, and do their endeavour not only to know but to obey, have no reason to distrust his care and great power to preserve, not only from being taken by the secret and subtle invasions of Satan, but also out of the hands of bloody and unreasonable men. These things I have experienced in the great deeps, and do certainly know that the Lord's arm is not shortened that it cannot save, nor is his ear heavy that it cannot hear. When I consider my own weakness and inability as a man, and as a servant engaged in so great a work, and also the grievous besetments and terrifying storms in which the subtle serpent arose against me, my mind is humbled; well knowing who preserved me in the depth of distress, when my soul was taken with fear, and my body almost given to the wild beasts of the wilderness: then the language of my soul was, Make haste, my beloved, for I am almost overwhelmed. I will make known to my brethren his wonderful works, and relate to them my travails and the exercise of my mind, and give the praise to the great God of power through his dear son Jesus Christ, who is worthy forever.

When we came near South Carolina, we were told that the country was all in an uproar. Scouting parties from both sides were riding to and fro, killing one another, and also peaceable men which they found travelling, except they knew them to be on their side: and that they had determined to take no prisoners, which we found to be in a great measure true. When I heard this sorrowful news, it took deep hold of my mind; for I had entertained a thought that I should die in that country, and as times were, I thought I should not die a natural death, but that I should be barbarously cut down by the light-horse. I searched deeply to know whether my concern was right, and my Master was pleased to manifest to me, that it was his will I should go forward. We travelled on, visiting meetings, and generally alone, inquiring the road. Friends were fearful. They were advised by the most moderate persons in power, to stay on their farms, except going to their particular meetings. We met with none of these cruel men, although we could hear of them almost every day, until we got within ten miles of the British garrison at Ninety-six. We then approached a large scouting party upon a hill: we could see them afar off, and when we came up to them, we found they were much afraid. We showed the major our certificates, and asked him if we might go forward. He said he would not hinder us, if we would venture our lives; for the rebels, (as they called them,) had got between them and their garrison, and were killing all before them. I told him that I did not trust altogether to man for preservation. We rode on, but had not gone far, until he and a negro came riding after us. He ordered his negro to ride on some distance before, and if he saw any man, to ride back and tell him. The major rode in between me and my companion. I felt uneasy in my mind while he rode there, and we endeavoured to shun his company, but could not. His negro wheeled round his horse, and hallooed to his master, "Rebels! rebels!" The major stopped, and turned about to run; then calling to his man, asked, "How many?" He answered, "two." He wheeled back again, and out with his pistols, and rode furiously towards them; but found they were his own men.

We travelled on, lay in the woods not far from the garrison, and next morning, passing through the town, were detained some time by the picket guard. Being conducted to the head officer, he appeared kind to us, and invited us to breakfast with them. I acknowledged their kindness, but told them I desired not to be detained then, for I expected to be called to an account for passing through that place. They, with sorrow, signified they would not detain us to our hurt; and we were told a few hours afterwards, that general Green surrounded the garrison. We visited the meetings on towards Georgia, and were told, it was as much as our lives were worth to go over Savannah river; that the Indians and white people were joined together in their bloody designs. We had been so remarkably preserved hitherto, that we did not much fear them: rode the river in great danger, the water being so rapid, and the bottom so rocky, that I never rode in such a dismal place before. It was well we had a pilot who led us amongst the rocks; for I thought if our horses had stumbled, they must have been washed away by the rapidity of the stream; but we got over safe, and travelled on towards the settlement of Friends: and while riding a small path in the wilderness, two men overtook us, and in a furious manner, with great rage, ordered us to stand, and with terrifying language were raising their guns to shoot us. I desired them to stop a little while, that we might clear ourselves of those high charges. They gave us a little time, but soon broke out in terrible rage, with blasphemous language, and one of them was cocking his gun. I desired them to have a little patience; I had something to say: and so we remained for about ten minutes. Then they turned round to consult between themselves privately. I heard one of them ask, if they should kill us; the other answered, "I hate to kill them": and after some more private discourse, turned to us, and ordered us off our horses; they got on ours, led their own, and so rode off.

Our pilot riding a mean beast, his habit also being mean, they said but little to him, and took nothing from him. Being now left in the wilderness, we soon came to a conclusion to return to Friends at Longcane, from whence we came; but how to cross that large and rapid river Savannah, we could not conceive: it looked unlikely that we could ride two at a time on so weak a creature, neither could we wade it. We sought for a canoe, and seeing one on the other side, called, in order to get over. A young man came to the canoe, and inquired who we were—asking if we were rebels. My companion told him we were friends to the rebels. He then said, we were damned tories, and should not come over. We then went down the river to a place where some had forded in low water. My companion and pilot stripped themselves, and being good swimmers, they got on the weak beast, with their clothes between them, intending, if the creature sunk, to swim out, and if they got safe over, one of them would come for me. I could see but little of the horse until they got to the other side, which was, I suppose, about two hundred yards: sometimes the water ran over the saddle, and my companion coming back for me, we also landed safe, then travelled on to William Miles's, from whence we came, and a kind friend he was to us.

This was a trying time to me; not so much on account of the loss of my property, as for the absence of my Beloved, who had been my preserver and conductor. I was afraid I had offended him in going so far. I endeavoured to keep still and quiet in my mind, and soon perceived I must return to that bloody place again: and when I made it known to my companion, it was grievous to him, and after a time of silence, he told me we had been so remarkably preserved whilst we were within our prescribed limits, he thought we had no business there; if we had, it appeared to him unlikely that we should have been stopped: and further, that I had not liberty by certificate to visit the meetings in Georgia. This discourse from a valuable friend, so highly esteemed by me, and also by his friends in general, struck me deeply. I told him I desired to look more deeply into it. This was the next morning after we came to the aforesaid friend's house. I inquired for work, and kept closely at it for two weeks, my companion not being able to do much; my desire was, to keep him and myself from being chargeable. At that time I could see no way home, nor the time to go back again. For several days I was in great distress, and there was none to help me; often looking towards my dear wife and children mourning for me, and I not knowing how long I should be detained there, or whether ever I should see them again.

One night as I lay bemoaning my sad condition, as though I had offended my Master, whom I had loved above all, I cannot express the anguish of my soul at that time; and in the depth of distress, a language livingly sprang in my mind, "Stand still": a language which I understood at Camden when a prisoner there, was now with life revived and renewed, "Fear not, my servant, I will be with thee." O, how was my troubled soul revived! All doubts and fears vanished away, and in this pleasant and favoured state I said, "It is enough, Lord! I want no further confirmation; I will go or will stay at thy word, only be with me." Indeed, the place where I was seemed so pleasant for some time after, that I thought I could live there all my days, if it was his will, without being much concerned about home.*
I soon informed my companion, that I intended to travel towards

---

* When relating this occurrence to a friend, he said in substance, That the room was so filled with light, attended with such consolation in the Divine presence, that in the flowings of heavenly joy and peace he felt no wants to be supplied.

Georgia, and that, as by his discourse a few days before, he thought he had no business there, I should leave him at his liberty; but desired he would stay here for me a certain time, and then return, if I came not. After serious consideration, he told me he could not be easy to let me go alone, and if I went, and died, he would die with me. A day soon appeared for me to travel on, and also to write a letter to general Green, who was then about thirty miles off, fighting against Ninety-six. He soon read my letter, and granted my request, as follows:

> *Mr. Abel Thomas, and Mr. Thomas Winslow, Long-cane.*
> *CAMP, before Ninety-six, June 7th, 1781.*

GENTLEMEN,

Your letter of the 6th is before me. From the good opinion I have of the people of your profession, being bred and educated among them, I am persuaded your visit is purely religious, and in this persuasion have granted you a pass; and I shall be happy if your ministry shall contribute to the establishment of morality and brotherly kindness among the people, than which no country ever wanted it more. I am sensible your principles and professions are opposed to war, but I know you are fond of both political and religious liberty. This is what we are contending for, and by the blessings of God, we hope to establish them upon such a broad basis, as to put it out of the power of our enemies to shake their foundation. In this laudable endeavour, I expect at least to have the good wishes of your people, as well for their own sakes as for ours, who wishes to serve them upon all occasions, not inconsistent with the public good.

> I am, Gentlemen,
>> Your most obedient
>> Humble servant,
>>> NATHANIEL GREEN.

> *Head-Quarters, June 7th, 1781.*

Abel Thomas has General Green's permission to pass and repass through this country, behaving with propriety.

> NATH. PENDLETON, *AID DE CAMP.*

We set out early in the morning on foot, serious and deep thoughts attending my mind. We seemed like sheep going a second time before the slaughter, without any outward obligation: travelled about twelve miles, crossed Savannah river, and came up with a colonel and his men, who had got there the night before. A captain looking earnestly at us, began to examine what our business was, and hearing the account we gave, (slender indeed in his views,) viz. "to visit our brethren at Wrightsborough," he appeared surprised and mistrustful; asked us for a pass, which we gave him: he ordered us to follow him, and led us to the colonel. Our certificates, general Green's friendly letter, and permission, being read to him, they asked why we were travelling on foot. We told them we were robbed not far from that place, about two weeks before. They said they had heard of us down at Augusta, and if we would stay, they thought they could find our horses, for they knew who had them. And as I was describing my horse, a soldier said, he thought my horse was in the company; and I soon found the horse, saddle, and bridle: for that wicked man had just ridden up. I informed the colonel, who had him immediately taken and put under guard, and then sent out a scout after the other, who had my companion's mare, saddle, and saddle-bags, and confined him also, which greatly surprised them. They sent for us, and desired we would forgive them. We inquired where our goods were. They readily informing us, we told them, that all we wanted was what we had lost, and that they would repent and amend their ways of living; that we could forgive them and do them a kindness if it lay in our power, although they had injured us. They appeared low in their minds, for the colonel declared they should be hanged, as many accusations of their wickedness and barbarity came against them.

We got the principal part of our goods, lodged with the soldiery that night, and next morning rode to Friends' settlement, I hope, with thankful hearts, and visited the meetings of Friends both at Wrightsborough and at New Purchase: and finding my mind clear, turned my face homewards, and as I rode, a hope renewedly revived, that I should see my little family again. I felt them near to my heart, although by computation eight hundred miles distant from them. We crossed Savannah river, and travelled towards Ninety-six, where the armies were fighting; and when we drew near, became doubtful how we should pass, as the cannon were firing fast, and the road we were in, leading immediately to the British garrison, we knew of no way to escape; but a friendly man

overtook us, and told us that he would pilot us round, and a difficult path it proved; sometimes we were close by where they were
fighting, or firing upon the garrison: and as we passed through the
skirts of general Green's army, the cross officer, whose prisoner I
had been when at Camden, saw me ride on as I before had told him.
He called to me: "What! old fellow, are you there?" I answered him
according to his question. He asked how I came to deceive him. I
replied, I had not, and that he knew it. He came to me, took me by
the hand in a friendly way, and said, he hoped I had done no harm.
I told him, I did not intend harm; and with some more friendly
conversation we parted. Just before we got round into the road,
general Green's men fell upon a fort or redoubt but a little way from
us, making a terrible noise. There was a great stir among the people, some running one way, and some another; some hiding behind
trees: we rode smartly on, and could hear them for about seven
miles without intermission. We passed on towards North Carolina,
without any other remarkable interruption. As for my service and
exercise in the ministry, I have left it to the judgment of my brethren. My Master had a service for me there, and I trusted my life in
his hand, travelled on, and so obtained a reward which is more
precious than gold.

ABEL THOMAS.
7TH MONTH, 7TH, 1781.

THE CIVIL WAR

RACHEL HICKS

The American Civil War presented many Friends with a wrenching dilemma. Few Friends had sympathies for the Confederacy, which they perceived as founded in treason to preserve human slavery. Some Friends were caught between contending armies. Many young Southern Friends fled north to avoid being conscripted into the Confederate army, and those who remained faced unsympathetic authorities when they professed objections to war.

One Friend who reflected on the war and its consequences was Rachel Hicks (1789–1878), a Hicksite Friend and minister from Long Island.

Memoir of Rachel Hicks, Late of Westbury, Long Island (New York, 1880).

4th mo., 1861.—Wars and rumors of wars are heard in our land! The nation seems to stand upon an awful precipice, ready to be plunged into the pit of deadly strife of brother against brother, in which, it is to be feared, rivers of human blood will flow. The groans of the dying on the field of battle, and the moans of the bereaved will ascend to Him who is just and holy, who has made man a free agent, and invites all to do His will and receive the reward of peace with Him, and of harmony with their fellow men; but leaves them at liberty, if they choose, to follow their own ways, and reap the sad consequences. In departing from the law of the Lord written in the heart, the seeds of calamity are sown in the pride, ambition, love of power and dominion, covetousness, oppression, frauds, and injustice, that spring up, until the cup of iniquity seems filled to the brim; and war, with all its horrors—the legitimate offspring of these evils—seems already begun.

In view of all this, I have been led in spirit to make a close investigation of myself and of my past life, desiring to see if I have contributed to the filling up of the full measure of iniquity that is now clothing the nation in mourning and woe. Although feeling myself the least of the flock of the companions of Christ, I have great consolation in the retrospect that I have ever endeavored to live in love to my God and love to my fellow man. For the last thirty years, by word and doctrine, as well as by example, I have labored to promulgate the peaceable principles of the Kingdom of Christ amongst men, according to the ability given of Him, who often makes use of weak instruments, who realize that without Him they can do no good thing. Knowing myself to be one of these, in humble gratitude, I acknowledge His goodness in giving me to stand acquitted in His holy sight, and that His power has enabled me to wash my hands in innocency from the blood of all men.

My soul is bowed in view of His majesty, His almightiness and justice, as well as His love and mercy. Blessed be His name! He sets bounds to the waves of the sea, He sets bounds to the raging of fallen man; and when by chastisements the people are humbled, and cry unto Him for help, He will say, "Peace, be still," and there will be a calm. I feel that a great weight of responsibility rests on the Society of Friends, a people called to stand before the world, "as a city set on an hill, that cannot be hid"; because, walking in the light of the Lord, they would have been instruments in His power and wisdom, in enlightening the minds of beholders, so that ere this they would have seen war to be inconsistent with the Christian religion. They would have seen that love to God, and love and forbearance toward man were the only sure basis of prosperity and happiness.

Had Friends all lived in the life and power of vital religion, we would have remained a united people, wise in the wisdom which God gives, standing aloof from all parties, and party feelings, giving evidence that we love all men of every nation, without distinction. These holy men and women, fearing God, and doing His will, mingling with the people in every part of the land, would have been as saviors on the mountain of the Lord, where nothing can "hurt or destroy." Our country would not then have sunk into its present sad condition; its people divided, and in many cases hating each other.

6th mo., 1861.—The Spirit of the Lord is upon me, and it said unto me, "Write"; and I said, "What shall I write?" and it said, "The day of the Lord is near that shall 'burn as an oven,' and the 'wicked' they that fear Me not, shall be as 'stubble,' and no man can prevent the bringing about the just and legitimate fruits of their backslidings, for they are many. The sins of the people have multiplied, their proud hearts are lifted up, they love this present world more than they love Me who gave it. In their love of money and power they oppress the weaker, and in every way which the wisdom of man can devise, they have defrauded their fellow creatures, committing the sins found in Sodom and Egypt. As I chastised them, so will I chastise those of this nation, which say, 'I will rule, I will not submit.' Hence brother is arrayed against brother, bathing the sword in each other's blood, in the pride and haughtiness of spirit, which have grown strong in them, because of the willful departure from My spirit in their souls. The crying, the sighing and the prayers of the oppressed and defrauded have come up before Me, and I have risen in My majesty to deliver them, and to chastise those who will not bow before Me in mercy, and who in the end will dare say 'What doest thou?'

"The South shall chastise the North for a season, for her participation in the oppression and injustice to the red man of the forest, and the black man of Africa; rivers of blood will erelong flow, and calamities sore and heavy will be experienced, until the people shall be humbled, and call on Me for help, acknowledging that these are My just judgments for sin and iniquity. Then will some of them learn righteousness."

1st mo., 1862.—This has been a day of rejoicing and giving thanks on the "banks of deliverance!" My soul has, for a long season, been plunged into deep exercise comparable to the bottom of the sea. The watery unstable elements of human nature have been permitted to buffet and beat against me, as if to try my hold on Heaven, and my faith in Him who alone can save. And now I can in humble reverence say, with the great apostle, through all "I have kept the faith, and maintained the warfare," oft saying in my heart, "if I die I will die a suppliant at Thy feet, oh! God, for to whom shall I go if I forsake Thee, and Thy Son, Thy power and wisdom in my soul that speak the words of eternal life?"

6th mo., 1862.—My spirit is covered with an awful solemnity in most of my waking hours. When I rouse from sleep in the morning this weight comes pressing upon me, and I query Why is it so? Then the battlefield is spread out before my mental vision, and I see brother arrayed against brother in mortal combat, and all for the sins of the nation, for they are very great. O South! Thy sin against thy brother of the African race is greater than Egypt's against Israel of old; thy darkness is felt, thy day of retribution is begun; when, and how it will end is known only to Him who sees in secret and whose "justice will not sleep forever." . . .

And the North has not escaped, and will not altogether escape; for in measure we are verily guilty concerning our brother. We have partaken of the spoils of his labor; his tears, his sweat, and his blood have cried against both the South and the North, and entered the ears of Him who permits rebellious man to go on until his own doings bring correction and deep suffering. O South! thou hast dug a pit for thyself, a pit of mire and thick clay, from which thou canst not be raised and cleansed until thou humblest thyself before the mighty God in repentance, seeking forgiveness, and forsaking thy sins. And O North! thou hast grown rich and powerful, and thy heart is lifted up. Oh! humble thyself, and come down into the low valley of humiliation, where the dew of Heaven lies long, and the pastures of Divine life are green. In reverence and thankfulness to God feed thereon, and thy light will shine before the world, and the nations of the earth will love and respect thee, and none of them shall be able to overthrow, or overpower thee. But if thou continue in pride, and in glorying in thy strength and thy skill, and shalt say, "By the might of my power" have I established this great nation, thy days ere long shall be numbered, and as Babylon, so shalt thou fall.

5th mo. 7th, 1864.—War still rages in our land. From its very commencement, although feeling its awfulness, and deep sympathy with its many sufferers, the command of my Divine Master has been, "Be still, and allow no anxious thoughts about the results," thus leaving all to Him who has power to say to haughty man, "Hitherto shalt thou come, and no further; and here shall thy proud waves be stayed." In humble submission my soul has rested, not daring to put up a petition for one party or the other, any further than that the eyes of all may be opened to see the glory and excellency of the religion which He came to promulgate, whose birth was proclaimed by the anthem of "Glory to God in the highest, and on earth peace, good-will to men." But for the past few days I have felt the spirit of prayer, and today I retired to my chamber, and on the bended knee put up the petition that He who has the power would give wisdom to the leaders of the North, that they may so move and manage as to bring to a close this fratricidal war and strife.

My spirit is clothed in mourning as I feel it to be a solemn truth that we as a people, raised up by the power of the Most High to show to the world the sufficiency of the Divine Spirit in man to do away with all sin and oppression, have not so dwelt under His teachings as a united whole as to be instruments in carrying the work of emancipation to the slave to a final issue in the spirit of love and peace. But we have in a great degree settled down in our ceiled houses, while those who have been actively engaged in the cause have taken reason as a sufficient guide and have failed to accomplish the work. Hence the sword has been taken up, and it appears that that will be done in judgment which would otherwise have been done in mercy without the shedding of blood, had all waited for qualification and command from the Most High. Do we not see that this iniquitous institution has produced its legitimate results? That through the exercise of authority over the slave by the slaveholder, a desire has been begotten amongst them as a people to take the reins of government in their own hands and rule the whole nation; thus perpetuating slavery and extending it into the territories of this country? But in the counsels of Infinite Wisdom the means taken to perpetuate this great evil have proved the means of its downfall. I fully believe that President Lincoln felt it to be his duty to God to make the proclamation of emancipation to the millions of slaves in the Southern States, and that those who held them in bondage had to realize in their own experience the truth declared by the Lord's prophet formerly, to a transgressing people, "Thine own wickedness shall correct thee, and thy backslidings shall reprove thee."

Many have rejoiced and do rejoice that the inhabitants of our nation can no longer make merchandise of their fellow-man, and for this may we render unto Thee, O holy Father, the tribute of thanksgiving and praise, for the work is Thine, the power is Thine, to turn the hearts of the children of men, therefore the praise is ever Thy due.

NORTH CAROLINA
YEARLY MEETING

Friends in North Carolina and Tennessee faced particular trials during the war. While the Confederacy, when it passed a conscription law, did make provisions for conscientious objectors, many Friends refused to accept its terms, since they required Friends to provide a substitute or pay an exemption fine. Refusal to comply brought forced induction, severe punishments, and even death. Among them were the Hockett brothers, Himelius M., Jesse D., and William B., of the Centre community of Friends in Guilford County, North Carolina.

An Account of the Sufferings of Friends of North Carolina Yearly Meeting, in Support of Their Testimony against War, from 1861 to 1865 (Baltimore, 1868).

In the spring of 1862 two brothers, H. M. H. and J. D. H., were drafted, arrested and taken to Raleigh. Being allowed to return home for ten days they faithfully reappeared. They were soon sent to Weldon, where they were required to drill, and were warned of their liability to be shot if they proved refractory. They were, however, only kept in close custody in the guardhouse, and the next month were discharged and sent home. About a year after this, they were included in the conscription. They were assigned to an artillery company at Kinston, and after various threats were sent to Gen. R, who declared that his orders should be carried out at all hazards. They were now confined in an upper room without food or drink. Various persons were allowed to converse with them, and, as day after day passed on, so far from sinking under the suffering they used their little remaining strength gladly in explaining their testimony, and telling of their inward consolation. They felt that, in this time of fiery trial, this did indeed turn to them for a testimony, and that they knew the promise fulfilled.

"It shall be given you in that same hour what ye shall speak."
Their sufferings from thirst were the most acute. On the third
night the brothers were wakened from a peaceful sleep by the
sound of rain. A little cup had been left in their room, and from
the open window they could soon have refreshed themselves. The
first thought of each was to do so. They were in nowise bound
to concur in this inhuman punishment. Yet an impression was
clearly made upon their minds, before consulting each other, that
they must withhold, and they scarcely felt the copious showers
tempt them. The next morning several officers entered the room
and questioned them closely. They claimed it to be impossible for
them to retain so much strength without any food, and charged
them with having secretly obtained it. They then, in much simplicity, told them of their not feeling easy to take even the rain that
fell. This evidently touched the hearts of the officers. Soon after
the end of four and a half days' abstinence, a little water was allowed, and about the end of five days their rations were furnished
again. This remarkable circumstance was widely spread and they
had constant opportunities of bearing an open testimony to
Christ, and not a few of those who crowded around, appeared to
be persuaded of the truth which they held. Even ministers of different denominations came and encouraged them to be faithful.
J. D. H. was next taken before General D, who said he would not
require him to bear arms, but would set him in the front of the
battle, and use him to stop bullets. On declining to work on the
streets as a part of the soldier's duty, he had a log of wood tied
on his shoulders and was marched around until quite exhausted.
He was next sent to a guardhouse, then placed in a dungeon for
a day—then in a prison cell. His persecutors seemed at their wits'
end, but they finally devised a rude and barbarous punishment. A
forked pole was thrust round his neck, and upon the prongs, as
they projected behind it, a heavy block of wood was fastened.
This they blasphemously called the Cross of Christ. The soldiers
and town's-people were looking on, while he was thus "made a
gazing stock by reproaches and afflictions." No sooner had the
Captain fairly completed this work than in a rage he pulled it off
again, and tied another log upon his shoulder, and marched him
about till exhausted, when he was sent back to jail.

Meantime his brother H. had been enduring a different punishment. At three different times he was suspended by his thumbs,

with his feet barely touching the ground upon the toes, and kept in this excruciating position for nearly two hours each time. They next tried the bayonet. Their orders were, they said, to thrust them in four inches deep; but, though much scarred and pierced, it was not so severely done as they had threatened. One of the men, after thus wounding him, came back to entreat his forgiveness. In the various changes of the next four months, some kindness was occasionally shown to them, but mingled with much cruelty. It was not till seven months had been passed in these fiery ordeals, that their release was obtained—another Friend thinking it right to pay their exemption money for them. The value of this tax, at that time, was only equal to a little more than a barrel of flour—a small sum indeed, could they have felt themselves easy to avail themselves of this provision. It was no small addition to their sufferings that their families at home were sharing in it. In the extreme scarcity of labor, their wives were compelled to toil hard in the fields to raise the food for the coming winter, and this proved not merely a passing hardship, but left one of them in greatly enfeebled health.

Another brother of the same family, W. B. H., was arrested on the 8th of Sixth Month, 1863. The officers to whose division he was assigned, were unusually rough and severe. Finally, after a full explanation of his views and the necessity he was under of refusing all military duties whatsoever, the Colonel said he should be shot, and the only favor allowed should be the choice of time— that night or the next morning. After a little pause, W. H. replied, that if it was his Heavenly Father's will that he should lay down his life, he would far rather do it than disobey one of his commands. But if it was not His will, none of them could take his life from him; however, they might give the order to do so. He then spoke of the three men who were cast into the burning fiery furnace, and of Daniel in the lions' den, who all trusted in God and He delivered them. As to the time of his death, he could make no choice. The officer seemed greatly at a loss, and sent him to the wagon yard for the night. The next morning he was ordered out with a foraging party. He explained that he had two objections to this. It was, in the first place, military work, and besides, it was taking the property of others. The Colonel, now greatly excited, came forward and had him laid on the ground, while a gun was tied to his back. He refused to rise with it on. The men were then ordered to run their bayonets into him, but they continued only to pierce his clothes. A squad of men was then drawn up in readiness to fire; but as the order was about being given W. H. raised his arms and said, "Father forgive them, for they know not what they do." Not a gun was fired, and some of the men were heard saying, "They could not shoot such a man." The enraged officer struck at his head, but missed his aim. He then spurred his horse repeatedly to ride over him, but the horse sprang aside at each attempt, and he remained unharmed. The officer then left, saying, he was not yet done with him—but was himself killed the same or next day in the battle of Gettysburg. As W. H. was sick at the time of this battle, no attempt was made to force him into it. He found in the retreat, with which he was unable to keep up, a shelter and kind care at a farmhouse, but was soon taken prisoner by the Union Cavalry and sent to Fort Delaware, as a rebel prisoner. He had been ill there a week before a message could reach Philadelphia. Application was at once made at Washington, and a telegram was promptly dispatched from the War Office ordering his release upon taking an affirmation of allegiance to the United States. But loyal as he had ever been, he could not promise "to support, protect and defend" the Constitution and Government. He had already suffered too much and been too marvelously preserved to flinch now from bearing any portion of his testimony. He was told, while thus apparently upon the eve of his release, that there were two alternatives—this affirmation or imprisonment until the close of the war. But upon a fuller explanation of the nature of his scruples, an alteration was promptly made in the form of the affirmation. He was released, and like many others, found a home in the West till the close of the war allowed him to return to his beloved family.

WEST BRANCH MONTHLY MEETING

The response of Friends in the North to young members who enlisted in the Union army was inconsistent. Some monthly meetings held to older practices and disowned them if they would not condemn their misconduct. Others ignored their soldiers entirely. Few faced the problem as squarely as the West Branch Monthly Meeting in western Ohio.

West Branch Monthly Meeting Men's Minutes, 5th Month 27, 1866 (Indiana Yearly Meeting Archives, Earlham College, Richmond, Indiana).

Those appointed at last meeting to consider what action might be best to be taken with those of our members who have served in the late war etc report as below—which was considered and was united with and its recommendations adopted and we appoint Thomas Jay, David M. Coate & Eli Jay—to inform those who have been engaged in military services the action of this meeting on the subject and extend to them such care as they think necessary and report when ready.

Report—We find that several of our young men have volunteered and engaged in the military service of the country, that some have paid commutation fees in lieu of military training required by the state laws—that nearly all our members having much property have either directly or indirectly paid money to aid in making up bounties for volunteers; and that all as far as liable have paid the county assessments and the special tax on incomes for bounty purposes as well as other requirements of the General Government for raising revenue to defray the expenses of the war—But while the facts are as has been stated, we think it due to our members: that we bear in mind that their actions have not been prompted by the existence of a war spirit amongst us, but mainly by a deep feeling of sympathy with the interests involved: viz—the preservation of our beloved government and the liberation of the enslaved African race from their unjust and cruel bondage.

And whilst none of us would have chosen to accomplish these objects by such means; yet when the issues were made and forced upon the country in war and the judgments of God for the sins of the nation were thus visibly abroad in the land; we know that many of our members could not see their way clear to stand aside in indifference; feeling that they had no part in these matters; and that none of the sufferings and sacrifices of their loyal fellow citizens were for them—But far as it was from the manner in which they would have preferred to act, they felt it was best to do something, even in the way presented; many also from a kindly feeling of sympathy with their neighbors in order to share the burden with them, gave of their means to aid in filling up the quotas of the townships, not from any fear of the draft on their own account, for if any of our members had been drafted; there were other means provided (let it be gratefully remembered) by the mercy and favor of the General Government by which they could have been relieved. These circumstances are mentioned, not to justify any actions of our members that conflict with the well known testimony of the Society of Friends against war; but to give a plain statement of the influences under which we have become so generally involved in this matter; and the impression appears to be general in the mind of Friends, that there is no real difference between paying the direct taxes for bounties above mentioned—which is commonly thought to be no violation of our discipline; and contributing to the same and similar purposes in other ways which are positively forbidden. In this respect, then as well as some others, the matter seems to be so involved in difficulty: that we see no way to proceed with disciplinary measures in the proper spirit of unity, harmony and consistency.

And it is our opinion that none of us are sufficiently clear, in regard to this subject "to cast the first stone"—And that the best thing we can do is for us all to say to one another, and in the collective capacity of the church, to say to each member: "neither do I condemn thee, go and sin no more"—Therefore whilst feeling that there has been serious departures amongst us from our testimony on war, the committee would recommend to dispense with disciplinary proceedings for *past* offenses of this kind, in all cases where there is a disposition apparent to uphold this highly important testimony of our society.

There are two objections to this course, which have been taken into consideration:

The first is that we thus violate our discipline and lay ourselves to be called to account by the yearly meeting. Though this may seem at variance with the letter of the discipline, *we do most sincerely believe* that the course recommended accords with its *spirit*, and the principles of Christian forbearance & mercy that we profess—And although the yearly meeting has a revisory power over our proceedings, it is yet apparent that it has delegated the *execution* of the discipline to the mo[nthly] meetings with a large *discretionary* power of their own, arising from modifying circumstances—and that it is the duty of our meetings in act in view of these.

And secondly: that in thus lightly passing over these violations we will compromise our professions; and balk our testimony against *war* with these—and especially these before whom we have plead for exemption on account of our conscientious scruples. We do not suppose however that the course pursued by the members of our society during the *war* has done this in the eyes of legislators & rulers, but rather that our earnest desire to do for our country in the time of her *trial* all that we could consistently do: and even to go beyond that rather than fall short of it; has been one great cause of the favorable disposition of our Government towards conscientious people—In evidence of this we thankfully refer to the recent act of our own Legislature "exempting from enrollment for military service *all members of religious denominations whose articles of faith prohibit them from performing military duty*"—Nor do we regard the course recommended as passing lightly over this subject—we know of no better or more truly Christian way to magnify our testimonies when we *all* have departed; but by mutual forgiveness and forbearance and by an endeavor to strengthen each other to do better in the future. And tho some who have gone farthest astray in this matter could not now make these concessions and adopt this resolution as fully as we might wish—yet *we* believe our present duty is to exercise *mercy* and *forbearance* and leave the rest with our Heavenly Father.

THE TWENTIETH
CENTURY

JESSE H. HOLMES

The twentieth century saw the first attempts of Friends to bring together representatives of all branches to work on common concerns. The first such conference was held in Philadelphia in 1901, and its focus was peace. It included representatives of all Quaker persuasions: pastoral, liberal, modernist, conservative, and evangelical. The address by Swarthmore College professor Jesse H. Holmes (1864–1942), a Hicksite Friend who would be a leader in the newly formed Friends General Conference, typifies how liberal Friends envisioned the Peace Testimony.

Jesse H. Holmes, "Attitude of Christians as to War and Peace," in *The American Friends Peace Conference Held at Philadelphia, Twelfth Month 12th, 13th, and 14th, 1901* (Philadelphia, 1902).

Christianity met with a great disaster early in its career—a disaster largely made possible by its rapid spread—in that it came to be officially recognized as a state religion. In its inception Christianity was particularly marked by its strong appeal to the individual. We cannot in our day fully grasp the originality displayed by its founders in turning their backs upon gods who dealt with mankind by the wholesale, as races or nations, and turning to God who speaks to the individual soul, and for whom not the nation, but the man, is the unit. Such conception is not, of course, a new one as presented by Jesus and his followers; it was present in the

minds of many of the prophets, and was not unknown among ancient philosophies.

But such idea of God was fundamental in Christianity. It was
not to Jews, not to Gentiles, not to rich or poor, not to great or
small, but to individual men that was preached the gospel of the
kingdom within us. For three centuries it made its way amid persecution and against opposition, passing on from soul to soul,
uplifting the slave and humbling the master, illuminating the
wrecks of old philosophies, and bringing back to life a zest and
interest which it had in large measure lost. In those three centuries
it had honeycombed the Empire. Slave had whispered the gospel
to his fellow-slave, or perhaps timidly to a kindly master. It circulated in the arteries of trade, it was talked in the streets, it grew
even when hunted into the catacombs. In all this it was taught
only as man to man. It was backed by no great official power, but
represented in all that it accomplished its own native force and energy. Where it won its way it was by mastering the consciences of
men. It had no prizes to offer by which to tempt the time-server.
Only a fervent conviction of truth, only a deadly (or, rather, a
truly living) earnestness could induce men to ally themselves with
a proscribed sect. We may hardly doubt that the Christian Church
of this time was made up of real Christians; they had stood the
test of fire, and with only a natural human alloy of baser metal,
they had been proved sterling.

It was under such circumstances that disaster fell upon it in the
form of an unhoped-for and dazzling success—the Empire became
officially Christian. The old and well-worn temptation rejected by
Jesus himself was now offered to his Church, and it fell. "All the
kingdoms of the earth will I give thee" might have been the language of Constantine when he made the Roman Empire Christian
in name. And what great things might not the Church of the
Christ do with all the kingdoms of the earth? The vision of a new
heaven and a new earth so dazzled the bishops of the fourth century that they forgot to notice the small and apparently insignificant condition annexed, "If thou wilt bow down and worship
me." Not for the first time was a distinctive price unnoticed in the
glory of immediate possession. Christianity received the kingdoms of the earth, and bowed down before Satan. Thenceforth
there were princes in the household of him who was "meek and
lowly"; thenceforth Christianity went forth, sword in hand, to

conquer heathendom, not for the Christ-spirit, but for a nominal Christianity. The Church turned from men to man. It baptized nations, indeed, after it had conquered them—baptizing with water—and, indeed, with fire also—but neglecting the baptism of the Holy Spirit. Only incidentally, and in small measure, did it spread abroad the spirit of the Master. Those methods which had made Christianity so great a power that the Empire was forced to adopt its name were neglected for those which had produced the very weakness under which the Empire suffered. The Church chose the way of the devil to reach the ends of God, taking no warning, as it might for the very ease of the journey, that it had left the straight and narrow for the broad and easy way.

Christianity broke up into warring sects. It dealt with principalities and powers; its eye became keen for estates, and it dealt in souls mainly by wholesale. Almost every generation, indeed, has seen small groups of individuals breaking away from the evil of official religion, and striving for a return to the spirit of Christianity—to a direct walk with God, a direct communing with his self-revealings. But, seeing the supreme success of the Master's failure, the crown of martyrdom is no longer offered beyond a certain point. So soon as Christianity becomes strong enough to be dangerous the kingdoms of the earth are offered again, and still this bait is taken. Protestantism, Calvinism, Puritanism, have in turn denied God in spirit while defining and explaining Him in words.

I would not be understood as indicating that Christianity has been altogether lost, altogether a failure—so far from it that it has always been and is today the leaven of human life. Its representatives have been, and are, few and weak, in worldly power, but they have been, and are, the hope of the world. And the long look over the centuries since Christianity was Romanized by a pretense of Christianizing Rome does not tend to discouragement. More and more, century-by-century, men have caught at God's personal fatherhood and man's brotherhood as the great facts of the divine message—at love, as the fulfilling of the law. "Not by might or by power, but by my Spirit" is now more than ever a triumphant note.

I wish to use this opportunity to make a distinct plea for the individual—the separate person—as the indivisible and indestructible unit in all matters of righteousness; that we shall undo the wrong of centuries and stand responsible to God alone. Christian churches and Christian nations are made of Christian men—are nothing apart from them or in addition to them. The whole is not greater than the sum of its parts. Nothing is right for us as Friends, as Christians, as citizens, which is wrong for us as individuals. There is no mysterious entity to be called a nation or a church which may cancel our duties as sons of God, and substitute another standard of right and wrong. If individuals making up a church represent a spirit of force, of violence, the church cannot represent a spirit of peace and goodwill. If missionaries are backed by gunboats, if they collect indemnities under threat of the bayonet, they are missionaries of that power which promised the kingdoms of earth in order secretly to destroy the kingdom of heaven. If citizens go forth to slay and destroy they may carry the name of civilization on their lips, but they are simply homicides and barbarians.

Men salve their consciences, yea, even benumb their consciences, by shifting the responsibilities of their deeds to a mythical something called a government, a church; but no power can release a man from the burden of his deeds. Not that all homicide and destruction is alike evil, not that men may not deceive themselves so that the worse appears the better. But this is only possible by avoiding the Christian attitude and shirking the Christian responsibility. I do not even say that all homicide and destruction are necessarily culpable; but only that what is wrong for each of us as a man cannot be right for each as a citizen, as a Christian. The righteous laws of nations are superadded to the moral law, not substituted for it. All our duties as members of churches, as citizens of nations, are based upon our duties as members of the human family, and stand for those higher duties consequent upon closer relations. They can never release us from the fundamental duty of a sense of universal brotherhood. We can no more, without violation of Christian principle, build our gain, our greatness, our exaltation, upon the loss of the Hindu or the Hottentot, the Spaniard or the Filipino, than upon that of our fellow-Quaker, or our fellow-American. And it is a neglect of this principle fundamental in Christianity; it is this placing metes and bounds upon our Christian charity, that marks the barbarizing of Christianity during sixteen centuries.

Some phases of this essential falsehood are these:

1. That Christianity is for peace, indeed; but that because of human weakness Christians must excuse war;
2. That peace tends to make cowards of us, and that we must have war in order to support the virility of the race;
3. That while violence for selfish ends is wrong, it is lawful to do evil that good may come;
4. That experience shows that many evils could not have been overcome without war.

(1) Christianity is for peace among men, but must defer to the weakness of humanity. Christianity must indeed stoop to the weakness of humanity, not to excuse that weakness, but to cure it. We must pardon the sinner—must we also accept the sin? Jesus, indeed, refused to punish the sinner; did he at the same time make light of the sin? Shall Christianity trail its white robe in the mire of sin to show its fellowship with sinners? Shall it do evil that it may draw near to evildoers? Not so do I understand the teaching of the Master or the teaching of the Spirit. The Christian is not called upon to be stupid, selfish, and sinful in order to reach those who are immersed in stupidity, selfishness and sin. Such doctrine could never have obtained except for the pagan idea that we are fractional parts of a nation or of a church, and must therefore assimilate ourselves to its average quality. But the Christian attitude is that of an independent unit, a partner with God in the work of subduing his earth. His duty to God transcends all temporary human relations. And, indeed, the conclusion at its best is a reversal of common sense. Because men are weak, let us be strong; because they are ignorant and violent, let us be wise and gentle. If they exalt force, let us show them how much more powerful is love. Of course, if our plea is that we are too weak to stand against the crowd, or that we believe the voice of the mob is the voice of God and to be obeyed— that is frankly an avowal of disbelief in Christianity, and should serve as an appeal to those who are Christians to convert us.

(2) Does peace make cowards of us? If it does, then Christian teaching is falsehood, and we should turn to a new and true gospel. It is the worst of hypocrisy to proclaim a gospel of peace as a theory and a gospel of war as a practice. And this is largely

the attitude of a nominal Christianity today. Numerous pseudo-Christian ministers have exalted the value of war as necessary to make men brave and self-sacrificing. In other words, they do not believe that the gospel they preach ex-officio tends to produce brave, true men. Occasional wars are necessary to serve as an antidote to the effects of periods in which Christian practices prevail. If for years we have been at peace—the condition longed for by prophet and Messiah—therefore, lest our manhood decline, let us burn cities; let us starve women and children, and kill men by thousands to avert the degeneration due to peace and the preaching of peace. Either Christianity is a mistake and a failure, and should be given up wholly or in part, or it is true and right, and should be applied in times of difficulty and danger as well as in times of ease and comfort. Indeed, unless it is a total failure, Christianity is needed especially at times when men differ and when passion tends to take the place of reason.

But, does peace make cowards of us? Let us turn first to war itself for answer. Peace made the men called heroes by the newspapers, who made up our armies in the Spanish[-American] war. Practically, all of them were born, educated and matured in a period of profound peace. But the courage of a soldier is not a very high type of courage. He is drilled beforehand, so that his own will shall have the smallest possible activity in the time of crisis. He risks being killed, indeed; but when did taking risks come to be a high type of courage? If it is so, truly, then, the gambler is somewhat of a hero too. I am not arguing against the courage of the American. I fully believe in his courage; but the taking of risks, even heavy risks, is not the best evidence of it. It is the motive, not the danger, that shows a hero. We have vastly better evidence in the heroes of peace, who never fail to appear in accidents, in wrecks at sea, in fires on land. These are they who take risks, often far greater than those of the soldier, to save life, not to destroy it. We have greater heroes than those of war, again, in those who face unflinchingly long years of monotonous labor, giving their strength ungrudgingly to win comfort and happiness for their families. We have heroes in our physicians, who so devote themselves to healing the sick and alleviating suffering that they deny themselves even the vacations which are their due. We have heroes in the pioneers who conquer the wilderness, in the explorers who expand the domain of human knowledge, in all those whose lives are self-dedicated to the good of others. We mistake deeply, we do injustice to our race, to our religion and to our civilization, when we grant our chief applause to the showy, organized national destroyers rather than to the unnoticed, miscellaneous saviours, who do their work, demanding no need of praise, who never claim to be heroes, but who support upon their bent shoulders the hope of the world. Glory to the builder, not to the destroyer.

(3) But shall we not do evil that good may come? If good come on the whole, then what we do is not evil. It is in the consequences of an act that exists its quality, whether good or evil. If an act has no consequences it has no moral element. But the flaw in the proposition that we may make war for a good purpose lies in its short view. The experience of the race and the teaching of our highest instincts unite in making clear that the total result of war is evil, and only evil continually. It is cheap and common to assert that war freed our nation from English domination, and that it struck the shackles from four millions of slaves. We leave out of account the heritage of bitterness and hatred not yet outlived that followed after the Revolution, to say nothing of the thousands of lives thrown away or made miserable. We skillfully avoid the question, which is a vital one, whether greater self-control, greater patience might not have accomplished more with less of evil. And we leave out of account the evident fact that the slavery question is not settled—that, indeed, it is perhaps less soluble as a race question embittered by the brutal years of violence and by sectional discord, than it was as a slavery question. Again, we fail to consider what self-restraint and patience might have done. And our fourth difficulty is involved in our third. War is sometimes necessary for the sake of others. The strong must be violent to help the weak—or, as before, the end justifies the means. Even so, friends, if what we look upon were the end—but there is no end. In a wave of nation-wide enthusiasm we went to war with Spain where men were governed badly and against their will, and where starvation and torture were used to enforce submission. After a harvest of suffering, disease, and crime had been reaped, we now look to a Cuba free from Spain, and we find ourselves immeshed in a war with a people whom we govern badly and against their will, and where starvation and torture are used to enforce submis-

sion.* Good may, indeed, come in spite of evil, for of unmixed evil there are few examples in the affairs of men, but good does not come because of it. If so much good has come in spite of all the evil, what would not the world be if it could be brought to Christianity?

There is no more fundamental atheism than is involved in a proclamation that God is too weak to win His way without calling in the devil to His help. There is no deeper infidelity than that which so distrusts the strength of righteousness that it must lean upon the arm of unrighteousness. It is from this attitude of apology that I would earnestly call Christians today. "Let us have faith that right makes might," and in that faith let us fare forward courageously in the path we are in. Let us no more evade and pretend. Are we ashamed of the Christ and his message? If not, let us speak it, and live it in spirit and in truth. May we not have in clear unmistakable tones the outspoken, uncompromising demand for righteousness on the part of each individual before God; the selfless plea for self-conquest; for the ruling of our own spirits? May we not have a definite rejection of compromise with evil, of deals with iniquity, a courageous and confident stand upon the power of the spirit of love to solve the hard problems of the world?

WORLD CONFERENCE OF FRIENDS

World War I was a turning point for Friends. In the British Isles and North America, Quakers had become so acculturated that many openly supported the war effort. Others went to prison rather than compromise what they saw as basic Christian teaching. Friends sought alternatives to military service for young members, the best known of which was the American Friends Service Committee, formed in 1917. In 1920, in the aftermath of war, the first World Conference of Friends was held in London to attempt to envision the future of Quakerism. Among its statements was this restatement of the Peace Testimony.

* [Holmes refers to American actions in the Philippines from 1898 to 1901. —ed.]

The Peace Testimony of the Society of Friends.
The Fundamental Basis (London, 1920).

I told them I knew from whence all wars arose, even from the lust, according to James's doctrine: and that I lived in the virtue of that life and power that took away the occasion of all wars.... I told them that I was come into the covenant of peace that was before wars and strifes were.

—ANSWER OF GEORGE FOX TO THE COMMONWEALTH
COMMISSIONERS, WHEN THEY OFFERED HIM
A COMMISSION IN THE ARMY, 1650.

We utterly deny all outward wars and strife, and fightings with outward weapons, for any end, or under any pretence whatever; this is our testimony to the whole world. The Spirit of Christ by which we are guided is not changeable, so as once to command us from a thing as evil, and again to move us unto it; and we certainly know, and testify to the world, that the Spirit of Christ, which leads us into all truth, will never move us to fight and war against any man with outward weapons, neither for the kingdom of Christ nor for the kingdoms of this world.

—FROM "A DECLARATION OF THE HARMLESS AND INNOCENT
PEOPLE OF GOD CALLED QUAKERS," PRESENTED TO CHARLES II, 1660.
RE-ISSUED 20 YEARS LATER WITH THE STATEMENT, "THIS WAS OUR TES-
TIMONY TWENTY YEARS AGO; SINCE THEN WE HAVE NOT BEEN FOUND
ACTING CONTRARY TO IT, NOR EVER SHALL; FOR THE TRUTH THAT IT IS
OUR GUIDE IS UNCHANGEABLE."

The Quaker Peace Testimony is "utterly to deny *all* outward wars, strife or fighting with outward weapons, for any end or under any pretence whatever." It has its basis in a new "life and power" that take "away the occasion of all wars." The early Friends, who asserted the Peace Testimony, had come into a new and living experience of God working within them. They could re-echo the words of Paul, "No longer I, but Christ liveth in me." This raised their whole life to a higher moral and spiritual level than they had before known. In particular it filled them with a passionate love for men (the working out in them of God's love within), and gave them an extraordinarily acute moral sensitiveness. This is seen on the one hand in the zeal with which they endeavoured to carry the message of light to all sorts and conditions of men, and on the other hand in their perception of moral issues both in the individual life and in the life of society. They were both missionaries and social reformers. And in both activities they showed a certainty of conviction in themselves and an assurance of response in others which were far beyond what was usual in their own day, or at any time. Their experience of the guidance of God was, they were convinced, not granted to them because they were special favourites of Heaven, but was intended for every one; it was God's gracious gift to *all* His children. They had heard God's voice within them. They were certain that that voice spoke in all men, and that if others but listened and obeyed it would lead them, too, to the same fulness of life and power. And this meant that they could with confidence appeal to *all* men, for God Himself was striving with *all*; and that when men turned to God and listened to the voice within, when they began to follow that Light, their experience and the line of conduct to which it led would in all essentials be identical with that which they themselves had found.

This conviction had as its consequence a belief not only that love ought to be paramount in the world, and must in the end gain control of the lives of all men, but also that now and always the true way of setting right the wrong was not coercion, but conversion. It had also two very practical consequences which showed themselves in everyday life and conduct. On the one hand, all fear of man was removed. They knew God and wholeheartedly served Him, and they relied implicitly upon His protection and guidance in all things. On the other hand, they renounced all action and desires which were out of accord with God's gracious will. They desired only and wholly to serve Him. This removed from their lives the pettiness, self-seeking and jealousy which so often form the breeding-ground of those passions which make for war. In place of these they manifested a large-hearted and unselfish charity towards all men which made directly for peace. They realised Epictetus' ideal of the free man: they feared nothing that man could do to them, and they desired nothing that man could withhold from them.

The belief in the Inward Light means that to every God-directed appeal from without there is a possibility of inward response in everyone. Therefore no one is hopeless. All can be led to the truth. And because this inward Light is no mere human endowment, but the very revelation of God Himself, it will always lead to Him and to the moral life which is in accord with the example and teaching of Christ. In short, it will lead to a life the basis of which is love.

When the early Friends said that the "Spirit of Christ would never move them to fight and war against any man with outward weapons," they not only testified that war was wrong, but they also indicated that there was a new and right way of dealing with men consonant with Love, and certain to be attended by a success far greater than had ever been attained by war. Instead of destroying or suppressing the evil-doers, the new method would transform them into children of light. These early Friends were come "into the Covenant of Peace which was before wars and strifes were," and by their lives lived in the power of the light they were helping others to enter that same covenant.

Translating the testimony from its intuitive form into terms of belief and into modern phraseology, we may say that it is founded upon (a) the belief in the Universal Light of Christ; (b) the actual results of following the Light in life and conduct; and (c) the aim for mankind which Christianity exists to achieve. That is to say, upon the essential character of the kingdom of God. All these principles consistently followed our lead to the testimony against all war.

(a) The Witness of the Light in the Individual.

Can anyone who is truly sensitive to the Spirit of God working in him kill another man in whom he is convinced that the Spirit is also working? If the answer is No, he will not therefore do nothing. He has found the ground common to both parties, and that ground the highest upon which an understanding and friendship may be built, namely, the common light and inspiration of God. Thus the belief in the Inward Light not only forbids war, but opens up the true way of peace. It is to be noticed, however, that no one can take this way while refusing to be guided by the Spirit of Truth. Even if the desires of his enemy are outspokenly unjust and aggressive, and his own are much better, as long as he is unwilling that perfect justice should reign he cannot in the power of truth overcome evil in another. The one victory over evil is a victory of the truth, and that cannot come through one who will not surrender himself to the truth. This does *not* mean, as has sometimes been stated, that only people of the highest spiritual attainments and perfect moral life can employ the method of overcoming evil with good. What is required is not attainment, but desire for good; not perfection, but sincerity.

(b) Living in Love and the Response.

The result of following the Light is a life lived in the power of Love, for God is Love. This does not mean a life full of sentimentality, or a soft and easy life, but a supremely unselfish life: one whose aim is not anything for oneself or immediate family only, but always the good of all with whom one comes into relations. Nor does it mean a coldly benevolent life. It is not simply that one desires—in a superior sort of way—the welfare of others, but that one is heartily interested in them, desiring both to gain from them and to give to them, to be in relations of mutual satisfaction with them. And this relation of mutual satisfaction can only be fully attained as both are founding their lives upon the love of God. But the fact that God is Love is a promise that such universal satisfactory relations can be universally attained, that the Brotherhood of Man is no mere dream, but is destined to be a reality, because it is in accord with the real constitution of the universe. Both the foundation and the aim of creation is love, and love is not only the fulfilling of the law but the final satisfaction of all human need. The task of the Christian in this world is the establishment of the kingdom of God, of the supremacy of love. The natural and obviously rational way to achieve this aim is for each to practise love to all. It has always been the Quaker conviction that this practice of love is incompatible with warfare, and that, if persisted in, it will in the long run achieve every right result that a war in the interests of justice has been held to achieve, and without the fatal drawbacks of war.

It is not, indeed, denied that while the enlightened and persistent practice of love to all men is the sure and only way of righting wrong and bringing good out of evil, the way of love may frequently mean suffering, and sometimes apparent defeat. For love took our Lord through Gethsemane to the Cross, where to all outward seeming evil triumphed. And both the Church and individual Christian have often had to tread the same path. But though, as Lacordaire says, "L'église est née crucifiée," it has also over and over again been true that "the blood of the martyrs is the seed of the Church," even though long patience be sometimes needed. For Christ "through death brought to nought him that had the power of death." Thus though suffering, disaster, death and apparent defeat may come to those who follow Christ's way of love, such sufferings are redemptive, and are on the direct road to the world's salvation. The Cross and the Grave were followed by the Resurrection and Pentecost.

Love naturally manifests itself in acts of kindness and helpfulness. Any acts of a contrary nature to these tend to convey the impression that their source is the opposite of love, and therefore, however good the intentions of the doer, are in reality liable to work against rather than for the enthronement of love. Any suggestion that coercion or injurious violence may have to be exercised upon men in order to make them amenable to love is a suggestion that love itself is weak and unable to win men. But this cannot be so if God is love. Moreover, it is denied by the final revelation of God in Jesus Christ. For He refused to take the methods of war and coercion which His countrymen expected the Messiah to take, and took instead the way of love, even to the last extreme of non-resistance.

To believe, then, that warfare and coercion are necessary to open the way to love is to believe that the methods of Jesus Christ were mistaken; in other words, that God was not really incarnate in Him.

(c) The Unity of Mankind.

The witness of the Inward Light in the individual, and of Love as the principle of living, both imply the unity of mankind. For the light in the individual is no individual possession, but a universal light. And unselfish love can overcome hatred and greed, because the most essential fact of human society is that we are members one of another. We are all the children of one Father, God; we may all share in the salvation brought by the one Lord, Jesus Christ; and the working of the same Holy Spirit may be, if we will have it, the guiding light of all. This unity is not realised. It is the ideal at which Christianity aims. Yet it is more than an unrealised ideal. It is the basal fact of human existence. For no man liveth to himself, and no man dieth to himself. We belong to God and to one another. It must therefore be the aim of the Christian not merely to work for unity and human brotherhood as a far-off goal, but to demonstrate it now as a fact—indeed, as the fundamental reality of human society. If one is fully convinced of this unity, and really regards all men as brothers, not only will one be unable to countenance the practice of war, but one will be inwardly impelled to live a life of unselfish service which will in truth go far to remove the occasion of all wars.

Printed in the United States
by Baker & Taylor Publisher Services